Depression

Second Edition

Depression

Causes and Treatment

Second Edition

Aaron T. Beck, M.D., and
Brad A. Alford, Ph.D.

PENN

University of Pennsylvania Press
Philadelphia

Copyright © 2009 Aaron T. Beck

Published by
University of Pennsylvania Press
Philadelphia, Pennsylvania 19104-4112

Printed in the United States of America on acid-free paper
10   9   8   7   6   5   4   3   2   1

Library of Congress Cataloging-in-Publication Data

Beck, Aaron T.
    Depression : causes and treatment / Aaron T. Beck and Brad A. Alford.—
2nd ed.
        p.   cm.
    Includes bibliographical references and index.
    ISBN 978-0-8122-1964-7 (alk. paper)
1. Depression, Mental.   I. Alford, Brad A.   II. Title.
[DNLM: 1. Depressive Disorder.   WM 171 B393d 2008]
RC537.B4   2008
616.85′27—dc22   2008025522

Contents

Preface to the Second Edition

The first edition of this book posed the question, "What has definitely been established regarding the nature, the causes, and the treatment of depression?" To answer it, Aaron Beck sifted through thousands of clinical and controlled studies and summarized representative research on the clinical, biological, psychological, and theoretical aspects of depression. Of greater significance, he described an original research program that, in retrospect, represented a breakthrough in understanding the cognitive components and treatment of depression.

Like the first edition, this one presents an update and overview of what is currently known about clinical depression, including developments that have taken place since the book was originally published 40 years ago and, also like that earlier volume, offers a historical perspective. Moreover, in Chapter 16 we review the randomized controlled trials that have built upon and elaborated cognitive theory and research.

What is new to the second edition? Definitions of the mood disorders have changed over the years, and new categories have been added. We now recognize major depression as the leading cause of disability worldwide, and it has received increased clinical and research attention. In the years since the book was first published additional types of bipolar disorder have been recognized, and research has been conducted on the relation between manic symptoms and life events. New drugs, such as the selective serotonin reuptake inhibitors, or SSRIs, have been developed. While comparable in efficacy (except in severe depression), they are chemically unrelated to tricyclic, heterocyclic, and other antidepressants discussed in the first edition, and they enjoy several advantages over those "first-generation" drugs. The newer medications can induce fewer adverse side effects and provide greater safety in case of overdose and improved tolerability and patient compliance. SSRIs may also be augmented with lithium, psychostimulants, and other agents.

There are even now many unresolved problems in pharmacotherapy. Drug treatment of depression—even using the newer SSRIs—still results in unwanted side effects, such as the sexual dysfunction that affects 60 percent of patients. There are potential lethal interactions between SSRI and MAOI drugs. Other unintended effects include gastrointestinal disturbance, nausea, and somnolence. Electroconvulsive therapy (ECT) causes side effects as well, and alternatives are under review, including transcranial magnetic stimulation (TMS). We describe the results and conclusions of preliminary studies on this new treatment.

Since this book first appeared we have made considerable progress in understanding the biological basis of depression. Steps have been taken in identifying the genetic basis of the mood disorders, including schizoaffective disorder. Research on changes in hippocampal neurons and amygdala enlargement appears promising. "Neurotrophic" (keeping cells alive) and "neurogenesis" (stimulating growth of new cells) theories abound and are being tested.

Many of the biological aspects of depression still remain uncertain, though progress continues. One research area explores specific brain changes that correspond to the effective pharmacological and psychological treatments of depression. For example, studies have focused on differential effects in recovery for paroxetine (Paxil) therapy and cognitive therapy in modulating specific sites in limbic and cortical brain regions.

Researchers have continued to identify the pathophysiological aspects of major depressive disorder, including alterations in various monoamine brain systems. Neuropeptides such as corticotropin-releasing hormone are under investigation, as are hormonal variables such as glucocorticoid secretion. Dexamethasone nonsuppression of plasma cortisol has been suggested as a marker, although the same effects have been induced experimentally by sleep deprivation and dietary fasting.

Several studies have tested whether genetic markers can predict differential drug response, thus leading to the possibility of individualized pharmacologic treatment of depression. Response to paroxetine in relation to the serotonin transporter gene polymorphism (5-HTTLPR) have found reductions in depression ratings to be more rapid for certain genotypes than for others, despite equivalent paroxetine concentrations. Future studies in pharmacogenomics will continue to identify genetic markers in the hope of better predicting individual drug response, and the reasons for such response. The end result will be the possibility of individualized pharmacologic treatment of depression.

Clinical and psychosocial approaches to depression have made major strides. We now know a great deal more about cognitive vulnerability, the interaction of genetic predisposition with childhood and adult stress, and relapse than we did a generation ago. Most aspects of the cognitive theory of depression and suicide have been confirmed empirically, including negatively biased cognitions about the self, the importance of hopelessness as a predictor, content specificity of themes, and mood-congruent recall. Cognitive priming studies and studies utilizing longitudinal designs now support the theory of cognitive vulnerability in adults, and evidence is emerging for children as well.

Around the world, exciting research programs on clinical depression are underway. Cognitive therapies that target neurobiological mechanisms are being tested as adjuncts to conventional treatment. There is growing appreciation for the biopsychosocial nature of the mood disorders, along with an increased sophistication concerning the action of psychological and somatic therapies across multiple dimensions. The dichotomy between the phenomenological and the "biological" are increasingly understood to be, in reality, two sides of the same coin. For example, we review one report that found changes in thyroid hormone levels in response to cognitive therapy of major depression, consistent with the effect on the thyroid axis found in various somatic antidepressant treatments. Future studies are needed to test the effects of the cognitive and the somatic therapies on neurogenesis, particularly in the granular cell level of the dentate gyrus (DG), the part of the hippocampus thought to be critical in laying down new cognitions.

As outlined above, depression research is vibrant and ever-changing. However, in addition to covering what is new, this Second Edition retains almost completely the original research and ideas of the First Edition. The basic theory of cognitive therapy was spelled out at that time. Part I, Clinical Aspects of Depression, keeps the naturalistic research on the cognitive aspects of depression (Chapter 2, "Symptomatology of Depression"). This work led to the cognitive content formulation which links the cognitive system to the affective, motivational, and physical phenomena of depression (Chapter 12, "Cognition and Psychopathology"). Part II, Experimental Aspects of Depression, includes the original tests of Freud's theory that led to an "anomalous finding,"[1] one that eventually generated a new system of treatment, cognitive therapy. This research is preserved also, as part of Chapter 10, including the dream study and the Negative Dreams ("Masochism") Inventory (see Appendix).

Part III, Theoretical Aspects of Depression, contains from the First Edition the original idea of the negative cognitive triad in depression, and the theory of mania and other disorders, including anxiety, phobia, somatization, paranoia, obsessive compulsive disorders, and psychosis. Likewise, Chapter 13, "Development of Depression," articulates the various causes of depression and has generated hundreds of studies. For these chapters, new sections add genetic findings, empirical support of the theory, and integrative theory that now underpins the general cognitive system of therapy. Thus, much of the first edition has been retained in the second, but the earlier work has been augmented and updated by the latest findings.

Part IV, Treatment of Depression, summarizes advances in somatic and psychological therapies. We review findings of randomized controlled trials, with special focus on comparisons between psychotherapy and antidepressant medication. Reviews of metaanalyses and conventional narrative reviews show certain psychological treatments and pharmacological therapy to be equally viable as clinical approaches to the mood disorders, with limited evidence suggesting the utilization of a combined approach. In addition, data now show the clear relapse prevention effect of cognitive therapy compared to medications. This includes group cognitive therapy for relapse of major depression, as well as for prevention of suicide reattempts in adults. Moreover, therapist experience with cognitive therapy is generally associated with better results.

Our comprehensive review of well-designed studies reveals that depressed patients treated with psychological interventions had a relapse rate of only 30 percent, compared to a relapse rate of 69 percent for patients treated with pharmacotherapy alone. We review studies that now support the routine use of maintenance treatment for depression. One major study calculated that half of all depression during the five years following a major depressive episode can be averted by using maintenance treatment, either cognitive behavior therapy or antidepressants.

In summary, where significant advances have occurred, we have incorporated these in this revision of Aaron Beck's classic text. In cases where terminology is new, as in the case of the classification of disorders, current terms replace earlier ones or are included alongside them. In the new edition, thus, we attempt to preserve the timeless material of the first edition and to distill all the timely advances that have occurred since then.

We would like to acknowledge the research assistance of Kathleen Shinko, Melissa St. Ledger, Sarah O'Neill, Rachel D'Agostino, Ruslan Denysyk, Mary Donohue, Jennifer Marsala, Patrick Orr, Sarah Tarquini, and James Yadavaia.

We thank Kenneth S. Kendler for his review and comments on the manuscript. Geary S. Alford suggested original source material for the section on cognitive neurobiology. Donna Rupp translated the manuscript into American Medical Association style. Krista McGlynn and Kavita Shah assisted with proofreading.

Finally, we express our appreciation to those at the Penn Press who added excitement and inspiration to the development of a Second Edition. Director Eric Halpern and Senior Editor Jo Joslyn deserve special mention. Alison Anderson, Managing Editor, played an important role in facilitating the goal of retaining the original classic material, and linking it to the more recent research that has flowed logically from it.

Chapter 16 is an extended version of Alford, BA, Beck, AT, Psychotherapeutic treatment of depression and bipolar disorder, in DL Evans & DS Charney (Eds.), *Physician's Guide to Depression and Bipolar Disorder*, New York, McGraw Hill, 2006. Portions of Chapters, 15, are adapted from the same source. Reproduced with permission of The McGraw-Hill Companies.

The following tables were reprinted or adapted by permission of the copyright holders:

Table 1-1 from Lopez AD, Murray CJL, The global burden of disease, *Nature Medicine* 1998;4:1241-1243.

Tables 1-2, 3-1, 4-1, 4-2, 4-3 , 4-4, 6-1, 6-2, 6-3, 8-1 from American Psychiatric Association, *Diagnostic and statistical manual of mental disorders*, 4th ed., textual revisions (DSM-IV-TR)(Washington, DC: APA, © 2000).

Table 1-3 from Kessler RC, Chiu WT, Demler O, Walters EE, Prevalence, severity, and comorbidity of 12-month *DSM-IV* disorders in the National Comorbidity Survey Replication, *Archives of General Psychiatry* 2005; 62, 616-627.

Tables 1-4, 1-5 from Kessler RC, Berglund P, Demler O, Jin R, Walters EE, Lifetime prevalence and age-of-onset distributions of DSM-IV disorders in the National Comorbidity Survey Replication *Archives of General Psychiatry* 2005;62,593–602.

Table 3.5 from Lundquist G, Prognosis and course in manic-depressive psychoses. *Acta Psychiat. Neurol. Suppl.* 1945;35.

Table 3-6 from Kiloh G, Andrews G, Neilson M, The long-term outcome of depressive illness, *British Journal of Psychiatry* 1988;153:752–757.

Table 3-7 from Riso LP, Blandino JA, Penna S, Dacey S, Grant MM, Toit PL, Duin JS, Pacoe EM, Ulmer CS, Cognitive aspects of chronic depression. *Journal of Abnormal Psychology* 2003;112:72–80 (by permission of American Psychological Association).

Tables 8-2, 8-3 from Bertelsen A, Gottesman II, Schizoaffective psychoses: genetical clues to classification. *American Journal of Medical Genetics* 1995;60:7–11.

Table 9-2 from McGuffin P, Rijsdijk F, Andrew M, Sham P, Katz R, Cardno A, The heritability of bipolar affective disorder and the genetic relationship to unipolar depression. *Archives of General Psychiatry* 2003;60:497–502.

Tables 14-2, 14-5 from Masand PS, Gupta S, Selective serotonin-reuptake inhibitors: an update. *Harvard Review of Psychiatry* 1999;7:69–84 (by permission of Taylor & Francis Group, LLC).

Table 14-3 from Johnson GF. Lithium in depression: A review of the antidepressant and prophylactic effects of lithium. *Australian and New Zealand Journal of Psychiatry* 1987;21:356–365.

Table 14-7 from Baldessarini RJ, Tonodo L, Hennen J, Viguera AC, Is lithium still worth using? an update of selected recent research. *Harvard Review of Psychiatry* 2002;10:59-75 (by permission of Taylor & Francis Group, LLC).

Part I
Clinical Aspects of Depression

Chapter 1
The Definition of Depression

Paradoxes of Depression

Depression may someday be understood in terms of its paradoxes. There is, for instance, an astonishing contrast between the depressed person's image of him- or herself and the objective facts. A wealthy woman moans that she doesn't have the financial resources to feed her children. A widely acclaimed movie star begs for plastic surgery in the belief that he is ugly. An eminent physicist berates herself "for being stupid."

Despite the torment experienced as the result of these self-debasing ideas, the patients are not readily swayed by objective evidence or by logical demonstration of the unreasonable nature of these ideas. Moreover, they often perform acts that seem to enhance their suffering. The wealthy man puts on rags and publicly humiliates himself by begging for money to support himself and his family. A clergyman with an unimpeachable reputation tries to hang himself because "I'm the world's worst sinner." A scientist whose work has been confirmed by numerous independent investigators publicly "confesses" that her discoveries were a hoax.

Attitudes and behaviors such as these are particularly puzzling—on the surface, at least—because they seem to contradict some of the most strongly established axioms of human nature. According to the "pleasure principle," patients should be seeking to maximize satisfactions and minimize pain. According to the time-honored concept of the instinct of self-preservation, they should be attempting to prolong life rather than terminate it.

Although depression (or melancholia) has been recognized as a clinical syndrome for over 2,000 years, as yet no completely satisfactory explanation of its puzzling and paradoxical features has been found. There are still major unresolved issues regarding its nature, its classification, and its etiology. Among these are the following:

1. Is depression an exaggeration of a mood experienced by the normal, or is it qualitatively as well as quantitatively different from a normal mood?

2. What are the causes, defining characteristics, outcomes, and effective treatments of depression?
3. Is depression a type of reaction (Meyerian concept), or is it a disease (Kraepelinian concept)?
4. Is depression caused primarily by psychological stress and conflict, or is it related primarily to a biological derangement?

There are no universally accepted answers to these questions. In fact, there is sharp disagreement among clinicians and investigators who have written about depression. There is considerable controversy regarding the classification of depression, and a few writers see no justification for using this nosological category at all. The nature and etiology of depression are subject to even more sharply divided opinion. Some authorities contend that depression is primarily a psychogenic disorder; others maintain just as firmly that it is caused by organic factors. A third group supports the concept of two different types of depression: a psychogenic type and an organic type.

Prevalence of Depression

The importance of depression is recognized by everyone in the field of mental health. According to Kline,[1] more human suffering has resulted from depression than from any other single disease affecting humankind. Depression is second only to schizophrenia in first and second admissions to mental hospitals in the United States, and it has been estimated that the prevalence of depression outside hospitals is five times greater than that of schizophrenia.[2] Worldwide, Murray and Lopez[3] found unipolar major depression to be the leading cause of disability in 1990, measured in years lived with a disability. Unipolar depression accounted for more than one in every ten years of life lived with a disability.

More than 40 years ago, a systematic survey of the prevalence of depression in a sharply defined geographical area indicated that 3.9 percent of the population more than 20 years of age were suffering from depression at a specified time.[4] According to the fourth edition of the *Diagnostic and Statistical Manual of Mental Disorders (DSM-IV)* of the American Psychiatric Association,[5] the probability during one's lifetime of developing a major depressive disorder is 5–12 percent for males and 10–25 percent for females. At any given point in time ("point prevalence"), 2–3 percent of the male and 5–9 percent of the female population suffer from a major depression. Piccinelli[6] reviewed the studies on gender differences in depression and found that the gender differences began at mid-puberty and continued through adult life.

TABLE 1-1. Leading Causes of Disability Worldwide, 1990

	Total years lived with disability (millions)	Percent of total
All causes	427.7	
1. Unipolar major depression	50.8	10.7
2. Iron-deficiency anemia	22.0	4.7
3. Falls	22.0	4.6
4. Alcohol use	15.8	3.3
5. Chronic obstructive pulmonary disease	14.7	3.1
6. Bipolar disorder	14.1	3.0
7. Congenital anomalies	13.5	2.9
8. Osteoarthritis	13.3	2.8
9. Schizophrenia	12.1	2.6
10. Obsessive-compulsive disorder	10.2	2.2

Adapted from Lopez and Murray 1998. For up-to-date WHO data, see http://www.who.int/mental_health/management/depression/definition/en/

TABLE 1-2. Prevalence of Major Depressive Disorder by Gender (%)

	Male	Female
Lifetime	5–12	10–25
Point prevalence	2–3	5–9

Adapted from *DSM-IV-TR*.

Prevalence and Severity by Types and Age at Onset

Lifetime prevalence rates for the other mood disorders (see Chapter 4 for distinctions among types) are reported in *DSM-IV*[5] as follows: Dysthymic disorder 6 percent; Bipolar I 0.4–1.6 percent; Bipolar II 0.5 percent; Cyclothymic 0.4–1.0 percent. The National Institute of Mental Health (USA)[7] reports that 18.8 million American adults (9.5 percent of the population age 18 or older) in a given year suffer from some form of depressive disorder. Major depressive disorder is the leading cause of disability in the established market economies around the world.[7]

Twelve-month prevalence and severity rates are provided by Kessler et al.[8] The U.S. National Comorbidity Survey Replication included a nationally representative face-to-face household survey conducted between February 2001 and April 2003. The study employed a structured diagnostic interview, the World Health Organization World Mental Health Survey Initiative version of the Composite International Diagnostic Interview. Participants included 9,282 English-speaking respondents 18 years and older. Twelve-month prevalence and estimates of mood disorders from this study are included in Table 1-3.

TABLE 1-3. Twelve-Month Prevalence and Severity of Mood Disorders (%)

	Total	Severity		
		Serious	Moderate	Mild
Major depressive disorder	6.7	30.4	50.1	19.5
Dysthymia	1.5	49.7	32.1	18.2
Bipolar I–II disorders	2.6	82.9	17.1	0
Any mood disorder	9.5	45.0	40.0	15.0

Adapted from Kessler et al. 2005.

TABLE 1-4. Ages at Selected Percentiles on Standardized Age-of-Onset Distributions of *DSM-IV/* WMH-CIDI Mood Disorders, with Projected Lifetime Risk at Age 75 Years

	Projected lifetime risk at age 75 (%)	Age at selected age-of-onset percentiles							
		5	10	25	50	75	90	95	99
Major depressive disorder	23.2	12	14	19	32	44	56	64	73
Dysthymia	3.4	7	11	17	31	43	51	57	73
Bipolar I–II disorders	5.1	11	13	17	25	42	50	57	65
Any mood disorder	28.0	11	13	18	30	43	54	63	73

Adapted from Kessler et al. 2005.

TABLE 1-5. Lifetime Prevalence (%) of Disorders by Age

	Total	Age			
		18–29	30–44	45–59	>60
Major depressive disorder	16.6	15.4	19.8	18.8	10.6
Dysthymia	2.5	1.7	2.9	3.7	1.3
Bipolar I–II disorders	3.9	5.9	4.6	3.5	1.0
Any mood disorder	20.8	21.4	24.6	22.9	11.9

Adapted from Kessler et al. 2005.

Age of onset and lifetime prevalence rates (the likelihood of experiencing a mood disorder at some time in one's lifetime) are presented in Tables 1-4 and 1-5.[9]

Descriptive Concepts of Depression

The condition that today we label depression has been described by a number of ancient writers under the classification of "melancholia." The first clinical description of melancholia was made by Hippocrates in the fourth century B.C. He also referred to swings similar to mania and depression.[10]

Aretaeus, a physician living in the second century A.D., described the melancholic patient as "sad, dismayed, sleepless. . . . They become thin by their agitation and loss of refreshing sleep. . . . At a more advanced stage, they complain of a thousand futilities and desire death." It is noteworthy that Aretaeus specifically delineated the manic-depressive cycle. Some authorities believe that he anticipated the Kraepelinian synthesis of manic-depressive psychosis, but Jelliffe discounts this hypothesis.

Plutarch, in the second century A.D., presented a particularly vivid and detailed account of melancholia:

> He looks on himself as a man whom the Gods hate and pursue with their anger. A far worse lot is before him; he dares not employ any means of averting or of remedying the evil, lest he be found fighting against the gods. The physician, the consoling friend, are driven away. 'Leave me,' says the wretched man, 'me, the impious, the accursed, hated of the gods, to suffer my punishment.' He sits out of doors, wrapped in sackcloth or in filthy rags. Ever and anon he rolls himself, naked, in the dirt confessing about this and that sin. He has eaten or drunk something wrong. He has gone some way or other which the Divine Being did not approve of. The festivals in honor of the gods give no pleasure to him but fill him rather with fear or a fright. (quoted in Zilboorg[11])

Pinel at the beginning of the nineteenth century described melancholia as follows:

> The symptoms generally comprehended by the term melancholia are taciturnity, a thoughtful pensive air, gloomy suspicions, and a love of solitude. Those traits, indeed, appear to distinguish the characters of some men otherwise in good health, and frequently in prosperous circumstances. Nothing, however, can be more hideous than the figure of a melancholic brooding over his imaginary misfortunes. If moreover possessed of power, and endowed with a perverse disposition and a sanguinary heart, the image is rendered still more repulsive.

These accounts bear a striking similarity to modern textbook descriptions of depression; they are also similar to contemporary autobiographical accounts such as that by Clifford W. Beers.[12] The cardinal signs and symptoms used today in diagnosing depression are found in the ancient descriptions: disturbed mood (sad, dismayed, futile); self-castigations ("the accursed, hatred of the gods"); self-debasing behavior ("wrapped in sackcloth or dirty rags . . . he rolls himself, naked, in the dirt"); wish to die; physical and vegetative symptoms (agitation, loss of appetite and weight, sleeplessness); and delusions of having committed unpardonable sins.

The foregoing descriptions of depression include the typical characteristics of this condition. There are few psychiatric syndromes whose clinical descriptions are so constant through successive eras of history (For descriptions of depression through the ages, see Burton.[13]) It is noteworthy that the historical descriptions of depression indicate that its manifestations are observable in all aspects of behavior, including the traditional psychological divisions of affection, cognition, and conation.

Because the disturbed feelings are generally a striking feature of depression, it has become customary to regard this condition as a "primary mood disorder" or as an "affective disorder." The central importance ascribed to the feeling component of depression is exemplified by the practice of utilizing affective adjective checklists to define and measure depression. The representation of depression as an affective disorder is as misleading as it would be to designate scarlet fever as a "disorder of the skin" or as a "primary febrile disorder." There are many components of depression other than mood deviation. In a significant proportion of the cases, no mood abnormality at all is elicited from the patient. In our present state of knowledge, we do not know which component of the clinical picture of depression is primary, or whether they are all simply external manifestations of some unknown pathological process.

Depression may now be defined in terms of the following attributes:

1. A specific alteration in mood: sadness, loneliness, apathy.
2. A negative self-concept associated with self-reproaches and self-blame.
3. Regressive and self-punitive wishes: desires to escape, hide, or die.
4. Vegetative changes: anorexia, insomnia, loss of libido.
5. Change in activity level: retardation or agitation.

Semantics of Depression

One of the difficulties in conceptualizing depression is essentially semantic, namely, that the term has been variously applied to designate a particular type of feeling or symptom; a symptom-complex (or syndrome); and a well-defined disease entity.

Not infrequently, normal people say they are depressed when they observe any lowering of their mood below their baseline level. A person experiencing a transient sadness or loneliness may state that he or she is depressed. Whether this *normal* mood is synonymous with, or even related to, the feeling experienced in the abnormal condition of depression is open to question. In any event, when a person complains of feeling inordinately dejected, hopeless, or unhappy, the term *depressed* is often used to label this subjective state.

The term depression is often used to designate a complex pattern of deviations in feelings, cognition, and behavior (described in the previous section) that is not represented as a discrete psychiatric disorder. In such instances it is regarded as a syndrome, or symptom-complex. The cluster of signs and symptoms is sometimes conceptualized as a psychopathological dimension ranging in intensity (or in degree of abnormality) from mild to severe. The syndrome of depression may at times appear as a concomitant of a definite psychiatric disorder such as schizophrenic reaction; in such a case, the diagnosis would be "schizophrenic reaction with depression." At times, the syndrome may be secondary to, or a manifestation of, organic disease of the brain such as general paresis or cerebral artereosclerosis.

Finally, the term depression has been used to designate a discrete nosological entity. The term has generally been qualified by some adjective to indicate a particular type or form, as for example: reactive depression, agitated depression, or psychotic-depressive reaction. When conceptualized as a specific clinical entity, depression is assumed to have certain consistent attributes in addition to the characteristic signs and symptoms; these attributes include a specifiable type of onset, course, duration, and outcome.

One such classification system, the diagnostic manual of the American Psychiatric Association (APA),[5] illustrates some of these aspects. The APA categorizes the mood disorders into (1) depressive disorders (unipolar depression) and (2) bipolar disorders. In the former, there is no history of a manic or hypomanic episode, and in the latter there is such a history.

The depressive disorders include major depressive disorder and dysthymic disorder. Major depressive disorder is defined by one or more major depressive episodes. Such episodes include 2 weeks of depressed mood or loss of interest, along with a minimum of four additional depression symptoms. Dysthymic disorder is defined in part by at least 2 years of low-level depressed mood, where the person is depressed for more days than not. The bipolar disorders are usually accompanied by major depressive episodes, and are divided into two types, Bipolar I and Bipolar II disorder.[5] The classification of the mood disorders will be considered in more detail in Chapter 4.

In medicine, a clinical entity or disease is assumed to be responsive to specific forms of treatment (not necessarily discovered as yet) and to have a specific etiology. There is a considerable body of evidence indicating that the clinical entity depression responds to certain drugs and/or electroconvulsive therapy (ECT), but there is no consensus as yet regarding its etiology. This issue will be further considered in Part II, "Experimental Aspects of Depression."

Depression and Normal Moods

There is little agreement among authorities regarding the relationship of depression to the changes in mood experienced by normal individuals. The term *mood* is generally applied to a spectrum of feelings extending from elation and happiness at one extreme, to sadness and unhappiness at the other. The particular feelings encompassed by this term, consequently, are directly related to either happiness or sadness. Subjective states, such as anxiety or anger, that do not fit into the happiness-sadness categories are not generally included. Some authors[14] believe that all individuals have mood swings and that normal individuals may have "blue" hours or "blue" days. This belief has been supported by systematic studies of oscillations in mood in normal subjects.[15]

The episodes of low mood or of feeling blue experienced by normal individuals are similar in a number of ways to the clinical states of depression. First, there is a similarity between the descriptions of the subjective experience of normal low mood and of depression. The words used to describe normal low mood tend to be the same used by depressives to describe their feelings—blue, sad, unhappy, empty, low, lonely. It is possible, however, that this resemblance may be due to depressed patients' drawing on familiar vocabulary to describe a pathological state for which they have no available words. Some patients, in fact, state that their feelings during their depressions are quite distinct from any feelings they have ever experienced when not in a clinical depression.

Second, the behavior of the depressed patient resembles that of a person who is sad or unhappy, particularly in the mournful facial expression and the lowered voice. Third, some of the vegetative and physical manifestations characteristic of depression are occasionally seen in individuals who are feeling sad but who would not be considered clinically depressed. A person who has failed an examination, lost a job, or been jilted may not only feel discouraged and forlorn, but also experience anorexia, insomnia, and fatigability. Finally, many individuals experience blue states that seem to oscillate in a consistent or rhythmic fashion, independently of external stimuli, suggestive of the rhythmic variations in the intensity of depression.[15]

The resemblance between depression and the low mood of normals has led to the concept that the pathological is simply an exaggeration of the normal. On the surface, this view seems plausible. As will be discussed in Chapter 2, each symptom of depression may be graded in intensity along a dimension, and the more mild intensities are certainly similar to the phenomena observed in normal individuals who are feeling blue.

In support of the continuity perspective, Hankin et al.[16] used Meehl's[17] taxometric procedures to examine the structure of depression in a sample of children and adolescents. Taking into account the skewness of depressive symptoms, the authors reported youth depression to be a dimensional, not categorical, construct. In discussing the implications of their findings, Hankin et al.[16] point out that by using continuously distributed scores, the statistical power of the research is enhanced, thus aiding the ability of researchers to ascertain correctly the true causes and consequences of depression.

Similar to the findings of Hankin et al.,[17] Haslam and Beck[18] used taxometric procedures to test for discreteness (discontinuity) of 5 hypothesized subtypes of major depression, including endogenous, sociotropic, autonomous, self-critical, and hopelessness forms. The study used self-reported symptom and personality profiles of 531 consecutively admitted outpatients diagnosed with major depression. The features of the respective subtypes were not found to covary as predicted, except for the endogenous subtype.[18]

It could be contended that many pathological states that seem to be on a continuum with the normal state are different in their essential character from the normal state. To illustrate this, an analogy may be made between the deviations of mood and deviations of internal body temperature. While pronounced changes in body temperature are on the same continuum as are normal temperatures, the underlying factors producing the large deviations are not an extension of the normal state of health: A person may have a disease, for example, typhoid fever, that is manifested by a serial progression in temperature and yet is categorically different from the normal state. Similarly, the deviation in mood found in depression may be the manifestation of a disease process that is distinct from the normal state.

There is no general consensus among the authorities regarding the relation of depression to normal mood swings. Some writers, notably Kraepelin and his followers, have considered depression a well-defined disease, quite distinct from normal mood. They have postulated the presence of a profound biological derangement as the key factor in depression. This concept of a dichotomy between health and disease has generally been shared by the *somatogenic school*. The *environmentalists* seem to favor the continuity hypothesis. In their view, there is a continuous series of mood reactions ranging from a normal reaction to an extreme reaction in a particularly susceptible person. The psychobiological school founded by Adolph Meyer tends to favor this view.

The ultimate answer to the question whether there is a dichotomy or continuity between normal mood and depression will have to wait until the question of the etiology of depression is fully resolved.

Chapter 2
Symptomatology of Depression

Previous Systematic Studies

As stated in Chapter 1, there has been remarkable consistency in the descriptions of depression since ancient times. While there has been unanimity among the writers on many of the characteristics, however, there has been lack of agreement on many others. The core signs and symptoms such as low mood, pessimism, self-criticism, and retardation or agitation seem to have been universally accepted. Other signs and symptoms that have been regarded as intrinsic to the depressive syndrome include autonomic symptoms, constipation, difficulty in concentrating, slow thinking, and anxiety. In 1953, Campbell[1] listed 29 medical manifestations of autonomic disturbance, among which the most common in manic depressives were hot flashes, tachycardia, dyspnea, weakness, head pains, coldness and numbness of the extremities, frontal headaches, and dizziness.

Very few systematic studies have been designed to delineate the characteristic signs and symptoms of depression. Cassidy et al.[2] compared the symptomatology of 100 patients diagnosed as manic depressive with a control group of 50 patients with diagnoses of recognized medical diseases. The frequency of the specific symptoms was determined by having the patient complete a questionnaire of 199 items. Among the symptoms that were endorsed significantly more often by those in the psychiatric group were anorexia, sleep disturbance, low mood, suicidal thoughts, crying, irritability, fear of losing the mind, poor concentration, and delusions.

It is interesting to note that Cassidy and his coworkers found that only 25 percent of the manic-depressive group thought that they would get well as compared with 61 percent of those who were medically ill. This is indicative of the pessimism characteristic of manic depressives: almost all could be expected to recover completely from their illness, in contrast to the number of incurably ill among the medical patients. Certain symptoms sometimes attributed to manic depressives, such as constipation, were found in similar proportions in the two groups.

Campbell reported a high frequency of medical symptoms, generally attributed to autonomic imbalance, among manic depressives. Cassidy's study, however, found that most of these medical symptoms occurred at least as frequently among the medically ill patients as among the manic-depressive patients. Moreover, many of these symptoms were found in a group of healthy control patients. Headaches, for instance, were reported by 49 percent of the manic-depressive patients, 36 percent of the medically sick controls, and 25 percent of the healthy controls. When the symptoms of manic depressives, anxiety neurotics, and hysteria patients were compared, it was found that autonomic symptoms occurred at least as frequently in the latter two groups as they did in the manic-depressive group. Palpitation, for instance, was reported by 56 percent of the manic depressives, 94 percent of the anxiety neurotics, and 76 percent of the hysterics. It therefore seems clear that autonomic symptoms are not specifically characteristic of manic-depressive disorders.

In the early 1960s, two systematic investigations of the symptomatology of depressive disorders were conducted to delineate the typical clinical picture, as well as to suggest typical subgroupings of depression.[3,4] But because the case material consisted primarily of depressed patients and did not include a control group of nondepressed psychiatric patients for comparison, it was not possible to determine which symptom clusters might be characteristic of depression or its various subgroupings and which might occur in any psychiatric patient or even in normals.

The following material is reprinted in its entirety from the first edition, with some minor updating of the language. The chapter ends with a brief section on variations in symptoms by age and culture as they are understood in the twenty-first century.

Following a review of the chief complaints, the symptoms of depression are described under four major headings: emotional, cognitive, motivational, and physical and vegetative. This is followed by a section on delusions and hallucinations. Some of these divisions may appear arbitrary, and it is undoubtedly true that some of the symptoms described separately may simply be different facets of the same phenomenon. Nonetheless, I think it is desirable at this stage to present the symptomatology as broadly as possible, despite the inevitable overlap. A section on behavioral observation follows the categorization of symptoms. The descriptions in this latter section were obtained by direct observation of the patients' nonverbal as well as their verbal behavior.

Chief Complaint

The chief complaint presented by depressed patients often points immediately to the diagnosis of depression; although it sometimes suggests a physical disturbance. Skillful questioning can generally determine whether the basic depressive symptomatology is present.

The chief complaint may take a variety of forms: (1) an unpleasant emotional state; (2) a changed attitude toward life; (3) somatic symptoms of a specifically depressive nature; or (4) somatic symptoms not typical of depression.

Among the most common subjective complaints[5] are "I feel miserable." "I just feel hopeless." "I'm desperate." "I'm worried about everything." Although depression is generally considered an affective disorder, it should be emphasized that a subjective change in mood is not reported by all depressed patients. As in many other disorders, the absence of a significant clinical feature does not rule out the diagnosis of that disorder. In our series, for instance, only 53 percent of the mildly depressed patients acknowledged feeling sad or unhappy.

Sometimes the chief complaint is in the form of a change of one's actions, reactions, or attitudes toward life. For example, a patient may say, "I don't have any goals any more." "I don't care anymore what happens to me." "I don't see any point to living." Sometimes the major complaint is a sense of futility about life.

Often the chief complaint of the depressed patient centers around some physical symptom that is characteristic of depression. The patient may complain of fatigue, lack of pep, or loss of appetite. Sometimes patients complain of some alteration in appearance or bodily functions, or that they are beginning to look old or are getting ugly. Others complain of some dramatic physical symptom such as, "My bowels are blocked up."

Depressed patients attending medical clinics or consulting either internists or general practitioners frequently present some symptom suggestive of a physical disease.[6] In many cases, the physical examination fails to reveal any physical abnormality. In other cases, some minor abnormality may be found but it is of insufficient severity to account for the magnitude of the patient's discomfort. On further examination, the patient may acknowledge a change in mood but is likely to attribute this to the somatic symptoms.

Severe localized or generalized pain may often be the chief focus of a patient's complaint. Bradley[7] reported 35 cases of depression in which the main complaint was severe localized pain. In each case, feelings of depression were either spontaneously reported by the patient or elicited on interview. In the cases in which the pain was integrally connected with the depression, the pain cleared up as the depression cleared up. Kennedy[8] and Von Hagen[9] reported that pain associated with depression responded to electroconvulsive therapy (ECT).

Cassidy et al.[2] analyzed the chief complaints of the manic-depressive patients. These complaints were divided into several categories which included (1) psychological; (2) localized medical; (3) generalized medical; (4) mixed medical and psychological; (5) medical, general and local; and (6) no clear information. Some of the typical complaints in each category are listed below:

TABLE 2-1. Chief Complaints of 100 Patients with Manic-Depressive Diagnosis and 50 Patients with Medical Diagnosis (%)

Type of complaint	Manic depressive	Medical controls
Psychological	58	0
Medical, localized	18	86
Medical, generalized		116
Medical, localized and generalized	2	0
Medical and psychological	2	6
No information	9	2

Adapted from Cassidy et al. 1957.

(1) *Psychological* (58 *percent*): "depressed"; "I have nothing to look forward to"; "afraid to be alone"; "no interest"; "can't remember anything"; "get discouraged and hurt"; "black moods and blind rages"; "I'm doing such stupid things"; "I'm all mixed up"; "very unhappy at times"; "brooded around the house."

(2) *Localized medical* (18 *percent*): "head is heavy"; "pressure in my throat"; "headaches"; "urinating frequently"; "pain in head like a balloon that burst"; "upset stomach."

(3) *Generalized medical* (11 *percent*): "tired"; "I'm exhausted"; "I feel all in"; "tire easy"; "jumpy most at night"; "I can't do my work, I don't feel strong"; "I tremble like a leaf."

(4) *Medical and psychological* (2 *percent*): "I get scared to death and can't breath"; "stiff neck and crying spells."

(5) *Medical, general and local* (2 *percent*): "breathing difficulty . . . pain all over"; "I have no power. My arms are weak"; "I can't work."

(6) *No information* (9 *percent*).

The authors tabulated the percentages of the various symptom types that were named by manic-depressive patients and by medically sick controls (Table 2-1). It is worthy of note that a medical symptom, either localized or generalized, was reported by 33 percent of the manic-depressive patients and 92 percent of the medically sick controls.

Symptoms

The decision as to which symptoms should be included here was made as a result of several steps. First, several textbooks of psychiatry and monographs on depression were studied to determine what symptoms have been attributed to depression by general consensus. Second, in an intensive study of 50 depressed patients and 30 nondepressed patients in psychotherapy, I attempted to tally which symptoms occurred significantly more often in the depressed than in the nondepressed group. On the basis of this tabulation, an inventory consisting of items relevant to depression was constructed and pretested on approximately 100 patients. Finally, this inventory was revised and presented to 966 psychiatric patients. Distributions of the symptoms reported in response to the inventory are presented in Tables 2-3–2-7.

One of the symptoms, namely *irritability*, did not occur significantly more frequently in the depressed than in the nondepressed patients. It, therefore, has been dropped from the list. Incidentally, Cassidy and his coworkers[2] found that this symptom was more frequent in the anxiety neurotic group than in the manic-depressive group.

Some of the symptoms often attributed to the manic-depressive syndrome are not included in the symptom descriptions in this chapter. For instance, *fear of death* was not included because it was not found to be any more common among the depressed patients than among the nondepressed in the preliminary clinical study. Cassidy, Flanagan, and Spellman[2] found, in fact, that fear of death occurred in 42 percent of patients with anxiety neurosis and only 35 percent of the manic depressives. Similarly, constipation occurred in 60 percent of the manic-depressive patients and 54 percent of the patients with hysteria. Consequently, this particular symptom does not seem to be specific to depression.

Conventional nosological categories were not used in our analyses of the symptomatology. Instead of being classified according to their primary diagnoses, such as manic-depressive reaction, schizophrenia, anxiety reaction, and so on, the patients were categorized according to the depth of depression they exhibited, independently of their primary diagnoses. There were two major reasons for this. First, in our own studies as well as in previous studies, it was found that the degree of interjudge reliability was relatively low in diagnoses made according to the standard nomenclature. Consequently, any findings based on diagnoses of such low reliability would be of relatively dubious value. The interpsychiatrist ratings of the depth of depression, by contrast, showed a relatively high correlation (.87). Second, we found that the cluster of symptoms generally regarded as constituting the depressive syndrome occurs not only in disorders such as neurotic-depressive reaction and manic-depressive reaction but also in patients whose primary diagnosis is anxiety reaction, schizophrenia, obsessional neurosis, and so on. In fact, we have found that a patient with the primary diagnosis of one of the typical depressive categories may be less depressed than a patient whose primary diagnosis is, for example, schizophrenia or obsessional neurosis. The sample, therefore, was divided into four groups according to the depth of depression: none, mild, moderate, and severe.

In addition to making the usual qualitative distinctions among the symptoms, I have attempted to provide a guide for assessing their severity. The symptoms are discussed in terms of how they are likely to appear in the mild,

TABLE 2-2. Distribution of Patients According to Race, Sex, and Depth of Depression

	Depth of depression				
	None	*Mild*	*Moderate*	*Severe*	*Total*
White males	71	98	91	15	275
White females	51	90	137	40	318
African American males	50	32	30	4	116
African American females	52	77	102	26	257
Total white	122	188	228	55	593
Total African American	102	109	132	30	373
Total male	121	130	121	19	391
Total female	103	167	239	66	575
Total	224	297	360	85	966

TABLE 2-3. Frequency of Emotional Manifestations Among Depressed and Nondepressed Patients (%)

	Depth of depression			
Manifestation	*None* ($n = 224$)	Mild ($n = 288$)	Moderate ($n = 377$)	Severe ($n = 86$)
Dejected mood	23	50	75	88
Self-dislike	37	64	81	86
Loss of gratification	35	65	86	92
Loss of attachments	16	37	60	64
Crying spells	29	44	63	83
Loss of mirth response	8	29	41	52

moderate, and severe states (or phases) of depression. This may serve as an aid to the clinician or investigator in making a quantitative estimate of the severity of depression. The tables may be used as a guide in diagnosing depression, since they show the relative frequency of the symptoms in patients who were considered to be either nondepressed, mildly depressed, moderately depressed, or severely depressed. The method for collecting the data on which the tables are based is described in greater detail in Chapter 10. The patient sample is described in Table 2-2.

Emotional Manifestations

The term *emotional manifestations* refers to the changes in the patient's feelings or overt behavior *directly* attributable to his or her feeling states (Table 2-3). In assessing emotional manifestations, it is important to take into account the individual's premorbid mood level and behavior, as well as what the examiner might consider the *normal* range in the patient's particular age, sex, and social group. The occurrence of frequent crying spells in a patient who rarely or never cried before becoming depressed might indicate a greater level of depression than it would in a patient who habitually cried whether depressed or not.

Dejected Mood

The characteristic depression in mood is described differently by various clinically depressed patients. Whatever term the patient uses to describe her or his subjective feelings should be further explored by the examiner. If the patient uses the word "depressed," for instance, the examiner should not take the word at its face value but should try to determine its connotation for the patient. Persons who are in no way clinically depressed may use this adjective to designate transient feelings of loneliness, boredom, or discouragement.

Sometimes the feeling is expressed predominantly in somatic terms, such as "a lump in my throat," or "I have an empty feeling in my stomach," or "I have a sad, heavy feeling in my chest." On further investigation, these feelings generally are found to be similar to the feelings expressed by other patients in terms of adjectives such as sad, unhappy, lonely, or bored.

The intensity of the mood deviation must be gauged by the examiner. Some of the rough criteria of the degree of depression are the relative degree or morbidity implied by the adjective chosen, the qualification by adverbs such as "slightly" or "very," and the degree of tolerance the patient expresses for the feeling (e.g., "I feel so miserable I can't stand it another minute").

Among the adjectives used by depressed patients in answer to the question "How do you feel?" are the following: miserable, hopeless, blue, sad, lonely, unhappy, downhearted, humiliated, ashamed, worried, useless, guilty. Eighty-eight percent of the severely depressed patients reported some degree of sadness or unhappiness, as compared with 23 percent of the nondepressed patients.

Mild: The patient indicates feeling blue or sad. The unpleasant feeling tends to fluctuate considerably during the day and at times may be absent, and the patient may even feel cheerful. Also the dysphoric feeling can be relieved partially or completely by outside stimuli, such as a compliment, a joke, or a favorable event. With a little effort or ingenuity the examiner can usually evoke a positive response. Patients at this level generally react with genuine amusement to jokes or humorous anecdotes.

Moderate: The dysphoria tends to be more pronounced and more persistent. The patient's feeling is less likely to be influenced by other people's attempts to cheer him or her up, and any relief of this nature is temporary. Also, a diurnal variation is frequently present: The dysphoria is often worse in the morning and tends to be alleviated as the day progresses.

Severe: In cases of severe depression, patients are apt to state that they feel "hopeless" or "miserable." Agitated patients frequently state that they are "worried." In our series, 70 percent of the severely depressed patients indicated that they were sad all the time and "could not snap out of it"; that they were so sad that it was very painful, or that they were so sad they could not stand it.

Negative Feelings Toward Self

Depressed patients often express negative feelings about themselves. These feelings may be related to the general dysphoric feelings just described, but they are different in that they are specifically directed toward the self. The patients appear to distinguish feelings of dislike for themselves from negative attitudes about themselves such as "I am worthless." The frequency of self-dislike ranged from 37 percent in the nondepressed group to 86 percent among the severely depressed.

Mild: Patients state that they feel disappointed in themselves. This feeling is accompanied by ideas such as "I've let everybody down . . . If I had tried harder, I could have made the grade."

Moderate: The feeling of self-dislike is stronger and may progress to a feeling of disgust with oneself. This is generally accompanied by ideas such as "I'm a weakling . . . I don't do anything right . . . I'm no good."

Severe: The feeling may progress to the point where patients hate themselves. This stage may be identified by statements such as: "I'm a terrible person . . . I don't deserve to live . . . I'm despicable . . . I loathe myself."

Reduction in Gratification

The loss of gratification is such a pervasive process among depressives that many patients regard it as the central feature of their illness. In our series, 92 percent of the severely depressed patients reported at least partial loss of satisfaction. This was the most common symptom among the depressed group as a whole.

Loss of gratification appears to start with a few activities and, as the depression progresses, spreads to practically everything the patient does. Even activities that are generally associated with biological needs or drives, such as eating or sexual experiences, are not spared. Experiences that are primarily psychosocial such as achieving fame, receiving expressions of love or friendship, or even engaging in conversations are similarly stripped of their pleasurable properties.

The emphasis placed by some patients on loss of satisfaction gives the impression that they are especially oriented in their lives toward obtaining gratification. Whether or not this applies to the premorbid state cannot be stated with certainty, but it is true that the feverish pursuit of gratification is a cardinal feature of their manic states.

The initial loss of satisfaction from activities involving responsibility or obligation, such as those involved in the role of worker, stay-at-home spouse, or student, is often compensated for by increasing satisfaction from recreational activities. This observation has prompted Saul[10] and others to suggest that, in depression, the "give-get" balance is upset; the patient, depleted psychologically over a period of time by activities predominantly *giving* in nature, experiences an accentuation of passive needs, which are gratified by activities involving less of a sense of duty or responsibility (giving) and more of a tangible and easily obtained satisfaction. In the more advanced stages of the illness, however, even passive, regressive activities fail to bring any satisfaction.

Mild: The patient complains that some of the joy has gone out of life. He or she no longer gets a "kick" or pleasure from family, friends, or job. Characteristically, activities involving responsibility, obligation, or effort become less satisfying. Often, patients find greater satisfaction in *passive* activities involving recreation, relaxation, or rest. They may seek unusual types of activities in order to get some of their former thrill. One patient reported that he could always pull himself out of a mild depression by watching a performance of deviant sexual practices.

Moderate: Patients feel bored much of the time. They may try to enjoy some former favorite activities but these seem "flat" now. Business or professional activities that formerly excited them now fail to move them. They may obtain temporary relief from a change, such as a vacation, but the boredom returns upon resumption of usual activities.

Severe: They experience no enjoyment from activities that were formerly pleasurable, and may even feel an aversion for activities they once enjoyed. Popular acclaim or expressions of love or friendship no longer bring any degree of satisfaction. The patients almost uniformly complain that nothing gives them any degree of satisfaction.

Loss of Emotional Attachments

Loss of emotional involvement in other people or activities usually accompanies loss of satisfaction. This is manifested by a decline in interest in particular activities or in affection or concern for other persons. Loss of affection for family members is often a cause for concern to the patient and occasionally is a major factor in seeking medical attention. Sixty-four percent of the severely depressed patients reported loss of feeling for or interest in other people, whereas only 16 percent of the nondepressed patients reported this symptom.

Mild: In mild cases, there is some decline in the degree of enthusiasm for, or absorption in, an activity. The patient sometimes reports no longer experiencing the same intensity of love or affection for spouse, children, or friends, but at the same time may feel more dependent on them.

Moderate: The loss of interest or of positive feeling may progress to indifference. A number of patients described this as a "wall" between themselves and other people. Sometimes a husband may complain that he no longer loves his wife, or a mother may be concerned that she does not seem to care about her children or what happens to them. A previously devoted employee may report no longer being concerned about his or her job. Both men and women may no longer care about their appearance.

Severe: The loss of attachment to external objects may progress to apathy. The patient may not only lose any positive feeling for family members but may be surprised to find that her or his only reaction is a negative one. In some cases, the patient experiences only a kind of cold hate, which may be masked by dependency. A typical patient's report is, "I've been told I have love and can give love. But now I don't feel anything toward my family. I don't give a damn about them. I know this is terrible, but sometimes I hate them."

Crying Spells

Increased periods of crying are frequent among depressed patients. This is particularly true of the depressed women in our series. Of the severely depressed patients, 83 percent reported that they cried more frequently than they did before becoming depressed, or that they felt like crying even though the tears did not come.

Some patients who rarely cried when not depressed were able to diagnose the onset of depression by observing a strong desire to weep. One woman remarked, "I don't know whether I feel sad or not but I do feel like crying, so I guess I am depressed." Further questioning elicited the rest of the cardinal symptoms of depression.

Mild: There is an increased tendency to weep or cry. Stimuli or situations that would ordinarily not affect the patient may now elicit tears. A mother, for example, might burst out crying during an argument with her children or if she feels her husband is not attentive. Although increased crying is frequent among mildly depressed women, it is unusual for a mildly depressed man to cry.[5]

Moderate: The patient may cry during the psychiatric interview, and references to his or her problems may elicit tears. Men who have not cried since childhood may cry while discussing their problems. Women may cry for no apparent reason: "It just comes over me like a wave and I can't help crying." Sometimes patients feel relieved after crying but more often they feel more depressed.

Severe: By the time they have reached the severe stage, patients who were easily moved to tears in the earlier phase may find that they no longer can cry even when they want to. They may weep but have no tears ("dry depression"); 29 percent reported that although they had previously been capable of crying when feeling sad, they no longer could cry—even though they wanted to do so.

Loss of Mirth Response

Depressed patients frequently volunteer the information that they have lost their sense of humor. The problem does not seem to be loss of the ability to perceive the point of the joke or even, when instructed, to construct a joke. The difficulty rather seems to be that patients do not respond to humor in the usual way. They are not amused, do not feel like laughing, and do not get any feeling of satisfaction from a jesting remark, joke, or cartoon.

In our series, 52 percent of the severely depressed patients indicated that they had lost their sense of humor, as contrasted with 8 percent of the nondepressed patients.

Nussbaum and Michaux[11] studied the response to humor (in the form of riddles and jokes) in 18 women patients with severe neurotic and psychotic depressions. They found that improvements in response to humorous stimuli correlated well with clinical ratings of improvement of the depression.

Mild: Patients who frequently enjoy listening to jokes and telling jokes find that this is no longer such a ready source of gratification. They remark that jokes no longer seem funny to them. Furthermore, they do not handle kidding or joshing by their friends as well as previously.

Moderate: Patients may see the point of a joke and can even force a smile, but are usually not amused. They cannot see the light side of events and tend to take everything seriously.

Severe: Patients do not respond at all to humorous sallies by other people. Where others may respond to the humorous element in a joke, they are more likely to respond to the aggressive or hostile content and feel hurt or disgusted.

Cognitive Manifestations

The cognitive manifestations of depression include a number of diverse phenomena (Table 2-4). One group is composed of the patient's distorted attitudes toward self, personal experience, and the future. This group includes low self-evaluations, distortions of the body image, and negative expectations. Another symptom, self-blame, expresses patients' notion of causality: they are prone to hold themselves responsible for any difficulties or problems they encounter. A third kind of symptom involves the area of decision-making: The patient typically vacillates and is indecisive.

Low Self-Evaluation

Low self-esteem is a characteristic feature of depression. Self-devaluation is apparently part of depressed patients' pattern of viewing themselves as

TABLE 2-4. Frequency of Cognitive and Motivational Manifestations Among
Depressed and Nondepressed Patients (%)

Manifestation	Depth of depression			
	None (n = 224)	Mild (n = 288	Moderate (n = 377)	Severe (n = 86)
Low self-evaluation	38	60	78	81
Negative expectation	22	55	72	87
Self-blame and self-criticism	43	67	80	80
Indecisiveness	23	48	67	76
Distorted self-image	12	33	50	66
Loss of motivation	33	65	83	86
Suicidal wishes	12	31	53	74

deficient in those attributes that are specifically important to them: ability, performance, intelligence, health, strength, personal attractiveness, popularity, or financial resources. Often the sense of deficiency is expressed in terms such as "I am inferior" or "I am inadequate." This symptom was reported by 81 percent of the severely depressed patients and by 38 percent of the nondepressed patients.

The sense of deficiency may also be reflected in complaints of deprivation of love or material possessions. This reaction is most apparent in patients who have had, respectively, an unhappy love affair or a financial reversal just prior to the depression.

Mild: Patients show an excessive reaction to their errors or difficulties and are prone to regard them as a reflection of inadequacy or a defect. They compare themselves with others and, more often than not, conclude they are inferior. It is possible, however, to correct these inaccurate self-evaluations, at least temporarily, by confronting patients with appropriate evidence or by reasoning with them.

Moderate: Most of the patients' thought content revolves about the sense of deficiency, and they are prone to interpret neutral situations as indicative of this deficiency. They exaggerate the degree and significance of any errors. When they look at their present and past life, they see their failures as outstanding and their successes as faint by comparison. They complain that they have lost confidence in themselves, and their sense of inadequacy is such that when confronted with tasks they have easily handled in the past, their initial reaction is: "I can't do it."

Religious or moralistic patients tend to dwell on their sins or moral shortcomings. Patients who placed a premium on personal attractiveness, intelligence, or business success tend to believe they have slipped in these areas. Attempts to modify distorted self-evaluations by reassuring the patients or by presenting contradictory evidence generally meet with considerable resistance; any increase in realistic thinking about themselves is transient.

Severe: Patients' self-evaluations are at the lowest point. They drastically downgrade themselves in terms of personal attributes and their role as parent, spouse, employer, and so on. They regard themselves as worthless, completely inept, and total failures. They claim they are a burden to family members, who would be better off without them. The severely depressed patient may be preoccupied with ideas of being the world's worst sinner, completely impoverished, or totally inadequate. Attempts to correct the erroneous ideas are generally fruitless.

Negative Expectations

A gloomy outlook and pessimism are closely related to the feelings of hopelessness mentioned previously. More than 78 percent of the depressed patients reported a negative outlook, as compared with 22 percent of the nondepressed group. This symptom showed the highest correlation with the clinical rating of depression.

Depressed patients' pattern of expecting the worst and rejecting the possibility of any improvement poses formidable obstacles in attempts to engage them in a therapeutic program. Their negative outlook is often a source of frustration to friends, family, and physician when they try to be of help. Not infrequently, for example, patients may discard their antidepressant pills because they believe a priori that they "cannot do any good."

Unlike anxious patients, who temper negative anticipations with the realization that the unpleasant events may be avoided or will pass in time, depressed patients thinks in terms of a future in which the present deficient condition (financial, social, physical) will continue or even get worse. This sense of permanence and irreversibility of one's status or problems seems to form the basis for consideration of suicide as a logical course of action. The relationship of hopelessness to suicide is indicated by the finding that, of all the symptoms that were correlated with suicide, the correlation coefficient of hopelessness:suicide was the highest.

Mild: Patients tend to expect a negative outcome in ambiguous or equivocal situations. When associates and friends feel justified in anticipating favorable results, their expectations lean toward the negative or pessimistic. Whether the subject of concern is health, personal problems, or economic problems, they doubt whether any improvement will take place.

Moderate: They regard the future as unpromising and state they have nothing to which to look forward. It is difficult to get them to do anything because their initial response is "I won't like it" or "it won't do any good."

Severe: They view the future as black and hopeless. They state they will never get over their troubles and that things cannot get better. They believe none of their problems can be solved. They make statements such as "This is the end of the road. From now on I will look older and uglier"; "There is nothing here for me any more. I have no place. There is no future"; "I know I can't get better . . . it's all over for me."

Self-Blame and Self-Criticism

Depressives' perseverating self-blame and self-criticism appear to be related to their egocentric notions of causality and penchant for criticizing themselves for their alleged deficiencies. They are particularly prone to ascribe adverse occurrences to some deficiency in themselves and then rebuke themselves for this alleged defect. In the more severe cases, patients may blame themselves for happenings that are in no way connected with them and abuse themselves in a savage manner. Eighty percent of the severely depressed patients reported this symptom.

Mild: In mild cases, patients are prone to blame and criticize themselves when they fall short of their rigid, perfectionist standards. If people seem less responsive to them, or they are slow at solving a problem, they are likely to berate themselves for being dull or stupid. They seem to be intolerant of any shortcomings in themselves and cannot accept the idea that it is human to err.

Moderate: Patients are likely to criticize themselves harshly for any aspects of personality or behavior they judge to be substandard. They are likely to blame themselves for mishaps that are obviously not their fault. Their self-criticisms become more extreme.

Severe: In the severe state, patients are even more extreme in self-blame or self-criticism. They make statements such as "I'm responsible for the violence and suffering in the world. There's no way in which I can be punished enough for my sins. I wish you would take me out and hang me." They view themselves as social lepers or criminals and interpret various extraneous stimuli as signs of public disapproval.

Indecisiveness

Difficulty in making decisions, vacillating between alternatives, and changing decisions are depressive characteristics that are usually quite vexing to the patient's family and friends as well as to the patient. The frequency of indecisiveness ranged from 48 percent in the mildly depressed patients to 76 percent in the severely depressed group.

There appear to be at least two facets to this indecisiveness. The first is primarily in the cognitive sphere. Depressed patients anticipate making the wrong decision: whenever they consider one of various possibilities they tend to regard it as wrong and think they will regret making that choice. The second facet is primarily motivational and is related to "paralysis of the will," avoidance tendencies, and increased dependency. Patients have a lack of motivation to go through the mental operations required to arrive at a conclusion. Also, the idea of making a decision represents a burden; they desire to evade or at least to get help with any situation they perceive will be burdensome. Furthermore, they realize that making a decision often commits them to a course of action and, since they desire to avoid action, they are prone to procrastinate.

Routine decisions that must be made in carrying out their occupational or household roles become major problems for the depressed patients. A professor cannot decide what material to include in a lecture; a householder cannot decide what to cook for an evening meal; a student cannot decide whether to spend the spring recess studying at college or go home; an executive cannot decide whether to hire a new assistant.

Mild: Patients who can ordinarily make rapid-fire decisions find that solutions do not seem to occur so readily. Whereas in their normal state they reach a decision "without even thinking about it," they now find themselves impelled to mull over the problem, review the possible consequences of the decision, and consider a variety of often irrelevant alternatives. The fear of making the wrong decision is reflected in a general sense of uncertainty. Frequently, they seek confirmation from another person.

Moderate: Difficulty in making decisions spreads to almost every activity and involves such minor problems as what clothes to wear, what route to take to the office, and whether to have a haircut. Often it is of little practical importance which alternative is selected, but the vacillation and failure to arrive at some decision can have unfavorable consequences. A woman, for example, spent several weeks trying to choose between two shades of paint for her house. The two shades under consideration were hardly distinguishable, but her failure to reach a decision created a turmoil in the house, the painter having left his buckets of paint and scaffolding until a decision could be made.

Severe: Severely depressed patients generally believe they are incapable of making a decision and consequently do not even try. A woman prodded to make a shopping list or a list of clothes for her children to take to camp insisted she could not decide what to put down. Patients frequently have doubts about everything they do and say. One woman seriously doubted that she had given her correct name to the psychiatrist, or that she had enunciated it properly.

Distortion of Body Image

Patients' distorted picture of their physical appearance is often quite marked in depression. This occurs somewhat more frequently among women than among men. In our series, 66 percent of the severely depressed patients believed that they had become unattractive, as compared with 12 percent of the nondepressed patients.

Mild: Patients begin to be excessively concerned with physical appearance. A woman finds herself frowning at her reflection whenever she passes a mirror. She examines her face minutely for signs of blemishes and becomes pre-occupied with the thought that she looks plain or is getting fat. A man worries incessantly about the beginnings of hair loss, convinced that women find him unattractive.

Moderate: The concern about physical appearance is greater. A man believes that there has been a change in his looks since the onset of the depression even though there is no objective evidence to support this idea. When he sees an ugly person, he thinks, "I look like that." As he becomes worried about his appearance, his brow becomes furrowed. When he observes his furrowed brow in the mirror, he thinks, "my whole face is wrinkled and the wrinkles will never disappear." Some patients seek plastic surgery to remedy the fancied or exaggerated facial changes.

Sometimes a woman may believe she has grown fat even though there is no objective evidence to support this. In fact, some patients have this notion even though they are losing weight.

Severe: The idea of personal unattractiveness becomes more fixed. Patients believe they are ugly and repulsive looking. They expect other people to turn away in revulsion: one woman wore a veil and another turned her head whenever anybody approached her.

Motivational Manifestations

Motivational manifestations include consciously experienced strivings, desires, and impulses that are prominent in depressions. These motivational patterns can often be inferred from observing the patient's behavior; however, direct questioning generally elicits a fairly precise and comprehensive description of motivations (see Table 2-4).

A striking feature of the characteristic motivations of the depressed patient is their *regressive* nature. The term regressive is applicable in that the patient seems drawn to activities that are the least demanding in the degree of responsibility or initiative or the amount of energy required. They turn away from activities that are specifically associated with the adult role and seek activities more characteristic of the child's role. When confronted with a choice, they prefer passivity to activity and dependence to independence (autonomy); they avoid responsibility and escape from their problems rather than trying to solve them; they seek immediate but transient gratifications instead of delayed but prolonged satisfactions. The ultimate manifestation of the escapist trend is expressed in the desire to withdraw from life via suicide.

An important aspect of these motivations is that their fulfillment is generally incompatible with the individual's major premorbid goals and values. In essence, yielding to passive impulses and desires to retreat or commit suicide leads to abandonment of family, friends, and vocation. Similarly, the patient defaults on the chance to obtain personal satisfaction through accomplishment or interpersonal relations. By avoiding even the simplest problems, moreover, the patient finds that they accumulate until they seem overwhelming.

The specific motivational patterns to be described are presented as distinct phenomena, although they are obviously interrelated and may, in fact, represent different facets of the same fundamental pattern. It is possible that certain phenomena are primary and the others are secondary or tertiary; for instance, it could be postulated that paralysis of the will is the result of escapist or passive wishes, a sense of futility, loss of external investments, or the sense of fatigue. Since these suggestions are purely speculative, it seems preferable at present to treat these phenomena separately, rather than prematurely to assign primacy to certain patterns.

Paralysis of the Will

The loss of positive motivation is often a striking feature of depression. Patients may have a major problem in mobilizing themselves to perform even the most elemental and vital tasks such as eating, elimination, or taking medication to relieve their distress. The essence of the problem appears to be that, although they can define for themselves what they should do, they do not experience any internal stimulus to do it. Even when urged, cajoled, or threatened, they do not seem able to arouse any desire to do these things. Loss of positive motivation ranged from 65 percent of the mild cases to 86 percent of the severe cases.

Occasionally an actual or impending shift in a patient's life situation may serve to mobilize constructive motivations. One notably retarded and apathetic patient was suddenly aroused when her husband became ill and she experienced a strong desire to help him. Another patient experienced a return of positive motivation when informed she was going to be hospitalized, a prospect she viewed as extremely distasteful.

Mild: Patients find they no longer spontaneously desire to do certain specific things, especially those that do not bring any immediate gratification. An advertising executive observes a loss of drive and initiative in planning a special sales promotion; a college professor finds himself devoid of any desire to prepare his lectures; a medical student loses her desire to study. A retiree who formerly felt driven to engage in a variety of domestic and community projects, described her loss of motivation in the following terms: "I have no desire to do anything. I just do things mechanically without any feeling for what I'm doing. I just go through the motions like a robot and when I run down I just stop."

Moderate: In moderate cases the loss of spontaneous desire spreads to almost all of the patient's usual activities. A woman complained, "There are certain things I know I have to do like eat, brush my teeth, and go to the bathroom, but I have no desire to do them." In contrast to severely depressed patients, moderately depressed patients find they can "force" themselves to do things. Also, they are responsive to pressure from other people or to potentially embarrassing situations. A woman, for instance, waited in front of an elevator for about 15 minutes because she could not mobilize any desire to press the button. When others approached the elevator, however, she rapidly pressed the button lest they think she was peculiar.

Severe: In severe cases, there often is complete paralysis of the will. Patients have no desire to do anything, even things that are essential to life. Consequently, they may be relatively immobile unless prodded or pushed into activity by others. It is sometimes necessary to pull patients out of bed, wash, dress, and feed them. In extreme cases, even communication may be blocked by the patient's inertia. One woman, who was unable to respond to questions during the worst part of her depression, remarked later that even though she "wanted" to answer she could not summon the "will power" to do so.

Avoidance, Escapist, and Withdrawal Wishes

The wish to break out of the usual pattern or routine of life is a common manifestation of depression. The office assistant wants to get away from paper work, the student daydreams of faraway places, and the stay-at-home spouse yearns to leave domestic tasks. Depressed individuals regard their duties as dull, meaningless, or burdensome and want to escape to an activity that offers relaxation or refuge.

These escapist wishes resemble the attitudes described as paralysis of the will. A useful distinction is that the escapist wishes are experienced as definite motivations with specific goals, whereas paralysis of the will refers to the loss or absence of motivation.

Mild: Mildly depressed patients experience a strong inclination to avoid or postpone doing certain things they regard as uninteresting or taxing. They tend to shy away from attending to details they consider unimportant. They are likely to procrastinate or avoid entirely an activity that does not promise immediate gratification or involves effort. Just as they are repelled by activities that involve effort or responsibility, they are attracted to more passive and less complex activities.

A depressed student expressed this as follows: "It's much easier to daydream in lectures than pay attention. It's easier to stay home and drink than call a girl for a date. . . . It's easier to mumble and not be heard than to talk clearly and distinctly. It's much easier to write sloppily than to make the effort to write legibly. It's much easier to lead a self-centered, passive life than to make the effort to change it."

Moderate: In moderate cases, avoidance wishes are stronger and spread to a much wider range of usual activities. A depressed college professor described this as follows: "Escape seems to be my strongest desire. I feel as though I would feel better in almost any other occupation or profession. As I ride the bus to the university, I wish I were the bus driver instead of a teacher."

Patients think continually of ways of diversion or escape. They would like to indulge in passive recreation such as going to the movies, watching television, or getting drunk. They may daydream of going to a desert island or becoming a hobo. At this stage, they may withdraw from most social contacts since interpersonal relations seem to be too demanding. At the same time, because of their loneliness and increased dependency, they may want to be with other people.

Severe: In severe cases, the wish to avoid or escape is manifested in marked seclusiveness. Not infrequently the patient stays in bed, and when people approach, may hide under the covers. A patient said, "I just feel like getting away from everybody and everything. I don't want to see anybody or do anything. All I want to do is sleep." One form of escape that generally occurs to severely depressed patients is suicide. They feel a strong desire to end their life as a way of escaping from a situation they regard as intolerable.

Suicidal Wishes

Suicidal wishes have historically been associated with a depressed state. While suicidal wishes may occur in nondepressed individuals, they occur substantially more frequently in depressed patients. In our series this was the symptom reported least frequently (12 percent) by the nondepressed patients, but it was reported frequently (74 percent) by the severely depressed patients. This difference indicates the diagnostic value of this particular symptom in the identification of severe depression. The intensity with which this symptom was expressed also showed one of the highest correlations with the intensity of depression.

The patient's interest in suicide may take a variety of forms. It may be experienced as a passive wish ("I wish I were dead"); an activity wish ("I want to kill myself"); as a repetitive, obsessive thought without any volitional quality; as a daydream; or as a meticulously conceived plan. In some patients, the suicidal wishes occur constantly throughout the illness, and the patient may have to battle continually to ward them off. In other cases, the wish is sporadic and is characterized by a gradual build-up, then a slackening of intensity until it disappears temporarily. Patients often report, once the wish has been dissipated, that they are glad they did not succumb to it. It should be noted that the impulsive suicidal attempt may be just as dangerous as the deliberately planned attempt.

The importance of suicidal symptoms is obvious, since nowadays it is practically the only feature of depression that poses a reasonably high probability of fatal consequences. The incidence of suicide among manic depressives ranged from 2.8 percent in one study with a 10-year follow-up[12] to 5 percent in a 25-year period of observation.[13]

Mild: Wishes to die were reported by about 31 percent of the mildly depressed patients. Often these take the passive form such as "I would be better off dead." Patients may state that they would not do anything to hasten death, but find the idea of dying attractive. One patient looked forward to an airplane trip because of the possibility the plane might crash.

Sometimes the patient expresses an indifference toward living ("I don't care whether I live or die"). Other patients may show ambivalence ("I would like to die but at the same time I'm afraid of dying").

Moderate: In these cases, suicidal wishes are more direct, frequent, and compelling; there is a definite risk of either impulsive or premeditated suicidal attempts. The patient may express this desire in the passive form: "I hope I won't wake up in the morning" or "If I died, my family would be better off." The active expression of the wish may vary from an ambivalent statement, "I'd like to kill myself but I don't have the guts," to the bald assertion, "If I could do it and not botch it up, I would go ahead and kill myself." The suicidal wish may be manifested by the patient's taking unnecessary risks. A number of patients drove their cars at excessive rates of speed in the hope that something might happen.

Severe: In severe cases, suicidal wishes tend to be intense, although the patient may be too retarded to complete a suicidal attempt. Among typical statements are the following: "I feel so hopeless. Why won't you let me die?"; "It's no use. All is lost. There is only one way out—to kill myself"; "I must weep myself to death. I can't live and you won't let me die"; "I can't bear to live through another day. Please put me out of my misery."

Increased Dependency

The term *dependency* is used here to designate the *desire* to receive help, guidance, or direction rather than the actual process of relying on someone else. The accentuated wishes for dependency have only occasionally been included in clinical descriptions of depression; they have, however, been recognized and assigned a major etiological role in several psychodynamic explanations of depression.[14,15] The accentuated orality attributed to depressed patients by those authors includes the kinds of wishes that are generally regarded as "dependent."

Since increased dependency has been attributed to other conditions as well as to depression, the question could be raised whether dependency can be justifiably listed as a *specific* manifestation of depression. Increased dependency wishes are seen in an overt form in people who have an acute or chronic physical illness; moreover, covert or repressed dependency has been regarded by many theoreticians as the central factor in certain psychosomatic conditions such as peptic ulcer, as well as in alcoholism and other addictions. However, it is my contention that frank, undisguised, and intensified desires for help, support, and encouragement are very prominent elements in the advanced stages of depression and belong in any clinical description of this syndrome. In other conditions, intensified dependency may be a variable and transient characteristic.

The desire for help seems to transcend the realistic *need* for help; that is, the patient can often reach his or her objective without assistance. Receiving help, however, appears to carry special emotional meaning for the patient beyond its practical importance and is often satisfying—at least temporarily.

Mild: The patient who is ordinarily very self-sufficient and independent begins to express a desire to be helped, guided, or supported. A patient who had always insisted on driving when he was in the car with his wife asked her to drive. He felt that he was capable of driving, but the idea of her driving was more appealing to him at this time.

As the dependency wishes become stronger, they tend to supersede habitual independent drives. Patients now find that they prefer to have somebody do things with them than to do them alone. The dependent desire does not seem to be simply a by-product of the feelings of helplessness and inadequacy or fatigue. Patients feel a craving for help even though they recognize that they do not need it, and when the help is received they generally experience some gratification and lessening of depression.

Moderate: The patient's desire to have things done for him or her, to receive instruction and reassurance, is stronger. The patient who experiences a wish for help in the mild phase now experiences this as a *need*. Receiving help no longer is an optional luxury but is conceived of as a necessity. A depressed woman, who was legally separated from her husband, begged him to come back to her. "I need you desperately," she said. It was not clear to her exactly what she needed him for, except that she wanted to have a strong person near her.

When confronted with a task or problem, moderately depressed patients feel impelled to seek help before attempting to undertake it themselves. They not infrequently state that they want to be told what to do. Some patients shop around for opinions about a certain course of action and seem to be more involved in the idea of getting advice than in using it. One woman would ask numerous questions about trivial problems but did not seem to pay much attention to the content of the answer—just so an answer was forthcoming.

Severe: The intensity of the desire to be helped is increased, and the content of the wish has a predominantly passive cast. It is couched almost exclusively in terms of wanting someone to do everything for the patient, including care-taking. Patients are no longer concerned about getting direction or advice, or in sharing problems. They want the other person to do the job and solve the problem for them. A patient clung to the physician and pleaded, "Doctor, you

TABLE 2-5. Intercorrelation of Physical and Vegetative Symptoms (n = 606)

Symptom	Fatigue	Loss of sleep*	Loss of appetite*	Loss of libido*
Depth of depression	.31	.30	.35	.27
Fatigability		.25	.20	.29
Sleep disturbance			.35	.29
Loss of appetite				.33

*Pearson product-moment correlation coefficients.

TABLE 2-6. Frequency of Vegetative and Physical Manifestations Among Depressed and Nondepressed Patients (%)

Manifestation	Degree of depression			
	None (n = 224)	Mild (n = 288)	Moderate (n = 377)	Severe (n = 86)
Loss of appetite	21	40	54	72
Sleep disturbance	40	60	76	87
Loss of libido	27	38	58	61
Fatigability	40	62	80	78

must help me." Her desire was for the psychiatrist to do everything for her without her doing anything. She even wanted the psychiatrist to adopt her children.

The patient may show dependency by not wanting to leave the doctor's office or not wanting the doctor to leave. Terminating the interview often becomes a difficult and painful process.

Vegetative and Physical Manifestations

The physical and vegetative manifestations are considered by some authors to be evidence for a basic autonomic or hypothalamic disturbance that is responsible for the depressive state.[1,16] These symptoms, contrary to expectation, have a relatively low correlation with each other and with clinical ratings of the depth of depression. The intercorrelation matrix is shown in Table 2-5. The frequency of the symptoms among depressed and nondepressed patients is shown in Table 2-6.

Loss of Appetite

For many patients, loss of appetite is often the first sign of an incipient depression, and return of appetite may be the first sign that it is beginning to lift. Some degree of appetite loss was reported by 72 percent of the severely depressed patients and only 21 percent of the nondepressed patients.

Mild: Patients no longer eat meals with the customary degree of relish or enjoyment. There is also some dulling of desire for food.

Moderate: The desire for food may be mostly gone and patients may miss a meal without realizing it.

Severe: Patient may have to force themselves—or be forced—to eat. There may even be an aversion to food. After several weeks of severe depression, the amount of weight loss may be considerable.

Sleep Disturbance

Difficulty in sleeping is one of most notable symptoms of depression, although it occurs in a large proportion of nondepressed patients as well. Difficulty in sleeping was reported by 87 percent of the severely depressed patients and 40 percent of the nondepressed patients.

There have been a number of careful studies of the sleep of depressed patients (see Chapter 9). The investigators have presented solid evidence, based on direct observation of the patients and EEG recordings during the night, that depressed patients sleep less than do normal controls. In addition, the studies show an excessive degree of restlessness and movement during the night among the depressed patients.

Mild: Patients report waking a few minutes to half an hour earlier than usual. In many cases, they may state that, although ordinarily they sleep soundly until awakened by the alarm clock, they now awaken several minutes before the alarm goes off. In some cases, the sleep disturbance is in the reverse direction: they find that they sleep more than usual.

Moderate: Patients awaken one or two hours earlier than usual and frequently report that sleep is not restful. Moreover, they seem to spend a greater proportion of the time in light sleep. They may also awaken after three or four hours of sleep and require a hypnotic to return to sleep. In some cases, patients manifest an excessive sleeping tendency and may sleep up to twelve hours a day.

Severe: Patients frequently awaken after only four or five hours of sleep and find it impossible to return to sleep. In some cases, they claim that they have not slept at all during the night, that they can remember "thinking" continuously during the night. It is likely, however, as Oswald et al.[17] point out, that the patients are actually in a light sleep for a good part of the time.

Loss of Libido

Some loss of interest in sex, whether of an autoerotic or directed toward someone else nature, was reported by 61 percent of the depressed patients and 27 percent of the nondepressed patients. Loss of libido correlated most highly with loss of appetite, loss of interest in other people, and depressed mood.

Mild: There is generally a slight loss of spontaneous sexual desire and responsiveness to sexual stimuli. In some cases, however, sexual desire seems to be heightened when the patient is mildly depressed.

Moderate: Sexual desire is markedly reduced and is aroused only with considerable stimulation.

Severe: Any responsiveness to sexual stimuli is lost and the patient may have a pronounced aversion to sex.

Fatigability

Increased tiredness was reported by 79 percent of the depressed patients and only 33 percent of the nondepressed. Some patients appear to experience this symptom as a purely physical phenomenon: the limbs feel heavy or the body feels as though it is weighted down. Others express fatigability as a loss of pep or energy. The patient complains of feeling "listless," "worn out," "too weak to move," or "run down."

It is sometimes difficult to distinguish fatigability from loss of motivation and avoidance wishes. It is interesting to note that fatigability correlates more highly with lack of satisfaction (.36) and with pessimistic outlook (.36) than with other physical or vegetative symptoms such as loss of appetite (.20) and sleep disturbance (.28). The correlation with lack of satisfaction and pessimistic outlook suggests that the mental set may be a major factor in the patient's feeling of tiredness; the converse, of course, should be considered as a possibility, namely, that tiredness influences the mental set.

Some authors have conceptualized depression as a "depletion syndrome" because of the prominence of fatigability; they postulate that the patient exhausts available energy during the period prior to the onset of the depression, and the depressed state represents a kind of hibernation, during which the patient gradually builds up a new store of energy. Sometimes the fatigue is attributed to the sleep disturbance. Against this theory is the observation that even when the patients do get more sleep as a result of hypnotics, there is rarely any improvement in the feeling of fatigue. It is interesting to note as well that the correlation between sleep disturbance and fatigability is only .28. If the sleep disturbance were a major factor, a substantially higher correlation would be expected. As will be discussed in Chapter 12, fatigability may be a manifestation of loss of positive motivation.

There tends to be a diurnal variation in fatigability parallel to low mood and negative expectations. The patient tends to feel more tired upon awakening but somewhat less tired as the day progresses.

Mild: Patients find that they tire more easily than usual. If they have had a hypomanic period just prior to the depression, the contrast is marked: whereas previously they could be very active for many hours without any feeling of tiredness, they now feel fatigued after a relatively short period of work. Not infrequently a diversion or a short nap may restore a feeling of vitality, but the improvement is transient.

Moderate: Patients are generally tired when they awaken in the morning. Almost any activity seems to accentuate the tiredness. Rest, relaxation, and recreation do not appear to alleviate this feeling and may, in fact, aggravate it. A patient who customarily walked great distances when well would feel exhausted after short walks when depressed. Not only physical activity but focused mental activity such as reading often increases the sense of tiredness.

Severe: Patients complain that they are too tired to do anything. Under external pressure they are sometimes able to perform tasks requiring a large expenditure of energy. Without such stimulation, however, they do not seem to be able to mobilize the energy to perform even simple tasks such as getting dressed. They may complain, for instance, that they do not have enough strength even to lift an arm.

Delusions

Delusions in depression may be grouped into several categories: delusions of worthlessness; delusions of the "unpardonable" sin and of being punished or expecting punishment; nihilistic delusions; somatic delusions; and delusions of poverty. Any of the cognitive distortions described above may progress in intensity and achieve sufficient rigidity to warrant its being considered a delusion. A person with low self-esteem, for instance, may progress in thinking to believing that he is the devil. A person with a tendency to blame herself may eventually begin to ascribe to herself crimes such as the assassination of the president.

To determine the frequency of the various delusions among psychotically depressed patients, a series of 280 psychotic patients were interviewed. The results are shown in Table 2-7.

Worthlessness

Delusions of worthlessness occurred in 48 percent of the severely depressed psychotics. This delusion was expressed in the following way by one patient: "I must weep myself to death. I cannot live. I cannot die. I have failed so. It would be better if I had not been born. My life has always been a burden . . . I am the most inferior person in the world . . . I am subhuman." Another patient said, "I am totally useless. I can't do anything. I have never done anything worthwhile."

TABLE 2-7. Frequency of Delusions with Depressive Content Among Psychotic Patients Varying in Depth of Depression (%; $n = 280$)

	Depth of depression			
Delusion	None ($n = 85$)	Mild ($n = 68$)	Moderate ($n = 77$)	Severe ($n = 50$)
Worthless	6	9	21	48
Sinner	11	19	29	46
Devil	3	4	3	14
Punishment	18	21	18	42
Dead	0	2	3	10
Body decaying	9	13	16	24
Fatal illness	5	6	14	20

Crime and Punishment

Some patients believe they have committed a terrible crime for which they deserve or expect to be punished. Of the severely depressed, psychotic patients, 46 percent reported the delusion of being very bad sinners. In many cases, patients feel that severe punishment such as torture or hanging is imminent; 42 percent of the severely depressed patients expected punishment of some type. Many other patients believed that they were being punished and that the hospital was a kind of penal institution. The patient wails, "Will God never give up?" "Why must I be singled out for punishment?" "My heart is gone. Can't He see this? Can't He let me alone?" In some cases patients may believe that they are the devil; 14 percent of the severely depressed psychotics had this delusion.

Nihilistic Delusions

Nihilistic delusions have traditionally been associated with depression. A typical nihilistic delusion is reflected in the following statement: "It's no use. All is lost. The world is empty. Everybody died last night." Sometimes patients believes that they themselves are dead; this occurred in 10 percent of the severely depressed patients.

Organ preoccupation is particularly common in nihilistic delusions. The patients complain that an organ is missing or that all their viscera have been removed. This was expressed in statements such as "My heart, my liver, my intestines are gone. I'm nothing but an empty shell."

Somatic Delusions

Sometimes patients believe that their bodies are deteriorating, or that they have some incurable disease. Of the severely depressed patients, 24 percent believed that their bodies were decaying and 20 percent that they had fatal illnesses. Somatic delusions are expressed in statements such as the following: "I can't eat. The taste in my mouth is terrible. My guts are diseased. They can't digest the food"; "I can't think. My brain is all blocked up"; "My intestines are blocked. The food can't get through." Allied to the idea of having a severe abnormality is a patient's statement, "I haven't slept at all in six months."

Poverty

Delusions of poverty seem to be an outgrowth of the overconcern with finances manifested by depressed patients. A wealthy patient may complain bitterly, "All my money is gone. What will I live on? Who will buy food for my children?" Many authors have described the incongruity of a man of means who, dressed in rags, goes begging for alms or food.

In our study, delusions of poverty were not investigated. Because of the very high proportion of low-income patients in the series, it was difficult to distinguish a delusion of poverty from actual poverty.

In Rennie's[13] study, nearly half of the 99 cases had delusions as part of their psychoses; 49 patients had ideas of persecution or of passivity. (The number of persons with each of these delusions is not given.) Typical depressive delusions were found in 25 patients; these dealt predominantly with self-blame and self-depreciation and with ideas of being dead, of their bodies being changed, or of immorality. Delusions were most common in the oldest age group (72 percent). In patients older than 50 the content revolved predominantly around ideas of poverty, of being destroyed or tortured in some horrible manner, of being poisoned, or of being contaminated by feces.

Hallucinations

Rennie found that 25 percent of the patients had hallucinations. This was most prominent in the recurrent depressive group. Samples of the types of hallucinations were as follows: "I conversed with God"; "I heard the sentence, 'Your daughter is dead'"; "I heard people talking through my stomach"; "I saw a star on Christmas Day"; "I saw and heard my dead mother"; "Voices told me not to eat"; "Voices told me to walk backward"; "Saw and heard God and angels"; "Saw dead father"; "Animal faces in the food"; "Saw and heard animals"; "Saw dead people"; "Heard brother's and dead people's voices"; "Saw husband in his coffin"; "A voice said, 'Do not stay with your husband'"; "Saw two men digging a grave."

In our study, we found that 13 percent of the severely depressed, psychotic patients acknowledged hearing voices that condemned them. This was the most frequent type of hallucination reported.

TABLE 2-8. Frequency of Clinical Features of Patients Varying in Depth of depression ($\%$; $n = 486$)

	Depth of depression			
	None	*Mild*	*Moderate*	*Severe*
Clinical feature				
Sad facies	18	72	94	98
Stooped posture	6	32	70	87
Crying in interview	3	11	29	28
Speech: slow, etc.	25	53	72	75
Low mood	16	72	94	94
Diurnal variation of mood	6	13	37	37
Suicidal wishes	13	47	73	94
Indecisiveness	18	42	68	83
Hopelessness	14	58	85	86
Feeling inadequate	25	56	75	90
Conscious guilt	27	46	64	60
Loss of interest	14	56	83	92
Loss of motivation	23	54	88	88
Fatigability	39	62	89	84
Sleep disturbance	31	55	73	88
Loss of appetite	17	33	61	88
Constipation	19	26	38	52

Clinical Examination

Appearance

The psychiatrists in our study rated the intensity of certain clinical features in the depressed and nondepressed patients. Many of these features would be considered *signs*; that is, they are abstracted from observable behaviors rather than from the patients' self-descriptions. Other features were evaluated on the basis of the patients' verbal reports as well as on the observation of their behavior. Some of the clinical features overlap those described in the previous section. This particular study provides an opportunity to compare the frequency of symptoms elicited in response to the inventory with the frequency of symptoms derived from a clinical examination.

The sample consisted of the last 486 patients of the 966 patients described in Table 2-2. The distribution of the clinical features among the nondepressed, mildly depressed, moderately depressed, and severely depressed are found in Table 2-8.

Most cases of depression can be diagnosed by inspection.[18] The sad, melancholic expression combined with either retardation or agitation is practically pathognomonic of depression. In contrast, many patients conceal their unpleasant feelings behind a cheerful façade ("smiling depression"), and it may require careful interviewing to bring out a pained facial expression.

The facies show typical characteristics associated with sadness. The corners of the mouth are turned down, the brow is furrowed, the lines and wrinkles are deepened, and the eyes are often red from crying. Among the descriptions used by clinicians are glum, forlorn, gloomy, dejected, unsmiling, solemn, wearily resigned.[5] Lewis reported that weeping occurred in most of the women but in only one-sixth of the men in his sample.

In severe cases, the facies may appear to be frozen in a gloomy expression. Most patients, however, show some lability of expression, especially when their attention is diverted from their feelings. Genuine smiles may be elicited at times even in the severe cases, but they are generally transient. Some patients present a forced or social smile, which may be deceiving. The so-called mirthless smile, which indicates a lack of any genuine amusement, is easily recognized. This type of smile may be elicited in response to a humorous remark by the examiner and indicates the patient's intellectual awareness of the humor but without any emotional response to it.

A sad facies was observed in 85 percent of the depressed group (including mild, moderate, and severe cases) and in 18 percent of the nondepressed group. In the severely depressed group, 98 percent showed this characteristic.

Retardation

The most striking sign of a retarded depression is reduction in spontaneous activity. The patient tends to stay in one position longer than usual and to use a minimum of gestures. Movements are slow and deliberate as though the body and limbs are weighted down. He or she walks slowly, frequently hunched over, and with a shuffling gait. These postural characteristics were observed in 87 percent of the severely depressed patients in our sample.

The speech shows decreased spontaneity and the verbal output is reduced. The patient does not initiate a conversation or volunteer statements and, when questioned, responds in a few words. Sometimes, speaking is decreased only when a painful subject is being discussed. The pitch of the patient's voice is often lowered and speech tends to be in a monotone. These vocal characteristics were observed in 75 percent of the severely depressed patients.

The more retarded patients may start sentences but not complete them. They may answer questions with grunts or groans. The most severe cases may be mute. As Lewis points out, it is sometimes difficult to distinguish the scanty talk of a depressive from that of a well-preserved, suspicious paranoid schizophrenic. In both conditions, there may be pauses, hesitations, evasion, breaking off, and brevity. The diagnosis must rest on other observations—of content and behavior.

In severe depressions patients may manifest signs of a syndrome that has been labeled *stupor* or *semi-stupor*.[19] If left alone, they may remain practically motionless whether standing, sitting, or lying in bed. There is rarely, if ever, any waxy flexibility as seen in catatonia or any apparent clouding of consciousness. The patients vary in the degree to which they respond to stimulation. Some respond to sustained efforts by the examiner to establish rapport; others appear oblivious. I questioned several patients in the latter category after they recovered from their depression, and they reported that they had experienced feelings and thoughts during clinical examination but had felt incapable of expressing them in any way.

In extreme cases, patients do not eat or drink even with urging. Food placed in the mouth may remain there until removed, and under such circumstances tube feeding becomes necessary as a life-preserving measure. Sometimes patients do not move their bowels and digital removal of feces or enemas are necessary. Saliva accumulates and drools out of the mouth. They blink infrequently and may develop corneal ulcers. A more complete description of these extreme cases will be found in the section on Benign Stupors in Chapter 8.

Bleuler (p. 209)[20] described the melancholic triad consisting of depressive affect, inhibition of action, and inhibition of thinking. The first two characteristics are certainly typical of retarded depression. There is, however, a strong question as to whether there is an inhibition of the thought process. Lewis[5] believes that thinking is active—or even hyperactive—even though speech is inhibited. Refined psychological tests, furthermore, have failed to show significant interference with thought processes (Chapter 10).

Agitation

The chief characteristic of agitated patients is ceaseless activity. They cannot sit still but move about constantly in the chair. They convey a sense of restlessness and disturbance in wringing the hands or handkerchief, tearing clothing, picking at skin, and clenching and unclenching fingers. They may rub their scalp or other parts of the body until the skin is worn away.

They may get out of the chair many times in the course of an interview and pace the floor. At night, they may get out of bed frequently and walk incessantly back and forth. It is just as difficult for them to engage in constructive activity as it is to stay still. Their agitation is also manifested by frequent moans and groans. They approach doctors, nurses, and other patients and besiege them with requests or pleas for reassurance.

The emotions of frenzy and anguish are congruent with their thought content. They wail, "Why did I do it? Oh, God, what is to become of me? Please have mercy on me." They believe they are about to be butchered or buried alive. They moan, "My bowels are gone. It's intolerable." They scream, "I can't stand the pain. Please put me out of my misery." They groan, "My home is gone. My family is gone. I just want to die. Please let me die."

The thought content of the retarded patient appears to revolve around passive resignation to his or her fate. The agitated patient, on the other hand, cannot accept or tolerate the torture envisioned. The agitated behavior appears to represent desperate attempts to fight off impending doom.

Variations in Symptoms

Children and Adolescents

Weiss and Garber[21] reviewed the empirical findings on whether children and adolescents experience and express depression in the same way as do adults. Although it is commonly accepted that depression occurs in this age group, and that developmental level has relatively little influence on the phenomenology of the depression, the developmental perspective predicts the possibility of unique manifestations and experiences of such. Thus, it is possible that a person's level of physiological, social, and cognitive development must be taken into account in defining depression.

Considering over a dozen studies relevant to the question, Weiss and Garber[21] concluded that the matter remains unresolved: It is not known how depression in childhood and adolescence may differ from that in adults. However, they did articulate the issues. In so doing, they distinguished between continuity within the individual and continuity of the form or nature of depression across developmental levels. Among other examples they provided was anhedonia (lack of pleasure), present at all developmental levels, but expressed differently in each. Young children may express anhedonia by lack of interest in toy play; adolescents may appear bored; adults may lose interest in sex.

It is important to note that the review and metaanalysis of the empirical literature[21] did not imply that there are no differences between children and adults in the experience and expression of depression; rather the current state of research is such that unequivocal outcomes have not yet emerged. If differences are found following properly controlled studies, the most essential research question is whether the differences result from the causes or consequences of depression. Before getting to that, however, "the fundamental question of whether there are developmental differences in the symptoms that comprise the syndrome of depression remains to be answered" (p. 427).

The official diagnostic manual of the American Psychiatric Association (APA)[22] is not as circumspect as the reviewers above, asserting instead that the "core symptoms" of a major depressive episode are the same for children and adolescents. However, it is stated that the prominence of characteristic symptoms may change with age: "Certain symptoms such as somatic complaints, irritability, and social withdrawal are particularly common in children, whereas psychomotor retardation, hypersomnia, and delusions are less common in prepuberty than in adolescence and adulthood" (p. 354).

Cultural Variations

Cultural context must be better understood in order to avoid underdiagnosis or misdiagnosis due to variation in the experience and communication of depressive symptoms.[22] The following may serve as concrete examples: "Complaints of 'nerves' and headaches (in Latino and Mediterranean cultures), of weakness, tiredness, or 'imbalance' (in Chinese and Asian cultures), of problems of the 'heart' (in Middle Eastern cultures), or of being 'heartbroken' (among Hopi) may [all] express the depressive experience" (p. 353).' Research is needed to more fully understand the symptoms of depression as expressed in different cultures around the world.

Chapter 3
Course and Prognosis

Depression as a Clinical Entity

In Chapter 2, depression was treated as a psychopathological dimension or syndrome. The clinical features of depression were examined in cross-section, that is, in terms of the cluster of pathological phenomena exhibited at a given point in time. In this chapter, depression is treated as a discrete clinical entity (such as bipolar disorder or dysthymia) that has certain specific characteristics occurring over time in terms of onset, remission, and recurrence. As a clinical entity or reaction type, depression has many salient characteristics that distinguish it from other clinical types such as schizophrenia, even though these other types may have depressive elements associated with them. The depressive constellation as a concomitant of other nosological entities will not be described in this chapter but will be considered later in terms of its association with schizophrenic symptomatology in the schizoaffective category (Chapter 8).

Among the important characteristics of the clinical entity of depression are the following: There is generally a well-defined onset, a progression in the severity of the symptoms until the condition bottoms out, and then a steady regression (improvement) of the symptoms until the episode is over; the remissions are spontaneous; there is a tendency toward recurrence; the intervals between attacks are free of depressive symptoms.

Importance of Course and Outcome

The *longitudinal* aspects of depression have been the subject of many investigations since the time of Kraepelin. Adequate information regarding the short-term and long-term course of depression is important, not only for practical management, but also for an understanding of the psychopathology and for evaluation of specific forms of treatment. Considerable data on the life histories of depressed patients were accumulated before the advent of the specific therapeutic agents—psychological treatments (such as cognitive and interpersonal therapy), electroconvulsive therapy (ECT), and drugs. These data are generally regarded as reflecting the natural history of the disorder, although it is difficult to separate out the effects of hospitalization.

The physician charged with making a determination of the prognosis in a given case is confronted with a number of questions.

1. In the case of a first episode of depression, what are the prospects for complete remission, and what is the likelihood of residual symptoms or of a chronic, unrecovered state?
2. What is the probable duration of the first attack?
3. What is the likelihood of recurrence, and what is the probable duration of any multiple attacks?
4. How long must one wait following a patient's remission from a given attack before ruling out the likelihood of recurrence?
5. What is the risk of death through suicide?

Answers to these questions can be provided by reference to research on early cases diagnosed as manic-depressive psychoses and subsequent studies that elaborated the prior findings. A number of fairly well-designed studies have been conducted to determine the fate of such patients. It should be emphasized that much of the available data applies primarily to hospitalized patients.

A series described by Paskind as "manic depressive" in 1930 undoubtedly contained a preponderance of cases that would later be diagnosed as "neurotic-depressive reactions." Since this study antedated the modern somatic therapies, the findings may be assumed to be relevant to the natural history of neurotic-depressive reactions.

Systematic Studies

Kraepelin[1] studied the general course of 899 cases of manic-depressive psychosis. The period of observation varied considerably; some patients were followed for brief periods and others for as long as 40 years. Moreover, since the follow-up depended largely on readmission to the hospital, the information on patients who were not readmitted is scanty. Despite these limitations, his study is of great value in providing solid facts regarding recurrent episodes, frequency and duration of the attacks, and duration of the intervals between attacks. His sample was as follows: single depression, 263; recurrent depression, 177; biphasic single episode, 106; combined, recurrent, 214; single manic episode, 102; recurrent manic, 47. *Biphasic* was used for cases in which both manic and depressive episodes occurred. These have been designated by terms such as compound, mixed, combined, double-form, cyclothymic, and cyclical. Alternating and circular refer to cases in which one phase follows immediately after the opposite without any free interval. "Closed circular type" refers to uninterrupted manic and depressive cycles.

Paskind's study[2,3,4] of cases of depression seen in private practice provides data on the course of depressions observed outside the hospital. Although there are many serious methodological deficiencies in this study, the data presented are relevant to milder episodes of depression. Paskind reviewed the records of 633 cases of depression in the private practice of Dr. Q. T. Patrick. Although all of these cases had been placed in the all-inclusive category of manic-depressive psychosis, a review of the case histories presented in the articles leaves little doubt that these cases are actually descriptive of the bipolar mood disorders rather than psychosis. In reviewing the tabulated data presented by the author, it is apparent that his findings are based on 248 cases abstracted from the original group. The cases were collected over a period of 32 years, but there is no mention of the average period of observation or of any systematic attempt to obtain follow-up material on these patients. Paskind noted that 88 cases (32 percent) could be classified as "brief attacks of manic-depressive psychosis," since the average duration of the episodes ranged from a few hours to a few days.

Paskind described the symptoms of the short attacks as exactly like those of longer attacks: profound sadness and unhappiness without obvious cause; self-reproach; self-blame; self-derogation; lack of initiative; lack of response to usual interests accompanied by keen awareness of this lack; avoidance of friends; a feeling of hopelessness; death wishes; and inclinations or desire to commit suicide. Paskind stated that the well-known antidotes for depression, such as a philosophic outlook, company of friends, amusements, diversions, rest, change of scene, and good news did not cause the attacks to disappear. "Instead one finds a person in a normal mood who without apparent cause becomes within a brief period profoundly sad and unhappy; in spite of all attempts to cheer him, the attack remains for from a few hours to a few days; when it does disappear it does so as abruptly and mysteriously as it came."

Rennie[5] did a follow-up study of 208 patients with manic-depressive reactions admitted to the Henry Phipps Psychiatric Clinic between 1913 and 1916. Atypical cases were not included because the author wanted to study only clear-cut manic-depressive (bipolar) reactions. Several patients having what seemed to be manic excitements at the time of admission developed schizophrenic reactions on long-term observation. These cases were excluded, as were cases of depression that had lost the preponderant depressive affect and had, in the course of years, evolved slowly into more automatic and schizophrenic-like behavior. Also excluded were depressive patients with hypochondriasis who had lost most of their depressive affect and who had sunk into a state of chronic invalidism with little depressive content. The material, consequently, can be regarded as following reasonably stringent criteria for diagnosing the manic-depressive syndrome.

Follow-up on these patients was obtained by letter, social service interview, physician's interview, newspaper notices of suicide, and records from other hospitals. In only one case were no follow-up data obtained. The follow-up period evidently ranged from 35 to 39 years.

In Rennie's study, the following clinical groups were described in order of frequency: (1) recurrent depression: 102 patients—15 had symptom-free intervals of at least 20 years between attacks, and 52 had remissions of at least 10 years; (2) Cyclothymic (biphasic), 49 patients in whom all combinations were observed, with elation and depression sometimes following each other in closed cycles; (3) single attacks of depression, recovered—26 patients; (4) single attacks of depression, unrecovered—14 patients, of whom 9 committed suicide; (5) recurrent manic attacks, 14 cases; (6) single manic attacks—two patients (These remained well for over 20 years after the attack. A third patient became manic for the first time at age 40 and was still hospitalized at age 64.)

A comparison of the relative frequency of depressed, biphasic, and manic patients observed in various studies is presented in Chapter 6.

Lundquist[6] conducted a longitudinal study of 319 manic-depressive patients whose first hospitalization for this disorder was at the Langbrö Hospital in 1912–31. The investigator reviewed the records and checked the appropriateness of the diagnoses to "satisfy all reasonable demands in regard to reliability." His sample consisted of 123 men (38 percent) and 196 women (62 percent).

After locating the discharged patients, follow-up was conducted by a personal examination of patients at the hospital, a home visit by a social worker if patients lived in Stockholm, a detailed questionnaire mailed to patients living outside of Stockholm, and a review of the hospital record of patients currently hospitalized elsewhere.

The period of observation varied considerably: 20–30 years, 42 percent; 10–20 years, 38 percent; less than 10 years, 20 percent.

The duration of an episode was defined as the time that elapsed between patients' recognition of their symptoms and their return to their former occupation. Remission was based on a rough gauge of patients' ability to resume their work and ordinary mode of life.

Onset of Episodes

The relative frequency of an insidious onset, as compared with an acute onset, was studied by Hopkinson[7] for 100 consecutive inpatients diagnosed as having an affective illness. All were more than 50 years of age on admission, and 39 had suffered previous attacks before age 50; 80 patients were examined personally by the author, and in the remaining 20 cases, the pertinent data were abstracted from the case histories.

When the onset of the illness was studied, it was found that 26 percent of the cases exhibited a well-defined prodromal period; the remaining 74 percent of the cases were considered of acute onset. Complaints made by these patients in the prodromal period were vague and nonspecific. Tension and anxiety occurred in all to some extent. The duration of the prodromal period before the onset of a clear-cut depressive psychosis ranged from 8 months to 10 years; the mean duration was 33.5 months.

In a later study,[8] Hopkinson investigated the prodromal phase in 43 younger patients (ages 16–48). Thirteen (30.2 percent) showed a prodromal phase of 2 months to 7 years (mean = 23 months). The clinical features of the prodromal period were chiefly tension, anxiety, and indecision.

In summary, 70–75 percent of the patients in both studies with an affective disorder had an acute onset.

The relationship of acuteness of onset to prognosis has been studied by several investigators, with contradictory results. Steen[9] found, in a study of 493 patients, that the remission rate was higher among manic depressives who showed an acute onset than among those with a protracted onset. On the other hand, Strecker et al.,[10] in a comparison of 50 recovered and 50 nonrecovered manic depressives, found that an acute onset occurred no more frequently in the recovered than in the chronic group. In a study of 96 cases grossly diagnosed as manic depressive, Astrup et al.[11] found that an acute onset favored remission.

Hopkinson[8] found a significantly higher *frequency* of attacks per patient among his cases with an acute onset (mean = 2.8) than among those patients with a prodromal phase (mean = 1.3).

Lundquist[6] reported that patients over 30 with an acute onset (less than a month) had a significantly shorter *duration* of their episodes than those with a gradual onset. In the age group of 30–39 years, the mean duration of the acute onset cases was 5.1 months and of the gradual onset cases, 27.2 months.

The average age of onset of depression varied so widely among these earlier studies that no definite conclusions could be drawn. The following statistics for the decade of peak incidence may serve as a rough guide: 20–30, Kraepelin[1]; 30–39, Stenstedt,[12] Cassidy et al.,[13] Ayd[14]; 45–55, Rennie[5]; 50 and older, Lundquist.[6]

Remission and Chronicity

There was considerable variation among the authors on the proportion of patients remaining chronically ill following the onset of depressive illness. It is difficult to make comparisons among the various studies because different diagnostic criteria were used, the definition of chronicity varied, the periods of observation varied, and in many studies, no distinction was made between those who became chronic after the first attack and those who became chronic only after multiple attacks.

The relatively well-designed retrospective study by Rennie indicated that approximately 3 percent were found on long-term follow-up to be chronically ill. Kraepelin reported that 5 percent of his cases became chronic. Lundquist reported that 79.6 percent of the depressives recovered completely from the first attack. Age of onset was a factor: the remission rate ranged from 92 percent for patients less than 30 years old to 75 percent in the 30–40 age group. It is probable that his percentages are lower than those of the others because of his more stringent definition of complete remission.

Astrup et al.[11] divided their group of manic-depressive patients into the categories of "chronic," "improved," and "recovered." Of the 70 "pure" manic depressives, 6 (8.6 percent) were still chronically ill at the time of follow-up. The majority had recovered completely, and a minority showed residual "instability" and were classified as improved. (Precise figures for the improved and recovered categories are not available because of the lumping together of manic-depressive and schizoaffective patients.) The follow-up period was five years or more.

It is noteworthy that a patient may have an initial manic or depressive episode from which she or he recovers completely and, after a long symptom-free interval, may relapse into a chronic state. Rennie reported the case of a patient who had an initial episode of mania followed by depression, the entire cycle lasting about a year. He was symptom-free for 23 years afterward and then lapsed into a state of manic excitement lasting 22 years.

Kraepelin[1] indicated that a patient may have chronic depression of many years' duration and still have a complete remission. He presented an illustrative case (p. 143) with a single attack lasting 15 years, from which the patient had made a complete remission.

Remission from Dysthymic Disorder

More recently, study of chronic, low-grade depression—referred to as "dysthymic disorder"—was reported by Klein et al.[15] The diagnostic criteria for dysthymic disorder are listed in Table 3-1. (More detailed information on the classification of the various mood disorders is provided in Chapter 4.)

To study recovery in dysthymic disorder, Klein et al.[15] used a prospective design and a naturalistic 5-year follow-up. Participants were 86 outpatients with early-onset dysthymic disorder, and 39 outpatients with episodic major depressive disorder. Follow-ups were conducted at 30 and 60 months. Only about half (52.9 percent) of the patients with dysthymic disorder had recovered after five years. Over an average of 23 months of observation, the relapse rate for this disorder was 45.2 percent.

Klein compared patients with dysthymic disorder and those with episodic

TABLE 3-1. Diagnostic Criteria for Dysthymic Disorder

A) Depressed mood for most of the day, for more days than not, as indicated by subjective account or observation by others, for at least 2 years. Note: In children and adolescents, mood can be irritable and duration must be at least 1 year.
B) Presence, while depressed, of two (or more) of the following:
   (1) poor appetite or overeating
   (2) insomnia or hypersomnia
   (3) low energy or fatigue
   (4) low self-esteem
   (5) poor concentration or difficulty making decisions
   (6) feelings of hopelessness
C) During the 2-year period (1 year for children or adolescents) of the disturbance, the person has never been without the symptoms in Criteria A and B for more than 2 months at a time.
D) No Major Depressive Episode has been present during the first 2 years of the disturbance (1 year for children and adolescents); i.e., the disturbance is not better accounted for by chronic Major Depressive Disorder, or Major Depressive Disorder, in Partial Remission.
E) There has never been a Manic Episode, Mixed Episode or Hypomanic Episode, and criteria have never been met for Cyclothymic Disorder.
F) The disturbance does not occur exclusively during the course of a chronic Psychotic Disorder, such as Schizophrenia or Delusional Disorder.
G) The symptoms are not due to the direct physiological effects of a substance (e.g., a drug of abuse, a medication) or a general medical condition (e.g., hypothyroidism).
H) The symptoms cause clinically significant distress or impairment in social, occupational, or other important areas of functioning.

major depressive disorder. The former spent 70 percent of the time over the 5-year follow-up meeting the criteria for a mood disorder; the latter spent less than 25 percent of the time meeting mood disorder criteria.

Those with dysthymia had more symptoms, lower functioning, and higher probability of attempting suicide and being hospitalized than those with major depressive disorder. By the end of the 5-year follow-up, 94.2 percent (81 of 86) of the dysthymic disorder group had at least one lifetime major depressive episode. This figure includes the 77.9 percent (67 of 86) of this group who had already experienced superimposed major depression at the onset of the study. Among those patients with dysthymic disorder who had not reported a major depressive episode before the study (19 of 86), the estimated risk of having a first lifetime major depressive episode was 76.9 percent (14 of 19). Overall, these findings suggest that dysthymic disorder is a chronic, severe condition with a high risk of relapse.[15]

Remission from Functional Impairments

Buist-Bouwman et al.[16] addressed the question of whether people who remit from a major depressive episode also recover from functional impairments.

These impairments were assessed by the Short-Form-36 Health Survey and included things like physical functioning, vitality, pain, social functioning, and general health.

The study used data from the Netherlands Mental Health Survey and Incidence Study, and depression was diagnosed using the hierarchical rules of *DSM-III-R*. Those who suffered major depressive episodes during the course of psychotic or bipolar disorders were excluded. A total of 165 people were included in the study.

Results showed that 60 to 85 percent of the respondents did better or showed no change in functioning after recovery from depression, compared to their functioning prior to depression. Still, the average levels of functioning after depression were lower compared to people from a nondepressed sample, people who had never been depressed. Those who suffered from substance abuse and anxiety disorders, physical illness, and low social support showed poorer functioning. The authors suggested that a limitation of the study was that nonprofessional interviewers were used to determine the diagnosis of depression by structured interviews, and functioning was obtained by self-report.

Duration

Some idea of the average or expected duration of an episode of depression is obviously important so that the physician can adequately prepare the patient and family psychologically and give them a basis for making decisions about the business affairs of the patient as well as appropriate financial arrangements for his or her care.

One aspect of the usual depressive episode that is of importance in treatment is the fact that the episode tends to follow a curve, that is, tends to progressively worsen, then bottom out, and then progressively improve until the patient returns to his premorbid state. By determining the time of onset of the depression, the physician can make a rough estimate as to when an upward turn in the cycle may be expected. It is particularly important when assessing the efficacy of specific forms of treatment to take into account the spontaneous start of the upward swing.

There is some variation in the findings of the numerous studies relevant to duration. Undoubtedly, these variations may be attributed to different methods of observation and to different criteria for making diagnoses and judging improvement. In general, the relatively unrefined clinical studies (which will be discussed presently) indicate a longer duration than do the systematic studies.

Lundquist[6] found that the median duration of the attack of depression in patients younger than 30 was 6.3 months, and for those older than 30, 8.7 months. This difference was statistically significant. There was no significant difference between men and women in regard to duration. (As noted previously, he also found acute onset associated with shorter duration.) Paskind[4] also found in his outpatient group a shorter duration of attacks occurring before age 30 than after age 30. Rennie's study yielded similar results, the first episode lasting on the average 6.5 months. He found, incidentally, that the average duration of hospitalization was 2.5 months. In Paskind's series of non-hospitalized depressives, the median duration was 3 months. He found that 14 percent of the episodes lasted one month or less, and that almost 80 percent were completed in six months or less.

The earlier, less refined studies predominantly reported a period of 6–18 months as the average duration of the first attack: Kraepelin,[1] 6–8 months; Pollack,[17] 1.1 years; Strecker et al.,[10] 1.5 years. The clinical impression of writers of monographs on depression published in the 1950s and 1960s shows similar variation. Kraines[18] stated that the average depressive episode lasts about 18 months. Ayd[14] reported that prior to age 30, the attacks average 6–12 months; between ages of 30 and 50, they average 9–18 months; and after 50, they tend to persist longer, with many patients remaining ill from three to five years.

In regard to the *duration of multiple episodes* of depression, there was a prevalent opinion among the earliest clinicians of a trend toward prolongation of the episodes with each recurrence.[1] Lundquist, however, performed a statistical analysis of the duration of multiple episodes and found no significant increase in duration with successive attacks. Paskind's[4] study of outpatient cases similarly showed that the attacks do not become longer as the disease recurs. The median duration for first attacks was four months, and for second, third, or subsequent attacks three months.

The differences in the findings between the rough clinical studies and the statistical studies may reflect a difference in samples and/or different criteria for recovery from the depression. It is probable that certain biases influenced the selection of cases in the less refined studies and, therefore, the samples cannot be considered representative.

Lundquist found a significant association between prolonged duration and the presence of delusions in younger but not older patients. The presence of confusion, however, favored a shorter duration.

Brief Attacks of Manic-Depressive Psychosis (Bipolar Disorder)

In 1929, Paskind[2] described 88 cases of depression of very brief duration, from a few hours to a few days. These patients had essentially the same symptoms as those in his other extramural cases of longer duration and constituted 13.9 percent of his large series of cases diagnosed as manic-depressive disorder. The case histories he presented leave little doubt that they would later be diagnosed as neurotic-depressive (dysthymia) reaction.

TABLE 3-2. Frequency of Single and Multiple Attacks of Depression

	Rennie		Lundquist	
Frequency	No.	%	No.	%
1 attack	26	21.0	105	61.0
2 attacks	33	27.0	45	26.0
3 attacks	28	23.0	11	6.5
4 + attacks	36	29.0	11	6.5
Total	123	100	172	100

Most of these patients with brief attacks also experienced longer episodes of depression. In 51, the brief attacks came first and were followed from months to decades later by longer attacks lasting from several weeks to several years. In 18, longer attacks occurred first, and were followed by the transient episodes. In nine, there were brief episodes only.

Recurrence

There is considerable variation in the older literature relevant to the frequency of relapses among depressed patients. Except as indicated, the statistics for manic-depressive psychosis include some manic patients in addition to the depressed patients. In the earlier studies, German authors reported a substantially higher incidence of recurrence than American investigators.[6] These differences may be attributed to more stringent diagnostic criteria and to longer periods of observation by the German authors.

Of the more refined studies, Rennie's reported relapse rate was closer to that of the German writers than to those of the other American investigators. He found that 97 of 123 patients (79 percent) initially admitted to the hospital in a depressed state subsequently had a recurrence of depression. (These figures do not include 14 patients who committed suicide after the first admission or who remained chronically ill.) When the cyclothymic cases (i.e., patients who had at least one manic attack in addition to the depression) are added to this group, the proportion of relapse is 142 patients of 170 (84 percent).

The Scandinavian investigators Lundquist[6] and Stenstedt[12] reported, respectively, a 49 percent and a 47 percent incidence of relapse. In comparing their studies with Rennie's, one can reasonably conclude that the more stringent diagnostic criteria employed by Rennie and the longer period of observation of his sample may account for the higher percentage of relapses in his report.

The differences in relapse rate are reflected in a striking difference in the rate of multiple recurrences. In Rennie's series more than half of the depressed patients had three or more recurrences (see Table 3-2). The frequency of multiple recurrences in the cyclothymic cases was particularly high in Rennie's series. Thirty-seven of the 47 patients in the group had four or more episodes.

In Kraepelin's series, 204 out of 310 cases of this type (67 percent) had one or more recurrences, with more than half having three or more attacks.

Another important aspect of the recurrent attacks is their duration. The opinion was frequently expressed that the episodes become progressively longer with each recurrence. Rennie, however, in analyzing his data, found that the second episode had the same duration as the initial episode in 20 percent, was longer in 35 percent, and was shorter in 45 percent. Paskind found that the median duration decreased with successive attacks.

Belsher and Costello[19] reviewed 12 published studies of relapse in unipolar as opposed to bipolar depression. They selected studies that included correlates of relapse, rates of relapse, and a naturalistic follow-up period with no controlled maintenance therapy. They found a number of methodological inadequacies, such as unclear and variable definitions of recovery and relapse, nebulous patient characteristics, and vague inclusion and exclusion criteria. Despite these uncertainties, they were able to conclude that the risk of relapse in unipolar depression goes down the longer a person stays well. Several factors did predict relapse: (1) a history of depressive episodes, (2) recent stress, (3) poor social support, and (4) neuroendocrine dysfunction. Other variables did not predict relapse, including marital status, gender, and socioeconomic status.

Intervals Between Attacks

In examining the older literature on the intervals between episodes of depression, one is struck by the fact that recurrences may occur after years, or even decades, of apparent good health. The systematic studies offer little encouragement for the notion of a permanent cure analogous to the 5-year cures reported for cancer treatment. Recurrences have been reported as long as 40 years after remission from an initial depression.[1]

The findings presented by Rennie, in particular, are noteworthy in that the highest proportion of relapses occurred 10–20 years after the initial episode of depression. His follow-up showed the following relapse rate for his 97 cases of recurrent depressions: less than 10 years after the first attack of depression, 35 percent; 10–20 years, 52 percent; more than 20 years, 13 percent. It should be emphasized that 65 percent had recurrences after remissions of 10–30 years.

In an earlier study, Kraepelin had tabulated the symptom-free intervals between 703 episodes of depression. Unlike Rennie's study, Kraepelin's included intervals after the second and later attacks (as well as intervals between the first and second episodes). He found that with each successive attack the intervals tended to become shorter. Since his series consisted of hospitalized patients, it is interesting to note the same trend among the extramural patients in Paskind's study. A comparison of the distribution of inter-

TABLE 3-3. Distribution of Time Intervals Between Manic-Depressive Episodes in Inpatients and Outpatients

Source	Intervals	Duration of intervals in years (%)				
		0–9	10–19	20–29	30–39	> 40
Kraepelin (1913) (inpatients)	703	80.5	13.5	4.8	1.1	0.14
Paskind (1930b) (outpatients)	438	64.0	27.8	5.7	1.6	0.92
Rennie (1942) (inpatients)	97*	35.0	52.0	15.0		

*Includes only first interval (between first and second episode).

TABLE 3-4. Median Intervals for Inpatients and Outpatients (years)

	Cases	First interval	Second interval	Third and subsequent intervals
Inpatients (Kraepelin 1913)	167	6	2.8	2
Outpatients (Paskind 1930b)	248	8	5	4

vals in ten-year categories is shown in Table 3-3. For the purposes of comparison, Rennie's results are also included. It should be emphasized that his findings applied only to the *first* interval. The tendency for his intervals to be longer than Kraepelin's and Paskind's may be explained by the fact that the later intervals included in their study were shorter than the first intervals. Kraepelin and Paskind showed a somewhat similar distribution of the intervals, with Paskind's outpatient cases having longer periods of remission than Kraepelin's hospitalized cases.

Another way of expressing the duration of the intervals is in terms of the median duration of the specific intervals. Table 3-4 shows that the median interval is longer in Paskin's outpatient cases, and also that in both outpatient and hospitalized cases the median intervals tended to be shorter with successive attacks. In Kraepelin's study, the biphasic cases showed consistently shorter symptom-free intervals than the simple depressions.

Further support for the observation that after the first recurrence the interval tends to become shorter is found in Lundquist's study. In the age group older than 30, the mean duration of the first interval was about seven years, and the second interval three years. This difference was statistically significant.

Lundquist's data, classified according to three-year intervals, showed that the overwhelming preponderance of relapses occurred in the first nine years. It should be pointed out that his follow-up period was as short as 10 years in some cases, as compared to 25–30 years in Rennie's series. Hence, it is probable that many of the cases in Lundquist's series would have shown a relapse if they had been followed for a longer period than 10 years. Lundquist computed the *probability* of a relapse after a patient has recovered from an initial

TABLE 3-5. Probability of Recurrence After Remission from First Attack (%)

Age at first attack	Years after first depression				
	3	6	9	12	15
< 30 years	12	13	4	—	—
30 + years	10	12	9	8	6

Adapted from Lundquist 1945.

TABLE 3-6. Outcome According to Clinical Criteria (%)

Clinical criteria	Endogenous depression	Neurotic depression	Total
Recovered and continuously well	26	14	20
Recovered with subsequent attacks	58	70	63
Always incapacitated or death by suicide	17	17	17

Adapted from Kiloh et al. 1988.

episode of depression (Table 3-5). These findings were tabulated separately for the young depressives and older depressives, but no significant difference was found between the two groups. It may be noted that the highest probability of recurrence was in the 3–6-year interval.

Outcome for "Endogenous" Versus "Neurotic" Depression

Kiloh et al.[20] studied the long-term outcome of 145 patients with primary depressive illness who were admitted to a university hospital between 1966 and 1970. Patients were categorized into endogenous and neurotic subtypes. The follow-up period was an average of 15 years later, and data were obtained on 92 percent of the patients. Table 3-6 shows the percentages of those who (1) recovered and remained well, (2) recovered but experienced subsequent depression, or (3) remained incapacitated or committed suicide.

Schizophrenic Outcome

In Rennie's 1942 sample of 208 cases of manic-depressive psychosis, four cases changed their character sufficiently to justify the conclusion of an ultimate schizophrenic development. A review of these cases suggested that there was a strong component of schizophrenic symptomatology at the time of the diagnosis of manic-depressive psychosis.

At about the same time, Hoch and Rachlin[21] reviewed the records of 5,799 cases of schizophrenia admitted to Manhattan State Hospital, New York City. They found that 7.1 percent of these patients had been diagnosed as manic depressive during previous admissions. Whether there was an alteration in the nature of the disorder, an initial misclassification, or a change in diagnostic criteria was not established by these writers.

Lewis and Piotrowski[22] found that 38 (54 percent) of 70 patients, originally diagnosed as manic depressives, had their diagnoses changed to schizophrenia in a 3–20-year follow-up. In reviewing the original records, the authors demonstrated that the patients whose diagnoses were changed were misclassified initially, that is, they showed clear-cut schizophrenic signs at the time of their first admission. Because of the very loose criteria used in diagnosing manic-depressive disorder in the early decades of the twentieth century, it is difficult to determine what proportion, if any, of the clear-cut manic depressives had a schizophrenic outcome.

Lundquist reported that about 7 percent of his manic-depressive cases eventually developed a schizophrenic picture.

Astrup et al.[11] isolated 70 cases of "pure" manic-depressive disorder and followed these 7–19 years after the onset of the disorder. They found that none had a schizophrenic outcome. In contrast, 13 (50 percent) of a group of 26 cases diagnosed as schizoaffective psychosis showed schizophrenic symptomatology on follow-up.

Suicide

At the present time, the only important cause of death in depression is suicide. (The general topic of suicide is broad, and many excellent monographs are available, e.g., Farberow and Schneidman,[23] Meerloo.[24]) Previously, inanition due to lack of food and secondary infection were occasional causes of death, but with modern hospital treatment such complications are less usual.

The actual suicide risk among depressed patients is difficult to assess because of the incomplete follow-ups and difficulties in establishing the cause of death. Long term follow-ups by Rennie[5] and by Lundquist[6] indicated that approximately 5 percent of the patients initially diagnosed in a hospital as manic depressive (or as having one of the other depressive disorders) subsequently committed suicide.

In the mid-twentieth century, several studies demonstrated comparatively higher suicide rates among depressed patients. Pokorny[26] investigated the suicide rate among former patients in a psychiatric service of a Texas veterans' hospital over a 15-year period. Using a complex actuarial system, he calculated the suicide rates per 100,000 per year as follows: depression, 566; schizophrenia, 167; neurosis, 119; personality disorder, 130; alcoholism, 133; and organic, 78. He then calculated the age-adjusted suicide rate for male Texas veterans as 22.7 per 100,000. The suicide rate for depressed patients, therefore, was 25 times the expected rate and substantially higher than that of other psychiatric patients.

Temoche et al.,[27] studying the suicide rates among current and former mental institution patients in Massachusetts, found a substantially higher rate of suicide among depressed patients than nondepressed patients. The computed ratio for depressives was 36 times as high as for the general population and about three times as high as for either schizophrenics or alcoholics.

The suicide rate among patients known to be suicidal risks is apparently high. Moss and Hamilton[28] conducted a follow-up study for periods of two months to 20 years of 50 patients who had been considered "seriously suicidal" during their previous hospitalization (average 4 years). Eleven (22 percent) of the 50 later committed suicide. In a retrospective study of 134 suicides, Robins et al.[29] found that 68 percent had previously communicated suicidal ideas and 41 percent had specifically stated they intended to commit suicide.

The figures available at that time clearly indicated that the suicidal risk was greatest during weekend leaves from the hospital and shortly after discharge. Wheat,[30] surveying suicides among psychiatric hospital patients, found that 30 percent committed suicide during the period of hospitalization, and 63 percent of the suicides among the discharged patients occurred within one month after discharge. Temoche et al.[27] calculated that the suicidal risk in the first six months after discharge is 34 times greater than in the general population and in the second six months about nine times greater. About half of the suicides occurred within 11 months of release.

Many earlier studies reported the observation that women depressives attempted suicide more frequently than men but that men were more often successful. Kraines[18] reported that, in his series of manic-depressive patients, twice as many women as men attempted suicide and three times as many men as women were successful suicides.

Although no data are available regarding the suicidal methods employed by depressives, recent statistics for the general population may be relevant. In 2001 intentional self-harm (suicide) by discharge of firearms was 16,869. By other and unspecified means, the number was 13,753. The ratio of male to female was 4.6 to 1; Black to White .5; Hispanic to non-Hispanic .5.[31]

There is evidence that the number of suicides each year in the United States is greater than the official 2001 report of 30,622. Many accidental deaths actually represent concealed suicides. For instance, in 1962 MacDonald[32] reported 37 cases of attempted suicide by automobile. Writers believed that the actual rate of suicide was three or four times as great as the official rate. The number of attempted suicides was believed to be seven or eight times the number of successful suicides.[33]

Homicide may occur in association with suicide among depressed patients.[34] Reports, for example, of parents killing their children and then themselves are not rare. One woman, convinced by her psychotherapist that her children needed her even though she believed herself worthless, decided to kill them as well as herself to "spare them the agony of growing up without a mother." She subsequently followed through with her plan.

Several factors contribute to the risk of attempted or completed suicide. Risk is especially high during a major depressive episode in those with psychotic symptoms, previous suicide attempts, a family history of completed suicides, and concurrent substance use.[35,36] The best indication of a suicidal risk is the communication of suicidal intent.[29] Stengel[33] pointed out that the notion that the person who talks about suicide will never carry it out is fallacious. Also, a previous unsuccessful suicidal attempt greatly increases the probability of a subsequent successful suicidal attempt.[36,37] Brown et al.[38] were able to reduce repeat suicide attempts by 50 percent through the application of cognitive therapy, compared to usual care of tracking and referral services. They also were able to reduce depression severity and hopelessness (see Chapter 15).

Over a 5-year follow-up period, Klein et al.[15] found that suicide attempts were made by 19 percent (16 of 84) of patients with chronic depression, and one of these resulted in actual suicide. In this study, there were no attempts among 37 patients with episodic disorder only. This suggests that the rate of suicide attempts increases in cases of chronic depressive illness (dysthymic disorder) compared to episodic major depression.

In addition to trying to elicit suicidal wishes from the depressed patient, the clinician should look for signs of hopelessness. In our studies we found that suicidal wishes had a higher correlation with hopelessness than with any other symptom of depression. Furthermore, Pichot and Lempérière,[39] in a factor analysis of the Depression Inventory, extracted a factor containing only two variables, pessimism (hopelessness) and suicidal wishes.

Suicide Risk in Bipolar Disorder

Fagiolini et al.[40] found suicidal thinking and behavior to be common in individuals with bipolar disorder. The people in the study were 175 patients with bipolar I disorder who were participating in a randomized controlled trial, the Pittsburgh Study of Maintenance Therapies in Bipolar Disorder. Suicide had been attempted by 29 percent of the patients prior to entering the study.

The method used in this study was to compare clinical and demographic characteristics of those who had attempted suicide before entering the study to those who had not attempted suicide. Among the conclusions was that greater severity of bipolar disorder and higher body mass predicted a history of suicide attempts. Severity was defined as a greater number of previous depressive episodes, as well as higher scores on an evaluator-rated measure of depression (Hamilton Rating Scale—25 items).[40]

Predictors of Chronic Depression

Riso et al.[41] reviewed the studies of determinants of chronic depression. They reported that such determinants have not been adequately elucidated, but that studies have considered six possible factors: (1) developmental factors such as childhood adversity (early trauma or maltreatment), (2) personality and personality disorders like neuroticism (emotional instability or vulnerability to stress) and stress reactivity, (3) psychological stressors, (4) comorbid disorders, (5) biological factors, and (6) cognitive factors. In what follows, we summarize their findings.

Developmental Factors

Among the developmental factors, there is some evidence for the importance of early trauma or maltreatment but not for early separation and loss.

Personality Disorders

In 11 studies comparing personality rates in dysthymia to major depression, patients with dysthymia were found to have higher rates of personality disorders. However, as of 2002 only one prospective study had been carried out. The two conditions may share causal factors, rather than dysthymia developing as a consequence of personality disorder.

Psychological Stressors

Concerning psychological stressors, the duration of chronic depression makes it more difficult to disentangle stressors that may lead to prolongation of depression from the effects of depression itself in generating stressors. Riso et al.[41] noted that the APA diagnostic manuals assert that dysthymic disorder is associated with chronic stress, but that it is possible that the two studies supportive of this may be confounded by patient perceptions of stressors rather than actual events. Supportive of this is that treatment with antidepressant medications modifies reports of daily hassles.

Comorbid Disorders

Findings on comorbid disorders include one study suggesting that chronic illness in a spouse can lead to dysthymia. Also, dysthymia has been found associated with several psychiatric conditions, including anxiety and substance abuse, with social phobia the most common.

TABLE 3-7. Cognitive Variables in Chronic Depression (CD), Nonchronic Major Depressive Disorder (NCMDD), and Never Psychiatrically Ill Controls (NPI)

Measure	Comparison group (M/SD)		
	CD	CNMDD	NPI
Schema questionnaire			
Disconnection and rejection	265.4 (70.4)	202.2 (84.9)	118.7 (54.5)
Impaired autonomy	137.0 (37.4)	103.0 (38.5)	67.7 (22.5)
Overvigilance	123.6 (29.0)	99.5 (37.7)	70.0 (24.6)
Impaired Limits	78.3 (21.7)	65.5 (19.8)	42.3 (17.7)
Dysfunctional Attitudes Scale	141.5 (38.5)	119.7 (30.7)	96.6 (26.2)
Attributional style questionnaire			
Stable	63.6 (10.6)	58.7 (12.2)	44.7 (19.0)
Global	63.2 (10.2)	31.7 (14.0)	38.1(18.4)
Response style questionnaire	56.5 (12.5)	54.4(12.9)	39.3 (10.3)

Adapted from Riso et al. 2003.

Biological Factors

Biological factors are considered more fully in Chapter 9. With respect to predicting a chronic course of depression, neuroendocrinology studies have found that the disturbances in the hypothalamic-pituitary-adrenocortical axis in chronic depression are similar to those in nonchronic types. Also, no consistent differences in sleep physiology have been found to be related to course. Immunology studies suggest increased natural killer cell activation in both dysthymia and major depression, but the overactive immune response in dysthymia may be more trait-like compared to nonchronic depression.

Cognitive Factors

The role of cognitive factors in chronic depression is "perhaps the most understudied area."[41] However, one study found that several cognitive variables differentiated chronically depressed individuals from those with major depression.[42] The study included 42 outpatients with chronic depression (CD), 27 outpatients with nonchronic major depressive disorder (NCMDD), and 24 never psychiatrically ill controls (NPI). The cognitive variables included a Schema Questionnaire, the Dysfunctional Attitudes Scale, the Attributional Style Questionnaire, and a ruminative response style questionnaire (see Table 3-7).

Results showed that the two depressed groups were elevated on every cognitive measure compared to the control group. The depressed groups were higher on the schema clusters, dysfunctional attitudes, stable and global attributional style, and rumination. Moreover, the chronic depression group compared to the nonchronic group was significantly elevated on all cognitive measures except for ruminative response and attributional style. In general, the chronic group of patients were more elevated on measures of cognitive variables even after taking into account (statistically controlling for) mood state and personality disorder symptoms. Thus, this preliminary study suggests that the cognitive perspective may be of some utility in distinguishing between those with chronic depression compared to nonchronic major depressive disorder.

Overall, Riso et al.[41] concluded by suggesting that continued research is needed with (1) better definitions of chronicity, (2) utilization of more appropriate comparison groups, and (3) prospective follow-up studies across longer time periods. To more completely ascertain the causes of chronic depression is one of the most important areas for researchers in the field of experimental psychopathology.

Conclusions

1. In naturalistic studies, complete remission from an episode of depression occurs in 70–95 percent of the cases. About 95 percent of the younger patients remit completely.

2. When the initial attack occurs before age 30, it tends to be shorter than when it occurs after 30. Acute onset also favors shorter duration.

3. After an initial attack of depression, 47–79 percent of the patients will have a recurrence at some time in their lives. The correct figure is probably closer to 79 percent, because this is based on a longer follow-up period.

4. Individuals who have experienced a major depressive disorder, single episode, have at least a 60 percent chance of having a second episode; those who have had two episodes have a 70 percent chance of a third; and those with three prior episodes have a 90 percent chance of having a fourth.[35]

5. The likelihood of frequent recurrences is greater in the biphasic cases than in cases of depression without a manic phase. Between 5 and 10 percent of individuals with major depressive disorder, single episode, later develop a manic episode.[35]

6. Although the duration of multiple episodes remains about the same, the symptom-free interval tends to decrease with each successive attack. In the biphasic cases the intervals are consistently shorter than in the simple depressions.

7. Approximately 5 percent of hospitalized bipolar patients subsequently commit suicide. The suicidal risk is especially high on weekend leaves from the hospital and during the month following hospitalization and remains high for six months after discharge.

8. The rate of suicide attempts appears to be higher among those with chronic depressive illness (dysthymic disorder) compared to episodic major depression.

9. The notion that a person who threatens suicide will not carry out the threat is fallacious. The communication of suicidal intent is the best single predictor of a successful suicidal attempt. Previously unsuccessful suicidal attempts are followed by successful suicides in a substantial proportion of the cases.

10. Suicide risk in patients with bipolar disorder is increased in those with greater severity and higher body mass.

11. The search for determinants of chronic depression includes developmental factors like childhood adversity (early trauma or maltreatment); personality, psychological stressors, comorbid disorders, biological factors, and cognitive factors. In studies of chronic depression, the strongest evidence of etiology is developmental factors, with some support for chronic stressors and stress reactivity.

12. The role of cognitive factors in chronic depression is "perhaps the most understudied area."[41] However, one study suggested the cognitive perspective may be of some utility in distinguishing between chronic and nonchronic forms of depressive disorder.

Chapter 4
Classifying Mood Disorders

The Official Nomenclature

Classification of the mood disorders has evolved in the more than 50 years since the American Psychiatric Association's first diagnostic and statistical manual was published. As research and theory have advanced, they have been reflected in the four editions and two revisions of the manual.

The current criteria for classifying Major Depressive Episodes and Manic Episodes are listed in Tables 4-1 and 4-2 from *DSM-IV-TR*.[1] It might be noted that the *DSM-IV* criteria for major depressive episode (as in Table 4-1) include "biological" or physiological symptoms along with cognitive ones. For example, these four symptoms are largely physiological in nature: (3) weight loss (or, in children, failure to make expected weight gains); (4) insomnia or hypersomnia; (5) psychomotor agitation or retardation; and (6) fatigue or loss of energy nearly every day. These five are cognitive or motivational symptoms: (1) depressed mood (or, in children and adolescents, irritability); (2) markedly diminished interest or pleasure in activities; (7) feelings of worthlessness or excessive or inappropriate guilt; (8) diminished ability to think or concentrate, or indecisiveness; (9) recurrent thoughts of death or suicidal ideation. The various types of mood disorder are listed in Table 4-3.[1]

To find the various types of depression in the earlier nomenclature of the American Psychiatric Association,[2,3] compared to subsequent versions,[1,4,5,6] it was necessary to hunt through many sections. This scattering of the affective disorders contrasted with the consolidation found in other classification systems (e.g., the British Classification).[7] This prior scattering of the mood disorders was a reflection of several historical trends, including the dissolution of Kraepelin's grand union of all affective disorders into the manic-depressive category, the isolation of new entities such as neurotic-depressive reaction, and the attempt to separate the disorders on the basis of presumed etiological differences.

Schizoaffective disorder, which has salient affective features, was at one

TABLE 4-1. Criteria for Major Depressive Episode

A. Five (or more) of the following symptoms have been present during the same 2-week period and represent a change from previous functioning; at least one of the symptoms is either (1) depressed mood or (2) loss of interest or pleasure. *Note*: Do not include symptoms that are clearly due to a general medical condition, or mood-incongruent delusions or hallucinations.
   (1) depressed mood most of the day, nearly every day, as indicated by either subjective report (e.g., feels sad or empty) or observation made by others (e.g., appears tearful). *Note*: In children and adolescents, can be irritable mood.
   (2) markedly diminished interest or pleasure in all, or almost all, activities most of the day, nearly every day (as indicated by either subjective account or observation made by others).
   (3) significant weight loss when not dieting or weight gain (e.g., a change of more than 5% of body weight in a month), or decrease or increase in appetite nearly every day. Note: In children, consider failure to make expected weight gains.
   (4) insomnia or hypersomnia nearly every day.
   (5) psychomotor agitation or retardation nearly every day (observable by others, not merely subjective feelings of restlessness or being slowed down).
   (6) fatigue or loss of energy nearly every day.
   (7) feelings of worthlessness or excessive or inappropriate guilt (which may be delusional) nearly every day (not merely self-reproach or guilt about being sick).
   (8) diminished ability to think or concentrate, or indecisiveness, nearly every day (either by subjective account or as observed by others).
   (9) recurrent thoughts of death (not just fear of dying), recurrent suicidal ideation without a specific plan, or a suicide attempt or a specific plan for committing suicide.
B. The symptoms do not meet criteria for Mixed Episode.
C. The symptoms cause clinically significant distress or impairment in social, occupational, or other important areas of functioning.
D. The symptoms are not due to the direct physiological effects of a substance (e.g., a drug of abuse, a medication) or a general medical condition (e.g., hypothyroidism).
E. The symptoms are not better accounted for by bereavement, i.e., after the loss of a loved one, the symptoms persist for longer than 2 months or are characterized by marked functional impairment, morbid preoccupation with worthlessness, suicidal ideation, psychotic symptoms, or psychomotor retardation.

Adapted from *DSM-IV-TR*.

time listed as a subtype of the schizophrenic reaction. In terms of its historical conceptualization, its course, and its prognosis, this disorder may be more closely allied to bipolar disorder (see Chapter 8).

Derivation of System of Classification

In its original development, the DSM system of classification represented a composite of the ideas of three schools of thought: those of Emil Kraepelin,

TABLE 4-2. Criteria for Manic Episode

A. A distinct period of abnormally and persistently elevated, expansive, or irritable mood, lasting at least 1 week (or any duration if hospitalization is necessary).
B. During the period of mood disturbance, three (or more) of the following symptoms have persisted (four if the mood is only irritable) and have been present to a significant degree:
  (1) inflated self-esteem or grandiosity;
  (2) decreased need for sleep (e.g., feels rested after only 3 hours of sleep);
  (3) more talkative than usual or pressure to keep talking;
  (4) flight of ideas or subjective experience that thoughts are racing;
  (5) distractibility (i.e., attention too easily drawn to unimportant or irrelevant external stimuli);
  (6) increase in goal-directed activity (either socially, at work or school, or sexual or psychomotor agitation;
  (7) excessive involvement in pleasurable activities that have a high potential for painful consequences (e.g., unrestrained buying sprees, sexual indiscretions, or foolish business investments).
C. The symptoms do not meet criteria for Mixed Episode.
D. The mood disturbance is sufficiently severe to cause marked impairment in occupational functioning or in usual social activities or relationships with others, or to necessitate hospitalization to prevent harm to self or others, or there are psychotic features.
E. The symptoms are not due to the direct physiological effects of a substance (e.g., drug of abuse, a medication, or other treatment) or a general medical condition (e.g., hyperthyroidism). *Note*: Maniclike episodes that are clearly caused by somatic antidepressant treatment (e.g., medication, electroconvulsive therapy, light therapy) should not be counted toward a diagnosis of Bipolar I Disorder.

Adapted from *DSM-IV-TR*.

Adolph Meyer, and Sigmund Freud. The division of the various nosological categories, particularly of the psychoses, reflected the original boundaries drawn by Kraepelin. The major modification in the terminology reflected the Meyerian influence. Meyer rejected the Kraepelinian concept of disease entities and formulated in its place a theory of "reaction types." The reaction types were conceived by him to be the result of the interaction between the specific hereditary endowment and the matrix of psychological and social forces impinging on the organism. The term *reaction* in the nomenclature reflected the Meyerian view.

Freud's influence was seen in the descriptions of the specific categories in the glossary section of the original APA manual.[2] Here the syndromes were outlined according to the psychoanalytic theories; the various affective disorders were presented in terms of the concepts of guilt, retroflected hostility, and defense against anxiety. More recently, Jerome Wakefield has contributed some important ideas on the concept of mental disorder as *harmful dysfunction*.[8,9,10]

TABLE 4-3. Types of Mood Disorder

Disorder	Characterizations
Depressive Disorders	
Major Depressive Disorder	One or more Major Depressive Episodes (i.e., at least 2 weeks of depressed mood or loss of interest accompanied by at least four additional symptoms of depression)
Dysthymic Disorder	At least 2 years of depressed mood for more days than not, accompanied by additional depressive symptoms that do not meet criteria for a Major Depressive Episode
Depressive Disorder Not Otherwise Specified	Included for coding disorders with depressive features that do not meet criteria for Major Depressive Disorder, Dysthymic Disorder, Adjustment Disorder with Depressed Mood, or Adjustment Disorder with Mixed Anxiety and Depressed Mood (or depressive symptoms about which there is inadequate or contradictory information)
Bipolar Disorders	
Bipolar I Disorder	One or more Manic or Mixed Episodes, usually accompanied by Major Depressive Episodes
Bipolar II Disorder	One or more Major Depressive Episodes accompanied by at least one Hypomanic Episode
Cyclothymic Disorder	At least 2 years of numerous periods of Hypomanic symptoms that do not meet criteria for a Manic Episode and numerous periods of depressive symptoms that do not meet criteria for a Major Depressive Episode
Bipolar Disorder Not Otherwise Specified	Included for coding disorders with bipolar features that do not meet criteria for any of the specific Bipolar Disorders defined in this section (or bipolar symptoms about which there is inadequate or contradictory information)
Other Mood Disorders	
Mood disorder due to a general medical condition	A prominent and persistent disturbance in mood that is judged to be a direct physiological consequence of a general medical condition
Substance-induced mood disorder	A prominent and persistent disturbance in mood that is judged to be a direct physiological consequence of a drug of abuse, a medication, another somatic treatment for depression, or toxin exposure
Mood Disorder Not Otherwise Specified	Included for coding disorders with mood symptoms that do not meet the criteria for any specific Mood Disorder and in which it is difficult to choose between Depressive Disorder Not Otherwise Specified and Bipolar Disorder Not Otherwise Specified (e.g., acute agitation)

Adapted from *DSM-IV-TR.*

Reliability and Validity of Classification

Early studies in the United States and the United Kingdom cast doubt on the reliability of the official nomenclatures. Some investigators, however, suggested at the time that the essential problem may be in the *application* of the nomenclature, rather than in its construction.[11,12,13] Substantial discrepancies were found among diagnosticians concurrently interviewing the same patients. Diagnostic agreement improved considerably by formulating operational definitions of the categories in the official nomenclature.

The validity of a nomenclature refers to the accuracy with which the diagnostic terms designate veridical entities. Unfortunately, in the case of the so-called functional psychiatric disorders, there has been no known pathology or physiological abnormality to provide guidelines in the construction of the nomenclature. The basic definition of the nosological categories has rested largely on clinical criteria.

In assessing the validity of a medical or psychiatric classification, it is appropriate to ask whether the specific groups or syndromes isolated from each other are different in ways that are of medical or psychiatric significance, that is, in terms of symptoms, duration, outcome, tendency to recur, and response to treatment. In general, the studies seem to justify the isolation of the group of depressive disorders from other psychiatric disorders; in addition, there is some support for the separation within the affective (now mood disorders) group of the *endogenous* depressions from the *reactive* (now *adjustment disorder*[1]) depressions.

In the early 1960s, Clark and Mallet[14] conducted a follow-up study of cases of depression and schizophrenia in young adults, in which 74 cases diagnosed as manic-depressive psychosis or reactive depression and 76 initially diagnosed with schizophrenia were followed for three years. During the follow-up period, 70 percent of those with schizophrenia were readmitted, as were 20 percent of the depressives. Thirteen (17 percent) of those with schizophrenia became chronic, compared with only one (1.3 percent) of the depressives. Of the 15 depressed patients requiring readmission to the hospital, four were considered to have schizophrenia at that time. Of the 76 patients initially diagnosed with schizophrenia, none were considered to have a depressive disorder on readmission.

Several inferences may be drawn from the clinical studies. Two major categories are distinguishable (as Kraepelin suggested) when rate of recovery and chronicity are examined as parts of the clinical picture. These are (1) depressive disorders having a relatively high rate of recovery, a moderate rate of relapse within three years of the initial diagnosis, and a moderate rate of chronicity; and (2) schizophrenia having a high rate of relapse and a high rate of chronicity. Some cases that initially evince the clinical picture of depression ultimately develop symptoms of schizophrenia. But it is rare for a patient who has symptoms of schizophrenia to develop bipolar disorder symptoms later. Lewis and Piotrowski[15] suggested that many cases are diagnosed incorrectly as bipolar disorder because of insufficient recognition of certain signs of schizophrenia.

Dichotomies and Dualisms: Past and Present

Aubrey Lewis[16] and Paul Hoch[17] regarded depression as essentially a single entity, while others sliced the syndrome along various planes to produce several dichotomies. This controversy reflected fundamental differences between the unitary and the separatist schools.[18] The unitary school (gradualists) maintained that depression is a single clinical disorder that can express itself in a variety of forms; the separatists stated that there are several distinguishable types.

Endogenous Versus Exogenous

This division attempted to establish the basic etiology of depression. Cases of depression were divided into those caused essentially by internal factors (endogenous) and those caused by external factors (exogenous). Although originally the exogenous group included such environmental agents as toxins and bacteria, writers have equated exogenous with psychogenic factors. This dichotomy will be discussed at greater length below.

Autonomous Versus Reactive

Some writers have distinguished between types of depression on the basis of degree of reactivity to external events. Gillespie[19] described several groups of depressed patients that differed in their responsiveness to external influences. He labeled those cases that followed a relentless course irrespective of any favorable environmental influences as "autonomous." Those that responded favorably to encouragement and understanding were labeled "reactive."

Agitated Versus Retarded

Depression has often been characterized in terms of the predominant activity level. Many authors considered agitation as characteristic of depressions of the so-called involutional period and retardation of activity as characteristic of earlier depressions. Several studies (see Chapter 7) have discounted this hypothesis.

Psychotic Versus Neurotic

Most authors have drawn a sharp line between psychotic and non-psychotic depressions. The gradualists, however,[16,17] believed that this distinction is artificial and that the differences are primarily quantitative. They asserted that the reported distinctions are based entirely on differences in the severity of the illness.

Endogenous and Exogenous Depressions

The focus of the controversy between the separatists and the gradualists was primarily on the etiological concepts of depression. The separatists favored two distinct entities. One category consisted of cases that were thought to be *endogenous*, that is, caused primarily by some biological derangement in the human organism. The second category, *reactive depressions*, consisted of cases caused primarily by some external stress (bereavement, financial reverses, loss of employment). The unitary school considered these distinctions artificial and did not recognize the validity of labeling some cases endogenous and others reactive.

The concept of two etiologically different types of depression was not new. In 1586 Timothy Bright, a physician, wrote a monograph, *Melancholy and the Conscience of Sinne*, in which he distinguished two different types of depression. He described one type "where the peril is not of the body" and requires "cure of the minde" (psychotherapy). In the second type, "the melancholy humour, deluding the organical actions, abuseth the minde"; this type requires physical treatment.

Origin of Endogenous-Exogenous Model

The words "endogen" and "exogen" were coined by the Swiss botanist Augustin de Candolle.[20] The concept was introduced into psychiatry toward the end of the nineteenth century by the German neuropsychiatrist P. J. Moebius (for a more complete discussion of the evolution of the concept, see Heron[22]). Moebius attached the label of "endogenous" to the group of mental disorders considered at that time to be due to degeneration or hereditary factors (internal causes). He further distinguished another group of mental disorders that he considered to be produced by bacterial, chemical, and other toxins (external causes); this group was given the label of "exogenous." The endogenous-exogenous view of psychiatric disorders was a completely organic dichotomy that left no room for a different order of causative agents, namely the social or psychogenic. The exclusiveness of this doctrine caused semantic difficulties when the concept later had to be adapted to include social determinants of abnormal behavior.

The dualism inherent in the endogenous-exogenous concept is apparent in Kraepelin.[21] He accepted Moebius's classification and stated that the principal demarcation of the etiology of mental disorders is between *internal* and *external* causes. He proposed that there was a natural division between the two major groups of diseases, exogenous and endogenous. In manic-depressive illness, "the real causes of the malady must be sought in permanent internal changes which very often, perhaps always, are innate." Environment could at most be a precipitant of manic-depressive disease, because by definition an endogenous illness could not at the same time be an exogenous illness.

"The Great Debates"

The controversy regarding the endogenous-exogenous concept was most prominent in Great Britain, and a number of outstanding authorities took part on both sides of the argument.[18] Earlier, Kraepelin had endeavored to include almost all forms of depression under one label, manic-depressive disorder. Later, German writers almost uniformly split depressions into endogenous and exogenous. The British, however, were sharply divided on this point, and as a result of the clash of opinions in a series of great debates, the concepts of depression were considerably refined (although unanimity has not as yet been attained).

The first of the debates was touched off by Mapother in 1926, when he attacked the notion of a clinical distinction between neurotic depressions and psychotic depressions. (This argument later shaded into the controversy of endogenous versus reactive depression.) He held that the only reason for making a distinction was the practical difficulties connected with commitment procedures. He claimed that he could "find no other basis for the distinction; neither insight, nor cooperation in treatment, nor susceptibility to psychotherapy." He attacked the notion that there are neurotic conditions that are purely psychogenic and psychotic conditions that are dependent on structural change. His view was that all depressions, whether ostensibly psychogenic or seemingly endogenous, are mediated by essentially the same means.

Mapother's concept is an interesting statement of the phenomenon of depression: "The essence of an attack is the clinical fact that the emotions for the time have lost enduring relation to current experience and whatever their origin and intensity they have achieved a sort of autonomy." There were a number of rebuttals in the discussion of Mapother's paper, and then another debate in 1930, which touched off another series of discussions and papers (see Partridge).

Klein and Wender[23] note that the labels "neurotic," "reactive," and "endogenous" depression are beginning to disappear. They speculate that one of the major reasons for their fading is the increasing evidence that diverse types of mood disorders are often triggered by life events, but nonetheless are treatable by "physical methods" (p. 93). However, as reviewed in Chapters 14, 15, and 16, the somatic and psychological therapies overall appear equally capable of providing treatment and prevention of the mood disorders.

Distinction Between Endogenous and Reactive Depressions

From the various conflicting as well as complementary opinions regarding the validity of differentiating endogenous from reactive or neurotic depressions, it is possible to make a composite picture of endogenous depression as it emerged from the debates. This may be helpful in understanding the referents of the term endogenous, which appeared widely in the earlier literature, although it was not included in any official nomenclature.

In general, there are two major defining characteristics of the category *endogenous depression.* First, it was generally equated with psychosis and consequently distinguished from neurotic depressions. Second, it was regarded as arising primarily from internal (physiological) factors and could thus be contrasted with reactive depressions produced by external stress. To complicate the distinctions, however, reactive depressions, although often equated with neurotic depressions, were sometimes distinguished from them.

The *etiology* of endogenous depression was ascribed to a toxic chemical agent, a hormonal factor, or a metabolic disturbance.[24,25] Autonomy from external environmental stimuli was considered an essential feature. Crichton-Miller likened the mood variation to the swinging of a pendulum, completely independent of the environment. Neurotic variations in mood, in contrast, were compared to the motion of a boat with insufficient keel, subject to the oscillations in its milieu.

The specific *symptomatology* was characterized as a diffuse coloring of the whole outlook, phasic morning-evening variation, continuity, detachment from reality, loss of affection, and loss of power to grieve.[26] To this should be added Gillespie's observation that the symptoms seemed alien to the individual and not congruent with her or his premorbid personality.

The role of *heredity* in endogenous depressions was stressed by a number of writers. Gillespie[19] reported that a family history of psychosis was common in this group, and Buzzard[26] suggested that suicide and alcoholism were frequent in the family background. *Constitutional factors* as reflected in body build were emphasized by Strauss.

Reactive depressions were distinguished from endogenous depressions because they were said to fluctuate according to ascertainable psychological factors.[19] In terms of symptomatology, the distinguishing features were seen to be a tendency to blame the environment and insight into the abnormal nature of the condition.

Systematic Studies

Several investigators tried to determine whether depressive illnesses are simply drawn from different points along a single continuum, or whether a number of qualitatively distinct entities exist. Kiloh and Garside[27] reported a study designed to differentiate between endogenous and neurotic (exogenous) depression. Their article reviewed the historical development of the controversy and the experimental literature and presented data collected by the authors.

They studied the records of 143 depressed outpatients and abstracted data relevant to their investigation; 31 of the patients had been diagnosed as having endogenous depression, 61 as having neurotic depression, and 51 as doubtful. Thirty-five clinical features of the illness were selected for additional study. A factor analysis was carried out, and two factors were extracted. The first was a general factor; the bipolar second factor was considered by the authors to differentiate between neurotic and endogenous depression. The second factor accounted for a greater part of the total variance than the general factor and was therefore more important in producing the correlations among the 35 clinical features analyzed.

Kiloh and Garside found significant correlation between certain clinical features and each of the diagnostic categories. The clinical features that correlated significantly ($p < .05$) with the diagnosis of neurotic depression were, in decreasing order of the magnitude of their correlations, reactivity of depression; precipitation; self-pity; variability of illness; hysterical features; inadequacy; initial insomnia; reactive depression; depression worse in evening; sudden onset; irritability; hypochondriasis; obsessionality. The features that correlated significantly with endogenous depression were early awakening; depression worse in morning; quality of depression; retardation; duration one year or less; age 40 or older; depth of depression; failure of concentration; weight loss of seven or more pounds; previous attacks.

Another study by Carney et al. [28] extended to inpatients the overall approach used by Kiloh and Garside in their study of outpatients. Carney and his coworkers studied 129 inpatient depressives treated with ECT. All patients were followed up for three months, and 108 patients were followed for six months. Initially, all were scored for the presence or absence of 35 features considered to discriminate between endogenous and neurotic depressions. Diagnoses were made before or shortly after treatment was started. Improvement was rated on a four-point scale at the termination of ECT, at three months, and at six months. At three months, only 12 of 63 neurotic depressives (19 percent) were found to have responded well to ECT, whereas 44 of 53 endogenous depressives (83 percent) had responded well.

A factor analysis of the clinical features produced three significant factors: a bipolar factor "corresponding to the distinction between endogenous and neurotic depression"; a general factor with high loadings for many features common to all the depressive cases studied; and a "paranoid psychotic factor." The bipolar factor closely resembled that which was extracted in the study by Kiloh and Garside. Among features with high positive loadings on the first factor, and thus corresponding to a diagnosis of endogenous depression, were adequate premorbid personality; absence of adequate psychogenic factors in relation to illness; a distinct quality to the depression; weight loss; pyknic body build; occurrence of previous depressive episode; early morning awakening; depressive psychomotor activity; nihilistic, somatic, and paranoid delusions; and ideas of guilt. Among features with a negative loading, corresponding to a diagnosis of neurotic depression, were anxiety; aggravation of symptoms in the evening; self-pity; a tendency to blame others; and hysterical features.

By means of multiple regression analysis, three series of 18 weighted coefficients for the differential diagnosis between the two varieties of depression and for the prediction of ECT response at three and six months were calculated. The multiple correlations between the summed features, on the one hand, and diagnosis and outcome at three and six months, on the other, were 0.91, 0.72, and 0.74 respectively. It was found that ECT response could be better predicted by the direct use of the weights for ECT response than from the diagnostic weights alone. The weights based on the 18 clinical features were complex, and therefore a table was constructed giving simplified weights based on ten features of diagnosis. When the weighted scores for each patient were computed, it was found that, of the patients with a score of six or higher, 52 had been diagnosed clinically as endogenous and three as neurotic. Those patients scoring below six included one endogenous and 60 neurotic depressives. The amount of overlap, consequently, was small, and the findings supported the two-type hypothesis.

Methodological Problems

Several methodological questions may be raised in connection with these studies. First, the reliability of the ratings of the clinical material was not reported. As has been pointed out in many papers, interjudge agreement tends to be relatively low when applied to clinical material; low reliability automatically imposes a limit on the validity of any findings based on these ratings. In addition, since the psychiatrists making the ratings were cognizant of the underlying hypotheses, the possibility of bias in making their judgments cannot be excluded.

The second methodological problem concerned the differences between the two groups studied with respect to uncontrolled variables of importance, such as age and sex. For example, relative sleeplessness and loss of appetite are characteristic of older patients. (We found a relatively high correlation between age and loss of appetite among our psychiatric patients.) There was also evidence that females and males reacted differently to stress. Since these studies did not control adequately for either age or sex (or for other demographic variables), we cannot be certain that the salient differences between the two groups are explained by the dualistic hypothesis.

There is also a problem in the interpretation of the factor analysis. The authors extracted a bipolar factor that seemed to indicate a division of the patient sample into two independent groupings. In order to prove that these groupings apply to different kinds of patients rather than simply to different clusters of signs and symptoms, it is necessary to show that there is a clear-cut splitting of the patient sample into two independent groups. Kiloh and Garside[27] did not present any information regarding the distribution of the cases. In the study by Carney, Roth and Garside,[28] however, a separation of the endogenous and neurotic groups was achieved by weighting items based on the statistical analysis.

Studies of Symptomatology

Hamilton and White[29] performed a factor analysis on data obtained from 64 severely depressed patients who had been evaluated with the use of Hamilton's rating scale.[30] The first of the four factors obtained included such clinical features as depressed mood, guilt, retardation, loss of insight, suicidal attempt, and loss of interest. It proved, according to the authors, to be correlated with a clinical diagnosis of retarded depression. Significantly different mean scores between the endogenous and reactive groups were obtained for this first factor. It should be emphasized, however, that this finding does not specify whether the difference is qualitative or merely quantitative.

Unfortunately, the so-called precipitating factors given to justify the diagnosis of reactive depression seemed unconvincing. In the three cases of reactive depression presented, the authors refer to the following as the psychological precipitating factors: one patient was left alone for prolonged periods while his wife went to look after their sick daughter; another was put in charge of a program that was beyond his capabilities; the third learned that the pulmonary tuberculosis he had had for nine years was bilateral.

Findings contradictory to those reported by Hamilton and White were contained in a study by Rose.[31] This investigator used the same clinical rating scale in studying 50 depressed patients. The patients were divided into endogenous, reactive, and doubtful groups. In contrast to Hamilton and White, Rose found no significant differences in symptoms among the three groups.

Physiological Responses and Tests

Kiloh and Garside referred to the work on sedation threshold by Shagass and Jones,[32] which indicated that cases of endogenous depression had lower sedation thresholds than those of neurotic depression. They also cited the work of Ackner and Pampiglione[33] and Roberts,[34] which failed to confirm Shagass's results. The work of Shagass and Schwartz[35] on cortical excitability following electrical stimulation of the ulnar nerve was also cited. They found that in 21 patients with psychotic depression, the mean recovery time was significantly increased. However, controls for age were not included in these early studies, thus confounding the variables of interest.

The Funkenstein test was cited by Sloan et al. as additional evidence supporting the distinction between these two types of depression.[36] Better designed studies failed to substantiate these findings (see Chapter 9). More recent research supports an interactive perspective on the development of depression, including cognitive vulnerability, stress, early experiences, and genetic components (see Chapter 13).

Body Build

Kiloh and Garside quoted a study by Rees[37] that demonstrated an association between neurotic depression and leptomorphic physique, and between eurymorphic physique and manic-depressive disorder. Here again, the mean age of the manic-depressive group was significantly higher than that of the neurotic-depressive group. As will be indicated in Chapter 9, body build becomes more eurymorphic with increasing age.

Response to Treatment

Kiloh and Garside cited several studies suggesting that exogenous depression reacts poorly to electroconvulsive therapy but endogenous depression reacts favorably. Some evidence to support this claim is contained in a study by Rose,[31] who found that better response was obtained only for the women who had endogenous depression. There was no difference in treatment response among the men in this study. (The study by Carney et al.[28] described in detail above helped substantiate the claim of a differential response.)

Depressive Equivalents

Many writers attempted to spread the umbrella of depression to cover cases showing clinical symptoms or behaviors different from those generally indicative of depression. The term *depressive equivalents* was introduced by Kennedy and Wiesel[38] to describe patients who had various somatic complaints but did not show any apparent mood depression. They reported three cases characterized by somatic pain, sleep disturbance, and weight loss, all of whom recovered completely after a course of ECT.

A number of other terms have been applied at various times to designate such cases of concealed depression. These include incomplete depression, latent depression, atypical depression, and masked depression. Various psychosomatic disorders, hypochondriacal reactions, anxiety reactions, phobic

TABLE 4-4. Diagnostic Criteria for Mood Disorder Due to General Medical Condition

A. A prominent and persistent disturbance in mood predominates in the clinical picture and is characterized by either (or both) of the following:
   (1) depressed mood or markedly diminished interest or pleasure in all, or almost all, activities;
   (2) elevated, expansive, or irritable mood.
B. There is evidence from the history, physical examination, or laboratory findings that the disturbance is the direct physiological consequence of a general medical condition.
C. The disturbance is not better accounted for by another mental disorder (e.g., adjustment disorder with depressed mood in response to the stress of having a general medical condition).
D. The disturbance does not occur exclusively during the course of a delirium.
E. The symptoms cause clinically significant distress or impairment in social, occupational, or other important areas of functioning.

Adapted from *DSM-IV-TR*.

reactions, and obsessive-compulsive reactions have also been implicated as masking the typical picture of depressive reactions.[39]

The use of such a term as depressive equivalents raised several difficult conceptual, semantic, and diagnostic problems. (1) How could a syndrome substitute for a depressive reaction? (2) Since the usual indices of depression are lacking, how can the diagnosis of masked depression, etc. be made? (3) Since the concept of depressive equivalent is so loose, it could be stretched to encompass practically any psychiatric or somatic syndrome.

One of the main criteria for diagnosing a depressive equivalent has been the response of patients with formerly intractable symptoms to ECT.[38] Denison and Yaskin,[40] in a report titled "Medical and Surgical Masquerades of the Depressed State," listed several criteria for the diagnosis of an underlying depression. These include previous attacks of somatic complaints similar to the present attack, with complete recovery after several months; disturbance of sleep cycle; loss of appetite; loss of energy disproportionate to the somatic complaints; diurnal variation in intensity of somatic symptoms; and feeling of unreality. In the consideration of disguised depressions, it is worth emphasizing the truism that depression may mask organic disease as well as vice versa.

Depressions Secondary to Somatic Disorders

It has long been understood that depressions are associated with a wide variety of nonpsychiatric disorders. In some instances, the depression appears to be a manifestation of the physiological disturbance caused by structural disease or toxic agents. The current American Psychiatric Association criteria for diagnosing depressions secondary to somatic disorders are in Table 4-4. In other instances, the depression seems to be a psychological reaction to being acutely or chronically ill—that is, the illness is a nonspecific precipitating factor. In either event, the depressive symptomatology per se, is not distinguishable from that observed in primary depressions.[1,41]

Conditions that specifically impair the normal functioning of the nervous system have long been known to produce depression.[42] These conditions may be acute (the acute brain syndromes) such as those associated with alcohol, drugs, head trauma, or post-ictal states. Or the conditions may be chronic (chronic brain syndromes) such as those associated with cerebral arteriosclerosis, dementia, neurosyphilis, multiple sclerosis, malnutrition, and various vitamin deficiency syndromes.

Depression as a complication of the use of the tranquilizing drugs has frequently been reported. Early reports of the use of reserpine in the treatment of hypertension implicated this drug as a causative agent in many depressions. Also, the phenothiazines have been suspected. Simonson,[43] for instance, interviewed 480 patients who were having their first acknowledged depression. He found that 146 (30 percent) had been taking a phenothiazine prior to the depression. Ayd,[44] however, was skeptical of the role of tranquilizers in producing a depression. He studied 47 cases of so-called drug-induced depression, and concluded that each case presented a history of predisposition to psychic disturbance and of physical and psychological stresses that helped precipitate the depression. This is not surprising, since the people in this study were presumably prescribed the tranquilizers due to some identified "psychic disturbance" in the first place.

Depressive symptomatology was found in a substantial proportion of patients hospitalized for medical disorders.[45] Yaskin[46] and Yaskin et al.[47] reported a high frequency in patients with organic disease of the abdominal organs, particularly carcinoma of the pancreas. Dovenmuehle and Verwoerdt[48] reported that 64 percent of 62 patients hospitalized for definitely diagnosed cardiac disease had depressive symptoms of moderate or severe degree.

Other types of generalized somatic disorders that, according to Castelnuovo-Tedesco, are likely to be complicated by depression are (1) certain infectious diseases—especially infectious hepatitis, influenza, infectious mononucleosis, atypical pneumonia, rheumatic fever, and tuberculosis; (2) so-called psychosomatic disorders such as ulcerative colitis, asthma, neurodermatitis, and rheumatoid arthritis; (3) anemias; (4) malignancies; and (5) endocrine disturbances.

In view of the longstanding theory that primary depression is caused by an endocrine disturbance, it is interesting that certain diseases of the endocrine glands are associated with a high frequency of depression. Michael and Gibbons[49] pointed out that the adrenocortical hyperfunction of Cushing's syndrome is almost always accompanied by mood change. The alteration in mood is generally depressive, but it may also be characterized by emotional lability and overreactiveness. In their review of the reports of psychiatric disturbance related to Cushing's syndrome, Michael and Gibbons stated that the incidence of psychiatric disturbance generally exceeded 50 percent. Severe mental disturbance, extreme enough to warrant the label *psychotic*, was found in 15–20 percent of the cases. In one series, 12 of 13 patients with Cushing's syndrome were reported to be consistently or intermittently depressed. There was, however, no close correlation between the symptoms of depression and the steroid output.

Michael and Gibbons also reviewed the incidence of depression in Addison's disease. They noted that depression occurred in 25 percent of the cases, and, somewhat surprisingly, euphoria occurred in 50 percent. Psychiatric disturbances have also been reported in cases of hypopituitarism. In longstanding untreated cases, the symptoms may appear in an extreme form. The most prominent symptom tends to be apathy and inactivity. Mild depression, occasionally interrupted by brief episodes of irritability and quarrelsomeness, is also prominent. Additional studies on the biological aspects are reviewed in Chapter 9.

Chapter 5
Psychotic Versus Nonpsychotic Depression

Historically, there was considerable controversy among authorities regarding the separation of psychotic and neurotic depressions. Although this cleavage was part of the official nomenclature for many years, authorities such as Paul Hoch[1] questioned the distinction, and it was eventually discarded. Hoch stated:

> The dynamic manifestations, the orality, the super-ego structure, etc., are the same in both, and usually the differentiation is made arbitrarily. If the patient has had some previous depressive attacks, he would probably be placed in the psychotic group; if not, he would be placed in the neurotic one. If the patient's depression is developed as a reaction to an outside precipitating factor, then he is often judged as having a neurotic depression. If such factors are not demonstrated, he is classified then as an endogenous depression. Actually there is no difference between a so-called psychotic or a so-called neurotic depression. The difference is only a matter of degree.

Hoch's statement epitomized the point of view of the *gradualists* as opposed to the concept of the *separatists*, who made a dichotomy between neurotic and psychotic depression. The historical precedent for the gradualist concept is found in Kraepelin's statement:[2]

> We include in the manic-depressive group certain slight and slightest colorings of mood, some of them periodic, some of them continuously morbid, which on the one hand are to be regarded as the rudiment of more severe disorders; on the other hand, passing over without sharp boundary into the domain of personal predisposition.

Paskind[3] also believed that the psychotic depressions were simply severe forms of the manic-depressive (bipolar) syndrome. They differ from the milder forms in terms of the dramatic symptoms, but not in terms of any fundamental factors. He stated (p. 789): "The situation is somewhat similar, for example, to what descriptions of diabetes would be if only hospital cases were described. Almost every case of diabetes would then show acidosis, coma, gangrene, and massive infection."

Separating depression into two distinct disorders would, according to Paskind, be analogous to separating diabetes into two distinct entities on the basis of severity.

Unlike the current system,[4] the preponderant opinion in the earlier literature favored the separation of the neurotic and psychotic depressions. Some support for the two-disease concept was provided by the studies of Kiloh and Garside[5] and Carney, Roth, and Garside.[6] These authors demonstrated, through the use of factor analysis, a bipolar factor, the poles corresponding to neurotic depression and endogenous depression respectively (see Chapter 4). Sandifer et al.[7] obtained a bimodal distribution of scores on their rating scale, which they interpreted as representing two types of depression. The bimodal distribution, however, may have depended on the type of instrument employed. Schwab et al.,[8] for instance, found a bimodal distribution of scores on the Hamilton Rating Scale but not on the Beck Depression Inventory.

"Psychoneurotic" Depressive Reaction

Definition

In the original American Psychiatric Association diagnostic manual,[9] this syndrome was characterized as follows:

> The reaction is precipitated by a current situation, frequently by some loss sustained by the patient, and is often associated with a feeling of guilt for past failures or deeds. . . . The term is synonymous with "reactive depression" and is to be differentiated from the corresponding psychotic reaction. In this differentiation, points to be considered are (1) life history of patient, with special reference to mood swings (suggestive of psychotic reaction), to the personality structure (neurotic or cyclothymic), and to precipitating environmental factors, and (2) absence of malignant symptoms (hypochrondriacal preoccupation, agitation, delusions, particularly somatic, hallucinations, severe guilt feelings, intractable insomnia, suicidal ruminations, severe psychomotor retardation, profound retardation of thought, stupor).

In addition to this statement regarding the manifest characteristics of this condition, the following psychodynamic formulation was included in the manual: "The anxiety in this reaction is allayed, and hence partially relieved, by depression and self-depreciation. . . . The degree of the reaction in such cases is dependent upon the intensity of the patient's ambivalent feeling towards his loss (love, possession) as well as upon the realistic circumstances of the loss."

Although not specified in the manual, the defining characteristics of psychoneurotic depressive reaction may be assumed to be the generally accepted features of depression. The more *malignant* symptoms indicative of a psychotic depression are mentioned above. It is noteworthy that the authors considered the presence of suicidal ruminations to exclude a diagnosis of neurotic depression. This notion is contradicted by the finding that this symptom was found in 58 percent of patients diagnosed as neurotic depressive reaction (Table 5-1). A patient with a low mood such as dejection, low self-esteem, indecisiveness, and, possibly, some of the physical and vegetative symptoms mentioned in Chapter 2, would have been considered to have a neurotic-depressive reaction.

In addition to the brief description of the manifest symptoms, the glossary also introduced two etiological concepts. The first, that the depression is precipitated by a current situation, is a derivative of the concept of reactive depression, the development of which will be discussed. The second etiological concept is that the depression is a defense against anxiety (pp. 12, 32), and that the ambivalent feelings toward the presumed lost object determine the intensity of the reaction.

This specific psychodynamic formulation represented an attempt by the authors of the manual to provide a psychological explanation for this condition. It is not clear whether the psychodynamic formulation was intended to be a defining characteristic of the category. In retrospect, the attempt should have been regarded as *experimental*, and the validity of the category not dependent upon the validity of the psychodynamic formulation or on whether it is possible to discern this particular configuration in a given case. Reports of investigators trying to apply the psychodynamic formulation questioned its usefulness in making the diagnosis.[10,11] The concept that neurotic depressive reaction is *reactive* seems to be more integral to the definition of this syndrome and some may have considered that if some external stress could not be demonstrated in a particular case, then the use of this diagnosis was not justified in that case.

Despite the inclusion of this category in many nomenclatures, it was by no means generally accepted. In fact, a large number of writers on depression continued to accept the *gradualist* or *unitary concept*, namely, that the difference between "neurotic" and "psychotic" depression was one of degree, and that there was no more justification for constructing separate categories than for dividing scarlet fever into two groups such as mild and severe. Proponents of this point of view included the authors who wrote most extensively about depression, such as Mapother[12] and Lewis[13] in England, and Ascher,[10] Cassidy et al.,[14] Campbell,[15] Kraines,[16] Robins et al.,[17] and Winokur and Pitts[18] in the United States.

Evolution of the Concept

There were a number of radical twists and turns in the gradual evolution and eventual displacement of the concept. In the earlier classifications, the reactive-depressive category was not fused with neurotic depression. Kraepelin recognized a condition similar to the notion of neurotic depression and allocated it to the category of congenital neurasthenia, which he listed under constitutional psychopathic states. He also referred to a group of "psychogenic depressions," which he considered different from manic-depressive psychosis. Patients with psychogenic depressions showed a high degree of reactivity to external situations and their depression tended to improve when the external situation improved. The manic-depressive attack, in contrast, was not then understood to result in part from external stress situations.

Bleuler[19] evidently allocated the milder depressions to the manic-depressive category, as indicated by his statement that "probably everything designated as periodic neurasthenia, recurrent dyspepsia, and neurasthenic melancholias belong entirely to manic-depressive insanity." He also conceded the existence of psychogenic depressions: "Simple psychogenic depressions, occurring in psychopaths not of the manic-depressive group and reaching the intensity of a mental·disease, are rare."

The most definite precursor of the concept of neurotic-depressive reaction was that of reactive depression. In 1926, Lange listed psychogenic and reactive depression separately in his classification of depression. He differentiated psychogenic depressions from the endogenous variety on the basis of greater aggressiveness, egocentricity, stubbornness, and overt hostility. In addition, he stated that there were no discernible variations in mood in the psychogenic depressions. Changes in the milieu influenced this condition, and it became better when the personality conflict was solved. Wexberg[20] described seven different groups of "mild depressive states." He included a "reactive group," but made no distinction between neurotic and psychotic in his classification.

Paskind[21] described 663 cases of mild manic-depressive disorder seen in outpatient practice. Harrowes[22] defined six groups of depression which included separate categories for the reactive and psychoneurotic types. Patients classified as psychoneurotic depressives showed "psychopathy, neuropathy, anxiety attacks, feelings of failure in life, sex trauma, unreality feelings and a greater subjectively than objectively depressed mood." This condition occurred in the third decade of life and, while mild, tended toward chronicity.

Aubrey Lewis,[13] in his classic paper on depression, stated that a careful analysis of 61 cases indicated that the neurotic symptoms appeared with equal frequency among the reactive and the endogenous forms of depression. He stressed that no sharp line could be drawn between psychotic and neurotic depressions.

It is apparent that despite the objections of authorities such as Lewis, there was a dominant tendency among nosographers to separate reactive and neurotic depressions from other types of depressions. The concepts of reactive and neurotic depressions gradually converged. The fusion of these categories occurred officially in 1934. At that time, the American Psychiatric Association approved a new classification in which reactive depression was subsumed under the psychoneuroses. This concept did not attain wide currency in the decade that followed, however, as indicated by the failure of most American textbooks and reference books on psychiatry to include a category of depression among the psychoneuroses.

The category *reactive depression* was defined in Cheney's *Outlines for Psychiatric Examinations*[23] as follows:

> Here are to be classified those cases which show depression in reaction to obvious external causes which might naturally produce sadness, such as bereavement, sickness, and financial and other worries. The reaction of a more marked degree and of longer duration than normal sadness, may be looked upon as pathological. The deep depressions with motor and mental retardation are not present, but these reactions *may be more closely related in fact to the manic-depressive reactions than to the psychoneuroses.* (emphasis added)

At this stage in its development, the concept of neurotic depression was still closely allied to the all-embracing category of manic-depressive disorder.

The next step in the evolution of the current concept was a major thrust in the direction of the current etiological concept. In the United States War Department classification, adopted in 1945, the term *neurotic depressive reaction* was used. The term *reaction* represented a clearcut deviation from the Kraepelinian notion of a defined disease entity, and it incorporated Adolph Meyer's psychobiological concept of an interaction of a particular type of personality with the environment. Since the presence of a specific external stress was more salient in an army at war than in civilian practice, the emphasis on reaction to stress seemed to gain increased plausibility.

The other significant departure in the definition in the army nomenclature was the introduction of two psychoanalytic hypotheses: that depression represents an attempt to allay anxiety through the mechanism of introjection, and that depression is related to *repressed aggression*. It states:

> The anxiety in this reaction is allayed, and, hence, partially relieved by self-depreciation through the mental mechanism of introjection. It is often associated with guilt for past failure or deeds. . . . This reaction is a nonpsychotic response precipitated by a current situation—frequently some loss sustained by the patient—although dynamically the depression is usually related to a repressed (unconscious) aggression.

The War Department classification received an extensive trial in the armed forces and was subsequently adopted in a slightly revised form by the Veterans Administration. The opinion of psychiatrists using the nomenclature, both in the army and at Veterans Administration clinics and hospitals, was evidently favorable, because this classification was subsequently used as the basis for the 1952 diagnostic manual of the American Psychiatric Association. The new categories of neurotic-depressive reaction and psychotic-depressive reaction had then become firmly established.

Severe Depression with Psychotic Features (Psychotic Depressive Reaction)

The term *psychotic depressive reaction* does not appear in any of the official American or European classifications prior to the end of World War II, but in 1951 the standard Veterans Administration classification included this term. In 1952, it was included in the official classification of the American Psychiatric Association. In the glossary accompanying this nomenclature, psychotic depressive reaction was characterized as including patients who were severely depressed and who gave evidence of gross misinterpretation of reality, including at times delusions and hallucinations.

The nomenclature distinguished this reaction from the manic-depressive reaction, depressed type, on the basis of the following features: absence of a history of repeated depressions or of marked psychothymic mood swings and presence of environmental precipitating factors. This category evidently was considered to be the analogue of the neurotic-depressive reaction and an updating of the reactive psychotic depressions described in the German literature in the 1920s.

Several features relevant to this diagnostic category troubled some authorities in the field, many of whom did not accept the distinction between neurotic-depressive reaction and psychotic-depressive reaction. As they saw it, the first depressive episode of a typical manic-depressive disorder might very well appear in reaction to some environmental stress.[2] On the basis of symptomatology, there were no criteria to distinguish the psychotic-depressive reaction from the depressed phase of the manic-depressive reaction.

The characteristics of psychotic-depressive reaction are illustrated in the following cases from Beck and Valin,[24] selected from a group of soldiers who experienced psychotic-depressive reaction after accidentally killing their buddies during the Korean War. The cases had the following common features relevant to the concept of psychotic-depressive reaction: (1) The psychosis followed a specific event that was highly disturbing to the patient; (2) there were clear-cut psychotic symptoms such as delusions and hallucinations; (3) the content of the patients' preoccupations, delusions, and hallucinations revolved around the dead buddy; (4) the typical symptoms of depression were present—depressed mood, hopelessness, suicidal wishes, and self-recriminations; (5) the patients recovered completely after a course of ECT or psychotherapy; and (6) there was no previous history of depression or mood swings.

Case 1

A 21-year-old soldier was referred to Valley Forge Army Hospital from a disciplinary barracks to which he had been confined for "culpable negligence." While near the line in Korea, he and his best buddy, Buck, had been working very hard laying wire. They paused to take a break and started "fooling around" and throwing water at each other. Buck threw a loaded carbine to him, and he accidentally discharged it into Buck's mouth and killed him. Buck and he had been best friends for a long time and had worked together as a solitary pair for several weeks. He had a clinging attachment to Buck, who was a very self-sufficient and adequate person. He subsequently stated, "Buck was the only person who ever understood or loved me."

Because of the negligence involved in the careless handling of a loaded gun, the patient had a general court martial three months later and was sentenced to confinement at hard labor for three years. At the time of the court martial he seemed to be struggling to contain his guilt feelings and had only a vague recollection of the details of the accident. However, he was able to maintain good contact with reality until nine months later. At that time he began to ruminate constantly about his offense. Within a few days, he experienced an acute psychotic break. He was transferred to Valley Forge Army Hospital in a very disturbed state. He was crying violently, attempted to strangle himself with his pajamas and then to slash his wrist on the window screen, and was extremely combative. He had visual hallucinations of Buck and carried on long conversations with him. He revealed that at times Buck told him "bad things" and at other times "good things." The "bad things" were that he should kill himself and the "good things" were that he should keep on living. He was given a series of 20 electroconvulsive treatments and experienced a complete remission of his psychosis.

Case 2

While examining a revolver behind the line in Korea, a 20-year-old soldier accidentally discharged the gun, shooting another soldier through the chest and killing him. He was sentenced to two years of hard labor for "culpable negligence." Eight months after the accident, while serving his term, he became increasingly upset and had to be hospitalized. He began to engage in obsessive rumination about the accident and in fantasies that would magically undo the deed. Within a few weeks, he became openly psychotic, suicidal, and violent. He had visual and auditory hallucinations involving the dead soldier. He saw the latter coming to him sitting on a cloud and holding a revolver in his left hand. The soldier would upbraid him for what he had done and would then "take off" in reverse. In the course of 20 electroconvulsive treatments, there was complete remission of symptoms.

Case 3

A 22-year-old rifleman accidentally shot his platoon sergeant while on patrol in Korea. He tried to conceal his emotional reaction to the event, but a month later he began to hear voices saying, "This is it . . . take a rifle and put a clip in and kill yourself." Another voice then said, "Don't do it, it won't do any good. Then there will be two of you [dead]." At the time of his transfer to Valley Forge Army Hospital he showed moderate agitation, depression, and tremendous anxiety. He frequently expressed the fear of losing his genitalia. In the course of psychotherapy, his symptoms largely abated.

Foulds[25] conducted a systematic study to determine what symptoms differentiated psychotic depressives. He administered an inventory of 86 items to 20 neurotic depressives and 20 psychotic depressives, all under sixty years of age. He found that 14 items occurred at least 25 percent more frequently among the psychotic than among the neurotic group. Using those 14 items as a scale, he was able to sort out correctly 90 percent of the patients diagnosed clinically as psychotic depressives and 80 percent of the neurotic depressives. In the list below, the frequency among the psychotics is stated first and among neurotics second in the parentheses after each item.

1. He is an unworthy person in his own eyes (12-3).
2. He is a condemned person because of his sins (12-3).
3. People are talking about him and criticizing him because of things he has done wrong (10-1).
4. He is afraid to go out alone (13-4).
5. He has said things that have injured others (9-2).
6. He is so "worked-up" that he paces about wringing his hands (11-4).
7. He cannot communicate with others because he doesn't seem to be on the same "wave-length" (10-3).
8. There is something unusual about his body, with one side being different from the other, or meaning something different (6-0).
9. The future is pointless (12-7).
10. He might do away with himself because he is no longer able to cope with his difficulties (8-3).
11. Other people regard him as very odd (8-3).
12. He is often bothered with pains over his heart, in his chest, or in his back (8-3).
13. He is so low in spirits that he just sits for hours on end (12-7).
14. When he does go to bed, he wouldn't care if he "never woke up again" (10-5).

Ideas or delusions relevant to being unworthy, condemned, and criticized, as well as the delusion of being physically altered, are the best differentiators between the two groups.

TABLE 5-1. Frequency of Clinical Features in Neurotic Depressive Reaction (NDR) and Psychotic Depressive Reaction (PDR) (%; $n = 50$)

Clinical feature	Feature present		Present to severe degree	
	NDR	PDR	NDR	PDR
Sad facies	86	94	4	24
Stooped posture	58	76	4	20
Speech: slow, etc.	66	70	8	22
Low mood	84	80	8	44
Diurnal variation of mood	22	48	2	10
Hopelessness	78	68	6	34
Conscious guilt	64	44	6	12
Feeling inadequate	68	70	10	42
Somatic preoccupation	58	66	6	24
Suicidal wishes	58	76	14	40
Indecisiveness	56	70	6	28
Loss of motivation	70	82	8	48
Loss of interest	64	78	10	44
Fatigability	80	74	8	48
Loss of appetite	48	76	2	40
Sleep disturbance	66	80	12	52
Constipation	28	56	2	16

Aside from delusions, the Beck Depression Inventory found that typical signs and symptoms of depression existed in a large proportion of both neurotic and psychotic depressives. As shown in Table 5-1, the features appeared with relatively high frequency in both conditions. This frequency distribution was obtained by abstracting the ratings and diagnoses made by psychiatrists on a random sample of psychiatric inpatients and outpatients. Each clinical feature was rated according to its severity as absent, mild, moderate, or severe. The records of 50 patients diagnosed as psychotic depressive reaction and of 50 diagnosed as neurotic depressive reaction were used in this analysis.

In almost all instances the signs and symptoms of depression were observed in the majority of both neurotic and psychotic depressives. Diurnal variation of mood occurred substantially more frequently among the psychotic depressives, but it was present in only a minority of these cases. Constipation occurred twice as frequently in the psychotic depressive group as might be expected because the patients in this group were generally in the older age category. Although almost all the clinical features were observed more frequently in the psychotic depressed group, the disparity in their relative frequency was not marked (with the exception of the two just mentioned).

Since each clinical feature was evaluated not only in terms of presence and absence but also in terms of severity, it was possible to ascertain the relative severity of the specific signs and symptoms in the two groups. It was found that the psychotic depressives tended to show a greater degree of intensity or severity on each of these signs and symptoms. This was expected, since the global rating of depth of depression was substantially higher in the psychotic depressive group. The frequency of *severe* ratings in the two groups is shown in Table 5-1. In every instance, the psychotic depressive group received substantially more severe ratings than the neurotic group.

Contemporary Diagnosis

The above historical line of reasoning has led us to where we are today. No specific signs or symptoms, aside from delusions, were found that distinguish psychotic from nonpsychotic depression. A distinction between "neurotic" and psychotic depression is no longer made. So far as specific depressive symptoms are concerned, the distinction is in terms of severity, or "quantitative" rather than qualitative factors. Currently, the diagnosis Major Depressive Disorder, Severe with Psychotic Features[4] is applied to designate cases that show definite signs of psychosis, such as loss of reality, delusions, and hallucinations.

Chapter 6
Bipolar Disorders

History and Definition

The contemporary clinical concept of bipolar disorder stems directly from the work of Kraepelin. When he started his ventures into the classification of the mental disorders, he was confronted with a collection of brilliantly described syndromes that were apparently unrelated. He consolidated the various disorders into two major categories: dementia praecox and manic-depressive insanity. He regarded dementia praecox as a progressive disorder leading eventually to a chronic state of intellectual deterioration; manic-depressive insanity was viewed as episodic (i.e., characterized by remissions and recurrences) and nondeteriorating. The new manic-depressive category ultimately was extended to almost all the recognized syndromes that included salient affective features. He stated,[1]

> Manic-depressive insanity comprehends on the one hand, the entire domain of so-called periodic and circular insanity, and on the other, simple mania, usually distinguished from the above. In the course of years I have become more and more convinced that all the pictures mentioned are merely forms of one single disease process. . . . Manic-depressive insanity, as its name indicates, takes its course in single attacks, which either present the signs of so-called manic excitement (flight of ideas, exaltation, and over-activity), or those of a peculiar psychic depression with psychomotor inhibition, or a mixture of the two states.

Kraepelin attempted to define his nosological groups according to the model of general paresis that had been shown to be due to syphilis of the nervous system. His model of manic-depressive disorder may be expressed in terms of the following hypotheses:

1. It is a definite disease entity. The concept of disease entity was challenged by a number of contemporary German writers and was attacked in the United States by Adolf Meyer,[2] who substituted the concept of "reaction-types" for "disease entities." Meyer's ascendancy in this

respect was reflected in the development of the official American nomenclature.[3]

2. It has a specific neuropathology and etiology. Kraepelin suggested that the basic cause was probably a metabolic instability that accounted for the affective symptoms and fluctuations.

3. It has a definite prognosis. He regarded complete recovery from a particular episode as characteristic of this disease. He believed that unlike dementia praecox, there is no intellectual deterioration. The view of complete recovery in all cases has been disputed by many authors, and Kraepelin himself conceded that about 10 percent of the cases became chronic.

4. It has a definite symptomatology. This consisted of the classic depressive and manic symptoms.

5. It is recurrent. The tendency to recurrence led Kraepelin to the concept of a chronic instability that makes the patient vulnerable to repeated attacks; recurrences were observed in only half of his cases, however.

6. The manic and depressive attacks were viewed as opposite poles of the same underlying process.

If Kraepelin's concept had been supported by subsequent experience, there would be little problem of classification today. Each of the hypotheses listed above has been attacked by subsequent writers on the basis of formal logical grounds, clinical experience, or experimental evidence.

Various authorities attacked the validity of the manic-depressive category. Zilboorg,[4] for example, asserted, "On the basis of my clinical experience I am under the definite impression that manic-depressive psychoses despite their age-long existence do not actually represent a separate clinical entity, but they are a pure culture, as it were, of that cyclical rhythm which is easily observed in hysterics, compulsive neuroses, and even in various forms of schizophrenia." It was possible, according to Zilboorg, that these alternations of mania and depression are but extreme expressions of a number of mental illnesses.

In the definition of terms in the first edition of the American Psychiatric Association diagnostic manual,[3] manic-depressive reactions were described as follows: "These groups comprise the psychotic reactions which fundamentally are marked by severe mood swings, and a tendency to remission and recurrence. Various accessory symptoms such as illusions, delusions, and hallucinations may be added to the fundamental affective alteration." It appears from this definition that the manic-depressive label was limited to those cases having a manic (or hypomanic) as well as a depressive phase. Thus, Kraepelin's great synthesis of the affective disorders under the manic-depressive label was splintered into the neurotic and psychotic depressive reactions, involutional reactions, and the schizoaffective type of schizophrenia. Only the hard core of the original manic-depressive category remained. This splitting was

TABLE 6-1. Diagnostic Criteria for Bipolar I Disorder, Single Manic Episode

A. Presence of only one Manic Episode and no past Major Depressive Episodes.
B. The Manic Episode is not better accounted for by Schizoaffective Disorder and is not superimposed on Schizophrenia, Schizophreniform Disorder, Delusional Disorder, or Psychotic Disorder Not Otherwise Specified.

Adapted from *DSM-IV-TR*.

reflected in the notable drop in the frequency of use of this diagnosis for first admissions to state hospitals throughout the United States from 12 percent in 1933 to 3 percent in 1953.[5]

Current Criteria for Bipolar Disorder

The current edition of the American Psychiatric Association diagnostic manual[6] provides specific criteria for the diagnosis of bipolar disorder, and distinguishes between two types, Bipolar I and Bipolar II Disorders. Bipolar I is defined by the experience of at least one manic or mixed episode and no past major depressive episodes. The diagnostic criteria for a Manic Episode are shown in Table 4-2.

Both Bipolar I and Bipolar II exclude common alternative causes of manic behavior, such as the presence of schizoaffective disorder (see Chapter 8), schizophrenia, schizophreniform disorder, delusional disorder, and other forms of psychosis. Bipolar II disorder is differentiated from Bipolar I in that (1) for Bipolar I there has been one manic episode or a mixed episode, and (2) for Bipolar II there has been no manic episode, but rather a "hypomanic episode," and one or more major depressive episodes (as defined in Chapter 1).

The distinction between manic and hypomanic episodes is that—despite an identical list of characteristic symptoms—the disturbances in hypomanic episodes are less severe and do not cause substantial impairment in social or occupational functioning, or require hospitalization. Sometimes hypomanic episodes become full manic episodes.[6] The diagnostic characteristics for one criteria set for bipolar I disorder are listed in Table 6-1. For a diagnosis of Bipolar I, the central criterion is that there has been previously (or is presently) at least one manic episode or mixed episode. The six separate criteria sets for Bipolar I are as follows: (1) single manic episode (as in Table 6-1); (2) most recent episode hypomanic; (3) most recent episode manic; (4) most recent episode mixed; (5) most recent episode depressed; and (6) most recent episode unspecified.[6]

The diagnostic characteristics for Bipolar II disorder are listed in Table 6-2. For Bipolar II, the criteria are (1) at least one major depressive episode; (2) never a manic or a mixed episode; and (3) at least one hypomanic episode.

In addition to Bipolar I and Bipolar II, there are other possible patterns of

TABLE 6-2. Diagnostic Criteria for Bipolar II Disorder

A. Presence (or history) of one or more Major Depressive Episodes.
B. Presence (or history) of at least one Hypomanic Episode.
C. There has never been a Manic Episode or a Mixed Episode.
D. The mood symptoms in Criteria A and B are not better accounted for by
   Schizoaffective Disorder and are not superimposed on Schizophrenia,
   Schizophreniform Disorder, Delusional Disorder, or Psychotic Disorder Not
   Otherwise Specified.
E. The symptoms cause clinically significant distress or impairment in social,
   occupational, or other important areas of functioning.

Adapted from *DSM-IV-TR.*

manic symptoms. If a person has not experienced both a hypomanic episode and at least one major depressive episode (Bipolar II), but has experienced two or more years of hypomanic symptoms and periods of depressed mood, then the term "cyclothymic disorder" is applied. Or, if there have been clinically significant manic or hypomanic symptoms that do not meet the criteria for Bipolar I, Bipolar II, or cyclothymic disorder, then the diagnosis "bipolar disorder not otherwise specified" is used in the APA classification system.[6]

Relationship of Manic to Depressive Episodes

The observation that manic episodes may occur in people who have had depressions (or vice versa) was noted two thousand years ago (Chapter 1). Despite the long history of this observation, there is still considerable uncertainty about the relationship of these two forms of mental illness. Kraepelin lumped together single depressions, multiple depressions, single manias, multiple manias, and cases of depression alternating with manias (the circular cases). This attempt to bring together all the diverse clinical pictures under the same rubric is still a subject of controversy. It is frequently argued that the biphasic cases are sufficiently different from the pure depressions to warrant the completely separate categorization found in the current APA nomenclature. However, Kraepelin's integration of all the affective disorders may ultimately prove to be analogous to the final crystallization of the concepts of tuberculosis and syphilis, both of which displayed a wide variety of clinical features but were eventually shown to be caused by a specific pathogenic agent.

Angst[7] studied the onset, course, and outcome of affective disorders in 406 patients admitted to the Psychiatric University Hospital in Zurich between 1959 and 1963. Patients were studied prospectively, at five-year intervals, until 1980. He found Bipolar I and Bipolar II disorders take a similar course. By contrast, median age of onset differed between unipolar depression (45 years) and bipolar disorder (29 years); more recurrence was found in bipolar illness, but shorter episodes than in unipolar depression; and, at follow-up in 1980, outcome was better for unipolar disorder compared to bipolar (42% versus 26% relapse-free for 5 or more years). However, Angst noted that these differences were identified in severe cases with at least one hospitalization, and no data were presented on the more common, milder forms of affective disorder.

Sharma et al.[8] conducted a diagnostic reevaluation of refractory "unipolar" patients. By using supplemental information from family, and extended follow-up, the diagnosis rate for bipolar disorder increased from 35 percent at intake to 59 percent at follow-up. The most frequent change in medications was to mood stabilizers alone,[9] and significant improvement was found from the time of initial consultation[8] (see also Chapter 14).

A problem is raised by the fact that a large proportion of depressed patients show a mild hypomanic tendency after recovering from their depressions. Especially in Bipolar II disorder, there is often confusion with unipolar depression.[10] Moreover, manic-like signs and symptoms are present to some extent in all mood disorders.[11] Psychiatrists who advocate the notion of a cyclical disorder would classify these cases as bipolar disorders. In the past, others have considered this transient hypomanic phase merely a compensatory phenomenon related to the depression and not a manifestation of a manic phase.[5] Classification problems such as these are considered in more detail below.[10,11,12]

Another problem is raised by the fact that, although the polarization of symptoms seems to support the two-phase concept, there is no evidence as yet that these two conditions are opposite in their biological substrates. Such physiological differences as have been observed appear to be secondary to the difference in activity level rather than to any primary difference in the underlying disorder.[13]

The relative frequency of depressed, manic, and circular cases depends to a large extent on the definition of the manic-depressive syndrome. In Kraepelin's series[1] the relative frequency was depression only, 49 percent; manic only, 17 percent; and circular or combined, 34 percent. Rennie[14] reported the following proportions: depression only, 67 percent; manic only, 9 percent; and combined, 24 percent. Clayton et al.[15] reported that of 366 patients diagnosed as having affective reaction, 31 (9 percent) had the diagnosis of mania.

The signs and symptoms of the depressed phase have been described in Chapter 2. The characteristics of the manic phase will now be described.

Symptomatology of Manic Phase

The symptomatology of the manic disorder presents a striking contrast to that of the depressive disorder. In fact, when one considers each of the symptoms they seem to be at opposite end points of a bipolar dimension. As is shown in

TABLE 6-3. Comparison of Manic and Depressive Symptoms

Manic	Depressive
Emotional manifestations	
Elated	Depressed
Increased gratification	Loss of gratification
Likes self	Dislikes self
Increased attachments	Loss of attachments
Increased mirth response	Loss of mirth response
Cognitive manifestations	
Positive self-image	Negative self-image
Positive expectations	Negative expectations
Blames others	Blames self
Denial of problems	Exaggeration of problems
Arbitrary decision-making	Indecisive
Delusions: self-enhancing	Delusions: self-degrading
Motivational manifestations	
Driven and impulsive	Paralysis of the will
Action-oriented wishes	Wishes to escape
Drive for independence	Increased dependency wishes
Desire for self-enhancement	Desire for death
Physical and vegetative manifestations	
Hyperactivity	Retardation/agitation
Indefatigable	Easily fatigued
Appetite variable	Loss of appetite
Increased libido	Loss of libido
Insomnia	Insomnia

Adapted from *DSR-IV-TR*.

Table 6-3, in which the various symptoms are categorized as primarily emotional, cognitive, motivational, or vegetative, in almost every instance the symptoms of the manic reactions are directly opposite to those of the depressive reactions. The major exception to this is difficulty in sleeping, which is encountered in both conditions.

Emotional Manifestations

Elation

Most manic patients convey a picture of complete lightness of heart and gaiety. They make statements such as, "I feel I am floating on air"; "I'm bursting with happiness"; "I've never felt so wonderfully happy in my life"; "I am bursting with joy." Some manic patients are aware of a false sense of well-being and may even feel uncomfortable with such an exaltation of spirit.

The euphoria of the manic patient is sharply contrasted with the feelings of the depressed patient, who is sad, morose, and unhappy: The difference may be expressed in terms of the contrast of pleasure and pain.

Increased Gratification

Manic patients, in contrast to depressed patients, are capable of getting gratification from a wide variety of experiences, and the intensity of the gratification far exceeds that of their normal phase. A leaf falling from a tree may cause feelings of ecstasy, or an interesting advertisement may produce a great thrill. In contrast, depressed patients get little or no gratification. Even activities that in a normal state could arouse great feelings of pleasure now "leave me cold." When they move into the manic phase, however, they not only respond to such experiences but react excessively to them.

Apparently only the pure manics experience consistent gratification. Manics who have mild paranoid trends generally experience irritation. This irritation is apt to be stimulated whenever they encounter any disagreement, criticism, or obstacle to their goals.

Self-Love

Whereas depressed patients often dwell on how much they dislike themselves, even to the extent of loathing or hating, manic patients experience a feeling of affection or love for themselves. They have the same type of intense amorous feeling toward themselves as does a person romantically involved with somebody else. They experience a sense of thrill when they think or talk about themselves and are very pleased and satisfied with all their attributes. In contrast to the self-deprecation of depressed patients, they tend to idealize themselves. They proclaim their great virtues and deeds and constantly congratulate themselves on them.

Increased Attachment to People and Activities

Whereas depressed patients complain that they no longer have any feelings for family or friends and that they have lost interest in their work and various favorite pastimes, manic patients often experience a surplus of fondness for other people and plunge into various interests with abundant zest. They experience a broadening as well as an intensification of their interests. Some manics are so stimulated that they jump from one activity to another. They are often extremely successful in pursuing a number of projects during the manic phase. I have observed a number of successful scientists, artists, and business managers who reached their peak performance during hypomanic or manic phases.

Manic patients tend to reach out to other people and enjoy their company. They strike up conversations with strangers and may influence a large number of people to their way of thinking. They are often a disruptive influence on a psychiatric ward because of their ability to stimulate other patients toward a particular goal of their own—for example, rebellion against hospital authority. On the other hand, some manic patients are unusually successful in breaking through the autistic barrier of withdrawn schizophrenics.

Increased Mirth Response

Depressed patients characteristically manifest a loss of sense of humor, but manic patients are full of fun. They tell jokes, compose rhymes and jingles, relate stories in an amusing way, and sing. They are often very witty and their good humor has an infectious quality. When presented at a case conference a manic patient can readily move the entire audience to laughter.

In contrast to the depressed patient's tendency to weep, cry, or moan, the manic patient laughs and exudes happiness.

Cognitive Manifestations

Positive Self-Image

It is immediately apparent in conversation that manic patients have a highly positive view of themselves. They not only overestimate the degree or significance of their physical attractiveness, but claim many other outstanding attributes; this is apparent in their use of superlatives. Some manics assert that they are the most beautiful people who ever lived and proclaim that they have great talents, ingenuity, insight, and understanding. This positive self-concept is in marked contrast to that of depressed patients, who see themselves as utterly devoid of positive attributes and as possessing only weaknesses and vices.

Positive Expectations

Manic patients are optimistic about the outcome of anything they undertake. Even when confronted with an insoluble problem, they are confident they will find a solution. This attitude contrasts with that of depressed patients, who attach a low probability of success to any attempts. With this tendency to overestimate prospects, manic patients often get involved in very risky business ventures and as a result may lose a considerable amount of money.

Assignment of Blame

In contrast to depressed patients, who tend to blame themselves for almost anything that goes wrong, manic patients tend to allocate the fault to other people, even though a particular error may be obviously the result of their own decisions or actions. The tendency to blame one's difficulties on others often makes it hard for other people to work with a manic patient.

Denial

Manic patients tend to deny the possibility of any personal weaknesses, deficiencies, or problems. They generally reject suggestions that their behavior is excessive or that they may have some psychiatric disorder. When confronted with difficult problems, they tend to gloss over them. They are likely to deny any obvious mistakes they make. The depressed patient, in contrast, tends to maximize problems and to see weaknesses and deficiencies where they do not exist.

Arbitrariness

Manic patients differ sharply from depressed patient, who are plagued by indecisiveness and vacillation. Manic patients tend to make decisions rapidly—often without any solid foundation. This quickness in making decisions is related to impulsivity. One woman would go off on buying sprees, for instance, whenever she was in the manic phase; when depressed, she would return all the purchases to the stores.

Delusions

The delusions of manic patients tend to be of the self-enhancing type. They firmly believe they are the most attractive person who ever lived, or the world's greatest genius, or possessed of prodigious physical abilities. They may regard themselves as superman or as the reincarnation of God, or believe they have billions of dollars and a vast empire. These delusions contrast with those of the depressed patient, which are concerned with ideas of unworthiness, poverty, deterioration, and sinfulness.

Motivational Manifestations

Impulse-Driven

Manic patients convey the impression of being driven by impulses over which they have little or no control. Even though they claim they do what they want to do, it is generally obvious that it is difficult to stop activities. In general, they appear to be overstimulated and to have an extraordinarily strong drive in a multitude of directions. Depressed patients, in contrast, experience paralysis of the will. They seem unable to mobilize spontaneously enough motivation to attend to even the basic amenities of living.

Action-Oriented

The wishes of manic patients generally have some objective that would provide a prospect of personal fulfillment. They want to impress people, to help them, to create something new or to be successful at a given task. The types of goals they have are similar to those of their contemporaries, though more extravagant and backed up by a compulsive drive. They want to move into life. Depressed patients, in contrast, desire to escape from life.

Drive for Independence

Patients in the manic phase shed the dependency that was manifest during the depressed phase. They no longer feel that they need help from other people and often assume the role of benefactor and helper. They want to assume responsibilities themselves and to demonstrate self-sufficiency.

Drive for Self-Enhancement

The desires of manic patients center around the wish to increase their prestige, popularity, and possessions. In their expansive way they wish to take in everything that life has to offer, and at the same time demonstrate to an increasingly greater extent their superior attributes. In contrast, depressed patients are driven to increasingly greater constriction of their sphere of experience and of their self-esteem.

Physical and Vegetative Manifestations

Hyperactivity

Patients in a manic phase engage in a much higher level of activity than in their normal period. They often talk endlessly, to the point that their voices become hoarse. Unlike agitated patients, however, whose activity is aimless, manic patients have specific goals. The overactivity, both in speech and action, is in marked contrast to the slowing down exhibited by the depressed patient.

High Tolerance for Fatigue

Manic patients seem to have a very high threshold for subjective fatigue. They claim they have endless energy and can go for many hours or even days without rest. Some seem to maintain a high level of activity for weeks on end, with only a few hours sleep at night. This is a marked contrast to the conspicuous fatigability of depressed patients.

Appetite

The appetite of manic patients is variable. In a case reported in 1911, Karl Abraham described the increased "orality" of manic patients. In some cases of mania the appetite may be voracious; in others it may be diminished. Depressed patients generally have a loss of appetite and may skip a meal without being aware of it.

Increased Libido

The sexual drive is generally increased in manic patients. They tend to be rather reckless and may be quite promiscuous during the manic phase. This characteristic of course is in marked contrast to the loss of libido experienced during a depressive episode.

Insomnia

As mentioned previously, manics have a tendency to have less than the average amount of sleep. There is no fixed pattern to their sleeping. In many cases they feel so charged up that they are unable to go to sleep. In others they may awaken three or four hours earlier than usual. An interesting feature of their subjective reactions to insomnia is the statement, "I woke up completely refreshed even though I had only two hours sleep." Insomnia is also characteristic of depressives, but usually follows the pattern of early morning wakening rather than great difficulty in falling asleep.

Behavioral Observations of Manic Phase

During the manic phase the behavior, speech, and temperament of the patient are so typical of this condition that it is generally easy to identify manic patients upon entering a ward. They tend to be energetic, aggressive, animated, and overactive. They present a demeanor of impulsivity, boldness, and lack of inhibition. They are generally sociable, genial, and exhibitionistic. A striking feature is the contagiousness of their humor and good spirits. People in contact with them often remark on how they can empathize very readily with them because of their free emotional expression.

When frustrated, however, manic patients may show a good deal of hostility and may launch vulgar tirades against people they regard as frustrators; at times they may be violent or assaultive. Some may show a dramatic alterna-

TABLE 6-4. Frequency of Clinical Features in Mania ($n = 31$)

Symptom	Patients with symptom recorded as positive (%)
Hyperactivity	100
Flight of ideas	100
Push of speech	100
Euphoria	97
Distractibility	97
Circumstantiality	96
Decreased sleep	94
Grandiosity and/or religiosity	79
Ideas of reference	77
Increased sexuality	74
Delusions	73
Passivity	47
Depersonalization and/or derealization	43

Adapted from Clayton, Pitts, and Winokur (1965).

tion between a cheerful, outgoing manner and being withdrawn, suspicious, paranoid. One patient had cycles of manic behavior alternating with paranoid behavior, each of about four to six hours' duration.

Spontaneous speech usually increases, and they generally find it difficult to stop talking. They may continue to talk or sing until they become hoarse or may lose their voice entirely. They frequently show a flight of ideas by moving rapidly from one subject to another. In contrast to the disconnected flight of ideas of the schizophrenic, manics usually demonstrate some unifying theme underlying their tangential associations.

Patients convey the impression of being extremely susceptible to stimuli rising from within themselves or the environment. They are prone to associate or to respond rapidly to any external stimulus or to any thought that may arise. They frequently resort to joking, making puns, rhyming, and humming or singing.

Manic patients do not show any intellectual deterioration. In the more advanced stages, however, there may be an increased tendency toward errors because of their distractibility.

Because of their decreased control and impulsiveness, manic patients often get themselves into difficult situations and require hospitalization to prevent them from giving away all their money, embarking on unwise financial schemes, or engaging in other forms of self-destructive behavior.

Clayton et al.[15] enumerated the frequency of 13 clinical features in 31 cases of mania. The results are presented in Table 6-4. It is notable that hyperactivity, flight of ideas, and push of speech occurred in all cases.

Periodicity of Manic-Depressive Behavior

Many authors have noted a regularity or rhythm (periodicity) in the behavior of some manic-depressive patients. This has been most notable in the consistent diurnal variations in mood and in the regularity of the recurrence of manic and depressive phases.

Richter[16] reviewed a number of case reports of patients who showed recurrences of their symptoms at relatively fixed time intervals. He postulated the existence of "biological clocks" to account for the regularities of the cycles. The timing of the cycles may vary from 24 hours to 10 years. He referred, for example, to a case reported by Kraepelin of a patient who experienced attacks of depression at the age of 30, 40, 50, and 60. Bunney and Hartmann[17] found 10 cases in the literature showing a regular cycle of 24 hours of mania alternating with 24 hours of depression and added a complete description of an additional case.

Richter also reports some interesting experiments to demonstrate biological clocks in animals with specific brain lesions. He was able to produce cyclical changes in rats through incision of the pituitary gland. He also showed that by bringing the animals almost to the point of complete physical exhaustion, he could induce marked cyclical changes in their activity level.

Unfortunately, neither the reports of periodicity in the manic-depressive patients nor the experiments cast much light on the nature of the disturbance. Only a very small percentage of the cases show a fixed cycle; in fact, wide variation in the interval between recurrences is the rule. Even the diurnal mood variation attributed to depression is not found with great frequency (see Chapter 2). At this time it seems premature to stretch the concept of a biological clock beyond the very few cases that do show periodicity. Many of the latter cases have been studied thoroughly, however, and do show interesting biochemical fluctuations (see Chapter 9).

Premorbid Personality of Manic-Depressive Patients

Many early writers emphasized the existence of a specific type of premorbid personality in patients who subsequently developed a manic-depressive reaction. The particular premorbid personality was alleged to be characterized by traits such as gregariousness, joviality, and cheerfulness. Despite the widespread acceptance of this concept of a characteristic premorbid personality, there have been no systematic studies that support this notion. Titley[18] rated manic-depressives and normals for the relative strengths of traits such as interests, sociability, and friendliness. He failed to find any differences between the two groups.

Further evidence against the notion of a specific type of premorbid personality in manic-depressive disorder is provided by a somewhat later study by

Kohn and Clausen.[19] The authors found that manic-depressives were as likely as schizophrenics to have been socially isolated in early adolescence. The proportion of social isolates in both groups was close to one-third while that in a normal control group was close to zero. These results contradict the conception that manic depressives are extroverted in their younger years and schizophrenics predominantly isolated.

Issues for Further Study

Classification Problems

Differential diagnosis between bipolar and unipolar mood disorder is often confusing, especially in the case of bipolar II disorder. For example, nearly 50 percent of all bipolar II patients would have been missed without prospective assessment on at least two points in time in a recent national French multisite study (15 sites, 48 investigators). Specifically, the rate of bipolar II disorder was found to increase—from 21 percent at intake to 39.7 percent after a month's time—as a result of systematically searching for *DSM-IV* criteria for hypomania.[10]

In a large national sample, Hantouche and Akiskal[10] evaluated the psychometric and phenomenological differences between unipolar ($n = 256$) and bipolar II ($n = 196$) depressions after carefully defining groups of each disorder. The bipolar II patients included major depression with both spontaneous and antidepressant-associated hypomania. Results showed that the unipolar group was higher on psychomotor retardation, loss of interest, and insomnia. The bipolar II patients scored higher on hypersomnia, and were characterized by psychomotor activation. Bipolar II had more mixed features than unipolar depression, and less agreement between clinician and self-ratings on various features of depression.[10] The authors suggested that these aspects help explain why bipolar II is often underdiagnosed or misdiagnosed by clinicians.

Other researchers on classification problems have evaluated whether mania and hypomania have different profiles, and have studied which of the manic phenomena are found in unipolar major depressive disorder (MDD). Serretti and Olgiati[11] used a sample of 652 inpatients (158 BP-I, 122 BP-II, and 372 MDD), and found that BP-I disorder compared to BP-II had a higher prevalence of reckless activity, distractibility, psychomotor agitation irritable mood, and increased self-esteem. In patients with MDD, more than 30 percent had one or two manic symptoms, and 18 percent experienced psychomotor agitation.

Finally, Akiskal and Benazzi[12] found the frequency of atypical depression to be 43.0 percent in a combined BP-II and MDD sample. Atypical depression was linked to higher rates of bipolar II, and was associated with bipolar family history. Family history was specifically associated with the atypical depression symptoms "leaden paralysis" and hypersomnia. The authors concluded that atypical depression is best considered a variant of BP-II.

Goal Achievement and Manic Symptoms

As presented above, the content of manic thinking includes an optimistic bias about one's ability to obtain rewards or achieve goals. Along these lines, Leahy[20] advanced a "portfolio theory" that included manic decision making, in which people in a manic phase operate with "market assumptions" of abundance and magnification. Treatment approaches have been developed to mitigate this specific cognitive vulnerability, the tendency toward dysfunctional, exaggerated optimism (see Chapter 15).[21]

An important question is whether or to what extent life events play a part in generating the symptoms of manic episodes in people susceptible to bipolar disorder. Johnson et al.[22] provide a test of this in a study of 43 people diagnosed with bipolar I disorder. They predicted that goal attainment—achieving a desired goal—would result in increases in manic symptoms.

Standardized symptom severity ratings were obtained monthly by telephone. Life events interviews were carried out at 6-, 12-, 18-, and 24-month face-to-face follow-ups. The Goal Attainment and Positivity scales of the Life Events and Difficulties Schedule were used to assess life events. To evaluate the possibility of confounding goal-attainment life events with demographic or illness characteristics, life events were correlated with a number of variables. These included age, gender, education, occupational status, age of onset, number of hospitalizations, number of episodes, number of depressions, and medication levels. No significant correlations were found.

Results supported their predictions. Manic symptoms increased in the 2 months following the achievement of goals. Symptoms of depression at goal attainment did not change. Moreover, general positive events were not related to increases in subsequent manic symptoms, and neither positive events nor goal attainment were linked to changes in depressive symptoms.

Many variables other than goal attainment predict mania, such as sleep deprivation, medication changes, and expressed emotion. Also, in this study[22] goal attainment life events predicted only a "modest" proportion of manic symptom variation. Therefore, the authors suggested the need for more research to better understand information processing and positive affect in bipolar patients in the context of goal achievement. Further studies are needed to replicate that the achievement of vital life goals increases manic symptoms in vulnerable individuals. If supported, then the relationship between life events and cognitive variables would best be described as one of reciprocal influence.

Chapter 7
Involutional Depression

In the history of clinical classification of the mood disorders, the concept of a depression that is specific for the involutional period was embodied in the term *involutional psychotic reaction* in the original version of the APA nomenclature.[1] The diagnostic manual specified five criteria, each of which, as will be seen, was subject to question. The *etiology* was definitely indicated by listing this condition under the heading "Disorders due to disturbance of metabolism, growth, nutrition, or endocrine function." The *age of onset* was specified as the "involutional period." The *symptomatology* consisted of "worry, intractable insomnia, guilt, anxiety, agitation, and somatic concerns." This nosological category included a primary paranoid type as well as the depressive type, our principal interest in this discussion. The *course* was described as "prolonged" and the *premorbid personality* as "compulsive." Some of the questions regarding the validity of this class designation, as well as its defining characteristics, will be discussed in this chapter.

History of the Concept

In his original formulation of the two great divisions of mental illness, dementia praecox and manic-depressive psychosis, Kraepelin[2] conceived of the agitated depression of middle life as a completely independent entity with a variable prognosis. Other clinicians, however, were not convinced of the validity of this distinction. Thalbitzer[3] contended that the so-called involutional melancholia properly belonged with the manic-depressive syndrome, and this point of view was buttressed by Dreyfus,[4] who made a detailed study of a series of 81 patients diagnosed by Kraepelin[2] as involutional melancholics. In reviewing this clinical material, Dreyfus decided that six cases were of questionable diagnosis and the other 75 were manic depressives. He concluded that the overwhelming majority of cases of agitated depressions in the involutional period correspond to mixed states of manic-depressive psychosis and that there is no justification for considering involutional melancholia a separate entity. He was evidently impressed by the relatively high frequency of recovery in these patients (66 percent) and, applying Kraepelin's criterion of prognosis, he reasoned that these cases belonged with other depressions of good prognosis that occurred in the earlier age group.[2] He observed, further, that 54 percent had had previous psychotic episodes.

Kraepelin accepted Dreyfus's findings and ultimately yielded to his point of view: In the eighth edition of his text, he included involutional melancholia in the category of manic-depressive psychosis.[2,4]

The controversy was hardly settled, however. In the United States, Kirby, having reviewed Dreyfus's monograph, commented, "In a number of cases, the manic-depressive symptoms were plainly in evidence, the cases having been improperly placed with the melancholias.[5,4] In a considerable number of other cases the author's conclusion that manic-depressive symptoms were present is based on extremely meager data." He consequently refused to accept Dreyfus's conclusions.

In another attack on Dreyfus's position, Hoch and MacCurdy[6] disputed the assertion that involutional melancholics almost always recovered. They demonstrated in their series of patients a group that did not improve. They separated two groups of cases: one, allied with manic-depressive psychosis, which generally improved; and one, allied with schizophrenia, which did not improve.

The outcome of the controversy was that although the official nomenclature in the United States followed the Kraepelinian system in its major outlines, it departed from Kraepelin's taxonomy in listing involutional melancholia as a distinct diagnostic entity.[7] Also, in England, despite the protestations of writers such as Aubrey Lewis, involutional melancholia was classified separately from manic-depressive psychosis.[8] This distinction was also made in the international classification of diseases of the World Health Organization, the Canadian nomenclature, the German classification (*Wurzberg Scheme*), the Danish nosology, the Russian classification, the Japanese classification, and the French standard classification.[9] It is apparent, however, from a perusal of recent publications, that the term is seldom used in systematic studies.

Etiology

The occurrence of this condition during the menopausal period in women (but presumably at a later age in men) led some authors to attribute a major factor to hormonal or biochemical changes at this time of life. This thesis received temporary support from some uncontrolled studies suggesting that this condition responded to estrogenic therapy. These findings were later contradicted by a better-designed study by Palmer, Hastings, and Sherman, who found estrogenic therapy less effective than electroconvulsive therapy.[10] The final blow to the hope of estrogenic therapy was delivered by Ripley, a clinical psychiatrist, Shorr, an internist, and Papanicolaou, an endocrinologist, who combined their skills in a study of depressions in the involutional period.[11] They found that estrogenic therapy did not directly modify the patient's depression, although it did provide some relief of the typical vasomotor symptoms associated with menopause. At the present time, transdermal estrogen patches are sometimes helpful for depressions in the perimenopausal (involutional) period.

There has been no solid experimental evidence linking abnormalities of growth, metabolism, or endocrine function to the occurrence of involutional depressions. For example, Henderson and Gillespie reported in 1963 that in their series at the Glasgow Royal Mental Hospital, 57 percent of the women and 70 percent of the men broke down as the result of psychic factors, whereas physical factors were of importance in only 21 percent of the women and 6 percent of the men.[12] Matthews et al.[13] studied the psychological and symptom consequences of the natural menopause in a longitudinal study of 541 premenopausal healthy women, and found that natural menopause led to few changes in psychological characteristics. They concluded that natural menopause had no negative mental health consequences for the majority of middle-aged healthy women. It is apparent that the etiology of the depressions in this period has not as yet been demonstrated and is still largely a matter of conjecture.

The main basis for ascribing an organic etiology to these depressions was their occurrence during the involutional period. The same fact, however, can be used as evidence of psychogenicity as stated by Cameron[14]: "There is a gradual decline in physical vigor and health. Chronic illnesses in oneself, or in one's kin and friends, grow commoner and call one's attention to the passage of time. The realization of ambitions becomes obviously less likely. There is apt to be less personal plasticity and less interest in new friends and new adventures. In women the loss of youth and the end of child-bearing, and in men the prospect of diminished powers and of retirement, undoubtedly operate as etiologic factors."

Thus, a distinction must be made between aging as such and the presence of health problems. It is well known that people in extended care homes have higher rates of depression. People in nursing homes who suffer from clinical depression have often lost many things that made their lives meaningful, things they love and that made their lives worthwhile. The issue of personal control is central and may be a core component in understanding depression in the nursing home environment. Unfortunately, the arrangement of contingencies of control in assisted living facilities in many cases assists too much, or controls too many things the residents would be better managing or deciding themselves. Where control or decision-making has been curtailed needlessly, restoring what is possible should be the highest priority.[15]

Age

During the time it was used as a diagnostic term, there was no general agreement on the age range for involutional depression beyond vague terms such as the "involutional period," or "climacterium." For reasons not completely clear, moreover, this period was assumed to occur about ten years later in men than in women. Henderson and Gillespie[12] stated that this syndrome occurs around ages 40–55 in women and 50–65 in men. In another place, however, they conceded that "a very similar syndrome may occur at an earlier age, in the twenties and thirties in women, and before the fifth decade in men."[12] Other writers stretched the age limits so far in both directions as to attenuate the claim for a depressive syndrome specific to the involutional period.

Another question relevant to the specified age period is whether there is any valid difference between involutional depressions and depressive episodes of bipolar disorder occurring in the same age period. There was the assumption among nosographers that the onset of manic-depressive disorder was earlier than that of involutional depression. Hence, the diagnosis was often decided on the basis of age. When one examines the tabulated frequencies of the cases diagnosed in the state hospitals in New York, it is apparent that diagnostic fashion may have been a factor. The tables in the *Annual Report* of the New York State Department of Mental Hygiene show that as the diagnosis of involutional melancholia increased, there was a corresponding drop in the diagnosis of manic-depressive disorder.[16]

Several studies of depressions occurring during the climacterium, furthermore, indicated that in a large majority of the cases a depressive episode had occurred earlier in life. Berger[17] found, in a study of 140 cases of climacteric psychosis, that only 14 of the patients were in their first psychosis, and he concluded that there was no specific psychosis of the climacterium. Driess,[18] in a study of 163 depressions in this age group, found only 17 patients who were experiencing their first depression.

Symptomatology

The symptomatology generally ascribed to involutional depression was essentially that of an agitated depression. A number of authors attempted to define various forms of this syndrome based on symptom variations but, as Henderson and Gillespie pointed out, these groups were largely artificial.

Since agitation was the main symptom that would tend to differentiate involutional depressions from other depressions, certain questions naturally follow:

1. What proportion of all *agitated* depressions have their onset during the climacterium? Also, what proportion of depressions during the climacterium are characterized by agitation, and what proportion show retardation?

2. Is there any essential difference in symptomatology between cases diagnosed as involutional depression and cases of manic depression that have their onset early in life and that recur in the involutional period? In other words, is there a change in their symptomatology from retardation to agitation?

When the relative frequency of agitation and retardation in depressed patients in the involutional period is compared, the significance of agitation as a distinguishing characteristic is vitiated. Malamud, Sands, and Malamud reported, in a study of 47 cases diagnosed as involutional psychosis, that 17 (36 percent) showed retardation and 24 (52 percent) showed agitation. The remainder presumably showed neither retardation nor agitation.[19]

Cassidy, Flanagan, and Spellman addressed themselves directly to the question of whether involutional patients could be distinguished from younger depressed patients on the basis of their symptomatology. They compared the relative frequency of 66 medical and psychiatric symptoms in two groups—20 female depressed patients aged 45 and older (with no previous episodes of depression) and 46 younger depressed females. There was no significant difference in the frequency of the symptoms. Retardation of thought, for instance, occurred with similar frequency in each group. Unfortunately, no data were presented regarding the relative frequency of agitation.[20]

The most relevant—and crucial—study in the literature was reported by Hopkinson. He investigated the characteristics of 100 consecutive cases of affective illness in patients aged 50 or more at the University Clinic of the University of Glasgow. He studied the 61 cases experiencing their first affective illness, who consequently would be diagnosed as involutional, and compared them with the 39 who, having had previous attacks, would be considered manic depressive. Contrary to the prevalent conception, he found that agitation occurred significantly more frequently in the manic-depressive group than in the involutional-depression group (61.5 percent versus 36.0 percent; $p <$ .02). This finding was strong evidence against the notion of a specific involutional syndrome distinguishable from other depressions on the basis of the symptomatology.[21]

In the course of our original systematic investigation of depression (which will be discussed further in Chapter 10), we collected data relevant to the question of the relationship of agitation to involutional depression. We found that of 482 patients rated by the psychiatrists as to the degree of agitation, 47 percent showed some degree of agitation (mild, moderate, or severe). The incidence of agitation among the various nosological categories was neurotic depressive reaction (95 cases) 57 percent; psychotic depressive reaction (27 cases) 70 percent; involutional reaction (21 cases) 52 percent; manic depressive, depressed phase (6 cases) 17 percent; schizophrenic reaction (161 cases) 42 percent; and all other nosological categories (172 cases) 44 percent.

It is notable that agitation was a common symptom that occurred among the nondepressed patients, such as the schizophrenics, as well as among the depressed. Also, agitation was more frequently observed in patients diagnosed as having psychotic depressive reaction or neurotic depressive reaction than in those diagnosed as having involutional reaction. This seemed to support the thesis that agitation is not specifically found among involutional depressives.

Another way of approaching the data is to determine whether agitation might be related to the involutional age period, irrespective of the specific diagnosis. When all the cases of the psychotic depressives were analyzed, it was found that there were 52 cases of agitated depression. Of these, 25 patients were younger than 45 and 27 patients were 45 or older, indicating that agitated depression occurs no more frequently among older psychotic depressives than among younger psychotic depressives. Similarly, among the 95 cases of agitation in the neurotic depressive category, 72 occurred before age 45.

Premorbid Personality

During the 1930s and early 1940s, several studies attempted to define the premorbid personalities of patients with involutional depressions. The first study, by Titley,[22] was methodologically superior to some of the later ones and will be described in greater detail. On the basis of histories obtained by other psychiatrists, he compared the relative strength of various traits such as overconscientiousness, meticulousness, and stubbornness in three groups of individuals: 10 involutional melancholics, 10 manic depressives, and 10 normal controls. Each was rated on a 5-point scale for each trait, and a trait score for each of the three groups was obtained by summing up the combined ratings of all the members of each group.

Titley found that the group scores of the involutionals were higher than those of the other two groups for the following traits: ethical code, saving, reticence, sensitivity, stubbornness, overconscientiousness, meticulousness about work, and meticulousness about person. The involutionals scored lower on the following: interests, adjustability, sociability, friendliness, tolerance, and sexuality.

Several limitations are apparent in this study, and these prevent ready acceptance of the findings. First, summing up the scores instead of presenting the median score in each group actually distorts the data in studies where there is no evidence of a normal distribution in the population. One or two extreme cases, particularly in such small groups, can radically alter the group score. Second, the normals scored slightly higher than the manic depressives on traits that have been generally described as indicative of the premorbid personality of manic depressives (interest, friendliness, sociability). This suggests either that the study disproved the hypothesis of a prevalent personality type among manic depressives or that this study is invalid. Third, there is a marked disparity in the mean age of the involutionals compared with the other two groups: involutional, 56.2 years; manic depressive, 29.2 years; and normal, 34.0 years. This finding suggests the possibility that the differences in premorbid personality may be a function of the age of the patients rather than of the type of illness. Fourth, the diagnostic categories used have a high degree of unreliability (see Chapter 10). In addition, the kinds of patient characteristics assessed are notoriously difficult to rate and generally have a high degree of interjudge unreliability. Finally, the number of each group (10) was relatively small, and in the absence of any tests of statistical significance there is no reason to ascribe the obtained differences to anything but chance.

Several other studies purportedly supported Titley's hypothesis of a typical premorbid personality in involutionals. Palmer and Sherman[23] reached this conclusion on the basis of a comparison of the protocols of 50 involutionals with those of 50 manic depressives. They did not, however, present any tabulation or statistical analysis of their data, so the validity of their conclusions cannot be evaluated.

Malamud, Sands, and Malamud[19] similarly endorsed Titley's profile of involutional traits, on the basis of a study of 47 involutional patients. An examination of their data indicates that the typical traits (conscientiousness, prudery, stubbornness) occurred in only a minority of the cases, and the characteristic of outgoingness occurred just as often as the most frequent other traits. In decreasing order of frequency, the traits ascribed to the involutionals were outgoing (15), introverted (15), sensitive (15), conscientious (9), prudish (7), stubborn (5), and frugal (3). Their own findings appear to contradict the contention of a specific personality organization in melancholics.

In summary, these early studies did not settle the problem of a specific premorbid personality in melancholia. The investigations were too loosely designed to permit any definite conclusions, and in at least one instance (Malamud et al.[19]) the findings, if taken at their face value, appear to invalidate the notion of a specific premorbid personality.

Conclusion

The following Conclusion appeared in the first edition of this volume:

> A survey of the systematic studies of involutional depression raises strong doubt regarding the usefulness of this nosological category. The widespread belief that involutional depression may be distinguished from other types of psychotic depression on the basis of symptoms (such as agitation) has not been supported by controlled studies. Furthermore, there is no evidence that hormonal changes

during the climacterium are in any way responsible for the depressions occurring during this period.

In the light of the currently available evidence, there is no more justification for allocating a special diagnostic label to depressions in the involutional period than there is for setting up other age-specific categories such as adolescent depressions or middle-age depressions. Moreover, the listing of the depressive and paranoid reactions of later life under the rubric of involutional reactions artificially binds together two clinically distinct disorders simply on the basis of age of the patient.[24]

Consistent with this analysis, a subsequent comprehensive review by Newmann[25] on aging and depression found no consistent support for a connection between the two. Some investigators have even found elderly persons to be relatively immune from depression, compared to their younger adult counterparts. In any case, diverse measurement, flaws in design, and faulty analysis have made it as yet impossible to draw any definitive conclusions regarding the age-depression relation at this time.

Chapter 8
Schizoaffective Disorder

Definition

The frequent association of prominent schizophrenic and affective symptoms, having engaged the interest of psychiatric nosographers for over a century, led to the inclusion of "schizo-affective reaction" (now schizoaffective disorder) in the first edition of the American Psychiatric Association nomenclature.[1] This category was then listed as a subtype of schizophrenia along with the more traditional subtypes such as hebephrenic (disorganized), catatonic, and paranoid, and its distinguishing characteristic was the occurrence of affective features (either pronounced depression or elation) in a setting of typical schizophrenic thinking and behavior.

As Clark and Mallet[2] pointed out in 1963, a large proportion of psychotic patients show a mixture of schizophrenic and affective features, and it is difficult to decide whether a given case should be regarded as schizophrenia with affective features, or as affective disorder with schizophrenia. In the United States it has been customary to assign these cases to the schizophrenic group, as described above. This practice is in keeping with the dictum of Lewis and Piotrowski[3] that "even a trace of schizophrenia is schizophrenia."

Two important questions are evoked by this nosology: (1) Is this group properly placed in the diagnostic hierarchy, does it belong with the bipolar group, or should it be classified as an independent entity? and (2) Is the prognosis for complete remission comparable to the affective disorders, or is it likely to be poorer, as in schizophrenia?

Evolution of the Concept

A review of the older literature indicates that three main streams converged to produce the current concept of schizoaffective disorder. The first consists of *new* subcategories of manic-depressive reactions; it includes Kirby's description of a "catatonic syndrome allied to manic-depressive insanity"[4] and

August Hoch's delineation of "benign stupors."[5] The second encompasses a number of syndromes with a symptomatology similar to schizophrenia but with a good prognosis; included here are Kasanin's "schizo-affective disorder"[6] and many other syndromes with common features but with different names.[7] The third consists of studies of cases initially diagnosed as manic-depressive psychosis but that later showed the typical symptomatology of chronic schizophrenia.[8]

Catatonia and Manic-Depressive Psychosis

Kirby[4] attempted to isolate from the dementia praecox category a group of cases showing catatonic symptoms that seemed to him to be more closely allied with the manic-depressive syndrome than with dementia praecox. In the introduction to his article he pointed out that Kraepelin's conception of catatonia as part of the dementia praecox group and as sharing its poor prognosis was contrary to Kahlbaum's previous formulation. Kahlbaum had stated that in catatonia there is a tendency to recover and that only certain cases become chronic and deteriorate. Kraepelin recognized that certain cases of catatonia recover, but he regarded the remissions as temporary.

Kirby reviewed the symptomatology of an unspecified number of cases and presented five case histories of a catatonic syndrome that seemed to him to be part of the manic-depressive category. He noted that during the catatonic episode the patients showed the same types of symptoms classically associated with catatonia. They showed complete inactivity, rigidity, mutism, insensitivity to pinprick, and waxy flexibility. He noted, however, that these catatonic attacks seemed to occur as part of a circular psychosis; that is, they alternated with manic attacks and thus could be regarded as having replaced the usual depressive phase in manic-depressive psychosis. Sometimes the catatonic episode seemed to be essentially an extension of a preexistent depression. The patients showed a thought content often found in depression, such as wishes to die, belief that they were dead, or preoccupation with the concept of hell. Later, when the patients were able to report their affect, they stated that they had felt depressed.

A striking feature of Kirby's cases was that they showed a complete recovery. The onset was generally acute and not of the insidious type associated with schizophrenia. The premorbid personality, moreover, was not of the schizoid type usually associated with patients developing schizophrenia. He concluded that the catatonic syndrome could be broken down into two main types: cases with an insidious onset and a poor prognosis allied to dementia praecox; and cases with an acute onset and a good prognosis allied to manic-depressive psychosis.

Benign Stupor

In his 1921 monograph, *Benign Stupors: A Study of a New Manic-Depressive Reaction Type*,[5] August Hoch presented 40 cases of benign stupors. The majority of the patients were within the age range of 15–25 years. He described the following classical features in the typical cases of deep stupor.

Inactivity

There was complete cessation or marked diminution of all spontaneous or reactive movement, including such voluntary muscle reflexes as contain a psychic component. For instance, there was interference with swallowing (resulting in accumulation of saliva and drooling), interference with blinking, and even interference with the inhibitory processes involved in holding urine and feces. Often there was no reaction to pinpricks. The inactivity frequently prevented the ingestion of food, so that spoon or tube feeding had to be used. The patient either kept the eyes covered or stared vacantly, the face presenting an immobile, wooden, or stolid expression. Complete mutism was the rule. When activity was not totally absent, the movements were slow. The patient often had to be pushed around.

Negativism

This consisted of marked stiffening of the body, either assumed spontaneously or appearing when attempts at interference were made. There was also more active turning away or even direct warding off, sometimes with scowling, swearing, or striking.

Affect

"Complete affectlessness" was an integral part of stupor reaction. The patient seemed basically indifferent, and only certain stimuli (some cheerful remark of a relative, or a comical situation) could elicit emotional reactions.

Catalepsy

Waxy flexibility (the tendency to maintain artificial positions) was a frequent but not an essential condition of the syndrome.

Intellectual Processes

According to Hoch, the deep-stupor patients did not betray any evidence of mentation and retrospectively spoke of their minds as being blank. Incompleteness and slowness of intellectual operations were characteristic of the partial stupors.

Ideational Content

Ideational content was elicited while the stupor was incubating, during interruptions, or from the recollections of recovered patients. Hoch found that 35 of the 40 patients showed a preoccupation with death, which was not only a dominant topic but often an exclusive interest. After recovery, the patient frequently spoke of having felt dead, paralyzed, or drugged. Hoch stated that 25 percent of the patients acknowledged having had the delusion of being about to die, or of being dead, or of being in heaven or hell. The delusion of death was accompanied by complete apathy. Related to this was a tendency to suicidal impulses that were ostensibly as planless and unexpected as other impulsive acts of catatonics.

The stupor reaction included the partial stupors as well as the complete stupors. Hoch made an analogy to hypomania and mania: The former is merely a dilution of the latter; both are forms of the manic reaction.

Hoch believed that the fundamental characteristic of the stupor symptoms is a change in affect that could be summed up in one word—apathy. The emotional poverty was evidenced by lack of feeling, loss of energy, and absence of the normal urge to live. He noted that inappropriateness of affect was not observed in a true, benign stupor.

He differentiated the catatonic type of schizophrenia from benign stupors by the presence, only in the former, of peculiarities such as empty verbalizations, giggling, and fragmented speech. Furthermore, in catatonic schizophrenia the onset is characterized by the pathognomonic symptoms of schizophrenia before the actual stupor occurs.

Follow-Up Studies

Rachlin[9] attempted to chart the progress of Hoch's benign stupor cases. Unfortunately, Hoch had provided sufficient identifying data for only 19 cases. Rachlin was able to locate only 13 of the 19, some of them as long as 30 years after their initial diagnosis by Hoch. Rachlin found that 11 of the 13 had been rehospitalized, and that six, after remissions lasting an average of 10 years, had developed the typical picture of dementia praecox (chronic schizophrenia). Rachlin believed that his study indicated the basic schizophrenic nature of the so-called benign stupors. In defense of Hoch's formulation, however, is the fact that, since Rachlin's follow-up tended to locate patients who had been rehospitalized, the patients who did well were not adequately represented in his tabulation.

Rachlin[10] later reported a follow-up of 132 cases diagnosed as benign stupor by many different psychiatrists at the Manhattan State Hospital over a 17-year period. Of these, 56 were available for further study, and 76 were not available. After reviewing the available cases, Rachlin concluded that 40 (71.4 percent) should have their diagnoses changed from benign stupor to dementia praecox. His available follow-up sample, however, was again biased in favor of patients who had not done well, namely, the rehospitalized group.

Although stupor was listed as a form of manic-depressive psychosis in the 1934 APA classification,[11] it has long been omitted from the official nomenclature and is rarely mentioned in the recent literature. The publication of Rachlin's work accelerated the abandonment of Hoch's concept of benign stupors. It should be emphasized, however, that although a significant proportion of cases formerly diagnosed as benign stupor belong in the schizophrenic category, there are a substantial proportion whose postdischarge behavior is similar to that of those with bipolar disorder.

Acute Schizoaffective Psychosis

Kasanin[6] described a group of nine patients he had personally studied who had aroused his curiosity because of the special clinical picture they presented. They had all been diagnosed as having dementia praecox. They were young men and women (in their twenties and thirties) in excellent physical health. Various biological tests of the urine, blood, and spinal fluid were negative. They had average or superior intelligence and had made a satisfactory educational or occupational adjustment prior to the onset of the illness. The attacks were preceded, however, by a difficult environmental situation that served as a precipitating factor. According to Kasanin, the environmental stress was chronic in some cases and acute in others. Examples listed by the author included the loss of a job, a state of anxiety over sudden promotion, a difficult love affair, an alien environment, and hostile in-laws.

Kasanin stated that the psychosis was usually ushered in by a latent depression, and a certain amount of rumination persisted for some time until the dramatic schizophrenic picture appeared. He observed that he was able to reconstruct the psychological significance of the psychosis through reviewing the various symptoms and behavior with the patient after his recovery, and that they then became quite intelligible. He found that there was comparatively little of the bizarre, unusual, or mysterious.

In his summary, Kasanin emphasized the following clinical features:

1. The psychosis was characterized by a very sudden onset in a setting of marked emotional turmoil with distortion of the outside world and, in some cases, false sensory impressions.
2. The psychosis lasted from a few weeks to a few months and was followed by complete recovery.

3. The patients were in their twenties or thirties and usually had a history of a previous attack in late adolescence.
4. The prepsychotic personalities of the patients showed the usual variations found in any other group.
5. A good social and vocational adjustment, the presence of a definite and specific environmental stress, an interest in life, and the absence of any passivity or withdrawal were considered factors favoring recovery.

It is of some interest that 30 years later Vaillant included three of these cases in his follow-up study of remitting schizophrenics;[12] one relapsed into chronic schizophrenia after about four years, one had five recurrences after about eight years of total remission, and one died of chronic brain syndrome ten years after remission.

Acute Remitting Schizophrenia

Vaillant[7] showed that since 1849 at least 16 different names had been attached to a condition characterized by an acute picture resembling schizophrenia, symptoms of psychotic depression, and recovery. Proceeding from Bell's mania in 1849, these have included melancholia with stupor (1861), acute dementia (1862), mixed conditions of manic-depressive psychosis (1903), catatonic syndrome allied to manic-depressive insanity (1913), homosexual panic (1920), benign stupor (1921), hysterical twilight state (1924), schizo-affective psychosis (1933), schizophreniform state (1937), Gjessing's syndrome (1938), reactive state of adolescence (1944), acute exhaustive psychosis (1947), oneirophrenia (1950), cycloid psychosis (1960), and adolescent turmoil (1964).

In addition to the symptoms of schizophrenia and depression with recovery, most of the writers described a good premorbid adjustment, psychologically understandable symptoms, ascertainable precipitating causes, confusion, and concern with dying. These characteristics are similar to those generally associated with bipolar disorder.

Studies of Revised Diagnoses

Some earlier studies presented evidence that certain patients who had initially been diagnosed as manic depressive, but who showed a component of schizophrenic symptomatology, would exhibit progressively more schizophrenic symptomatology on each subsequent admission. Lewis and Hubbard[13] studied a group of 77 patients originally diagnosed as manic-depressive psychotics who were followed for a number of years and finally diagnosed as schizophrenics. These writers observed that, regardless whether the first psychosis was characterized by elation or depression, there was an increasingly greater tendency for the content to become schizophrenic in subsequent attacks. They stated, "These schizophrenic developments were so pronounced that should the psychiatrist, making a diagnosis on the basis of affect, have seen the patient in a later attack he would not have the least hesitation in making a diagnosis of dementia praecox." The picture generally became one of schizophrenia with deterioration. The early schizophrenic signs occurred in the first observed attack but were minimized by the diagnosing physician. These signs consisted of odd somatic feelings, hypochondriacal ideas, strange attitudes, and auditory hallucinations subjected by the patients to a mystical interpretation.

A later report by Lewis and Piotrowski[3] was based on a study of patients who, after a first admission to the New York State Psychiatric Institute in New York City, had received discharge diagnoses of manic-depressive psychosis. They were rediagnosed by Lewis at least three years and not more than 20 years after discharge. For more than 90 percent of the patients the follow-up interval was at least seven years long. The new diagnosis was made on the basis of historical data and of a personal examination, except in the case of a patient hospitalized elsewhere at the time of the study.

Of 70 patients initially discharged as manic depressives, 38 (54 percent) were considered to have developed clear-cut schizophrenia. The authors located 10 signs that appeared much more frequently in the records of patients who later developed obvious schizophrenia than in the records of those who remained genuine manic-depressive psychotics. By assigning a score of one point for each of these 10 signs, the writers found a clear-cut cleavage between the two groups. Patients with more than two points were schizophrenics; those with fewer than two points were almost all manic depressives.

Hoch and Rachlin[8] examined the records of approximately 5,800 cases of schizophrenia admitted to the Manhattan State Hospital in New York City. From this pool they found 415 cases whose initial diagnosis of manic-depressive psychosis could not be confirmed on later admission to the hospital. In other words, 7.1 percent of the cases of schizophrenia had originally been misclassified as manic-depressive psychosis. The authors mentioned a number of points that should be considered in making the differential diagnosis.

Differentiation of Depression and Schizophrenia

In his paper on benign stupors, Rachlin[9] pointed out that one rarely sees a true depressive patient throwing furtive glances or a manic patient refusing to answer questions verbally but choosing to write the reply instead; similarly, the incongruity of a patient in a state of playfulness laughing at his pranks and drooling saliva at the same time is indicative of a schizophrenic process rather than of a manic-depressive disorder. Sudden changes in behavior with impulsiveness (refusal to eat one meal and then eating the next ravenously) are also more suggestive of schizophrenia. Finally, evasiveness and reticence upon improvement may be seen in schizophrenia but not in manic-depressive psychosis.

Hoch and Rachlin[8] pointed out that, although periodicity or repeated attacks of a short duration are frequently considered a characteristic of manic-depressive psychosis, many cases of schizophrenia show complete remissions with apparent well-being between psychotic episodes. The authors suggested that in many of the so-called good recoveries a careful examination will "disclose defects in the affectivity or in the behavior."

Hoch and Rachlin also emphasized the importance of careful evaluation of the patient's ideation. Illogical remarks or incongruous statements with bizarre elaboration should arouse a suspicion of schizophrenia. Even a slight dissociation between affect and thought content is indicative of schizophrenia.

The authors pointed out that cases of mania with auditory hallucinations and paranoid delusions end up as schizophrenia. They emphasized particularly the importance of ideas of reference or of persecution as indicative of the schizophrenic process. Also indicative of schizophrenia is the rapid changing of the delusional and hallucinatory content accompanied by fluctuating affect: A patient who rapidly alternates between laughing and crying would be more likely to be schizophrenic than manic depressive. In the pure affective disorders, the mood tends to be relatively consistent and does not show notable fluctuations over brief periods. Lewis and Piotrowski[3] also emphasized this differential characteristic.

The ten signs listed by Lewis and Piotrowski[3] as indicative of an underlying schizophrenic process in cases initially diagnosed manic depressive are as follows.

Sign 1. Physical sensation with dissociation. This sign denotes delusions of perception rather than delusions of judgment. The authors cite as an example, "There is a steel plate in my forehead." "I have the skin of a monkey and I'm going to be a human being turned into an animal." "I feel as though a piece of meat is sticking out of my rectum." Also allocated to this category were electrical sensations in the body, especially in the genitals, the feeling that one is growing thinner or smaller (contrary to evidence), and the impression that the neck is crooked when it is not. These were also treated as instances of "physical sensation with dissociation."

Sign 2. Delusions regarding others. These include misidentification and misrecognition of people. One patient felt that her parents had risen from the dead and were physically present whenever she quarreled with her husband. Another believed that some of his fellow patients on the ward were his close relatives. One patient was convinced that her baby was dead, even though it was alive and was being shown to her. Another patient, hearing someone cough, became convinced that the person would die, and began to cry from grief.

Sign 3. Delusions regarding physical objects. One patient felt at times that objects in her environment had become unreal. Other patients had the idea that the walls, beds, etc., were changing size or shape. Another patient spoke to objects as though they were human beings.

Sign 4. Feeling of physical isolation and personal unreality. Some patients were anxiously aware of being separated from everything else by space or air. These patients stated either that the distance was greater than it actually was or that the air or space was impenetrable. Complaints of unreality, such as are indicated by a patient's impression of living in a dream world, were also classified in this category.

Sign 5. Inability to concentrate. This sign was credited to patients who had complained spontaneously of inability to concentrate. It was not credited to patients who, because they were preoccupied with worries or fears, could not concentrate on a subject suggested by the examiner.

Sign 6. Feelings of having changed. The feeling of having changed applied to complaints such as "Something slipped in my mind. Some nerve jumped." "I see myself in an institution for the rest of my life." "My mind has just disintegrated and gone down until it is nothing."

Sign 7. Speech disturbance and intellectual blocking. This sign was applied to inability to complete a sentence in the absence of physical fatigue or emotional tension, or a change in the subject matter of the patient's talk. Also classified as speech disturbance was a sudden and unintelligible mumbling, not only if it interrupted the patient's speech but also if it occurred after the patient had been silent. Other instances of speech disturbance in this category were staring ahead in an attempt to collect one's thoughts before answering questions or before making spontaneous remarks; opening the mouth to talk but remaining mute; complaining that "the thoughts are not just right," because the patient had intended to say something else.

Sign 8. Uncontrolled repeated interrupting and anxious thought. This sign included auditory and visual hallucinations. One patient complained that while he was trying to think of words his thoughts were telling him to kill people.

Sign 9. Ideas of reference and/or feelings of being controlled by inimical outside forces (paranoid ideas). This sign was credited to patients who clearly accused other persons of some external forces (magic or real) of definite attempts at harming them. This sign was particularly applicable if it implied bizarre, involved, or magical thinking.

Sign 10. Seclusiveness maintained or increased in hospital. The patient was credited with this sign if he or she had stayed in the hospital at least a month without becoming less seclusive, despite psychotherapy and other forms of treatment and despite participation in some organized activities on the ward. Practically all the patients who maintained or increased their seclusiveness were eventually diagnosed as schizophrenic.

The authors tabulated the frequency of each sign in schizophrenics who had originally been misdiagnosed as manic depressive and in those manic depressives who retained their diagnosis. Signs that discriminated most effectively between the two groups are 1, 6, and 9 (physical sensation with dissociation; feelings of having changed; and ideas of reference).

The concept of schizoaffective disorder as outlined in the APA[14] nomenclature differs in at least one significant way from Kasanin's description.[6] In the present nomenclature, the condition is unequivocally classified with Schizophrenia and Other Psychotic Disorders category rather than in the borderland between the schizophrenic and bipolar disorders. This classification placement implies that the prognosis is not better than that of schizophrenia generally. This is at variance with the previous descriptions of a remitting schizoaffective disorder.

Vaillant,[12] on the basis of his long-term follow-up study of remitted schizophrenics, suggested that the term be used as defined by Kasanin. Thus, schizoaffective disorder would cover cases of good premorbid adjustment and acute onset, manifesting affective features, confusion, and preoccupation with death.

Henderson and Gillespie[15] were dubious about the use of the term schizoaffective psychosis and offered the opinion that it created more diagnostic difficulties than it solved. They asserted that in the majority of cases the term has been applied incorrectly to cases that should have been diagnosed as manic depressive disorder, mixed type, in which the admixture of depressive and manic symptoms had given rise to some apparent incongruity of affect.

Prognosis

A 1963 study by Clark and Mallet[2] attempted to determine the relative frequency of readmissions for patients initially diagnosed as schizophrenic, schizoaffective disorder, or depressive disorder. The proportions in each group requiring readmission within three years of discharge from the hospital were: schizophrenic, 70 percent; schizoaffective, 53 percent; and depressive, 20 percent. This finding was in keeping with the report of Hunt and Appel[16] that the recovery rate for cases of psychosis "lying midway between schizophrenia and manic-depressive psychosis" was twice as good as in schizophrenia and 50 percent poorer than in pure manic-depressive psychosis.

The "acute, remitting schizophrenias" described by Vaillant,[7] characterized by acute onset of typical schizophrenic symptoms, affective components, and complete remission, would probably be classified today as schizoaffective disorder. A 50-year follow-up study by Vaillant[12] of a group of 12 of those patients provides valuable information about the ultimate prognosis of such cases. Eight of the 12 led independent, useful lives for at least 25 years. The ultimate prognosis was not good, however; eight eventually required chronic hospitalization.

The prognosis of schizoaffective disorder may be further illuminated by examining studies of the relationship of affective factors to outcome in schizophrenia. Since most of these studies were conducted before the subcategory "schizoaffective type" was officially adopted, the cases of schizophrenia with depression, "intrapunitive tendencies," self-degrading delusions, and so forth undoubtedly correspond to the new category. The findings of these earlier studies may therefore be used as a basis for establishing the prognosis of schizoaffective disorder. These studies are discussed in the next section.

Affective Factors and Prognosis in Schizophrenia

Diverse studies have indicated that in cases diagnosed as schizophrenia, the presence of depressive features in the individual or in the family history is a favorable prognostic factor. Among the examples of the relationship of depression to improved prognosis in schizophrenia have been studies of the manifest affect,[17] the content of delusions,[17,18] the content of hallucinations,[17] family history of affective illness,[17,19] the specific subtypes of schizophrenia,[17] and studies of the overt behavior of the patients.[20,21,22]

Manifest Affect

Zubin and his coworkers[17] reviewed 800 studies of the outcome of schizophrenia. In 159 studies the relationship of affect to prognosis was reported. In all 159 the presence of overtly expressed affect, regardless of its quality or direction, generally led to a good outcome. The types of affect mentioned were elation, depression, anxiety, and general emotional reactivity. The presence of guilt, either overt or inferred, was associated with a good outcome in all 15 studies in which it was noted.

Content of Delusions

Zubin reported that in two studies in which intrapunitive delusions were distinguished from extrapunitive delusions, the presence of the former favored a good prognosis. As pointed out in Chapter 2, delusions of the intrapunitive type are characteristic of depression. Albee[18] studied the outcome of 261 patients with schizophrenia admitted to a mental hospital. He distinguished self-condemnatory delusions from other types of delusion. In the former category he included delusions of heinous crimes, horrible sins, ugliness, worthlessness, contamination, deformity, and diseases; also delusions that horrible odors that were offensive to other people emanated from the patient. Albee used as a criterion of outcome whether the patients were improved or recovered one year after admission to the hospital. He found that there was a relationship between recovery and self-condemnatory delusions significant at the

.01 level. Persecutory delusions, in contrast, were found to be significantly related to poor prognosis.

Hallucinations

Zubin found that the presence of hallucinations contributed to a bad outcome in five of six studies. In one study, however, where the content of the hallucinations was of a self-accusatory nature, the prognosis was improved. As pointed out in Chapter 2, when hallucinations occur in depression, they tend to be self-accusatory.

Manic-Depressive Heredity and Outcome in Schizophrenia

Zubin noted that in six of seven studies there was a positive relationship between a family history of manic-depressive psychosis and a favorable prognosis in schizophrenia. In one study he found that there was no relationship between family history and outcome. Vaillant[19] also studied the relationship of manic-depressive heredity and outcome of schizophrenia. He found that among schizophrenics who recovered completely from their illness, the frequency of relatives with affective psychosis was significantly higher than among those schizophrenics with an unfavorable prognosis.

Presence of Depression

Vaillant, in a prospective prediction of schizophrenic remission,[23] found that the presence of depression was associated with full remission in 77 percent of the cases. This was significant at the .01 level.

Patterns of Aggression in Overt Behavior

Zubin and his coworkers[17] reported that patients with "self-directed aggression," as opposed to those with externally-directed aggression, showed a good prognosis. In 8 of 9 studies the prognosis was favorable for patients showing internally directed aggression. This contrasted with 8 of 13 studies that showed a bad prognosis when externally directed aggression was present.

Albee[20] studied 127 psychiatric patients in a mental hospital in regard to the relation of the direction of aggression to outcome of treatment. Patterns of aggression were classified as extrapunitive or intrapunitive according to whether patients were involved in injuries inflicted on someone else or on themselves. He found that when the aggression was intrapunitive the improvement rate was significantly higher than when the aggression was extrapunitive. Albee analyzed the data on the 81 schizophrenics in the group to determine whether the relationship held when they were considered separately from the nonschizophrenic group. He found that more than half of the schizophrenics classified as intrapunitive improved, but only one-seventh of the extrapunitive schizophrenics improved ($p < .001$).

Feldman et al.[21] also studied the direction of aggression as a prognostic variable in mental illness. A group of 486 hospitalized patients were categorized as improved or unimproved one year after discharge from the hospital. It was found that patients who tended to direct blame or hostility toward themselves rather than toward others had a significantly better prognosis than those who directed hostility exclusively onto the environment.

Phillips and Ziegler[22] studied the case histories of 251 patients to investigate the relationship between the symptom clusters and two outcome measures, length of hospitalization and rehospitalization. As predicted by the authors, the patients whose symptomatology was characterized by a "turning against himself" had a shorter period of hospitalization than patients whose symptoms fell into the "avoidance of others" category.

Zubin noted that the reason for the improvement in cases with internally directed aggression was not clear. He suggested that one should take into account the possibility that the hospital might have been more willing to release patients with internally directed aggression, since they might be more readily tolerated by the community than patients with externally directed aggression. However, many studies indicated that complete recovery, rather than simple discharge from the hospital, was associated with the presence of various characteristics of depressive illness.

Albee[18] proposed that self-condemnatory patients evaluate themselves on the basis of social standards and therefore operate at a higher level of maturity than patients with externally directed aggression. Phillips and Ziegler similarly postulated that people who assume a "turning against the self" role have incorporated the values of society and, consequently, experience guilt when they do not successfully meet these values. They conjectured that a pathological solution to life's demands (e.g., pronounced withdrawal) would be unacceptable to such a person, who would hence have an improved prognosis.

Present Classification of Schizoaffective Disorder

In the current APA diagnostic manual, schizoaffective disorder is listed as a separate disorder within the general category Schizophrenia and Other Psychotic Disorders. The APA manual states that the diagnosis is not always straightforward, since some medical conditions—as well as substance abuse—can lead to combined psychotic and mood symptoms. Also, differential diagnosis is said to be difficult in distinguishing between schizoaffective disorder and schizophrenia, and between schizoaffective disorder and mood disorder with psychotic features.[14]

An example of a "typical pattern" of symptoms would be as follows. An

TABLE 8-1. Diagnostic Criteria for Schizoaffective Disorder

A. An uninterrupted period of illness during which, at some time, there is either a Major Depressive Episode, a Manic Episode, or a Mixed Episode concurrent with symptoms that meet Criterion A for Schizophrenia. *Note*: The Major Depressive Episode must include Criterion A1: depressed mood.
B. During the same period of illness, there have been delusions or hallucinations for at least 2 weeks in the absence of prominent mood symptoms.
C. Symptoms that meet criteria for a mood episode are present for substantial portion of the total duration of the active and residual periods of the illness.
D. The disturbance is not due to the direct physiological effects of a substance (e.g., a drug of abuse, a medication) or a general medical condition.
   Specify type:
   Bipolar Type: if the disturbance includes a Manic or a Mixed Episode (or a Manic or a Mixed Episode and Major Depressive Episode.
   Depressive Type: if the disturbance only includes Major Depressive Episodes.

Adapted from *DSM-IV-TR*.

individual may have pronounced psychotic symptoms—such as auditory hallucinations and persecutory delusions—for two months before the onset of a major depressive episode. The psychotic symptoms and the full major depressive episode may then be present together for the next three months, after which time the person recovers entirely from the depressive episode. The psychotic symptoms remain for another month. In this example, the symptoms met *at the same point in time* both criteria for a major depressive episode and characteristic symptoms for schizophrenia. Auditory hallucinations and delusions were present both before and after the depressive phase, with the total period of illness lasting for six months. Psychotic symptoms alone were observed during the first two months, both depressive and psychotic symptoms during the next 3 months, and psychotic symptoms only during the last month (p. 320).[14]

The defining diagnostic criteria of schizoaffective disorder are listed in Table 8-1.

Unresolved Issues for Continuing Research

Further research is needed on the question of how—and whether it is meaningful—to differentiate schizoaffective disorder from the mood and schizophrenic disorders. Three areas for further research remain most relevant to these questions, including differences in course of illness,[24] unique symptom and cognitive profiles,[25] and genetic distinctions.[26,27,28] In this section, we consider these issues, with special attention to the literature reviews of symptom differences[28] and genetics.[29]

Course of Illness

As noted above, additional research is needed to illuminate whether schizo-affective disorder is a variant of schizophrenia, deviation of mood disorder, or an independent, distinct entity. Comparative long-term outcome studies are pertinent to this question. The course of illness may illuminate distinctive characteristics.

Along these lines, Williams and McGlashan[24] compared patients with schizoaffective psychosis ($n = 68$) to those with schizophrenia ($n = 163$), bipolar disorder ($n = 19$), and unipolar disorder ($n = 44$) on multiple premorbid, morbid, and outcome dimensions. They found that among samples of long-term inpatients, those who satisfied diagnostic criteria for both schizophrenia and affective disorder displayed a demographic and premorbid profile like that of patients with unipolar disorder. However, at 15-year (on average) follow-up, the profile of schizoaffective psychosis paralleled that of schizophrenia. They concluded that—at least among samples of long-term inpatients—schizoaffective disorder appears more like schizophrenia than affective disorder. Research on a wider range of samples is needed in order to properly interpret this finding.

Symptom and Cognitive Profiles

Taylor[28] provides a selective review of studies that support a "continuum" perspective on the question of whether schizophrenia and affective disorder are distinct disease entities. Numerous family, twin, and adoption data document the cooccurrence of schizophrenia and affective disorder in some families. It is possible that this cooccurrence may reflect true overlap (continuity) between the two disorders, contrary to the "Kraepelian" view.

Taylor[28] identified 14 published family studies of schizoaffective disorder that assessed the risk in relatives for schizophrenia, schizoaffective disorder, and affective disorder. These studies were selected based on the criteria that all had more than 40 probands and adequate methodology. The risks in relatives of those with diagnosed schizoaffective disorder were found to be as follows: 3.72 percent for schizophrenia, 5.30 percent for schizoaffective disorder, and 15.68 percent for affective disorder. Based on his overall review of family, twin, and adoption studies, the risk for schizophrenia among relatives of those with affective disorder is 0.5–3.5 percent, and the risk for affective disorder in first-degree relatives of those with schizophrenia is 6–8 percent.

A study by Evans et al.[25] compared outpatients aged 45 to 77 years who were diagnosed with schizoaffective disorder ($n = 29$), schizophrenia ($n = 154$), or nonpsychotic mood disorder ($n = 27$). All were given a neuropsychological test battery designed to comprehensively measure cognitive performance, as well as standardized measures of psychological dysfunction. A statistical analysis (discriminant function) was used to make comparisons based on their cognitive functioning. The aim was to determine the similarities and differences of patients with schizoaffective disorder and with schizophrenia or nonpsychotic mood disorder.

Evans et al.[25] found the schizoaffective and schizophrenic patients to have the following (among other) differences from mood disorder patients: (1) a weaker family history of mood disorder, (2) more frequent hospitalizations for psychiatric reasons, (3) more prescriptions for neuroleptic and anticholinergic medication, (4) less severe depressive symptoms, and (5) more impaired neuropsychological performances than the nonpsychotic mood disorder patients. They concluded that schizoaffective disorder and schizophrenia should be combined into a single patient category when cognitive performance is the variable of interest.

Family and Genetic Studies

A study by Maj et al.[27] assessed the risks for schizophrenia and major affective disorders in the first-degree relatives of patients with schizoaffective disorder. The participants were recruited from outpatient clinics of a university psychiatry department. Comparisons were made to students and nurses with no diagnosed mental disorder.

A psychiatrist blind to information about relatives conducted the interviews of probands (people who have the disorder of interest in a family history study). Likewise, the relatives were interviewed by two psychiatrists blind to the probands' diagnoses. When direct interviews were not possible, the direct interview was replaced by family history data. This was the case in 24 percent of the interviews.

Probands included 21 patients with schizoaffective disorder, depressive type; 22 patients with mood-incongruent psychotic depression; 19 with mood-congruent psychotic depression; 27 with nonpsychotic depression; and 28 diagnosed with schizophrenia. The comparison group included 18 normal subjects. The first-degree relatives of probands with schizoaffective disorder had a significantly lower risk for major affective disorder than relatives of those with nonpsychotic depression. The risk for schizophrenia was found to be the same in relatives of schizoaffective patients as in relatives of those with schizophrenia, suggesting that schizoaffective disorder may share genetic overlap with schizophrenia.

A study by Kendler et al.[26] assessed whether schizoaffective disorder differs from schizophrenia and affective illness in clinical features, outcome, and familial psychopathology. They also evaluated the validity of subtyping systems for schizoaffective disorder, including bipolar versus depressive (distin-

TABLE 8-2. Schizoaffective Psychosis: Family Studies

	Diagnostic criteria	Morbid risk in first-degree relatives (%)		
		Schizophrenia	Schizoaffective	Affective
Angst et al. 1979	ICD	5.3	3.0	6.7
Scharfetter & Nüsperli 1980	ICD	13.5	2.5	9.6
Baron et al. 1982	RDC	2.2	2.2	18.9
Gershon et al. 1982	RDC	3.6	6.1	31.3
Kendler et al., 1986	DSM-III	5.6	2.7	11.0
Maier et al. 1991	RDC	4.1	5.3	25.8
Kendler et al. 1993a,b,c	DSM-III-R	5.7	1.84	9.7

Adapted from Bertelsen & Gottesman 1995.

guished by presence or absence of a previous full manic syndrome) and good versus poor recovery.

Contrary to the findings of Maj et al.,[27] where higher risk for affective disorder was found in relatives of depressive versus schizoaffective probands, relatives of probands with schizoaffective disorder in Kendler et al.[26] had a significantly higher risk for major affective disorder than relatives of schizophrenic probands. They were also found to have higher rates of schizophrenia than relatives of probands with affective illness.

The distinction between bipolar and depressive schizoaffective disorder was not supported. These categories (bipolar versus depressive) did not differ on psychotic symptoms, negative symptoms, outcome, or family history. The distinction between good versus poor interepisode recovery did not show differences in familial psychopathology. Overall, the conclusion was that schizoaffective disorder incorporates a high liability to both schizophrenia and affective illness.

Bertelsen and Gottesman's Review

As illustrated by the above, a comprehensive review by Bertelsen and Gottesman[29] concluded that the genetic studies (family, twin, and adoption studies) are "divergent" (p. 7). Also, they note that the diagnostic classification of schizoaffective psychoses has varied since Kasanin introduced the concept in 1933. Moreover, symptom number, quality, and sequence vary even in recent classifications like RDC, DSM-III-R, and ICD-10.

Despite these unsettled issues, and although the etiology of schizoaffective disorder remains undetermined, there is evidence for a strong genetic factor. Consider the earlier and more recent family studies on first degree relatives of those with schizoaffective disorder, as shown in Table 8-2.

Bertelsen and Gottesman[29] note that the family studies of relatives of

TABLE 8-3. Dual Mating Studies on Parent Combinations of Schizophrenia and Manic-Depressive Disorder

| | | Morbid risk in offspring (%) | | |
	n	Schizophrenia	Schizoaffective	Affective
Schulz 1940	49	14	6	18
Elsasser 1952 (incl. Schulz)	85	13	4	20
Gottesman and Bertelsen 1989	25	4	4	32

Adapted from Bertelsen & Gottesman 1995.

schizoaffective probands suggests that schizoaffective disorder is composed of independent genetic components of affective disorder and schizophrenia. This is the case because the relatives of those with schizoaffective disorder show moderate to high risks of schizophrenia and affective disorders, but a low to moderate risk of schizoaffective disorder. The argue that if schizoaffective disorder is a continuum psychosis or an independent psychosis, then higher risks for schizoaffective disorder would have been observed (p. 8).

Three studies have been conducted of one parent with bipolar disorder and the other schizophrenia, as in Table 8-3. The low risks for schizoaffective disorder observed are inconsistent with the continuum hypothesis, which would predict that most of the resulting mentally ill relatives would have schizoaffective disorder. It is also inconsistent with a completely independent genetic psychosis, where few if any schizoaffective disorders would have resulted.[29] Summarizing the data, Bertelsen and Gottesman state: "Results from family, twin, and adoption studies are divergent, but all the same, support a separate classification of broadly defined schizoaffective psychoses as possibly being phenotypical variations or expressions of genetic interforms between schizophrenia and affective psychoses" (p. 7).

Conclusion

It is apparent from the review of the pertinent literature that the presence of affective factors significantly increases the probability of improvement in cases of schizophrenia. This finding was reported in a study of the schizoaffective subtype of schizophrenia, as well as in numerous studies conducted prior to the official adoption of this new subcategory. The improvement in this type of schizophrenia is greater than in the other types at all levels: In terms of the degree of improvement (mild, moderate, or marked); in terms of the proportions showing total remission; in terms of frequency of recurrence (measured by frequency of rehospitalization); and in terms of chronicity (measured by duration of hospitalization). The prognosis for schizoaffective disorder is somewhat better than for schizophrenia but worse than for mood disorders. When precipitating events or stressors are present, there is a better prognosis.[14]

These observations could be expressed graphically by viewing the cases of *functional* mental illness in terms of a spectrum: at one end are the pure manic-depressive cases with a relatively good prognosis; at the other are the pure schizophrenic cases with a poorer prognosis. In between are varying blends of these disorders (the schizoaffective cases) with a fair prognosis. This relationship between diagnosis and prognosis may be conceptualized in terms of the operation of two variables: the schizophrenic variable linked to a poor prognosis and the affective variable to a good prognosis. The cases at either end of the spectrum represent one of these variables—schizophrenic or affective. The cases between the poles contain both variables, and the resultant prognosis depends on the relative strength of each.

The nature of these two diagnostic-prognostic variables has not been determined. It seems likely, however, that the determinants of schizophrenic and affective disorders include some factor (or factors) responsible for the prognosis. It could be conjectured that the schizophrenogenic determinants include a factor inhibiting recovery or promoting chronicity. The determinants of the affective disorders, in contrast, could contain a factor promoting recovery. When the two variables are mixed, as in schizoaffective disorder, the cases also show a mixture of the recovery-inhibiting and recovery-promoting factors. The resultant prognosis is based on the balance between these two factors.

Despite progress in understanding schizoaffective disorder, as reviewed above, many questions remain. In part because of the complexities of the disorder, research has yet to determine fundamental facts, such as prevalence rates. For example, on the question of prevalence, *DSM-IV-TR*[14] notes that "detailed information is lacking," but it appears to occur less frequently than schizophrenia (p. 321). Many such basic questions and issues await further research on the nature, causes, and proper classification of this mixture of psychosis and mood disturbance.

References for Tables 8-1, 8-2 are as follows:

Angst J, Felder W, Lohmeyer B. Schizoaffective disorders: results of genetic investigation I. *Journal of Affective Disorders* 1979:1;139–153.

Baron M, Gruen L, Asnis L, Kane J. (1982). Schizo-affective illness, schizophrenia and affective disorders: morbidity risk and genetic transmission. *Acta Psychiatrica Scandinavica* 1982:65;253–262.

Elsässer G. *Die Nachkommen Geisteskran er Elternpaare.* Stuttgart: G Thieme;1952.

Gershon ES, Hamovit J, Guroff JJ, Dibble E, Leckman JF, Sceery W, Targum SD, Nurnberger JT, Goldin LR, Bunney WE. A family study of schizoaffective, bipolar I, bipolar II, unipolar and normal control probands. *Archives of General Psychiatry* 1982:39;1157–1167.

Gettesman II, Bertelsen A. Dual mating studies in psychiatry: offspring of inpatients with examples from reactive (psychogenic) psychoses. *International Review of Psycho-Analysis* 1989:1;287–296.

Kendler KS, McGuire M, Guirenberg AM, O'Hare A, Spellman M, Walsh D. The Roscommon Family Study. I. Methods, diagnosis of probands and risk of schizophrenia in relatives. *Archives of General Psychiatry* 1993a:50;527–540.

Kendler KS, McGuire M, Guirenberg A.M, O'Hare A, Spellman M, Walsh D. The Roscommon Family Study. II. The risk of nonschizophrenic non-affective psychoses in relatives. *Archives of General Psychiatry* 1993b: 50;645–652.

Kendler KS, McGuire M, Guirenberg AM, O'Hare A, Spellman M, Walsh D. The Roscommon Family Study. IV. Affective illness, anxiety disorder and alcoholism in relatives. *Archives of General Psychiatry* 1993c: 50;952–960.

Scharfetter C, Nüsperli M. The group of schizophrenias, schizoaffective psychoses and affective disorders. *Schizophrenia Bulletin* 1980:6;586–591.

Schulz, B. Kinder von Elternpaaren mit einem schiophrenen und einem affectivepskotischen Partner. *Zeitschrift Neurologische Psychiatrie* 1940:170;441–514.

Part II
Experimental Aspects of Depression

Chapter 9
Biological Studies of Depression

Early Studies

The biological aspects of depression have received considerable attention. Thousands of studies have been reported in the literature; tests have been made of almost all the known constituents of the blood, the urine, and the cerebrospinal fluid; and careful pathological studies of the brain and other organs have been conducted. Yet, few "positive" findings have stood the test of time, and there is still very little basic knowledge of the biological substrate of depression.[1]

The concluding words in this chapter as originally written by Beck (p. 153)[2] were as follows: "With the tightening of the experimental methods it may be expected that much of the uncertainty surrounding the biological aspects of depression will be dissipated." This has not yet occurred.

In 1995, addressing the question of causality in biological processes of depression, Thase & Howland[3] wrote that "few conclusions can yet be reached with certainty, even after 30 years of research" (p. 216). This judgment is consistent with that of other experts in biological studies of depression.

Dubovsky and Buzan[4] reviewed several factors that contribute to the complexity. One problem is the enduring diversity of phenomenology and comorbidity within the definitions of the various disorders, despite progress made in *Research Diagnostic Criteria* and in *DSM-IV*. Another is that there is no reason to think there is a single cause of any mood disorder.

Even if there were a single cause, that would not mitigate the complexity of identifying it. As an example, Dubovsky and Buzan pointed out that in researching inherited factors, one abnormal gene may lead to a protein that causes a positive symptom, yet another gene may fail to produce a protein that would regulate the positive symptom produced by the first.

Another difficulty is that a specific neurotransmitter may lead to a cascade

TABLE 9 1. Biological Studies of Depression

Area of study	Finding	Validity
Constitution	Relation to pyknic physique	Doubtful
Identical twins	Concordant for depression	Uncertain
Glucose metabolism	Decreased glucose tolerance	Uncertain
Electrolytes	Sodium retention	Uncertain
Steroids	Increased secretion	Probable*
Mecholyl test	Abnormal vascular response	Doubtful
Salivation	Decreased secretion	Doubtful
Sedation response	Decreased threshold	Doubtful
Sleep EEG	Decreased stage 4 sleep	Probable
Photoconvulsive response	Decreased threshold	Uncertain
EMG	Increased residual activity	Uncertain

* Finding not specific for depression.

of events that overlaps an identical sequence initiated by another transmitter. In this case, there may be the appearance of specificity where none actually exists.[4] The only way to demonstrate specificity would be to measure at the same time all independent and interacting neurotransmitters and event sequences. The unique contribution of any single cause, apart from the contribution of other factors and in interaction with them, has yet to be identified.

Despite these obstacles, progress continues. The biological studies of depression are reviewed in this chapter. As in earlier studies, the initial positive findings have often been discounted by later negative findings. One of the problems contributing to contradictory results has been the lack of adequate control of such factors as age, sex, weight, state of nutrition, and type of diet. The lack of control for age, in particular, has been responsible for many positive findings that were later disconfirmed. It has been amply demonstrated that changes in metabolism and physiological responses occur with advancing age; since depressed patients tend to fall into the older age groups, they tend to show responses different from younger control groups.

The major early biological studies of depression are summarized in Table 9-1. In the first edition I attempted to assess the validity of the various findings using a scale: certain, probable, uncertain, and doubtful. None of the findings had as yet had sufficient confirmation to justify the label "certain." To qualify for "probable" validity, a particular finding had to be based on a well-designed study with both proper controls and attention to known sources of error such as diagnostic unreliability. Furthermore, the finding must have been corroborated by well-designed studies by other investigators. When earlier findings based on loosely designed studies were contradicted by well-designed studies, or when a positive finding was more readily explained on the basis of some variable other than depression, the finding was classified as doubtful.

The "uncertain" label applies to areas of conflicting results, inadequate experimental design, or lack of independent confirmation.

Only two findings were assigned the label "probable." The increased steroid secretion warranted this designation, but was not specific for depression. The EEG studies with one exception showed decreased periods of deep sleep; the single contradictory finding may be explained by the administration of sedatives during the testing period.

Manic-Depressive Disorder and Constitution

An early line of research explored the relationship between physical "body type" and manic-depressive psychosis. In this section, we consider correlations that have been found among physique, manic-depressive psychosis, and schizophrenia. A review of methodological limitations is also provided.

The name Ernst Kretschmer has been intimately associated with the theory of the relationship between various types of psychoses and physical type. On the basis of his clinical observations, he postulated that there is a biological relationship between pyknic physique (corresponding to *endomorphic* and *eurymorphic* in later reports) and manic-depressive psychosis. He reported[5] that 81 of 85 schizophrenic patients had a leptosomatic habitus, whereas 58 of 62 manic depressives had a pyknic physique.

A large number of studies were carried out in the ensuing years. Some of these strongly supported Kretschmer's findings, but others provided only partial support or did not support his theory. A thorough critical review of the literature was presented by Rees.[6]

In a study of 100 cases of manic depression, 100 normals, and 100 people diagnosed with schizophrenia, Clegg[7] found only partial support for Kretschmer's theory. Burchard[8] compared a group of 125 manic depressives and 125 schizophrenics. The patients were initially classified on the basis of a global impression of the examiner into pyknic, athletic, and asthenic types. He found an association between the pyknic type and manic-depressive psychoses and between the leptosomatic type and schizophrenia. He was also able to find a statistically significant relationship between the classification of the leptosomatic physique based on anthropometric indices and schizophrenia. He reported, however, that the physical type is influenced by the age of the patient; this finding, of course, casts some doubt on the significance of his results. Wittman, Sheldon, and Katz[9] also found a significant correlation (0.51) between endomorphic (pyknic) physique and manic-depressive disorder. Age was not properly controlled, however.

Anastasi and Foley[10] found a definite tendency toward a more pyknic body build with advancing age; this finding held for both manic depressives and schizophrenics. A similar observation was made by Farber,[11] who studied a number of physical dimensions and ratios in 18 manic depressive patients and

81 schizophrenics. He found that the pyknic physique becomes more common with increasing age. He also suggested that the greater likelihood of physical deterioration among schizophrenic patients could account for their appearing leptosomatic.

Rees[12] compared 42 manic-depressive patients with a group of normal subjects and 49 schizophrenics. Using a variety of physical measures and body-build ratios, he found a greater tendency to eurymorphic (pyknic) build in the manic-depressive group. Rees concluded that this relationship could be explained only partly—not completely—on the basis of age differences, and that there was a hard-core relationship between body build and affective disorder.

In evaluating the aforementioned studies, certain methodological problems should be taken into account: (1) The schizophrenic patients in the studies were younger than the manic depressives. Since there is a transition from leptosomatic to pyknic physique with advancing age, the differences in physique may be due to age. (2) Nutritional status may affect body-build indices. It might be expected that chronic schizophrenics would exhibit more pronounced physical effects than manic depressives as a result of longer duration of hospitalization.[13] Furthermore, if the reports of a relationship between high social class and manic-depressive disorder are valid, the manic depressives might be expected to have had better nutrition during their developmental period. (3) The possibility of contamination or bias was present to some degree in most of the studies. An investigator making ratings of physical indices cannot be oblivious of the presence or absence of affect in the patients and may be influenced by his or her theoretical preconceptions. Furthermore, in making the clinical diagnosis, the investigator may be influenced by the clinical stereotype of the lean, sallow schizophrenic and the rotund cyclothymic (manic depressive). (4) As Rees[6] showed, there are no disparate types corresponding to pyknic and leptosomatic, but there is a continuous graduation from one extreme to the other. (5) Concerning the finding that higher body mass index (BMI) predicted a history of suicide attempts in individuals with bipolar disorder, Fagiolini et al.[14] speculated in 2004 that increased suicide risk may reflect the generally poorer treatment outcome in patients with high BMI. Another possibility is that obesity may independently increase the risk of suicide through its negative psychosocial consequences. These negative consequences could include stigmatization, discrimination, and general negative impact of higher BMI on general physical and psychological well-being.[14]

In sum, there was never a well-designed study to test Kretschmer's findings. With our present state of knowledge it seems clear that the association of endomorphic or eurymorphic physique with depression is an artifact resulting from intermediate variables such as age and nutritional status.

Heredity in Manic-Depressive Disorder

Over half a century ago, a number of writers presented evidence in favor of the theory that some persons are *carriers* of a specific predisposition or vulnerability to manic-depressive psychosis.[15,16] These investigators attempted to demonstrate that the tendency to develop this disease increases in proportion to the degree of blood relationship to a patient with this disorder. The early studies of manic-depressive disorder in general yielded concordance rates consistent with the theory of transmission of the disorder via a dominant gene.[15]

On the basis of his survey of 461 persons, Kallmann used the *twin family* method to compute the following expectancy rates of manic-depressive psychosis among blood relatives of patients with manic-depressive psychosis:

0.4 percent in general population
23.5 percent in parents
16.7 percent in half siblings
23.0 percent in full siblings
26.3 percent in nonidentical twins
100.0 percent in identical twins

Identical Twin Studies

Kallmann[15] isolated a group of 23 manic-depressive patients who were distinguished by their having identical (monozygotic) twin siblings. In 22 cases, the co-twin was also diagnosed as manic depressive. The essential diagnostic feature was the presence of "acute, self-limited, and unadulterated mood swings before the fifth decade of life and no progressive or residual personality disintegration before or following manic or depressive episodes."

A number of problems are raised by Kallmann's twin studies.

The problem of diagnostic unreliability. The possibility of bias by the investigator in making a diagnosis of one twin while having full knowledge of the psychiatric status of the twin-partner must be considered. In Kallmann's study the degree of concordance is surprisingly high in view of the demonstrated low reliability of psychiatric diagnoses. It would be expected that diagnostic variability would have substantially reduced the concordance if completely independent diagnoses were rendered.

The problem of ascertainment of twins. Reliance on the patient's own report for ascertainment of the twins is a source of error. Moreover, the selection of material from resident hospital populations introduces a sampling bias; for example, concordant cases are more likely to come to a hospital than discordant cases because it is a heavier burden for a family to take care of twin psychotics than one psychotic at home.[16] It is possible, furthermore, that Kallmann's attention was more likely to be called to cases in which manic-depressive disorder existed in both twin partners than to cases in which only one partner had the disease. This selective factor could spuriously inflate the obtained concordance.

The problem of determination of zygosity. As Gregory[17] pointed out, there is considerable inaccuracy in the older methods of zygosity determination (identical vs. fraternal twins) used in the psychiatric studies cited above. These inaccuracies have ranged as high as 30 percent as compared with more refined serological typing.

Slater[18] collected a much smaller group of identical twins with affective disorders. He used more refined methods for determining zygosity than did Kallmann, and he also presented more complete data. Of the eight twin pairs, four were concordant for affective disorder. Of the discordant co-twins, three were diagnosed as normal and one as neurotic. The author points out that among the concordant twins there were many dissimilarities in the clinical picture. Although this series is too small to draw any definite conclusions, it should be noted that the degree of concordance (50 percent) was substantially less than the 100 percent expectancy rate presented by Kallmann.

Tienari[17] attempted to correct the methodological inadequacies and plug the loopholes in the previous investigations of mental illness in twins has been reported. His data consisted of all recorded live births in Finland in 1920–1929. The establishment of twinship was based on the birth register. For zygosity determination he used refined serological techniques in addition to the older methods. The investigator found 16 schizophrenic cases and one case of reactive psychosis among the identical twins (no case of affective psychosis was found). The most striking feature of the report is that in not a single instance did the co-twin of a schizophrenic patient also have schizophrenia; the degree of concordance was zero! This finding is remarkable in view of Kallmann's report of a corrected expectancy rate for schizophrenics of 86.2 percent.

The relevance of Tienari's findings to the twin studies of depression is that Kallmann used the same techniques for twinship ascertainment, zygosity determination, and diagnostic labeling in his investigation of manic-depressive psychosis as in his investigation of schizophrenics. If the results of his studies of schizophrenia are invalid, then his findings in manic-depressive psychosis are subject to serious doubt.

Identical Twins Reared Separately

Shields[19] conducted an investigation into genetic and environmental factors and variation in personality. He organized his study so that twins volunteered for the study by sending their names to the British Broadcasting Corporation. Among the volunteers were 44 monozygotic pairs separated in early life and brought up apart. Shields matched this group with 44 nonseparated monozygotic twin pairs who served as controls.

Shields found that the twins reared together were more alike on various personality ratings than the separated pairs. This difference, however, was not statistically significant. He also found that the separated as well as the nonseparated twins had considerable similarity in mannerisms, voice, temperament, and tastes. Certain extreme personality variables, such as quick temper, anxiety, emotional lability, rigidity, and cyclothymic tendencies, showed approximately the same degree of concordance in the separated group as in the nonseparated group.

On a test for extraversion, both the separated and nonseparated pairs showed significant correlations. The correlation coefficient for extraversion was higher (.61) in the separated group than in the control group (.42). Since extraversion is claimed to have some relationship to the premorbid personality of manic-depressive patients, this finding may be of some significance. The separated twins also showed a higher interclass correlation coefficient on a test for neuroticism (.53) then did the nonseparated twins (.38).

The data regarding the concordance of psychiatric disorders among the twins are inconclusive, but it is worthwhile to mention them here. One set of separated twins had psychiatric disturbances with depression and tenseness after the age of 40 and were advised to have treatment in a mental hospital. In three cases, one twin had neurotic-depressive episodes. In summary, one set of twins was concordant for affective disorder and three sets were discordant for affective disorder. Obviously the sample is too small to draw any conclusions.

Pedigree Studies

Stenstedt[20] studied 288 manic-depressive cases. He found that morbidity among the siblings, parents, and children of the patients was 11.7 percent for the males and 11.8 percent for the females. The patients in this study had been admitted to psychiatric hospitals from a Swedish rural area during the years 1919–1948. Various sources of information were explored regarding the patients and their relatives. When there was a possibility of psychiatric disturbance in a relative, the relative was examined. Fourteen families were excluded because of insufficient information. The period of observation ranged from 14 months to more than 20 years.

The morbidity risk for manic-depressive disorder in the investigation district was calculated to be about 1 percent if uncertain cases were included. The morbidity risk among the relatives of the patients was as follows: parents, 7.5 percent; siblings, 14.1 percent; children, 17.1 percent.

Using data from structured interviews of 748 consecutive patients admitted to a psychiatric hospital, Winokur and Pitts[21] attempted to determine the prevalence of affective disorders among relatives of patients diagnosed as having manic-depressive reaction, psychotic-depressive reaction, neurotic-depressive reaction, or involutional reaction. Of the initial sample, 366 patients received one of these diagnoses. Information regarding the prevalence of affective disorders among the relatives of the patients was received either from a relative accompanying the patient or from the patient.

The investigators found a prevalence of affective disorder in 22.9 percent of the mothers of the patients and 13.6 percent of the fathers. They determined that the prevalence of affective disorders in the siblings was much greater when one or both parents had an affective disorder than when neither did. According to the authors, neither a single recessive gene nor a single dominant gene hypothesis is supported by the data.

The study has limitations. (1) Information regarding the prevalence of affective disorder in the relatives was obtained either from a single relative accompanying the patient or from the patient; no other relatives were examined. This leaves a wide area of uncertainty regarding the validity of diagnoses based on data that could be incomplete or biased. (2) The presence of a positive family history of affective disorder could have exerted some influence on the diagnosis of the patient, particularly when the clinical picture was ambiguous. (3) The follow-up of family members did not cover sufficient time to ensure that all members had passed through the *risk period*. (The age of risk as proposed by Fremming[22] ranges from 20 to 65 years.)

A much more recent review by Taylor et al.[23] concludes that, although molecular genetic research has yet to unequivocally identify the specific genes, family, twin, and adoption studies show a clear genetic pathway to bipolar disorder. They report the lifetime prevalence of bipolar disease in the general population to be about 1 percent, compared to family studies that have shown the risk in a first-degree relative of a bipolar proband to be 5 to 10 percent. In monozygotic twins, the probability of developing bipolar disorder is as much as 75 times greater than in the general population. They conclude that future research should take into account multiple genetic loci and the role of environmental factors.

McGuffin et al.[24] explored the genetic etiological overlap of bipolar affective disorder and unipolar depression. *DSM-IV* operational criteria were used to obtain lifetime diagnoses of each mood disorder. They found that the majority of the genetic variance in the development of mania (approximately 71 percent) is specific to the manic syndrome, rather than shared with depression. Concordance rates in their study for Unipolar and Bipolar Disorder are shown in Table 9-2.[24]

TABLE 9-2. Probandwise Concordance for Unipolar (UPD) and Bipolar (BPD)
Affective Disorder (AD)

Proband diagnosis	Co-twin diagnosis Monozygotic (%)				Dizygotic (%)			
	n	UPD	BPD	Total AD	n	UPD	BPD	Total AD
BPD	30	26.7	40	66.7	37	13.5	5.4	18.9
UPD	68	44.1	1.5	45.6	109	20.2	0.0	20.2

Adapted from McGuffin et al. (2003).

Summary

Bipolar Disorder

In reviewing the genetic contribution to bipolar illness, Sevy et al.[25] found strong support for a genetic factor in bipolar illness. In twin and adoption studies, their review reported the mean concordance rate for bipolar disorder to be 69.3% in monozygotic twins, with variation between 50 and 92.5 percent. Mean concordance in dizygotic twins was reported as 20 percent, with variation from 0 to 38.5 percent. Moreover, Sevy et al.[25] cite research showing that bipolar illness expresses itself independently of early environment, since identical twins reared apart tend to be concordant for the disease.

Unipolar Depression

In a review of the genetics of unipolar depression, Wallaceet al.[26] concluded that the genetic contribution is quite substantial. They suggested that, because common general experience leads us to identify apparent reactive or situational causes of depression, the genetic contribution has been neglected. Two recent reports in the *American Journal of Psychiatry* agree very well on the overall heritability of major depression. These include a meta-analysis by Sullivan, Neale, and Kendler (2000), and then a large Swedish national study by Kendler, Gatz, Gardner, and Pedersen (2006). The 2006 study is the only major twin study published after the 2000 review and meta-analysis, and both together suggest a heritability of major depression of about 38 percent.

Biochemical Studies of Depression

Early Studies (1903–1939)

Despite the hundreds of studies of manic-depressive disorder performed during this period, there were no unequivocal findings that related this disorder to any biochemical abnormalities. Cleghorn & Curtis[27] summarized this as follows:

The work of the early twentieth century was performed mainly in the search for somatic pathology to account for manic-depressive psychosis as described by Kraepelin. These can be summarized quickly by saying that every accessible cell, tissue, and fluid was studied by every technique available at the time with negative results. Certain abnormalities of the glucose tolerance curve were found but in no respect did this differ significantly from that found in patients suffering from schizophrenia, anxiety, or the all-inclusive "emotional tension."

In 1939 McFarland and Goldstein[28] presented an exhaustive review of the biochemical studies of manic-depressive psychosis up to that date. These authors presented in tabulated form the negative results, and in descriptive form the positive results, of 134 studies. These studies are summarized below.

Blood Glucose

The authors tabulated 19 studies in which blood glucose was within normal limits. The largest study, by Whitehorn, included 520 cases: 345 were depressed, 151 were manic, and 24 were mixed. In 6 studies the blood glucose was above normal limits.

Glucose Tolerance

The glucose tolerance curve was normal in 5 studies and abnormal in 16 otherss. Kooy found an elevated tolerance curve in cases of melancholia, but he also found equally elevated curves in cases of marked anxiety.

Acidity and Alkaline Reserve

The pH of the blood of manic depressives was within normal limits in 7 studies. One study by Poli of 12 depressives and 10 manics reported constant and marked lowering of pH in excitable states and normal or slightly lowered pH in depressive states. The alkaline reserve was markedly diminished in excitable states and almost normal in depressive states.

Serum Calcium and Phosphorus

These constituents of the blood were found to be normal in 9 studies, but 5 other studies failed to confirm these normal values in the manic depressives. Klemperer, for example, reported that calcium was diminished in agitated melancholia. Cases of melancholia with stupor also had low calcium, but cases of mania had high calcium.

Nitrogenous Substances

Ten studies indicated that the nitrogen metabolism of the manic depressive was within normal limits. Two studies, however, reported abnormal findings.

Looney, for example, tested 30 cases of depression and reported a high plasma content of nitrogenous substance. He expressed the opinion that toxic amines were present in the blood of markedly depressed cases.

Lipoidal Substances

Normal cholesterol values were obtained in 4 studies, and abnormal values in 12 studies. In general, the investigations reporting abnormal values showed hypocholesteremia, and the abnormality could usually be attributed to the degree of activity of the patient.

Chlorides

Blood chlorides were reported as within normal limits in 5 studies. In one study of 11 anxious and depressive psychotics, however, the chloride values in whole blood and in plasma were increased above normal.

Critique of Studies

In analyzing the results of the biochemical studies, McFarland and Goldstein pointed out that manic-depressive patients tended to show both intraindividual and an interindividual variability greater than that by normal controls. Furthermore, there seemed to be indications of a slightly greater variability in the personal constants of the depressive when compared with those of the manic patient. Critical reviews and subsequent, more systematic, studies have substantially discounted the few positive findings reported above.

The abnormal glucose tolerance curve, as pointed out by Cleghorn and Curtis,[27] did not differentiate manic-depressive psychosis from other psychiatric disorders. The defective glucose tolerance was considered by Gildea et al.[29] as an artifact, produced by delayed absorption of the test glucose from the gastrointestinal tract. When they administered glucose intravenously instead of orally, they did not obtain an abnormal glucose tolerance curve. This finding was disputed by Pryce,[30] who also used the intravenous route but found decreased tolerance among depressed patients as compared with a control group. Since glucose tolerance decreases with age, deficiency of carbohydrates in the diet, and chronic malnutrition, the finding of abnormal glucose tolerance in the depressed patients must be interpreted cautiously. The finding of hypocholesteremia was contradicted by Whittier et al.[31]

More Recent Studies (1940–2004)

Differences Between Manic and Depressive Phases

In 1942, Cameron[32] presented a thoughtful review of comparisons of biochemical findings in mania and depression. He criticized the studies primarily on the basis that the so-called clinical entities in the studies had been a collection of many diverse phenomena.

> The usual laboratory experimental reports simply throw together all the results obtained from patients with mood disorders, get an average and perhaps state the deviations and range of determinations and then compare such figures with similar ones obtained from unselected groups diagnosed as schizophrenic. Often no indication whatever is given as to whether individual patients included are overactive or stuporous, resentful or cooperative, fearful or secure, even though the possible effects of such differences are well known to any clinician. No amount of refined statistical treatment can make data presented in such a way of any significance.

Emotional state, especially anxiety and stress reactions, must be considered in making causal attributions. A 2001 review of biological studies in depressed children and adolescents concluded that the effects of stress and reactivity to stress need to be considered in future studies "because these factors by themselves may affect the same biological systems that have been implicated in the aetiology of MDD" (p. 153).[33]

Cameron came to the following conclusions. (1) There is no correlation between basal metabolism and mood but there is some evidence that the basal metabolic rate in affective disorders is related to the degree of general activity, anxiety, and fear. *Manic and depressive patients do not give determinations at opposite ends of the scale.* (2) The blood pressure shows no relation to mood; variability of pressure may be marked in a given person, but the degree of lability does not correlate with lability of mood. (3) Blood pressure reaction to adrenaline indicates some difference between stupors and excitement but not between elation and depression. (4) Blood glucose level determinations after administration of ephedrine produce no significantly different results. (5) Glucose tolerance curves are not correlated with the direction of the mood disorder. (6) Evacuation of barium from the gastrointestinal tract shows differences; depressed patients have considerably delayed evacuation. (7) Significant differences are reported for the rate of parotid gland secretion, with the manic rates falling within the normal range and depressive rates falling well below it. (8) Elevated gastric acidity is reported for manic and agitated depressives and low values for retarded depressives.

In conclusion, Cameron emphasized the fact that the studies did not differentiate between mood disorders as such:

> The contrast most often made in the reports seemed to be associated not with mood differences but with differences in the kind and degree of action involved. Tense or agitated persons thus may show more in common in their biological function with elated and excitable persons than they do with other depressive syndromes. This is not compatible with the hypothesis that elation and depression are fundamentally opposed metabolical processes.

In the 1950s and 1960s there was much investigation of water and electro-lyte metabolism in depression, although the exhaustive reviews of the litera-ture by McFarland and Goldstein in 1939[28] indicated that plasma electrolytes are within normal limits in depressed patients.

Studies of Continued Cycles

A systematic attempt to ascertain changes in metabolism in association with changes in the mental status was first made by Gjessing[34] in cases of *periodic catatonia*. By placing his patients on a fixed intake of food and fluid over a period of many months, it was possible for him to make a detailed balance study during several cycles of the biphasic illness.

Other researchers applied Gjessing's technique to a number of manic-depressive patients who showed rapid alterations of mood. In these cases, a period of depression and retardation of a few days' duration was followed by a normal interval of one or more days and then by a short period of elation and overactivity. These cycles continued to repeat themselves over many months or years.

The first studies in depressives were stimulated by the ancient observation that the urinary output tends to be low during the depressed phase and high during the manic phase. Despite the obvious explanation that the difference may be attributed to the fact that manic patients tend to drink more than depressed patients, investigators sought a more important reason to account for the differences in urinary output.

Klein and Nunn[35] studied a 67-year-old patient who had unfailing regularity of the rhythm of his manic-depressive cycles each week for 14 years. Clinical observation, continued over a period of months, had shown a period of five days of depression followed by two of mania. The writers undertook parallel clinical and biochemical investigations to correlate metabolic changes coinci-dental with the variations in his mental state. Various autonomic changes were associated with the mood changes; during the manic phases there was a defi-nite rise in blood pressure, pulse, and respiratory rate.

For a period of several months, this patient was given a constant balanced diet and a constant fluid intake. Urine collections were made at 12-hour inter-vals. He showed a cyclic metabolic fluctuation consisting of retention of water and salt in the depressive phase and release in the manic phase. This was accompanied by weight gain during the depression and corresponding weight loss during the manic phase. The sudden rise in the flow of urine started when the patient was still in his depression and was maintained at this high rate during the early stages of his manic phase. By the time he had reached the most excited state, however, the rate of urinary excretion had already decreased.

Klein described a second case in 1950. The patient was a 40-year-old male who had recurrent attacks of depression and mania, varying in duration over a period of five years. A depressive attack usually lasted about 13 days and was followed by a manic phase lasting 18 days. The manic phase was followed by about 14 days of normal mood. This patient was also studied on bed rest, with a constant diet of food and fluid. In contradistinction to the first case, there was no evidence of any fluid or electrolyte retention at any stage of the cycle.

In 1959, Crammer[36] reported a metabolic study of two chronic psychotic patients with recurring mental disturbances who showed periodic weight losses and gains associated with the particular phases of the illness. Weight loss was accompanied by polyuria with increased urinary excretion of sodium chloride, weight gain by oliguria and sodium retention. In one patient, weight loss occurred at the beginning of an attack of depression; in the other, weight loss began just before emergence from a depressive, semistuporous state into a hypomanic state.

Studies During Depressive Episodes

A number of researchers pursued biochemical correlates of depression in the 1960s. Gibbons[37] investigated a group of 24 patients who "showed the clinical picture of so-called endogenous depression." He found that upon recovery from depression there was a decrease in exchangeable sodium. No consistent change in total exchangeable potassium was found. The author concluded that the results supported the hypothesis that depression is accompanied by retention of sodium that is excreted during recovery.

Russell[38] investigated 15 depressed patients by the metabolic balance technique for periods of two to five weeks, during which time they received electroconvulsive treatment. He found that the patients showed a slight loss of sodium that was not statistically significant during the period of recovery.

Coppen and Shaw[39] studied 23 patients with "severe unremitting depressions." They found that residual sodium, which includes intracellular and some bone sodium, was very significantly increased during depression. Exchangable sodium and extracellular sodium did not change significantly. The total body water, extracellular fluid, and extracellular chloride were all greater after recovery.

Lobban et al.[40] studied chloride, sodium, and potassium excretion in 20 depressed patients and compared them with 25 neurotic controls. It was found that the depressives excreted less sodium and chloride than the control groups during the day and more at night. They concluded that depressed patients showed a disturbance of the diurnal rhythm of electrolyte excretion that is not secondary to changes in behavior or diet. Of course, it could be argued that the differences between the two groups could be a sign of disturbance of the diurnal rhythm of the control group of neurotics rather than of the depressed patients.

Anderson and Dawson[41] reported that about half of a series of 98 depressives had a high blood level of acetylmethylcarbinal. This finding was contradicted by a study by Assael and Thein[42] that did not reveal a significant increase of this acetaldehyde metabolite in depression.

Flach[43] investigated the calcium metabolism in 57 patients maintained on a constant control diet on a metabolic unit. He found that following the administration of electroconvulsive treatment or imipramine therapy for the alleviation of depression, there was an associated significant decrease in the urinary excretion of calcium. This change was also noted in paranoid schizophrenic patients, but not in patients diagnosed as psychoneurotic. The changes, moreover, were apparent in patients who improved on therapy but were lacking among those who failed to improve clinically during the period of study.

Cade[44] reported a significant elevation of plasma magnesium levels in schizophrenia and depressive states but not in manic patients. This finding, which persisted after clinical remission, could be the result of age differences, which were not controlled in this study.

The many reports of successful treatment of manic patients with lithium ion gives further evidence that changes in electrolytes may be important in affective disorders. During the manic phase the patients have an unusually high tolerance for lithium. With the resolution of the mania this tolerance disappears and is accompanied by a massive excretion of lithium.[45] Although the mechanisms of action of the lithium ion in the treatment of mania have no immediate explanation, these findings are under investigation.

An Experimental Test of Biological Markers

According to Gibbons,[46] any electrolyte changes in depression are probably *secondary effects* of the illness. Some may result from changes in the amount and composition of the diet or from the variation in motor activity. Others may be the result of the affective disturbance.

Consistent with Gibbons's[46] point on differentiating "secondary" from primary effects of depression, two decades later Mullen et al.[47] conducted an experimental investigation of two common biological markers of depression, the dexamethasone suppression test (DST) and the rapid eye movement (REM) latency test.

Accompaniments of depression often include sleep disorder and poor appetite with concomitant weight loss due to reduced calorie intake. Yet decreased REM latency and cortisol responses to dexamethasone have been used in clinical practice as diagnostic aids, or "biological markers," of depression. Mullen et al. asked whether the DST and REM latency tests could be artifacts arising from dietary and sleep disturbances, rather than specific markers for clinical depression.

To answer this query, 28 normal volunteers were assigned to either sleep deprivation or calorie restriction. The sleep deprivation imitated the pattern of sleep disturbance typical of major depressive disorders. They first maintained a regular sleep-wake cycle for two weeks, then sleep time was delayed by an hour and they were wakened two hours earlier than usual.

The calorie restriction procedure limited calorie intake for 18 days to 1,000 to 1,200 kcal per day.

Sleep disruption shortened REM latency, thus replicating the shortened latency used clinically as a diagnostic indicator of depression. In addition, calorie restriction was found to induce a response to dexamethasone like that which had been considered diagnostic of clinical depression.

Despite the fact that this study proved nonspecificity, the authors conceded the possibility that the biology of depression and calorie restriction may be mediated separately. Put differently, nonsuppression of cortisol levels in response to dexamethazone may be caused by either depression or weight loss, but with causal connections through independent mechanisms. Regardless whether this is the case, the coexistence of sleep disruption and calorie restriction during depressed states eliminates any clinical utility of the DST to provide independent diagnostic information on the presence of depression.[47]

Responses of Normal Subjects to Stress

Schottstaedt et al.[48] found that depression-inducing life experiences, whether occurring in the natural course of events or artificially in the laboratory, are associated with abnormal patterns of renal excretion of water and electrolytes. The evoked reactions in the five subjects consisted of reduced physical activity, attitudes of futility or hopelessness, and feelings of depression or exhaustion. These were associated with decreased rates of excretion of water, sodium, and potassium, as compared with the excretion rates observed during neutral and tranquil periods.

It seems that in some cases of alternating mania and depression, variations of water and sodium metabolism parallel the fluctuations in mood. But studies using the metabolic balance technique in single attacks of depressive illness have failed to reveal such variation. Some studies with radiosodium indicate that there may be some alteration in sodium metabolism. In general, the investigations provide equivocal evidence of disturbance of water and mineral metabolism in depression. The specific findings reported above need further confirmation by independent studies. Even in the case of confirmed positive findings, it is difficult to assess the significance of changes in water and mineral metabolism because these may be secondary to abnormalities known to be associated with the depression. Among these deviations are poor food and fluid intake; reduction in physical activity; and increased steroid secretion. With regard to food intake, Mullen et al.[47] demonstrated experimentally that caloric restriction causes identical effects on cortisol levels in response to dexamethazone compared to that found in clinical depression.

Endocrine Studies

Steroid Metabolism

There is substantial evidence that changes in steroid metabolism accompany certain phases of depression as well as other psychiatric disorders. Some evidence suggests that an excess of adrenal hormones may produce psychiatric disturbances. Other evidence suggests that the excess adrenal hormones may be the result of, rather than the cause of, a psychiatric disturbance.

A possible association between the "humours" and mental disorder has been postulated since ancient times. Almost every newly isolated hormone has been used in an effort to treat psychiatric disorders, with inevitable failure. The development of techniques for isolating steroids in the blood and urine, as well as the introduction of steroids into the treatment of various medical conditions, has focused attention in the last half-century on the relationship between steroids and psychiatric disorders.

In 1963, Michael and Gibbons[49] presented a comprehensive review of the relationship of steroids to psychiatric disorders. They pointed out that the experience of emotion by healthy subjects is associated with a rise in the plasma level of 17-hydroxycorticoids. This increase in adrenocortical activity occurs both when the emotional arousal is produced spontaneously in response to naturally occurring environmental events and when it is induced experimentally. An increase in the plasma level of cortisol or the urinary excretion of 17-hydroxycorticoids, for instance, has been reported in the following stressful situations: in hospitalized patients just prior to major surgical procedures; in relatives accompanying severely ill or injured members of their family to the emergency room of a hospital; in students anticipating or following examinations; and in boat-race crews just prior to a race. Increases in steroid secretion have also been noted in reaction to experimentally induced stress in the laboratory. Subjects admitted to the hospital for a sleep deprivation experiment were found to have a rise in their blood steroid levels before beginning the actual experiment. Moderate rises in the steroid level have been reported among patients subjected to stressful interviews. The level of the plasma steroids correlates more closely with the intensity of the affect (anxiety, anger, or depression) aroused than with any specific affect. Emotional arousal, in general, rather than any particular type of emotional reaction or any particular type of stress-inducing stimulus, seems to be responsible for the increased steroid levels.

Michael and Gibbons point out that notable increases in plasma steroids occur in anxious and depressed patients and in acute schizophrenic patients showing emotional turmoil. Chronic schizophrenic patients, however, displaying no appreciable disturbance of affect, have steroid levels within the normal range. Improvement of depressed patients seems to be accompanied by a decrease in the adrenal cortical activity. Adrenalectomized patients who are maintained on adequate doses of steroids experience a more serene emotional life and less fluctuation in moods than before their illness. This finding suggested to Michael and Gibbons that the changes in adrenocortical function that accompany emotion may have a role in determining the emotional experience.

Board et al.[50] demonstrated that plasma cortisol levels were higher in depressed patients than in normal controls. The more emotional stress observed in the patient, the higher the observed steroid level. On subsequent testing, the steroid level generally fell, although a few patients who had received electroconvulsive therapy showed increasing levels. Curtis et al.[51] investigated the relationship between urinary 17-hydroxycorticoids and various affective states. They found steroid excretion higher in the anxiety cases than in the depressed patients.

Gibbons and McHugh[52] measured the plasma cortisol at weekly intervals in 17 depressed patients during 18 periods of stay in the hospital. The authors found elevated levels of plasma cortisol. In general, the more severe the depression the higher the cortisol level. The 18 cases' recovery from depression was accompanied by a decline in cortisol level. Kurland[53] conducted serial studies of urinary steroid excretion in five neurotic-depressed patients and five manic-depressed patients. He found the excretion of 17-ketogenic steroids for the total group of 10 patients significantly correlated with the clinical depressive symptomatology. He also reported that the diurnal variation in the excretion of these compounds followed the usual diurnal variation recorded in the mood of depressed patients: the highest rate occurred during the early morning hours and decreased progressively throughout the day and night.

Gibbons[54] measured plasma cortisol in 15 depressed patients. Elevated secretion rates were found before treatment; these were higher in the more severely depressed patients. In 10 patients, relief of depression was accompanied by a substantial decrease in the secretion rate.

In a series of studies, Bunney and his coworkers demonstrated the relationship between steroid secretion and depression. In one study Bunney et al.[55] investigated the relationship between urinary steroid excretion and behavioral ratings. Seven patients were followed during periods of psychotic depressive crises. In general, they found that the onset of a depressive crisis was accompanied by a substantial increase in 17-hydroxycorticoid excretion.

In another investigation, Bunney et al.[56] studied the behavioral and biochemical changes in a patient with 48-hour manic-depressive cycles. The 17-hydroxycorticoid excretion levels were found to alternate regularly every other day in the opposite direction from 24-hour ratings of mania. On the high manic days the 17-hydroxycorticoid levels were low, and on the immobile depressed days the levels were high.

Bunney and Fawcett[57] also investigated the relationship between successful suicide and previous excretion of excessive 17-hydroxycorticoid levels. Three patients who committed suicide but who had previously showed relatively low ratings of suicidal behavior revealed high mean 17-hydroxycorticoids just prior to their suicides.

A 2003 review by Tiemeier[58] suggests that the most reliable finding in biological psychiatry is the association between depression and disturbance of the hypothalamic-pituitary-adrenal axis. Moreover, a review of longitudinal studies indicates that an increased risk of relapse correlates with endocrine dysfunction.

Despite the large body of studies on the biological correlates, little is known about causal relations. Thus, there is a need for prospective population-based studies to help elucidate etiological mechanisms. Such studies must include cohorts free of depression at baseline.[58] In addition, the neuroendocrine aspects of acute depressions may differ from that found in chronic mood disorders.[59] This requires independent studies of acute and chronic depression, rather than mixing patients of both types into one analysis.

Thyroid Function

There has been no consistent evidence of thyroid dysfunction in depression. Brody and Man[60] found that the serum protein bound iodine (PBI) of depressed schizophrenics did not differ significantly from that of nondepressed schizophrenics or normals. Gibbons et al.[61] found no significant differences between 17 depressives and normal controls. Most patients showed a slight decline in PBI upon recovery from the depression.

However, more recently, Joffe et al.[62] did report changes in thyroid hormone levels in response to cognitive therapy for major depression, consistent with the effect on the thyroid axis found in various somatic antidepressant treatments of depression. Decreases in levels were found in 17 patients who responded to therapy, and increases in 13 who did not respond. The implications of this finding are not clear, with two possible interpretations suggested by the authors: decreases in thyroid hormone levels may be epiphenomenal and not related to the biological activities that result in treatment response, or they may be one part in a cascade of biological actions that lead to improvement in depression.[62]

From a large number of investigations it is apparent that increased steroid output is associated with depression, and that the greater the degree of depression the greater the steroid output. It has also been observed that the steroid levels decrease substantially following improvement or recovery. But the increase in adrenal steroid output is by no means specific for depression. It has also been found in cases of anxiety and in disturbed schizophrenics. It seems to be related more to the intensity of the affect than to the specific kind of affect. An exception, however, is the finding that the steroid levels are low in many cases of mania.

No significant abnormalities of thyroid function have been demonstrated in depressed patients.

Autonomic Function

Blood Pressure Responses to Mecholyl

In 1954, Funkenstein[63] reported that he and his coworkers had demonstrated a relationship between blood pressure reactivity and depression. Although a number of techniques were used, the one that was employed by most subsequent investigators measured the response in blood pressure to an injection of Mecholyl. This procedure was referred to as the *Funkenstein test.*

The test consists of measurement of blood pressure at specific intervals before and after intramuscular administration of Mecholyl. A positive response is defined as an excessive drop in blood pressure and a prolonged rate of return to the normal level. Funkenstein reported this effect in 32 of 36 (88.9 percent) manic-depressive or involutional patients. He attributed this response to an excessive secretion of an epinephrine-like substance. He regarded the remaining 4 cases as showing evidence of an excessive secretion of norepinephrine. He also reported a relationship between an epinephrine-like response and a favorable outcome after electroconvulsive therapy. Another related finding was that students showing intrapunitive behavior in response to stress had an epinephrine-like pattern, whereas those showing extrapunitive responses had a norepinephrine pattern.

As has often been observed in the history of medicine, the early reports were enthusiastic and tended to support Funkenstein's findings. After several years, however, discrepant results were reported, and serious doubts were raised regarding the reliability of the test procedures and the validity of the findings. In a critical review of the literature up to 1958, Feinberg[64] summarized the methodological inadequacies of the studies and the contradictory results. He also suggested that the relationship between the epinephrine-like pattern and depression might be a reflection of the fact that the depressed patients tended to be older than the patients in the comparison groups. Since an epinephrine-like pattern is shown in elderly normals as well as in patients in the older age groups, the relationship between depression and the particular physiological response could be spurious. Attempts were made to improve the methodology and the design of investigations using the Funkenstein Test; these improved investigations used more objective criteria in estimating the degree of depression and assessing the changes in blood pressure. Hamilton[65] found a correlation of .42 between age and the drop in blood pressure following the injection of Mecholyl.

A critical review of the literature by Rose[66] in 1962 failed to quell any of the doubts raised by Feinberg[64] and Hamilton[65] regarding the validity of Funkenstein's findings. In a well-designed study incorporating a partial blockade of the autonomic ganglia, Rose demonstrated that the drop in blood pressure following Mecholyl administration could not be attributed to central autonomic activity but was probably related to peripheral end-organ sensitivity. This finding tends to vitiate Funkenstein's thesis that depressed patients secrete excessive amounts of epinephrine.

Further doubt of the validity of the theory underlying use of the Funkenstein Test was raised by direct measurement of the output of adrenaline and noradrenaline. Funkenstein postulated that the vascular responses of depressed patients resemble those induced by an injection of adrenaline and are, therefore, indicative of excessive adrenaline secretion. Curtis et al.,[51] however, found that the adrenaline excretion of depressed patients was *lower* than that of other psychiatric patients; in addition, contrary to Funkenstein's thesis that adrenaline excretion was higher in depression than in other psychiatric states.

Salivation Studies

Complaints of dryness of the mouth have been noted by psychiatrists examining depressed patients. Between the late 1950s and early 1960s, a number of studies were conducted to determine whether there is any objective evidence of diminution of salivary secretion among depressed patients.

Strongin and Hinsie[67] attempted to compare the parotid gland secretory rate in manic-depressive patients with that of deteriorated schizophrenics and normal controls. A suction cup was applied to the parotid duct, and saliva was collected. The authors concluded that the depressed patients showed decreases in salivation as compared to the nondepressed sample. In a more refined study, Peck[68] used dental swabs to absorb the total salivary flow. Three dental rolls were placed in the mouth of each subject for a period of two minutes. Allowances were made for evaporation, and the rolls were weighed to determine the amount of salivary absorption. The test was applied to a heterogeneous group containing depressed and nondepressed patients. It was found that the depressed patients showed a diminished salivary secretion.

Gottlieb and Paulson[69] applied Peck's technique to 18 hospitalized patients with the diagnosis of depressive reaction. The patients were tested again following recovery from the depression. It was found that 8 patients had increased salivary secretions and 10 had decreased salivary secretions after recovery; there was no significant difference between salivation rates when ill and recovered.

Busfield and Wechsler[70] studied 87 patients. Of the 45 judged to be significantly depressed, 20 were diagnosed as having schizoaffective reaction and 25 as having neurotic or psychotic-depressive reaction; 23 were rated as mildly depressed, 14 as moderately depressed, and 8 as severely depressed. The depressed group was compared with 42 nondepressed patients (16 diagnosed as schizophrenic and 26 with other diagnoses). Salivary secretion was measured by using dental rolls. It was found that the depressed hospitalized patients showed significantly less salivation than did the nondepressed hospitalized patients or the normal controls. There was not, however, any significant difference among the mildly, moderately, and severely depressed patients. In another report, Busfield et al.[71] attempted to differentiate between reactive and endogenous depressions on the basis of the salivation. They found that the group of endogenous depressions showed a significantly lower salivation rate than did the reactive group.

Davies and Gurland[72] found that 30 depressed patients had slightly *higher* salivation than 11 schizophrenics. Both groups, however, secreted significantly less saliva than normal controls (age not stated). Palmai and Blackwell[73] measured the salivary flow in 20 female patients with a diagnosis of depressive illness. Controls were selected from the female nursing staff and, according to the authors, were "matched for age and weight." However, no statement was made as to the range of weight or mean weight in the two groups. The investigators found that the depressed patients showed significantly diminished flow throughout the 24 hours compared to controls. There was a gradual recovery in flow on return to the normal diurnal rhythm during treatment with ECT.

Critique of Salivation Studies

(1) Studies in which comparison groups were used did not adequately control factors such as age, sex, diet, or state of oral hygiene. Many of the differences shown, such as the difference between endogenous and reactive groups, may be accounted for in part or in total by the age discrepancy. It has been well established that in the older age groups there is a notable decrease in the salivation rate of normal people.[74] (2) The longitudinal studies (Gottlieb vs. Davies) show a definite discrepancy. In the former there was no significant change in salivation with recovery, whereas the latter reported an increase in salivation was reported. (3) Age-specific values for the excretion of saliva had not been established and there is no evidence, in any event, that the degree of salivation reported was abnormally low. (4) No consideration was given to the

presence of oral disorders such as pyorrhea (periodontitis), dental caries, and stomatitis, frequently found in chronic mental disorders, especially depression; these certainly may influence the activity of the salivary glands. (5) There was no attempt to control for smoking habits. Experimenters have found that the amount of saliva in the mouths of smokers is substantially increased. (6) The nature of food ingested prior to the salivation tests could influence the results. It is well known that depressed patients ingest less water and food than normals.

Neurophysiological Studies

Sedation Threshold

In a series of articles, Shagass reported on the use of a procedure designed to differentiate among various psychopathological groups. The procedure consists of determining the sedation threshold of the patient in terms of the amount of amobarbital sodium required to produce a specified increase in frontal EEG activity. In a study of 182 patients reported in 1956, Shagass et al.[75] found that the threshold for the psychotic depressives was low, and that for neurotic depressives and anxiety states was high. Shagass concluded that the *sedation threshold test* could be used as an objective test to differentiate between neurotic and psychotic depressions.

A number of studies since the original reports by Shagass cast some doubt on the validity of his conclusion. Ackner and Pampiglione[76] performed the sedation threshold test on 50 psychiatric patients. They failed to find any significant relationship between the sedation threshold and any of the diagnostic groups. Nymgaard[77] reported that the mean sedation threshold of a group of 44 psychotic depressives was significantly lower than that of a group of 24 neurotic depressives. It is noteworthy, however, that the mean age of the psychotic depressives was 49, whereas that of the neurotic depressives was 37. Martin and Davies[78] determined the sleep threshold by intravenous sodium amytal for 30 depressed patients and 12 normal controls. The depressed patients were categorized as endogenous, reactive, or indeterminate. The writers found no significant difference in the sedation threshold among the various groups. Martin and Davies reported another study on the sedation threshold in 1965. As in their previous report, they failed to find any difference between the neurotic and psychotic depressions in the sedation threshold. Friedman et al.[79] measured the sedation threshold in a group of paranoid and depressed patients. In an initial comparison, it was found that the depressed sample had a significantly lower sedation threshold than the paranoid sample. Friedman[80] found, however, that the difference disappeared when the two groups were equated for age. Friedman, incidentally, found a correlation of 0.22 between age and sedation threshold score.

The work on the sedation threshold yielded contradictory results. On the basis of the findings, it seems there was no solid experimental support for the hypothesis that there is a significant difference in the sedation threshold of the neurotic and psychotic depressions. Whatever differences were reported may be attributed to the age difference between the neurotic and psychotic depressives and to the fact that the sedation threshold tends to increase with age.

Anatomical Studies

More recently, several preliminary studies have explored the possibility that depression is related to neurological damage to specific areas of the brain. In 2004, Farley[81] provided a review of several studies of such changes associated with depression. He cited research by psychiatrist Yvette Sheline, in which brain scans were performed on 10 women suffering from recurring bouts of severe depression. The hippocampus was found to be up to 15 percent smaller in the women with recurrent depression, compared to 10 women who served as matched controls. Moreover, there was a positive correlation between reduced hippocampal size and the length of time the women had suffered depressive episodes.[82]

Farley's review[81] suggests that there are at least two ways to account for this finding. McEwen and Sapolsky[83] suggest that hippocampal neurons may be reduced in response to stress and the consequent increase of cortisol. Another possibility relates to findings that show an enlarged amygdala in people prone to depression. The same neuropeptide that triggers cortisol release during stress is also produced by the amygdala. Thus, enlargement and over-activity in this brain structure could be responsible for the activation of the cycle leading to damage to the hippocampus.[81]

Frodl's Study

Frodl et al.[84] conducted a study entitled "Hippocampal and Amygdala Changes in Patients with Major Depressive Disorder and Healthy Controls During a 1-Year Follow-Up." The study was intended to help determine whether depression relates to reduction of hippocampus size, or whether a smaller hippocampus might predispose a person to the development of depression.

From March 2000 through August 2002, 30 patients with *DSM-IV* major depressive disorder were compared to 30 healthy people of comparable age, gender, and handedness. High-resolution magnetic resonance imaging (MRI) was used to examine these 60 individuals at admission to the hospital and one year later. The imaging compared changes in the two groups on hippocampal and amygdala volumes. No volume changes were found in either group overall between baseline and one-year follow-up.

However, in the 12 (of 30) depressed patients who had not improved at the time of follow-up compared to those who had improved (18 of 30), significantly reduced left and right hippocampal volumes were detected by MRI at both baseline and follow-up. Also, people in the healthy control group were found to have significantly larger right hippocampal volumes compared to people whose depression had not improved during the one-year follow-up period. Thus, smaller hippocampal size predicted poor outcome.[84]

Frodl et al. (p. 498)[84] speculated that their study could have contained a bias in that more patients who had a good treatment outcome may have participated in the follow-up part of the study. This would account for the finding that, overall, the two groups did not differ on changes in hippocampal and amygdala volumes between baseline and one-year follow-up. They conclude by suggesting that their study is consistent with the possibility that smaller hippocampal volume predisposes to depression, that the number of previous depressive episodes may correlate with extent of hippocampal volume loss, and that such loss is then implicated in the recurrence of depression. This is in accord with the finding that the patients whose mood did not improve (nonremitted patients) were primarily those with recurrent depression, and that nonremitted, depressed patients showed reduced hippocampal volumes at baseline and follow-up (p. 497).

Other studies have found further anatomical differences in other brain regions in people with clinical depression. These include abnormally small neurons and fewer glial cells in the prefrontal cortex. It is not clear whether stress could be responsible as well for these anatomical anomalies, but, in any case, the observed neurodegeneration may account for many of the negative ruminations and other cognitive patterns observed in depression.[81]

Neurotrophic and Neurogenesis Theories

Related to the line of research on anatomical aberrations noted above, Farley[81] cited other research and theorizing about "neurotrophic" (keeping cells alive) and "neurogenesis" (stimulating growth of new cells). Duman et al.[85] proposed that antidepressant medications may work through the mechanism of keeping cells alive in the hippocampus. Consistent with this hypothesis, Santarelli et al.[86] found in mice that disrupting antidepressant-induced neurogenesis blocks behavioral responses to fluoxetine.

The possibility that antidepressants could have a neuroprotective effect was investigated by Sheline et al.[87] In 38 female outpatients with major depression, high resolution magnetic resonance imaging was used to compare hippocampal gray matter volumes during times when antidepressant treatment was received and times when it was not. Results showed that longer durations of untreated depressive episodes were associated with reduced hippocampal volume, suggesting that antidepressants may have a neuroprotective effect during depression.

Duman suggested that the time it takes to induce neurogenesis is equivalent to the time (three to four weeks) it takes depressed mice to improve in response to the antidepressant Prozac. The apparent causal sequence is as follows. (1) Prozac raises serotonin levels; (2) elevated serotonin increases the protein CREB in nerve cells; (3) CREB augments the level of growth factor BDNF (brain-derived neurotrophic factor); (4) BNDF stimulates the development of new hippocampal cells. Consistent with this line of thought, several other treatments that have been shown to alleviate depressive symptoms (other classes of antidepressants and ECT) likewise have been found to increase BDNF.[81,88,89]

On a cautionary note, Duman[90] reminds us of several inconclusive aspects of this line of research. (1) verification that adult neurogenesis facilitates brain function is based mostly on correlational studies; (2) the degree of neurogenesis in the adult human brain is inconclusive, and the functional relevance in primates still an open question; (3) the influence of neurogenesis and hippocampal volume in depression has not been determined; and (4) atrophy and cell loss in mood disorders are not limited to the hippocampus.

Jacobs[91] outlined the research program necessary to test the present theory. He provided several questions for empirical evaluation. (1) the dentate gyrus (DG) is the part of the hippocampus thought to be critical in the laying down of new cognitions. Does DG neurogenesis slow when patients are in depressive episodes and return to normal when depression remits? New imaging techniques must first be developed to test this question. (2) If such correlative data were found through adequate imaging techniques (i.e., definitive correlation between neurogenesis and depressive episode), the next test would be to observe whether experimental manipulation of cell proliferation affects depressive episodes. (3) Finally, researchers would need answers to other related questions, such as the following. (a) Do effective depression treatments lose their potency if neurogenesis is pharmacologically suppressed? (b) Do new drugs that facilitate neurogenesis serve as potent antidepressants? (c) Will the nonpharmacological therapies known to augment neurogenesis be more fully tested to determine antidepressant efficacy? (d) Does the neurogenesis theory explain equally all the different types of clinical depression? (e) Is DG cell loss mediated exclusively by adrenal hormones, or are other neurochemicals involved that can likewise become targets for biological therapies? (f) Will the specificity of neurogenesis to the hippocampus be tested?[91]

Electromyograph (EMG) Studies

In 1959, Whatmore and Ellis[92] reported their measurment of "residual motor activity" of depressed patients by means of the electromyograph. They found that in either an agitated or a retarded state the residual motor activity of the depressed patients was at abnormally high levels. The investigators also found, however, that the *invisible* motor activity tends to increase with age. This finding again indicates the importance of controlling for age in studies of this type.

Three years later, Whatmore and Ellis[93] presented a longitudinal study of depressed patients with severe recurrent depressions. They found that during the period of depression the EMG readings were markedly elevated. Accompanying treatment there was a temporary drop in the readings. During the period of well-being following treatment and prior to relapse the readings were markedly *elevated*.

Goldstein[94] made basal recordings of muscle action potential during 15 minutes of rest and also in response to a noise stimulus. She found that of the various psychiatric patients the depressed patients showed the most pronounced skeletal muscular response during the noise. Autonomic activity during both rest and stimulation was also heightened in the depressed patients.

Electroencephalogram (EEG) Sleep Studies

In 1946, Diaz-Guerrero et al.[95] performed continuous sleep recordings of the entire night's sleep of six patients diagnosed as having manic-depressive psychosis, depressive type, and compared the data with those obtained from normal subjects. The investigators found considerable variability among the patients in terms of the percentage of time that each type of electroencephalographic (EEG) tracing appeared during the entire night's recording. This variability became less when the waking records were excluded and only the tracings that occurred during sleep were considered.

The authors found that the patients had almost twice as much low voltage activity as the normal controls and approximately one-half as much spindle plus random activity as the normal controls. In a comparison of the minute-by-minute fluctuations from one EEG pattern or level to another, they found that the fluctuations for the patients were more frequent than those for the controls. The percentage of the minutes that contained two or more of the EEG sleep levels during the night's sleep was nearly twice as great for the patients as for the normal controls.

The authors concluded that the disturbed sleep of patients with manic-depressive psychosis is characterized not only by difficulty in falling asleep and by early or frequent awakening but also by a greater proportion of light sleep. In addition, the patients showed more frequent oscillation from one level of sleep to another than did the normal controls.

Almost 20 years later, Oswald et al.[96] conducted a study of the sleeping patterns of depressive patients compared to those of matched normals. Continuous nocturnal recordings of EEG, eye movement, and bed movement were carried out on six normal controls. The six psychiatric patients, ranging in age from 33 to 67 years, had in common a depressive component of their illness, although they differed considerably in terms of the rest of the psychiatric picture. Each patient was matched with a corresponding paid control of the same sex. Four women and two men were in each group, and the age differences between patient and control ranged from three to eight years.

According to the authors, all patients were suffering from an autonomous melancholia. In an expanded definition of this condition, the authors stated that the patient had

> an illness of a kind which we believe may sometimes develop in the absence of severe environmental stress, while in others it may be clearly provoked by circumstances. But the illness as it develops may take on a form which becomes largely independent of the environmental circumstances, and may continue even when the provoking factors are past. It has become an *autonomous melancholia.* It will be apparent that by autonomous melancholia we mean an illness shown by clinical experience to respond especially well to electroplexy.

The experiment was carried out over a period of five nights. On the first night, intended for adaptation to the laboratory setting, electrodes were attached but no recording was made. On the following four nights recordings were made. The investigators were interested not only in natural sleep but also in the effects of barbiturates on sleep patterns. Consequently, the patients and the control group received either heptabarbitone or dummy tablets. A total of 48 records were obtained. "Blind interpretation" of the EEG was carried out by the senior author. There were several significant findings. (1) The patients spent significantly more minutes awake than did the controls; (2) the percentage of time spent by the patients in paradoxical sleep (REM sleep) and frequency of shifts in the depths of sleep were not significantly different from those of the controls; and (3) when the patients did sleep, they spent a significantly larger percentage of time in the *deeper* stage of sleep (Stage E) than did the controls. Heptobarbitone greatly decreased the duration of REM periods and also the frequency of eye movements within these periods. The drug decreased the duration of time awake, especially in patients in the early hours of the morning, and decreased the frequency of body movement.

In addition to substantiating clinical observations that depressed patients sleep less than do normals, the study was notable in that it showed that when the patients did sleep, they showed a higher percentage of sleep in the deeper stages than did the normals (contrary to the findings of Diaz-Guerrero et al.). The authors explained this particular finding as a kind of compensation for the sleep deprivation. Among the limitations of this study are (1) the small number of patients included; (2) the broad criteria for inclusion of patients in the psychiatric group; (3) the use of a normal control group rather than nondepressed psychiatric controls (consequently, it is difficult to know whether the findings are specific for depressed patients or characteristic of psychiatric patients generally); and (4) since all the patients had electroconvulsive therapy at some times during their illness, there is a question as to whether these treatments might have in some way influenced the EEG recordings.

Another study, reported in 1964, of the effect of depressive disorders on sleep EEG responses was conducted by Zung et al.[97] The sample consisted of 11 hospitalized men ranging in age from 37 to 69 years. The characteristics of the normal control subjects are not specified. In one part of the study the patients served as their own controls. The diagnostic criteria were more rigorous than those in Oswald's study. "The diagnosis of the depressive disorder was made clinically, based upon the presence of a pervasive depressed affect and its physiological and psychological concomitants." The specific criteria used were specified and included 20 indices of depression; no reliability studies were cited, however. In addition, the patients quantitated the severity of their own symptoms by means of a self-rating depression scale.

Observations and analyses were made of continuous EEG records obtained from an entire night's undisturbed sleep. On the second consecutive night, pretaped sounds of approximately equal intensity were played at various stages of sleep. For six of the patients these studies were repeated after remission of the symptoms.

Results were as follows. (1) Mean time from retiring to sleep state was 20 minutes (range 7.5–63 minutes); mean duration of sleep, seven hours; and the number of fluctuations between Stage E (the deepest stage) to Stage A (the lightest stage), 11 per patient. (2) The distributions of the sleep recorded in A, B, C, D, and E were 26.6, 20.2, 20.5, 23.1, and 9.0 percent respectively. These findings are consistent with those of Diaz-Guerrero but not with those of Oswald et al., quoted above. The present study, unlike the Oswald one, showed a smaller percentage of time in the deepest levels of sleep.

Responses to auditory stimulation by the depressed patient group indicate that the patients' responses in the B, C, D, and E stages of sleep before treatment were 79.2, 77.1, 61.8, and 54.4 percent respectively. A comparison with the results obtained from normal control subjects indicates that the depressed patient group showed a significantly higher degree of response at all stages of sleep. This was interpreted by the authors as indicating a *heightened arousal response*. After treatment, the responses to auditory stimulation in the B, C, D, and E stages were 62.5, 34.8, 31.8, and 25.0 percent, respectively. Comparison of the post-treatment responses with those obtained from normal control subjects indicates that they did not differ significantly.

The findings of these authors indicate that the patients' duration of sleep was similar to that recorded in a normal population. The patients, however, spent more time in the lighter stages of sleep. The responses to auditory stimulation are consistent with the suggestion that the depressed patients have a greater responsivity during sleep than do normals.

Other possible interpretations of the data are possible. It is conceivable, for instance, that the increased responsivity of the depressed patients to auditory stimuli may be due to a lower degree of physical fatigue because of lessened activity during the day that is not due to the depressive illness itself, but is related more to the low activity level of depressed patients. The normalization of the records after ECT and drug treatment should be considered in terms of the effect of these treatments on the electrical rhythm of the brain, quite apart from whether the patient was in the depressed or nondepressed state. When a control group was used, age and sex were not adequately controlled. In addition, since psychiatric controls were not used, there is no indication that the findings are specific for depressive illness.

Gresham et al.[98] conducted a more refined study than any previously reported. Instead of relying on clinical impressions alone to determine the depressed group, they used a variety of clinical and psychometric measures. Eight depressed psychiatric inpatients were selected on the basis of six tests and were compared with closely matched controls for four consecutive nights in a laboratory controlled for noise, temperature, and lighting, with continuous, all-night recordings of EEG and eye movements.

The first night's records were not used for analyses. The duration of the stages of sleep over three nights was estimated by observers other than the experimenter. The investigators found that the patients showed more wakefulness, less Stage 4 sleep, and a slightly longer sleep latent state than the controls. Four patients were available for reexamination after their depressions were substantially reduced by therapy; they showed a change in the direction of the values obtained by the controls.

Mendels et al.[99] also reported a deficiency in Stage 4 sleep. This correlated with the severity of the depression.

More recent researchers have also studied EEG variables as correlates of clinical improvement in response to treatment. For example, in attempting to predict treatment outcome with cognitive therapy, Simons et al.[100] found that patients with longer REM latency took longer to achieve remission of depressive symptoms. There was an interaction between REM latency and life events, with a positive association between REM latency and number of weeks to remission in those patients who had experienced a negative life event.

Thase et al.[101] tried to differentiate state-dependent (temporary) versus trait-like (stable) EEG sleep abnormalities in depressed patients. Their experimental method was to examine the sleep profiles of depressed patients before and after a standard 16-week course of cognitive behavior therapy. They then looked to see which sleep abnormalities improved following therapy and which did not.

Based on pretreatment EEG results, a sample of 78 unmedicated patients was divided into abnormal and normal sleep subgroups. All were diagnosed by *DSM-III* criteria as nonbipolar, nonpsychotic major depression. Type 1 sleep disorder was defined by reduced rapid eye movement latency, decreased delta sleep ratio, and decreased slow wave sleep. This type of disturbance was found to be stable across time, with no improvement following psychological treatment. They noted that type 1 sleep disturbance in other studies has been associated with a reduction in the secretion of nocturnal growth hormone, and that this likewise is assumed to be a traitlike or stable correlate of depression.

By contrast, type 2 disturbance was defined in terms of rapid eye movement latency, density, and sleep efficiency. This type of disturbance improved in response to treatment. Thase et al.[101] concluded that it is possible to divide electroencephalographic sleep correlates of depression into state-independent and partly reversible subgroups.

The consensus regarding the studies of the sleep EEGs of depressed patients is that depressed patients tend to have excessive periods of light or restless sleep and a shorter period of total sleep. In addition, they tend to be more sensitive to noises when they are asleep. The studies reported to date are hampered by the small number of patients in each study, the use of normal controls instead of nondepressed psychiatric patients, and the lack of age-specific values for the various EEG patterns. Some studies, moreover, have not excluded the possible influence of sedation on the EEG tracings.

EEG Arousal Response

In 1961, Paulson and Gottlieb[102] reported on a longitudinal study of the electroencephalographic arousal response in 11 depressed patients. The rationale behind their study was that the depressed patient seems in general to be self-absorbed and preoccupied and has a corresponding impairment in alertness to environmental stimulation. The presence of an apparent deficit in attention provided the basis for the following hypotheses: (1) If the patients' thresholds for responding to environmental stimulation are excessively high during depression, then the EEG arousal response to environmental stimulation should occur less frequently during depression than upon recovery. (2) If the peripheral rate of responsiveness is retarded during depression, then the latency of the arousal response should be longer during depression than upon recovery. (3) If the central responsiveness and integrative activities are retarded during depression, then the duration of the arousal response should be longer during depression than upon recovery.

The investigators found that 8 of the 11 patients showed more frequent arousal upon recovery but that the latency was unchanged. The average duration of the arousal response was shortened. The writers interpreted these results as being consistent with the assumption that the attentional threshold is higher than usual during depression and the central integrative processes are slower.

Shagass and Schwartz[103] investigated the cerebral cortical reactivity in psychotic depressives. The mean cortical reactivity cycles were determined for 21 psychotic-depressive patients and 13 nonpatient control subjects. The nonpatient subjects showed an early phase of response recovery, whereas early recovery was much less in the psychotic depressives before treatment. As the depressed patients improved, however, they showed progressively more early response recovery.

Wilson and Wilson[104] investigated the duration of photically elicited arousal responses in psychotic depressed patients. They found that the mean arousal response duration for 16 patients was significantly increased when compared with the control group of normal subjects.

Some contradictory evidence was presented in a study by Driver and Eilenberg.[105] The investigators measured the photoconvulsive threshold in 27 patients with a severe depressive illness. The findings are not different from those reported elsewhere for other nosological syndromes and also for normal subjects. The authors concluded that the threshold had no clinical differentiating value. The estimation was repeated in 18 patients after they had received a course of ECT. No change was found in the photoconvulsive threshold. The investigators concluded that it was unwise to assume that any aspect of diencephalic function was assessed by an estimate of the photoconvulsive thresholds.

The results of the studies of reactivity of the central nervous system are contradictory. Many of the studies have serious methodological shortcomings. The most frequent finding (contradicted by one study) has been an increased threshold for external stimulation during depression and a reduction in the threshold upon recovery. Also, the duration of the arousal response was increased during depression but decreased after recovery. Further confirmatory work is necessary.

Recent Studies of Children and Adolescents

Birmaher and Heydl[33] reviewed biological studies on depressed children and adolescents. They focused on research studies of growth hormone, the serotonergic system, the hypothalamic-pituitary axis (HPA), sleep, and neuroimaging. They also reviewed the findings of biological studies of children at high risk to develop MDD but who have never been depressed.

As for most of the studies with adults, Birmaher and Heydl[33] found abnormalities in the secretion of growth hormone, prolactin, and cortisol levels after pharmacological stimulation in depressed children and adolescents. The stimulating agents in such studies included clonidine, L-dopa, desipramine, insulin, and growth hormone-releasing hormone, all thought to act in part through hypothalamic receptors. Studies in children never depressed but at high genetic risk for MDD showed identical responses, suggesting that alteration in certain hormonal systems may be trait markers for MDD.

The correct interpretation of these observations remains to be worked out. The authors identified many factors that were not controlled in the studies reviewed. These include age, sex, maturation, severity of symptomatology, melancholic symptoms, inpatient versus outpatient patient setting, psychiatric family history, and reactivity to stress. Such variables can affect the same bio-logical systems associated with the onset of clinical depression. For this rea-son, it remains unclear whether the identified uncontrolled factors (or others)—or the identified biological variables (or others)—are the actual causes of clinical depression.[31]

Neuropsychological Studies

Quraishi and Frangou[106] reviewed 42 neuropsychological studies of bipolar disorder published between 1980 and 2000. To be included in their analysis, a study had to have (1) a psychiatric or normal comparison group or standard-ized tests, (2) rigorous diagnostic procedures, (3) inclusion of the clinical status of patients at the time of assessment, and (4) standardized or well-estab-lished cognitive assessment procedures with clear statistical presentation of cognitive functioning.

They found substantial and persistent cognitive impairment. No major dif-ferences were found in cognitive profile between bipolar and unipolar depres-sion. While general intellectual function was largely conserved, cognitive deficits were as follows: (1) attentional abnormalities, (2) impaired verbal memory that persisted in remission, (3) impaired verbal memory (even in euthymic patients), and (4) all facets of executive function (planning, abstract concept formation, set shifting).[106]

Consistent with these findings, the neuropsychological theories of depres-sion were reviewed by Shenal et al.[107] They speculated that dysfunction in any of three neuroanatomical divisions (left frontal, right frontal, and right poste-rior) is associated with mood disorder, and they suggested further research to confirm specific predictions (see Chapter 11, "Theories of Depression").

Conclusions

Despite the thousands of studies in this area, there is little solid knowledge of the specific biological substrate of depression.[1] No laboratory findings that are diagnostic of a major depressive episode, or of a manic episode, have been identified.[108] Results of studies on the neurobiology of suicidal behavior like-wise remain unclear.[109] With almost monotonous regularity, initial positive results have failed to be confirmed by later investigations. Many of the widely accepted findings are clouded with doubt because of methodological inadequacies in the original studies.

Among the positive findings that have been consistently associated with depression have been excessive levels of steroids, sodium retention, and changes in sleep EEG patterns. However, excessive steroid secretion is not a specific characteristic of depression and appears to be associated with many states of emotional arousal. Sodium retention has so far been demonstrated in only a few studies. Several EEG studies have indicated a deficit in the deeper levels of sleep.

Historically, numerous sources of error have been present in the biological studies. These include inadequate, heterogeneous samples; diagnostic methods of dubious reliability and validity; and inadequate control for variables such as age, sex, diet, state of nutrition, and activity level. The lack of control for age may be singled out as one of the most frequent factors responsible for initial positive findings that were disconfirmed by later better controlled studies.

Nevertheless, some progress has been made in elucidating the biological bases of depression, such as identifying the genetic basis of the mood disorders, including that of schizoaffective disorder (see Chapter 8). Research on changes in hippocampal neurons and amygdala enlargement appears promising. "Neurotrophic" (keeping cells alive) and "neurogenesis" (stimulating growth of new cells) theories abound and are being tested.

One research area explores specific brain changes that correspond to the effective pharmacological and psychological treatments of depression. For example, studies have focused on differential effects in recovery for paroxetine (Paxil) therapy and cognitive therapy in modulating specific sites in limbic and cortical brain regions.[110]

Biological researchers have continued to identify the pathophysiological aspects of major depressive disorder, including alterations in various monoamine brain systems (see also Chapter 11). Neuropeptides such as corticotropin-releasing hormone are under investigation, as well as hormonal variables such as glucocorticoid secretion. Dexamethasone nonsuppression of plasma cortisol has been suggested as a marker, although the same effects have been induced experimentally by sleep deprivation and dietary fasting.

Chapter 10
Psychological Studies: Tests of Psychoanalytic Theory

This chapter provides a summary of selected early psychological studies of depression. The studies include psychological performance comparisons between depressed and nondepressed individuals, and Beck's original investigations of depression, which led to the cognitive formulations.[1,2,3,4] The more recent psychological studies on reactivity, vulnerability (diathesis), and the empirical status of somatic and psychological treatments are covered in subsequent chapters.

The studies included here are those, included in the first edition, that have conceptual links to Beck's systematic investigation of depression and led directly to the development of cognitive theory. A comprehensive review of other psychological studies not directly relevant to this topic can be found in texts on mood disorders such as Beckham and Leber,[5] Dubovsky and Buzan,[6] and Paykel.[7]

Early Tests of Psychological Functioning

Psychomotor Performance

Clinical descriptions of depression have included psychomotor retardation. Early researchers merely assumed that patients' complaints of being slowed down in their thinking indicated inhibition of thought. In 1945, Rapaport[8] reported testing this assumption by comparing a depressed group with a schizophrenic group; he found lowered digit-symbol scores in the depressed group. However, Rapaport's depressed group was significantly older than his schizophrenic group, so age difference might have accounted for the inferior performances by the depressed patients.

To control for age and intelligence, Beck et al.[9] tested by digit-symbol and vocabulary a sample of 178 psychiatric patients. Consistent with their hypothesis, digit-symbol scores decreased in a stepwise fashion with increasing age and increased in the same fashion with increasing vocabulary scores. When age and intelligence were taken into account, there was no relationship between digit-symbol scores and depression.

Granick[10] performed a comparative analysis of performance on the Wechsler Adult Intelligence Scale Information and Similarities tests and on the Thorndike-Gallup Vocabulary Test of 50 psychotic depressives and 50 normals matched for age, sex, race, education, religion, and nativity. No differences were found between the psychotically depressed and the normal group. Similarly, Friedman[11] found no differences on 33 cognitive, perceptual, and psychomotor tests between 55 depressed and 65 nondepressed individuals after matching for age, sex, education, vocabulary score, and nativity. The depressed individuals ranked lower than did the normal group in only 4 percent of the test scores, a finding that could be due to chance. The author concluded that actual ability and performance during severe depression are not consistent with the depressed patient's unrealistically low self-image. This is consistent with Loeb et al.,[12] who compared 20 depressed and 20 matched nondepressed male patients on two card-sorting tasks. The depressed patients tended to underestimate their performance, which was actually as good as that of the nondepressed patients.

Likewise, Shapiro et al.[13] found that depressed patients following recovery (produced by ECT) did not show any significant change in performance on a battery of psychomotor tests when compared to a control group.

Tucker and Spielberg[14] compared the Bender-Gestalt scores of 17 depressed outpatients with those of 19 nondepressed psychiatric outpatients. In general, the various Bender-Gestalt scores did not discriminate between the two groups. Of 20 items, only 2, tremor and design distortion, were significant at the 5 percent level in discriminating between the depressed and nondepressed groups. Surprisingly, the depressed patients showed a *faster* mean reaction time to test cards compared to the nondepressed group, but this finding was short of statistical significance.

In summary, although the depressed patients tended to complain of cognitive inefficiencies, they performed as well in test situations as did nondepressed patients.

Conceptual Performance

Payne and Hirst[15] investigated conceptual thinking in depressed patients. The authors administered the Epstein Overinclusion Test to 11 depressed patients and 14 normal controls matched for age, sex, and vocabulary level. Their findings indicated that depressives showed a significantly greater tendency toward overinclusion than the normals. They found, in fact, that depressed patients seemed to be more extreme with respect to overinclusion of thinking than schizophrenics. The authors suggested that the overinclusion tendency may be related to psychosis generally, rather than to any specific psychosis such as schizophrenia or depression.

Perceptual Threshold

Hemphill et al.[16] measured the pain and fatigue tolerance of depressed patients as compared with other psychiatric patients. The depressed patients showed a significantly higher threshold for both pain and fatigue than the other groups. However, the mean age of the depressed patients was substantially higher than that of the other groups, which could account for the differences in thresholds for perception of fatigue and pain. Hemphill et al.[16] found the depressed patients more persevering in a fatiguing task than the nondepressed patients, yet Wadsworth et al.[17] found no difference in fatigability or work performance between those with depression and schizophrenia.

In an attempt to relate perceptual regulation to mental disorders, Dixon and Lear[18] measured the visual threshold for one eye while presenting neutral and emotive material below the awareness threshold to the other eye. The five depressive patients showed a consistent raising of threshold ("perceptual defense") as compared to the six schizophrenics, who showed a lowering of threshold ("perceptual vigilance"). Caution is necessary in interpreting these results because of the small samples and because all the patients were on drug therapy.

Distortion of Time Judgment

Many writers have described a distortion of the time sense in affective disorders. The existential writers in particular have commented on the relevance of time distortion to the existential experience of the patient (Chapter 11). Mezey and Cohen[19] investigated the subjective experience of time and the judgment of time of 21 depressed patients. The study included introspective statements about time experience as well as objective tests involving projection-reprojection and verbal estimation of time intervals ranging from one second to 30 minutes. The authors found that about three-fourths of the patients felt that time was passing more slowly than normal; this feeling tended to disappear on recovery. The objective tests, in contrast, indicated that the verbal estimation of time under experimental conditions was as accurate during the depressed phase as during the recovery phase.

Distortion of Spatial Judgment

A number of articles suggested that psychiatric patients experience some changes in spatial perception, such as distortions in the perceived distance between themselves and others. Other phenomena have been the assignment of different qualities to the right and left aspects of space and fading of the third-dimensional aspect of objects.[20]

Depression was shown to be related to up-down perception in several studies. Rosenblatt[21] found that in contrast to manic patients, depressed patients had a tendency to focus on the downward rather than upward aspect of a spatial situation. Wapner et al.,[22] in a parallel study of college students, related the experience of academic failure to a consequent downward effect on the subjective judgment of eye level ("apparent horizon"). Fisher[20] tested the specific hypothesis that the degree of downward bias of perception is positively related to the level of sadness or depression. Fifty-two subjects were evaluated. The measure of sad affect was made in terms of the number of sad terms used in describing a series of faces. Upward versus downward directionality of perception was estimated by means of the autokinetic phenomenon and by judgments requiring the adjustment of a luminous rod to the horizontal. The results supported the proposition that subjects with a sad affect showed a downward bias in perception, whereas subjects with a neutral affect showed an upward bias.

Early Experimental Studies

An intriguing study concerned with the effect of serum from manic-depressed patients on the behavior of dogs was reported in the Russian literature. Polyakova[23] reported that the time taken for five dogs to negotiate a labyrinth increased from a mean of 6.37 seconds to 19 seconds when the dogs received serum from depressed patients. The time decreased to a mean of 5.8 seconds when the blood came from patients in the manic phase. The profound implications of this study certainly would warrant independent replication.

In the first of several studies in which depressed patients were exposed to varying experimental conditions, we randomly assigned a group of 20 depressed and 22 nondepressed patients to an experimentally induced superior and inferior performance condition.[24] Prior to and immediately following the experimental task, the patients rated their own mood. Indices of self-confidence were also obtained. The depressed patients tended to be more affected by task performance than the nondepressed patients when estimating how they would do in a future task. The groups did not differ, however, in performance effect on self-ratings.

In a later study, we measured the effects of success and failure on mood, motivation, and performance.[12] Twenty depressed and 20 nondepressed male patients were selected on the basis of their having, respectively, high or low scores on the Depression Inventory *and* high or low ratings of depression made independently during a psychiatric interview. In an experiment designed as part of the psychiatric outpatient evaluation procedure, the depressed patients were significantly more pessimistic about their likelihood of succeeding and tended to underrate the quality of their performances, although their actual output was the same as that of nondepressed patients. On a second task the previous experience of success and failure had contrasting effects on the actual performances of the two groups. Success improved the performance of the depressed patients, and failure improved the performance of the nondepressed patients.

Harsch and Zimmer[25] selected 62 male and 34 female college students on the basis of their performance on the Zimmer Sentence Completion Test; 48 students were considered to exhibit a predominantly extrapunitive behavior pattern, and 48 to exhibit a predominantly intrapunitive behavior pattern. Since the intrapunitive behavior pattern was considered characteristic of depression, this experiment was relevant for understanding depression. The experiment endeavored to produce abandonment of the characteristic behavior pattern and adoption of a different behavior pattern. This was attempted by rewarding subjects for statements contrary to the basic behavior pattern or punishing the subjects for statements conforming to the behavior pattern. As a result of the experimental manipulation, both groups showed significant shifts in behavior pattern as measured by the Zimmer test. The experimentally induced changes in a direction opposite from the starting points persisted over an eight-day follow-up period.

Family Background and Personality

Wilson[26] investigated the role of family pressures in the socialization of manic depressives. On the basis of his review of case records and the intensive study of 12 patients and their families, he concluded that during childhood the manic depressives felt excessive pressure to conform to the attitudes of their parents and had less freedom than did the control group.

In 1954, Cohen et al.[27] reported the results of an intensive psychoanalytic investigation of 12 cases of manic-depressive psychosis. A consistent finding in all 12 patients was that during their childhood their families felt set apart by some factor that singled them out as "different." Among these factors were membership in a minority group, serious economic reversals, or mental illness in the family. In each case, the patient's family felt the social distinction keenly and reacted to it by trying to improve its acceptability in the community. The family placed a high premium on conformity and made a great effort to improve its social status by raising its economic level or achieving other symbols of prestige. In order to reach that goal, the children were expected to conform to a high standard of behavior, based primarily on the parents' concepts of what the neighbors expected. The patient's role was experienced by him as being in the service of the family's social striving.

The responsibility for winning prestige was generally delegated by the mother to the child who was later to develop a manic-depressive psychosis.

The reason a particular child was selected was because the child was exceptional in terms of intelligence or other gifts or was the oldest, the youngest, or only child. The emphasis on achievement and competition usually caused the child to have serious problems with envy.

Gibson[28] used a more refined technique to test the findings of Cohen's study. He studied a group of 27 manic-depressive patients and 17 schizophrenic patients from St. Elizabeth's Hospital in Washington, D.C., to determine whether Cohen's description of early life history and family background could differentiate manic-depressive from schizophrenic patients. Hospital records and interviews with the families by specially trained social workers provided the basic data. The data were evaluated according to a questionnaire specifically designed to measure the degree to which a patient's history conformed to the concepts formulated by Cohen and her group. The 12 patients of the original Cohen study were also evaluated according to the questionnaire.

The two manic-depressive groups were differentiated from the schizophrenic groups on three of the five scales of the questionnaire. The manic depressives were statistically different from the schizophrenics in terms of the following characteristics. (1) The manic depressive came from a family in which there was marked striving for prestige and the patient was the instrument of the parents' prestige needs. (2) The manic-depressive patient had a background in which there was intense envy and competitiveness. (3) The parents of the manic-depressive patients showed a high degree of concern about social approval.

Certain methodological inadequacies are apparent in this study. Among these are the possibility of contamination in the social workers' evaluations of their data and the lack of control for age.

Becker and his associates, in a series of systematic studies, attempted to test the hypotheses derived from Cohen's study and the systematic investigation by Gibson. According to their reformulations of Cohen's findings, persons who develop manic-depressive reaction in adulthood have experienced excessive parental expectations for conformity and achievement as children. They react to these demands by adopting the prevailing values of their parents and other authority figures in order to placate them and win approval. The authors attempted to investigate the extent to which chronic dependence on others for guidance and approval is manifested in the opinions and attitudes of the manic-depressive patient. In an initial study, Becker[29] compared 24 remitted manic depressives with 30 nonpsychiatric controls who were matched for age, education, and literacy level. The manic depressives scored significantly higher than the controls on measures of value achievement, authoritarian trends, and conventional attitudes. The manic depressives did not differ from the nonpsychiatric controls in direct self-rating of achievement motivation or on performance output.

In another study, Spielberger et al.[30] essayed a broader investigation of the formulations derived from the studies of Cohen, Gibson, and Wilson. The subjects of this investigation consisted of 30 remitted manic depressives and 30 nonpsychiatric controls. Four objective psychological scales or tests were administered. These consisted of the California Fascism Scale, the Traditional Family Ideology Scale, the Value Achievement Scale, and the Need Achievement Scale. The manic depressives obtained significantly higher scores than the controls on all these experimental measures except need achievement. The authors interpreted their findings as indicating that the adult personality structure of manic depressives is characterized by conventional authoritarian attitudes, traditional opinions, and stereotyped achievement values, but not by internalized achievement motives.

Some doubt of the specificity of these findings was raised by another study by Becker, Spielberger, and Parker.[31] In this study, the scores of manic depressives on various attitude measures were compared with the scores of neurotic depressives, schizophrenics, and normal controls. No significant difference in value achievement or authoritarian attitudes was found between the psychiatric groups, although they differed significantly from the normal controls. The investigators found, however, that age and social class significantly affected the scores; this indicates the need for empirical or statistical control of these variables in personality studies of this kind.

Self-Concept

A self-concept test was developed by Beck and Stein,[32] consisting of traits and characteristics such as appearance, intelligence, sex appeal, selfishness, and cruelty. Patients rated themselves on each of these traits using a five-point scale. They also made ratings of how they felt about having each of these traits (the self-acceptance score). We found a significant correlation (− .66) between self-concept scores and Depression Inventory scores; the correlation between self-acceptance scores and DI scores was also significant (− .42). This study indicated that depressed patients tended to give themselves low ratings on socially desirable traits and high ratings on undesirable traits. We concluded that the self-concept is low in depressed as compared with nondepressed patients. The self-concept test has been revised, and its psychometric properties may be found in Beck et al.[33]

Laxer[34] used the Semantic Differential Test to investigate changes in the self-concept of neurotic depressive and other psychiatric patients. The depressives showed a low self-concept on admission to a hospital but moved to a higher self-concept at the time of discharge. The paranoids, however, began with a relatively high self-rating and did not change appreciably at the time of discharge.

One interesting group of findings demonstrated that in test situations the depressed patient is able to perform as effectively as matched controls. Experimental studies indicated that the experience of success significantly improves the performance of depressed patients. These findings suggested that the inertia in depression may be related more to factors such as loss of motivation than to physiological inhibition. The studies also indicated that depressed patients greatly underestimate their capacity and actual performance.

The finding of a high threshold for fatigue also suggested that in actual work situations the depressed patent does not become as fatigued as is generally believed. No objective evidence was obtained to substantiate the notion of a disturbance of judgments of time. Some studies, however, suggest that the depressed patient tends to have a downward bias in spatial perception.

Studies of the personality and family backgrounds of depressed patients have not fulfilled early expectations. Efforts to test the hypothesis generated by the clinical studies of M. B. Cohen and her group provided some initial support. Investigations using a tighter design, however, suggested that the obtained differences between depressed and nondepressed patients might have been due to extraneous factors such as age, social class, and educational level. Studies of self-concept indicated that depressed patients rate themselves much lower than nondepressed patients but return to average ratings upon recovery from the depression.

Beck's Systematic Investigation of Depression

Psychodynamic Factors

The psychodynamic factors in depression have engaged the interest of psychiatric writers since Abraham's first exploration of this subject in 1911. The early psychiatric literature contains a wide variety of theories of depression including increased orality,[35] retroflected hostility,[36] and the need to manipulate significant persons in the environment.[37]

At the time Beck began his systematic investigation, in view of the numerous clinical papers on depression,[38] the paucity of controlled studies testing the various hypotheses was surprising. A major factor was the number of highly complicated conceptual and methodological problems confronted in subjecting these hypotheses to systematic test. One problem—perhaps the greatest obstacle—was specificity: The same psychodynamic formulations that had been provided to explain the phenomena of depression were also applied to quite different conditions. The concept of oral fixation, for instance, had been applied not only to depression but also to a diversity of conditions including schizophrenia, alcoholism, and peptic ulcer. Another problem was that many of the theories, such as Freud's formulation of depression in *Mourning and Melancholia*,[36] are so complex and remote from observables in the clinical material that they are not readily reduced to operational terms for systematic study.

In undertaking a study of the psychodynamic factors of depression, it was necessary to satisfy two prerequisites. First, it should be possible to isolate a particular psychodynamic constellation or construct that has a meaningful relationship to depression but not to other syndromes. Second, it should be possible to develop methods for identifying the referents of this construct in the clinical material.

History of the Investigation

The evolution of Beck's studies may be of interest. In an earlier study, data had been collected from five soldiers who became psychotically depressed after having accidentally killed a comrade[39] (see Chapter 5). A detailed examination of the ideational productions of these patients (hallucinations, fantasies, dreams, and obsessive ruminations) revealed direct evidence of self-punitive tendencies. In a typical case, for example, the patient had a visual hallucination of the dead buddy in which the buddy told him to kill himself. All the patients expressed a desire to be punished for their deeds, and all but one had made suicide attempts.

The next event in this evolution was the observation that the dreams of neurotically depressed patients in intensive psychotherapy or analysis showed a particularly high frequency of themes of being disappointed, thwarted, injured, punished, incompetent, or ugly. These themes occurred occasionally in the dreams of nondepressed patients, but much less frequently.

This observation of the dreams of depressed patients suggested the possibility that there might be a particular psychodynamic variable or constellation that was characteristic of depression but not of other psychiatric conditions. The common denominator of these dream themes was that the dreamer experienced some unpleasantness or suffering in the manifest dream. Proceeding on Freud's theory that dream content represents wish fulfillment, Beck speculated that these dreams represented a wish to suffer.

When this observation of the dreams of depressed patients was aligned with the previous observation of the punishment themes in the ideational productions of the psychotically depressed soldiers, there appeared to be one feature common to both, namely, self-imposed suffering. Beck conjectured that the unpleasant dream themes might reflect the same psychological variables as the self-punitive hallucinations and verbal statements of the psychotically depressed soldiers. This formulation led to the formal hypothesis that a central feature in depression is the need to suffer. The term "negative dreams" was employed to designate this particular variable. To confirm this hypothesis experimentally, it was necessary to demonstrate that depressed patients show a significantly higher degree of "negative dreams" than nondepressed patients.

To develop a method for measuring this, it was first necessary to obtain a kind of data that could be readily defined, collected, and analyzed. Dreams seemed to fit these requirements. The reported dream is a discrete entity, in contrast to other types of clinical material (such as discursive responses to questions, free associations, or nonverbal behavior). In addition, it is relatively easy to subject dreams to content-scoring systems that have a high degree of interjudge reliability.[40]

In attempting to provide a theoretical framework to explain the negative tendencies in depressed patients, Beck considered two alternative conceptualizations. (1) "Negative dreams" could be regarded as a manifestation of inverted hostility. In accordance with Freud's thesis in *Mourning and Melancholia*,[36] patients are primarily angry at somebody else (the lost love-object), but turn this anger against themselves. The insults and rebukes initially intended for the lost love-object are focused on themselves. (2) The need to suffer could be viewed as a direct expression of self-punishment tendencies. (This thesis is different from the first in that it does not presuppose the presence of hostility.) According to the second formulation, the patient has either done something contrary to his or her primitive moral code (superego), or has some unacceptable wish. This deed or wish arouses guilt in the patient, and the guilt then leads to the wish for self-punishment.

Several objections were immediately apparent. The first formulation was concerned with inverted hostility, but the presence of hostility could not be demonstrated in the manifest content of the dream of the depressed patient or in the feeling experience during the dream. The second formulation assumed the presence of guilt over some unacceptable wishes or deeds. Neither guilt nor the unacceptable wishes or deeds could be directly identified in the manifest content of the dreams. Since these elements could not be demonstrated directly in the clinical material, the formulations could not be subjected to direct test.

Another problem was that Freud's theory of dreams is based on the assumption that the dream represents a wish fulfillment of some kind, that is, the content of the dream represents a particular wish or set of wishes. If this assumption is invalid, then the whole formulation of the need to suffer collapses.

As the research developed, we attempted to circumvent these problems by adopting a different approach. It seemed more satisfactory to stay at the level of the patients' experiences than to infer some underlying process. If patients dream that other people are frustrating them, it would be more economical to consider this a conception of people as being frustrating rather than to read into the dream an underlying wish. This revised conception also fitted in with some later observations of the thematic content of the verbalized statements of patients. Focusing on the material in terms of the patients' perception of self and of external reality gradually shifted the emphasis from an unconscious motivational to a cognitive model.

The first stage in the systematic investigation of depression was a content analysis of the dreams of patients in psychotherapy. The hypothesis that depressed patients show a greater frequency of negative dreams than a control group of nondepressed patients was confirmed.

This initial finding seemed to warrant a more complete investigation, using a much larger patient sample and more refined techniques. In order to provide a more solid empirical basis for the large-scale investigation, we carried out a number of preliminary studies. The first stage consisted of a series of studies evaluating current methods of clinical diagnosis. On the basis of these studies, we decided to use psychiatrists' ratings and various psychometric techniques to isolate the depressed group. The second stage was the development of an inventory for measuring depression,[41] and a refinement of the clinical rating scale.

In the third stage, the studies were oriented to testing the hypothesis that depressed patients are characterized by a number of distinctive patterns that lead to suffering disproportionate or inappropriate to the reality situation. We took two major approaches to demonstrate these self-suffering patterns. Ideational material (dreams, responses to structured projective tests, and free associations) was analyzed to determine whether depressed patients show a greater frequency of negative themes in these productions than nondepressed patients; and controlled experimental stress situations were set up, to determine whether the reactions of depressed patients were more self-debasing than those of nondepressed patients.

In a collateral study to determine whether there were any significant differences in the backgrounds of depressed and nondepressed patients, we computed the relative incidence of parental loss during childhood. In addition, we studied the verbal productions of depressed patients in psychotherapy to determine whether there were any patterns that were characteristic of depression.

Testing the Hypothesis

Once we had established reasonably reliable measures of depression, we were ready to proceed with determining whether the self-defeating patterns could be identified in dreams and other ideational productions (early memories and storytelling), responses to verbal tests, and reactions to experimentally induced stresses. The major hypothesis to be tested was: There is a significant association between self-defeating patterns and depression.

Definition of Negative

We defined negative in terms of a cluster of related behaviors. Some typical repetitive behavior patterns observed in individuals considered self-defeating but not necessarily depressed are the tendency to interpret the lack of complete success as failure; to have self-doubts even when successful; to magnify the importance of personal defects; to react to criticism with self-debasement; and to expect rejection. This type of behavior pattern was conceptualized as either a manifestation of *a need to suffer* or a manifestation of an enduring cognitive distortion which negatively biases the individual's evaluation of self-worth, adequacy, social acceptability, or achievements. Which of these formulations is more applicable still remains to be demonstrated empirically. In either case, the individual tends to structure personal experiences in such a way as to react to life situations with inappropriate or excessive suffering. The type of dysphoria experienced includes feelings of humiliation, deprivation, frustration, and social isolation.

Previous clinical experience, and a systematic study based on this experience,[42] indicated that dreams in which the dreamer is deserted, frustrated, deprived, or injured are characteristic of depression-prone people. As a broad test of this finding, we attempted to determine whether the self-representation of the depressed patient as degraded, impotent, or deprived may be found consistently in various types of ideational material. Since there is no definitive criterion of the concept, it was necessary to make a series of predictions and to design tests and experiments to confirm or disconfirm these predictions. As a first step, we predicted a priori that the scores on various tests that were designed to facilitate negative response would correlate significantly with measures of depression. Since these tests (an inventory and a self-concept test) dealt with various forms and levels of behavior including dreams, memories, storytelling, and self-reports, a fairly broad area of verbal behavior was tapped. That scores on each of these measures showed a significant relationship to measures of depression offer supporting evidence for the hypothesis.

Dream Study

In our preliminary study, we devised a scoring system for identifying negative dreams. In our large-scale study, this system was applied to the dreams of 219 patients. The depressed group was found to have a significantly higher number of negative dreams than the nondepressed group.

Assumptions and interpretations. A major problem in using dreams, memories, and storytelling responses to projective tests concerns whether the basic assumptions regarding the identification and measurement of constructs in this material are justified. Dreams, for instance, have been postulated to express a wide variety of personality processes. Some of the specific assumptions regarding dream content that were most relevant to our research and that we considered in interpreting our findings were that dream content is (a) an expression of motivations, such as hostility, dependency, the need to suffer, and so on.; or (b) a representation of the individual's concept of himself and/ or of his concept of personal and impersonal forces in the environment; or (c) an expression of characteristic patterns of behavior; or (d) a translation of affects, such as sadness, into pictorial imagery; or (e) a manifestation of an attempt at problem-solving; or (f) a condensation of random waking impressions, thoughts, worries, and memories.

Two more general assumptions interwoven with those listed above are that dream imagery may be regarded as (g) a symbolic, indirect, or disguised representation of a psychological process, or (h) a direct, uncamouflaged representation that can be appraised at its face value—that is, relatively little inference is required to categorize it. The various assumptions are not necessarily mutually exclusive.

As mentioned previously, our utilization of dreams in the project originally rested on at least two of the above assumptions. The first (assumption a), was that the construct, would be expressed in dreams because of its motivational properties. Thus we regarded the dream of being subjected to a painful experience as the expression of a motivation, the need to suffer. The second (assumption b), was that the dream could be usefully categorized on the basis of its superficial content and the specific themes may be taken literally (irrespective of any possible symbolic or disguised meaning). These two assumptions (which also appear to underlie research with the TAT in which Murray's "need system" is used) were made in our work with the projective tests.

After we had determined that there was a significant relationship between our measures of depression and the incidence of negative dreams, the question of how to interpret these findings arose. Since any interpretation is dependent on the underlying assumptions, these were reexamined. Our assumption that the dream is an expression of a motivation led to the interpretation of the dream as the representation of a need to suffer. However, an equally (or more) plausible explanation had to be considered. This was that the behaviors characterized by suffering disproportionate to the reality situation are the results of the specific way these individuals structure their experiences. As a result of particular conceptual systems, they might introduce a systematic bias (against themselves) in evaluating specific experiences; they would, for example, be prone to interpret any difficulties or disappointments as manifestations of their own inadequacies. In accordance with this formulation, the negative dream would be regarded as a manifestation of the individual's distorted self-concept, negative interpretation of experience, and unpleasant expectations.

Our other initial assumption was that the dramatic action and imagery in the dream could be analyzed in a relatively literal way on the basis of the superficial themes. Thus, the dream of being betrayed by a spouse would be assigned to the category of *rejection*. A corollary is the assumption that the themes in the dreams have observable counterparts in waking behavior or conscious mental activity. Thus, individuals who dream of themselves as ugly would be expected to show unusual concern about appearance as manifested by, say, frequently looking into the mirror or worrying about their physical attractiveness.

Dreams and overt behavior. Since we were relying on the assumption that dream themes reflect specific behavior patterns, we considered it important to determine whether this assumption is tenable. One approach to the problem was to ascertain whether the thematic content of dreams bears any relevance to overt behavior. An initial line of inquiry was to select individuals whose actions had been unusual or extreme in some regard and to attempt to predict this behavior on the basis of their dreams. For this reason, we conducted a study of the dreams of various types of convicts (sexual offenders, murderers, and burglars) to determine whether their manifest dreams were significantly related to the type of offense for which they were imprisoned.

We collected ten consecutive dreams from each of eight prisoners convicted of sexual offenses against children and from a matched control group of eight prisoners with no history of sexual offenses,[43] then employed a scoring system for identifying undisguised sexual elements and *criminal sexual activity* in the manifest content of dreams. Agreement between two judges as to whether a dream contained a sexual element or a theme relating to sexual offenses was 99 percent on 200 dreams that were scored. We found that there was a significantly higher frequency of dreams with both uncamouflaged sexual elements and *criminal* sexual activity in the sexual offender group than in the control group ($p < .01$, Wilcoxon Matched-Pairs Signed-Ranks Test). We regarded these findings as consistent with the assumption that dream themes are relevant to observable patterns of behavior.

Early Memories

Each patient in our studies was routinely asked to report his or her three earliest memories, and in about 80 percent of the cases it was possible to obtain at least three early memories. We found that the same categories used in scoring the dreams could be adapted to a scoring manual to identify relevant themes in the early memories. Agreement between independent ratings of two judges was 95 percent. The verbal reports of 25 patients who reported their three earliest memories were analyzed blindly for the presence of negative themes; we found that the frequency of negative early memories reported by patients in the depressed group was significantly higher than for patients in the nondepressed group. The association between the scores on the Depression Inventory and the frequency of negative early memories was evaluated statistically by the Mann-Whitney U Test and was found to be significant at the 0.05 level.[1]

Focused Fantasy Test

This test consists of a set of four picture cards. Each card has four frames that portray a continuous sequence of events. The action in the sequence centers essentially around two male figures who are sufficiently similar to make it equivocal which figures in one frame correspond to those in the subsequent frames. One of the two figures is subjected to an unpleasant experience; the other avoids the unpleasant experience or has a pleasant experience.

The subject is presented one of the pictures and asked to tell a story about the sequence. After listening to the story, the examiner determines which of the two characters in the story is the main character or hero. The hero, by definition, is the character who is present in all four frames in the story, that is, he is identified as the solitary figure in the first frame. The outcome is labeled negative or not depending on whether the hero or the secondary character is identified with the figure hurt in the final frame.

This test was administered to 87 patients. Since four cards were used, the score for each patient ranged from 0 to 4. The patients were divided according to their Depression Inventory scores into depressed and nondepressed groups and ranked according to the scores on the Focused-Fantasy Test. We found that the scores were significantly higher ($p < 0.0003$, Mann-Whitney U test) among the depressed than among the nondepressed patients.[1]

Negative Inventory

This inventory consists of 46 items relevant to the following behaviors: negativity (20 items), hostility (20 items), and submission (6 items). The items were primarily clinically derived. The negativity items were based on clinically observed behaviors considered consistent with the definition and observed in patients who were not clinically depressed. Each item in the inventory consists of a statement that is read aloud to the patient, who is then asked to select one of five alternative phrases to complete the statement. The alternatives are scaled on a frequency dimension as follows: never (0), sometimes (1), often (2), usually (3), always (4).

This test was administered to 109 patients. The scores on the negativity items were then compared with the scores on the Depression Inventory. It was found that there was a Spearman rank correlation of 0.51 between these two tests ($p < 0.001$). The correlation between scores on the Depression Inventory and on the hostility items was substantially lower, the coefficient being 0.24.[1]

Self-Concept Test

Another interviewer-administered schedule was developed to index negative self-concept. We observed clinically that negative and depressed patients tended to downgrade themselves in regard to attributes that are of special importance to them; we also observed clinically that other types of attributes, such as the conventional virtues (kindness, goodness, generosity), were often selected by depressed patients as characteristics in which they were superior to others. The inventory consists of 25 personal attributes such as personal appearance, conversational ability, sense of humor, and success. The patient compares her- himself with other people on a five-point scale ranging from "worse than anybody I know" (1) to "better than anybody I know" (5), and similarly indicates "how I feel about being this way." The items are keyed so that a low total score indicates a low self-regard.

This test was administered to a sample of 49 psychiatric inpatients and out-patients. The product-moment correlation between scores on this self-concept test and the scores on the Depression Inventory was − .66 ($p < .01$). A similar negative correlation (− .42) was found between self-acceptance scores on the Self-Concept Test and scores on the Depression Inventory. The results support the hypothesis that depressed patients have a negative view of themselves and reject themselves for presumed failings.

Experimental Studies

Another approach we used to investigate the relationship of specific psycho-dynamic constructs to depression and to develop measures of the constructs was through manipulation of the specific variables in a controlled experiment. In two of the experiments described below, we made predictions regarding the expected response of depressed patients when the experimental situation was designed to elicit "negative behavior."

Effects of inferior performance on depressed patients. One characteristic behavior is the tendency to be disproportionately affected by inferior perform-ance. To test this assumption empirically, we designed an experiment to deter-mine the differential effects of superior and inferior performance on the reported mood of depressed and nondepressed patients.[24] The Depression Inventory was individually administered to 32 male patients on the intensive treatment ward of a Veterans Administration neuropsychiatric hospital. On the basis of their inventory scores, patients were divided into three groups: high-depressed, moderate-depressed, and low-depressed. On the same day that they were given the Depression Inventory, subjects were scheduled in groups of three for the experiment. Patients rated their present mood on an 11 point scale (with "extremely sad" and "extremely happy" as the anchor points) both before and after the experimental manipulation of success and failure. In addi-tion, a post measure on the level of expectation (in regard to the estimated number of words they could write in three minutes) was obtained from all subjects.

During the experiment, the patients worked on a series of four word-com-pletion tasks that they believed were identical but that in reality varied in dif-ficulty. Consequently, in each group of three, one subject consistently scored high (superior), one medium (neutral), and one low (inferior). The moderate-depressed were always assigned to the neutral position and are not considered in the results. Half the high-depressed were assigned to the inferior performance group and half to the superior performance group; the low-depressed were treated in the same way. After each word-completion task, scores were posted on a blackboard to dramatize the relative performance of the subjects. After the final posting of scores, the patients rated their mood for the second time.

The results indicated that the high-depressed patients showed a greater drop in mood level (as indicated by self-ratings) following failure, and a greater increase after success, than did the low-depressed patients. This difference was short of statistical significance ($p = .10$). The high-depressed had a significantly higher level of expectation (number of words they estimated they could write in three minutes) following superior performance than the other three groups; following inferior performance, the high-depressed had a lower level of expectation than the other groups.

Effects of success and failure on expectancy and performance. We designed a study to determine the effects of success and failure on the probability-of-success estimate, level of aspiration, and actual performance of depressed and nondepressed patients. Twenty depressed and 20 nondepressed patients were individually given two card-sorting tasks. The experimenter deliberately interrupted the second task so that all the subjects "failed."

We found that the depressed patients were more sensitive to failure than the nondepressed patients. They reacted with significantly greater pessimism (as measured by probability-of-success estimates) and a lower level of aspiration. Despite consistently greater pessimism than the nondepressed patients, the depressed patients' actual performance was consistently as good as that of the nondepressed patients.[12]

Collateral Studies

Cognitive Patterns in Verbal Material

While the systematic studies of patients newly admitted to the psychiatric outpatient clinics or hospitals were proceeding, we reviewed the case records of depressed and nondepressed patients in psychotherapy to determine whether any consistent differences could be detected in the verbal (non-dream) material. We found that the depressed patients tended to distort their experiences in an idiosyncratic way: They misinterpreted specific events in terms of failure, deprivation, or rejection. They also tended to make negative predictions of the future. There was, however, no tangible evidence of a need to suffer. Such a need, if it exists, could not be identified directly in the clinical material nor in any of the systematic studies.

Since the studies could not demonstrate (or rule out) that the depressed patient is motivated by a need to suffer, we considered alternative explanations for the findings in the dream studies and the studies of the verbal materials. In both the dreams and in the reports of waking experiences, the patients frequently pictured themselves as thwarted, deprived, defective, and so on. This led to the conclusion that certain cognitive patterns could be responsible for the patients' tendency to make negatively biased judgments of themselves, their environment, and their future. These cognitive patterns, although less prominent in the nondepressed period, became activated during the depression.

Longitudinal Studies

In another approach to understanding depression, we obtained past-history information to determine whether the depressed patients had been exposed to particular types of developmental stresses that might account for their sense of deprivation and hopelessness. We anticipated that the death of a parent in childhood, because of the intensity and finality of the loss, might be expected to sensitize the child to react to future life situations in terms of deprivation and hopelessness. We found that in a group of 100 severely expressed adult patients, 27 percent had lost one or both parents through death before age 16, whereas in a control group of nondepressed psychiatric patients, only 12 percent had been orphaned before 16. It appeared that these results were consistent with the concept that depressed patients may develop through traumatic life experiences certain cognitive-affective patterns which, when activated, produce inappropriate or disproportionate reactions of deprivation and despair.

Patterns in Dreams of Depressed Patients

This section summarizes the original dream studies reported by Beck in the first edition of this book.[4] Statistical techniques began to be used in the content analysis of dreams in the 1930s. In 1935, Alexander and Wilson[44] applied quantitative techniques to the manifest dreams of patients for the purpose of quantifying psychoanalytic material. Twenty years later, Saul and Sheppard[40] devised a rating scale for measuring hostility in the manifest dream. In a later paper,[45] they outlined a comprehensive rating system for estimating ego functions in dreams. These studies provided a stimulus for the investigations reported in this chapter.

Preliminary Study

In the course of the psychotherapy of outpatients, we noted that the manifest content of the dreams of neurotically depressed patients contained a relatively high frequency of unpleasant themes; these unpleasant themes were observed much less frequently in other types of neurotic patients. The striking characteristic of the unpleasant dream was the presence of a particular kind of thematic content: that the patient had dreamed of a painful experience such as being rejected, thwarted, deprived, or punished. The affect, when reported, was consistent with the dream theme and described as a feeling of sadness, loneliness, or frustration.

On the basis of the associations to the dream, as well as the other clinical material, we concluded that the unpleasant dreams were the outcome of certain personality processes in the depressed patient that produced suffering disproportionate to his or her reality situation. The dreams were regarded as analogous to the kind of suffering the depressed patient experienced in waking life. Because of the salience of suffering in these dream themes, the term "masochistic" was selected originally to designate this type of negative dream. We now refer to these dream contents more simply as "negative dreams."

In order to determine whether this clinical observation was valid, we began a systematic study of the dreams of depressed patients. Data for the subsequent investigation were limited to the manifest content of the dream; the free associations to the dream and other clinical material were excluded from consideration for methodological reasons. The hypothesis for this study was: Consecutive dreams of neurotic depressed patients in psychotherapy show a greater incidence of manifest dreams with negative content than a series of dreams in a matched group of nondepressed patients.

In order to test this hypothesis, Beck began a systematic study in collaboration with Dr. Marvin S. Hurvich. Relying primarily on clinical observations, we developed a provisional scoring manual. We then reviewed several hundred dreams of patients diagnosed as depressed or nondepressed. Examples of unpleasant themes that were found frequently in the dreams of the depressed patients but that were found infrequently in the dreams of the nondepressed patients provided the basis for expanding and refining scoring categories. (It should be noted that the dreams of the 12 patients who were the subject of this investigation were not included in the construction and refinement of the scoring manual.)

The typical theme consisted of something unpleasant happening to the patient. The unpleasantness might be *static*: the patient appeared deformed; or *dynamic*: in the course of the dream the patient is thwarted or subjected to direct or indirect psychic or physical trauma. The scoring categories are listed below:

1. Deprived, disappointed, or mistreated
2. Thwarted
3. Excluded, superseded, or displaced
4. Rejected or deserted

TABLE 10-1. Identifying Data on Depressed and Nondepressed Patients

	Age		Marital status		
Pair	Dep.	Nondep.	Dep.	Nondep.	Diagnosis of nondep.
A	23	20	S	M	Anxiety reaction
B	28	28	M	M	Character neurosis
C	31	29	M	M	Spastic colitis
D	31	33	M	M	Cardiac neurosis
E	36	36	M	M	Character neurosis

   5. Blamed, criticized, or ridiculed
   6. Legal punishment
   7. Physical discomfort or injury
   8. Distorted appearance
   9. Being lost
  10. Losing something of value

No score was given for dreams with "threat" or "shame" content unless there was a specific negative element or theme as indicated above. The complete scoring manual is found in the Appendix.

After the scoring system was developed and we had attained a high degree of agreement in scoring dreams, we applied the system to our experimental and control groups. The records of six female patients with the diagnosis of neurotic depression and those of six nondepressed female patients were selected from Beck's files. The two groups were matched patient-for-patient as closely as possible on the basis of age, marital status, and an estimate of the severity of the illness. The characteristics of all the patients are listed in Table 10-1.

The first 20 dreams were abstracted in treatment from each case record and typed on individual sheets of paper. The total sample was 240 dreams (20 per patient for 12 patients), arranged in random order. These were then presented to Dr. Hurvich, who rated each dream according to the negative theme scale. He had no knowledge of any of the patients; this ensured an unbiased blind scoring procedure. These blind ratings were subjected to the statistical valuation reported below. In order to obtain an estimate of the reliability of the ratings, Beck also rated the dreams, and the percentage agreement between our ratings was calculated.

The criteria for establishing the diagnosis of neurotic-depressive reaction in these patients were as follows: depressed mood, feelings of discouragement, unwarranted self-criticism and self-reproaches, inertia or apathy, sleep disturbance, anorexia, and suicidal wishes. The following signs were also considered in the diagnosis: psychomotor retardation, weight loss, and melancholic faces associated with weeping and crying. Each patient showed at least 11 of

TABLE 10-2. Frequency of Negative Dreams of Matched Depressed and Nondepressed Patients

	Dreams out of 20 scoring negative	
Pair	Depressed	Nondepressed
A	13	1
B	9	3
C	14	3
D	13	3
E	7	3
F	9	2

$p < .025$ (one-tailed test).

the 13 diagnostic signs and symptoms. The absence of any evidence of conceptual disorganization, inappropriate affect, or bizarre behavior ruled out a psychotic process.

The estimate of severity of illness was based on the intensity of the symptoms and the degree of impairment of social adjustment. An estimate of socioeconomic standing indicated that all subjects would probably be labeled upper-middle or lower-upper class. A rough clinical estimate of intelligence suggested that all patients in both groups were of at least bright average intelligence. The range of social class and intelligence was thus somewhat restricted; there were no systematic differences between the two groups on either continuum.

For the 240 dreams, the raters agreed regarding the presence or absence of a negative or self-defeating element in 229, slightly in excess of 95 percent agreement. This indicates that the scoring procedure is highly reliable. The results of the comparison between the two groups are listed in Table 10-2. There was no overlap between the groups: more than half (54 percent) of the dreams of the depressed patients contained one or more "negative elements," whereas in the nondepressed group, one-eighth (12.5 percent) of the dreams contained one or more of these elements. Statistical evaluation of the frequency differences between groups with the Wilcoxon Matched-Pairs Signed-Ranks test resulted in a probability figure of .025 (one-tailed test).

The obtained differences between the depressed group and the control group were statistically significant and clear-cut. On the basis of these results, the hypothesis that the depressed patients showed a greater incidence of dreams with negative dream content than the nondepressed patients appeared to be clearly confirmed.

Several qualifications of the scope of these results should be stressed, however. The smallness of the sample, the use of the dreams of females only, and the restricted socioeconomic and IQ ranges represented by these private patients all limited the possible generalizability of the findings. Furthermore, although this sample was not explicitly used as a basis for construction of the rating scale, it is probable that some aspects of the scale were at least partly based on the dreams of patients in the present sample, since the dreams were known to me when the scoring manual was developed.

Principal Study

In view of the obvious limitations of the initial study, we considered it desirable to test the findings on a substantially larger patient sample and to employ more refined procedures as well as a tighter experimental design. The larger study was designed to eliminate the possibility of suggestion by the data collector, as well as the possibility of biased reporting of the dreams; these possibilities of contamination had not been excluded in the first study. In addition, by using a substantially larger sample we were able to test the generalizability of the findings to patients of different nosological, socioeconomic, age, and intelligence categories from those represented by private patients in psychotherapy. Moreover, we could determine whether the findings applied to males as well as to females, who were the sole subjects in the first study. Finally, by using a standardized inventory for measuring depression, in addition to clinical ratings, we were able to circumvent a number of the complex problems associated with the low reliability of psychiatric diagnoses.

A precise replication of the original study was not feasible. Although we had planned to collect dreams at weekly intervals from the patients in the sample, this was not possible because of a number of insuperable problems. We had to limit our collection of dreams, consequently, to the first dream reported by the patient on admission to the outpatient clinic or the hospital.

The likelihood of the introduction of any systematic bias by the data collector was minimized by using a group of interviewers who were not aware of the hypothesis under investigation. A blind scoring procedure by two judges was used to classify the dreams.

In order to determine the reliability of the conventional clinical methods of classifying patients according to nosological categories, a group of four experienced psychiatrists interviewed a series of patients and rendered independent diagnoses according to the first edition of the APA *Diagnostic and Statistical Manual*. Degree of agreement obtained on the primary diagnosis of depression, as well as on diagnoses of the other nosological categories, was considered to be too low for the purposes of this study. Consequently, psychiatrists' ratings of the depth of depression were used, since they had a higher degree of reliability. The Depression Inventory was used as another index of the degree of depression.

The 287 patients in the initial sample were drawn from random admissions to the psychiatric outpatient department of the Hospital of the University of Pennsylvania and the psychiatric outpatient and psychiatric inpatient service of Philadelphia General Hospital. The outpatients were interviewed during the period of evaluation prior to starting treatment; the hospitalized patients were interviewed during their first full day in the hospital. The sample was 61 percent female and 39 percent male; 65 percent white and 35 percent African American. The age range was from 15 to 60, with a median age of 38. The social index, as derived from the Two-Factor Index of Social Position,[46] indicated that the patients were for the most part from the lower socioeconomic groups (15 percent in groups I, II, and II; 38 percent in group IV; 47 percent in group V); 66 percent were outpatients, 34 percent inpatients. Cases of mental deficiency were automatically excluded from the series. All 287 patients received a complete work-up.

The distribution of the patients among the major diagnostic categories was psychotic disorders 41 percent; psychoneurotic disorders 43 percent; personality disorders 16 percent. The diagnoses were schizophrenic reaction, 28 percent; neurotic-depressive reaction 25 percent; anxiety reaction 16 percent; psychotic-depressive reaction 10 percent; personality disorder 10 percent; miscellaneous 11 percent.

The Depression Inventory was administered by a trained interviewer (a clinical psychologist or sociologist), who read each statement in each category aloud to the patient, who was then instructed to select the statement that seemed to fit best. The patient also had a copy of the inventory, so that he or she could read each statement while the interviewer read the statement aloud.

After administering the Depression Inventory, the interviewer asked the patient to tell his or her most recent dream. This was reported orally and recorded. Only the first dream reported by a patient was used in this study. Following this procedure, the interviewer administered a short intelligence test and several other short projective and questionnaire-type tests.

Either immediately before or immediately after the above procedure, one of the four psychiatrists in our research group saw the patient, conducted a thorough psychiatric evaluation, and made a psychiatric diagnosis and a rating of the depth of depression.

The scoring manual used is described in detail in the Appendix. The reliability was shown to be high: the agreement between the two raters in the earlier study was approximately 95 percent. A further check by Dr. Clyde Ward and Beck on the scoring of the present data revealed a similarly high degree of agreement (96 percent).

The most recent dreams collected from the patients were typed on individual sheets identified only by the patients' file numbers. We scored the dreams independently, and differences were resolved by the conference method. A dream was considered scorable so long as there was a subject and a verb in the dream text. An example of a short, scorable dream is "My mother was sick." The following would not be scorable: "It was about my cousin. That's all I can remember."

TABLE 10-3. Comparison of Incidence of Negative Dreams with Depression Inventory Scores (DI)

DI score range	n	Reporting negative dreams	Reporting non-negative dreams
26–45	73	22 (30%)	51 (70%)
15–25	73	21 (29%)	52 (71%)
0–14	72	8 (11%)	64 (89%)

Total distribution: $\chi^2 = 9.08$, $p = 0.01$. Upper vs. lower third: $\chi^2 = 8.00$, $p < 0.01$.

TABLE 10-4. Incidence of Negative Dreams Using Two Measures of Depression as Criterion: Clinical Ratings of Depth of Depression (D of D) and Depression Inventory Scores (DI)

D of D /DI score range	n	Reporting negative dreams	Reporting non-negative dreams
D of D: moderate or severe DI: 26–45	51	16 (31%)	35 (69%)
D of D: none DI: 0–14	38	4 (11%)	34 (89%)

$\chi^2 = 5.43$, $p \leq 0.02$.

Results. Of the 287 patients who received the complete clinical and experimental evaluation, dreams were obtained from 228. Ten dreams were not scorable because of brevity or unintelligibility; thus 218 patients reported scorable dreams. The cases were ranked according to the scores on the Depression Inventory and divided into three groups of approximately equal size. A comparison of the incidence of negative dreams in these groups is presented in Table 10-3. It was found that significantly more negative dreams occurred in the high depressed group than in the nondepressed group ($p < 0.01$). An analysis of the overall association between the degree of depression and the incidence of negative dreams indicated a relationship significant at the 0.01 level.

When we used both psychometric and clinical measures to demarcate the extreme groups, the incidence of negative dreams in the depressed groups was again found to be significantly greater than in the nondepressed groups. With the more stringent criterion, the proportion of negative dreams in each group remained approximately the same as in the previous analysis, although there was some decrease of significance ($p < 0.02$) due to the smaller number of cases. The results of this analysis are shown in Table 10-4.

Another approach to analyzing the data divided all the cases into groups reporting and not reporting negative dreams. When the data were organized in this way, we found that 84 percent of the negative dreams were obtained from patients whose scores placed them in the mildly to severely depressed range. When we evaluated the differences in the ranks of the DI scores with the Mann-Whitney U test, we obtained a highly significant difference between the two groups ($p < .003$).

Specific analyses were performed to determine any significant differences in the distribution of negative dreams attributable to age, sex, race, IQ, or socioeconomic position. None were obtained.

In the initial study we evaluated a series of 20 consecutive dreams collected from each of six depressed patients and from a matching group of six nondepressed patients (total number of dreams, 240). We found that whereas all the patients reported dreams, the proportion of negative dreams was significantly higher for the depressed patients. In contrast, the data of this investigation consisted of only one dream per patient from a much larger patient sample (218). On the basis of the previous findings, it was expected that the probability of any single dream's being negative would be greater if the patient were depressed than if not. This was borne out by the finding of a significantly higher percentage of depressed than nondepressed patients who reported negative dreams.

Almost as many mildly or moderately depressed as severely depressed patients reported negative dreams. This suggests that the negative dream is associated with the presence of depression, regardless of its intensity. However, this finding may be due to the fact that, since the scoring procedure permitted only a dichotomy of dream content, quantitative differences in the degree of negativity could have been obscured.

A consideration of the general significance of the negative dream raises certain important issues. Since many individuals who have never had a clinical depression or other psychiatric illness stated that they occasionally had dreams of this nature, the dream itself is not necessarily a sign of illness. Moreover, many patients with recurrent depressions continued to report self-defeating or negative dreams with the same frequency during the symptom-free intervals. Furthermore, some patients recalled having had repetitive dreams of this nature long before having been depressed. Consequently, the negative dream cannot be construed as being associated only with the state of depression. It seems more likely to be a correlate of certain personality characteristics of individuals who are prone to develop depressions.

The dynamic relationship of the negative (self-defeating) dream to depression may be further explored by comparing the typical dream themes with other behaviors observable in the depressed patient. For example, the dreams of failing, of being rejected, or of losing something of value may be compared with the depressive's waking feelings of inadequacy, of undesirability, and of deprivation. Another characteristic dream is that of trying to attain some goal and of being consistently thwarted by circumstances. This type of dream is suggestive of the depressive's constantly seeing barriers to any goal-directed activity, a kind of behavior that conveys a general attitude of indecisiveness or of hopelessness.

In the course of the psychotherapy of patients with neurotic-depressive reactions, we noted that there was a high incidence of dreams with unpleasant content. This unpleasant content was of a particular kind: rejection, disappointment, humiliation, or similar unpleasant experiences.

We constructed a rating scale for the objective identification of these unpleasant themes. This scale was applied to the first 20 dreams in treatment of six patients who were diagnosed as neurotic depressives, and six matched but nondepressed patients. The depressed patients showed a significantly higher number of dreams with negative content than did the nondepressed patients.

Because of the findings of this preliminary study, we carried out a large-scale investigation to test these findings in a more carefully designed study. The dreams of 218 patients were rated independently by two judges for the presence or absence of self-defeating themes. There was 96 percent agreement between the judges. Patients were divided into three groups according to their scores on the Depression Inventory: nondepressed, moderately depressed, and severely depressed. The moderately and severely depressed groups reported significantly more negative dreams than the nondepressed group. Analysis of background factors such as age, sex, race, intelligence, and socioeconomic position indicated that these variables were not responsible for the attained results.

Child Bereavement and Adult Depression

The association of early parental deprivation with the subsequent development of psychopathology has been reported by many authors. By the mid-1960s, more than 50 papers in this area had been published. The systematic studies published before 1958 were well summarized in a critical review by Gregory,[47] who focused particularly on their sources of error.

In a study of orphanhood in England, Brown[48] reported a significant relationship between parental loss in childhood and adult depression. He found that 41 percent of 216 depressed adult patients had lost a parent through death before the age of 15; this incidence was found to be significantly greater than the incidence of orphanhood in the general population (12 percent) and in a comparison group of 267 nonpsychiatric medical patients (19.6 percent).

Most studies of orphanhood and psychopathology had methodological defects that pose difficulties in evaluating the obtained relationships. First, when the isolation of the criterion group depends on the conventional system of diagnosis, many complex problems related to the variability of psychiatric diagnoses are introduced and restrict the ability to generalize the findings. In

Brown's study, the basis for diagnosing depression was "the presence of an unpleasant affect, not transitory, and without schizophrenia or brain disease." Such a broad definition could make clinical identification of the depressed patients particularly vulnerable to inconsistency and overinclusiveness. A second problem encountered in this type of investigation is the comparison of a specific nosological group with a normal control group. In Brown's study, for example, the use of nonpsychiatric medical patients as the control group raises a question as to whether the high incidence of orphanhood was a specific characteristic of his depressed group or was associated with psychiatric disorders in general. A third difficulty is presented by the fact that there is considerable discrepancy in the base rates of parental death for the various demographic classes in the general population from which samples of patients are drawn. These variations need to be taken into account in any epidemiological studies.

Childhood Bereavement Study

Our bereavement study presented further findings regarding the relationship of the development of depression in late adolescence and adulthood to the death of a parent in childhood. To circumvent the difficulties posted by the variability of psychiatric classifications, the Depression Inventory was used as the major criterion measure. As an additional measure of depression, we obtained clinical ratings of the depth of depression, irrespective of the specific diagnostic category. Nondepressed psychiatric patients were used as the comparison group, and provision was made to determine the influence of background variables such as age, race, and sex.

A total of 297 patients were selected from routine admissions to the psychiatric outpatient clinic of the University of Pennsylvania and the psychiatric outpatient clinic and psychiatric wards of Philadelphia General Hospital. Cases diagnosed as having brain damage were excluded from the study.

Each patient was studied by the research team during an initial period of evaluation at the outpatient clinic or on the day following admission to the psychiatric ward. The research study included a thorough psychiatric evaluation by one of four psychiatrists who made both a diagnosis according to the 1952 edition of the *Standard Nomenclature of the American Psychiatric Association* and also a rating on a four-point scale of the depth of depression irrespective of the nosological category. The Depression Inventory was administered to each patient by a trained interviewer. Each patient was specifically questioned about whether his or her parents were living and, in the case of the death of a parent, the interviewer attempted to determine the patient's age at the time of the death.

We divided the patient sample into three groups of approximately equal size according to the scores on the Depression Inventory. In the formulation of the research design, however, we had decided that the comparison would be made only between the extreme groups, since previous experience with the inventory indicated that there was a considerable overlap of clinically depressed and nondepressed patients in the middle group.

We found that 27 percent of the patients in the high-depressed group (DI score 25 +) reported the loss of a parent before the age of 16 as compared with 12 percent in the nondepressed group (DI score 0–13). The difference in incidence between these two groups was found to be highly significant ($p < 0.01$).

We performed a similar analysis to determine the incidence of parental loss when clinical judgments of the depth of depression were used as the criterion measure. When the extreme groups were compared, it was again found that the severely depressed groups showed a significantly higher proportion of parental death (36.4 percent) than the nondepressed group (15.2 percent). There was no significant difference in incidence among the groups judged clinically to be moderately depressed, mildly depressed, or nondepressed.

When we compared the sex of the patient with the sex of the dead parent, we found that for both males and females loss of the father occurred appreciably more frequently than loss of the mother. This frequency held for both sexes across all levels of depression. Furthermore, when the extreme groups are compared, loss of father was overrepresented in the high-depressed group for both males and females. It should also be noted that the overall incidence of orphanhood was significantly higher in the African American than in the white group and in the older (31–60) than in the younger (16–30) group.

Within each demographic class, the incidence of orphanhood was consistently higher for the high-depressed than for the nondepressed patients. A χ^2 analysis indicated that these differences between extreme groups were significant in the following categories: inpatients ($p < 0.02$); African Americans ($p < 0.02$); females ($p < 0.02$); and younger age group ($p < 0.05$). The differences between the extreme groups in the remaining categories were in the predicted direction, the p-value in each case being <0.20. Age was also associated with depression as well as with orphanhood. There was also a suggestion of a relationship between sex and depression, since females were overrepresented in the high-depressed group.

In order to evaluate statistically the significance of the relationship among orphanhood, age, and depression, the data were reorganized with the Depression Inventory scores as the dependent variable. An appropriate number of cases were randomly eliminated from each age category in the nonorphan group in order to make the cells proportional for the analysis of variance. The total number thus was reduced from 297 to 162 for this analysis. The F value of 3.81 for the comparison of depression with orphanhood falls just short of the 0.05 level of significance (when $F = 3.84$, $p < 0.05$), indicating that the major portion of the variance in the Depression Inventory scores was attributable to the association between these scores and orphanhood. The interaction between age and orphanhood was not significant.

To explore the possibility that the obtained differences between the high-depressed and nondepressed patients might be related to the specific nosological classes, the patients were grouped according to their specific formal diagnoses as well as according to their scores on the Depression Inventory. Only those diagnostic categories that contained at least 12 cases were included; the remaining 53 cases were distributed among various diagnostic categories, predominantly those in the generic class of "personality disorders," as given in the *Standard Nomenclature.*

Within each nosological category, the group scoring highest on the Depression Inventory consistently showed a greater incidence of orphanhood than the low-scoring group. This consistent difference across all categories was evaluated by the Sign test and was found to be significant at the 0.03 level. Although the overall incidence of orphanhood in the psychotic-depressed group was higher than in any other category, the difference was not significant when this group was compared with the schizophrenic group. The overall incidence of orphanhood in the neurotic-depression group approximated that in the schizophrenic group.

To determine whether any of the late adolescent depressions occurred during the mourning period following bereavement, we reviewed the cases who lost their parents just before age 16. Of the four who lost a parent at age of 14 or 15, three reported symptom-free intervals of 15, 29, and 30 years between time of bereavement and onset of the depression. The remaining patient, age 15 when his parent died, was 19 at the time of admission to the hospital. At that time he reported a one-year symptom-free interval between the loss of the parent and the onset of depression.

Comment. The finding of a significantly greater incidence of loss of a parent during childhood in the high-depressed as compared with the nondepressed patients is consistent with the results reported by Brown. We dealt with some of the methodological problems presented by his study by using a comparison group of nondepressed psychiatric patients and employing a standardized instrument to identify the depressed group rather than relying on clinical diagnoses of uncertain reliability. In addition, in analyzing the data, we attempted to control certain relevant background variables. Although the incidence of both orphans and depressed patients was increased in the older age groups, we found that age did not account for the obtained relationship between orphanhood and depression.

The finding of significant differences in the incidence of orphanhood between various demographic groups (e.g., whites versus African Americans) underscores the necessity for introducing methods in the design of such studies for controlling background characteristics. For instance, many earlier studies overlooked the fact that during the past century there has been a gradual decline in the incidence of orphanhood in the general population. Gregory's[47] abstract of the census data for the Province of Ontario (1961) showed an appreciable drop in frequency of death of a parent before age 16 when individuals born in 1921 were compared with those born a decade later. This decrease was reflected in our comparisons of the relative incidence of orphanhood in the older and younger groups.

The use of an inventory as the principal measure of depression naturally presents problems. In view of the demonstrated vulnerability of some inventories to noncontent variables such as response styles, a researcher must be careful in interpreting the scores on instruments that consist of self-descriptive items. Nevertheless, the obtained differences between the extreme groups were confirmed when a different measure of depression, namely, psychiatrists' ratings of the depth of depression, was used. The Depression Inventory was selected as the preferred criterion measure because it has the major advantage over clinical ratings of being easily applied by different investigators, a characteristic that facilitates replication of the study.

Another feature that may justify further elaboration is the conceptual basis for defining the criterion group. The concept of depression as a psychopathological state that may exist to varying degrees irrespective of the formal diagnosis is more congruent with the "polydimensional model" described by Lorr[49] than with the model on which the *Standard Nomenclature* is based. It seemed a priori that for the purposes of this investigation the former model was more appropriate than the latter. In fact, when the patients were grouped according to the conventional nosological system, no significant relationships were found between specific diagnostic categories and the incidence of orphanhood; however, within each diagnostic category there was a consistent tendency for high scorers on the Depression Inventory to show a greater incidence of orphanhood than low scorers.

After this study was completed, two relevant controlled studies, also conducted in the 1960s, were published by other investigators. These did not show a significant relationship between parental loss and clinical diagnosis of depression. In this respect, their findings are similar to ours in that we did not find any association between orphanhood and the *nosological category* of depression. Although neither of these studies employed the same approach or methods as did our study, the findings raised doubts about the relationship of orphanhood to depression.

Pitts et al.[50] did not find a significant association between childhood bereavement and any diagnostic category in their adult patients. However, their control group consisted of medical inpatients. Several studies have shown that depressive symptomatology is widely distributed among medical inpatients.[51,52] Hence, it is necessary to control for the presence of depression even when nonpsychiatric patients are used as the comparison group. Gregory[53] made systematic comparisons of parental loss and psychiatric diagnoses.

Using clinical diagnoses and MMPI high points as his criterion measures, he was unable to establish a significant association between parental loss and any of the diagnostic groups.

A group of 297 inpatients and outpatients were studied during their initial period of evaluation on a psychiatric ward or at a psychiatric clinic to determine the relationship of orphanhood to depression. The state of depression was investigated as a psychopathological dimension, irrespective of specific diagnoses, by the use of the Depression Inventory and by clinical ratings by experienced psychiatrists.

The 100 patients who received high-depressed scores on the Depression Inventory showed a significantly higher incidence of orphanhood before age 16 (27 percent) than did the 100 low scorers (12 percent). A similar difference between the extreme groups was obtained when psychiatrists' ratings of the intensity of depression were used as the criterion measure.

The obtained difference in the incidence of orphanhood between the high-depressed and nondepressed groups provides evidence that the death of a parent in childhood may be a factor in the later development of a severe depression in a significant proportion of psychiatric patients.

Cognitive Distortions in Depression

Prior to Beck's studies that led to the publication of the first edition of this book, clinical and theoretical papers dealing with the psychological correlates of depression generally used a motivational-affective model for categorizing and interpreting the verbal behavior of patients. The cognitive processes as such received little attention except insofar as they were related to variables such as hostility, orality, or guilt.[38]

This lack of emphasis on thought processes in depression may have reflected of—or possibly contributed to—the widely held opinion at the time that depression is an affective disorder and any impairment of thinking is a result of the affective disturbance.[54] This opinion was buttressed by the failure to demonstrate any consistent evidence of abnormalities in the formal thought processes in the responses to the standard battery of psychological tests.[55] Furthermore, the few experimental studies of thinking in depression revealed no consistent deviations other than a retardation in the responses to speed tests[56] and a lowered responsiveness to a Gestalt completion test.[57]

In his book on depression, Kraines[58] described, on the basis of clinical observations, several characteristics of a thought disorder in depression. The objective of our study was to ascertain the nature of the thought processes of depressed patients. An important corollary of this objective was the specification of the differences from, and similarities to, the thinking of nondepressed psychiatric patients. The remainder of this chapter focuses on the following areas: (1) the verbalized thought content indicating distorted or unrealistic conceptualizations; (2) the processes involved in the deviations from logical or realistic thinking; (3) the formal characteristics of the ideation showing such deviations; and (4) the relationship between the cognitive distortions and the affects characteristic of depression.

The data for this study were accumulated from interviews with 50 psychiatric patients seen in psychotherapy or formal psychoanalysis. Four of these patients were hospitalized for varying periods during treatment. The rest were ambulatory.

The frequency of interviews varied from one to six a week, with the median number three a week. The total length of time in psychotherapy ranged from six months to six years; the median was two years. In no case did a single episode of depression last longer than a year. Many patients continued in psychotherapy for a substantial time after the remission of their initial depressive episode. Thirteen either had recurrent depressions while in psychotherapy or returned to psychotherapy because of a recurrence. In this recurrent depression group, six had completely asymptomatic intervals between the recurrences, and seven had some degree of hypomanic elevation. It was, therefore, possible to obtain data from these patients during each phase of the cycle.

Of the 50 patients in the sample, 16 were men and 34 were women. The age range was 18 to 48, with a median of 34. An estimate of their intelligence suggested that all were of at least bright average intelligence. Their socioeconomic status was judged to be middle or upper class. Twelve were diagnosed as having psychotic-depressive or manic-depressive reactions, and 38 as having neurotic-depressive reactions.

To establish the diagnosis of depression, we employed the following diagnostic indicators: objective signs of depression in face, speech, posture, and motor activity; a major complaint of feeling depressed or sad; and at least 11 of the following 14 signs and symptoms: loss of appetite, weight loss, sleep disturbance, loss of libido, fatigability, crying, pessimism, suicidal wishes, indecisiveness, loss of sense of humor, sense of boredom or apathy, overconcern about health, excessive self-criticism, and loss of initiative.

Patients showing evidence of organic brain damage or of a schizophrenic process, and those in whom anxiety or some other psychopathological state was more prominent than depression, were excluded from this group.

In addition to the group of depressed patients, a group of 31 nondepressed patients was also seen in psychotherapy. This group was similar to the depressed group in respect to age, sex, and social position, and constituted a control group for this study.

Beck conducted face-to-face interviews when the depressions were regarded as moderate to severe and was active and supportive during these periods. Other than during periods of severe depression, formal analysis was employed for the long-term patients; Beck utilized the couch, encouraged free association, and followed the policy of minimal activity. The recorded data used as the basis for this study were notes handwritten during the psychotherapeutic interviews. These data include retrospective reports by the patients of feelings and thoughts prior to the sessions, as well as spontaneous reports of their feelings and thoughts during the sessions. In addition, several patients regularly kept notes of their feelings and thoughts between psychotherapeutic sessions and reported these.

While these data were collected, handwritten records of the verbalizations of the nondepressed patients were also collected, and these notes were compared with the notes on the depressed group.

We found that the depressed patients differed from the nondepressed group in the preponderance of certain themes outlined below. Moreover, each nosological group showed an idiosyncratic ideational content that distinguished it from each of the others. Depression was characterized by themes of low self-esteem, self-blame, overwhelming responsibilities, and desires to escape; anxiety state by themes of personal danger; hypomanic state by themes of self-enhancement; hostile paranoid state by themes of accusations against others.

Although each nosological group showed particular types of thought content specific for that group, the formal characteristics and processes of distortion involved in the idiosyncratic ideation were similar for each of these nosological categories. The processes of distortion and the formal characteristics will be described.

Thematic Content of Cognitions

The types of cognitions outlined below were reported by the depressed patients to occur under two general conditions. First, the typical depressive cognitions were observed in response to particular kinds of external stimulus situations. These were situations that contained an ingredient, or combination of ingredients, whose content had some relevance to the content of the idiosyncratic response. This stereotyped response was frequently irrelevant and inappropriate to the situation as a whole. For instance, any experience that touched in any way on the subject of the patient's personal attributes might immediately make him think he was inadequate.

A young man responded with self-derogatory thoughts to any interpersonal situation in which another person seemed indifferent to him. If a passerby on the street did not smile at him, he was prone to think he was inferior. Similarly, a woman consistently had the thought she was a bad mother whenever she saw another woman with a child.

Second, the typical depressive thoughts were observed in the patients' ruminations or free associations, that is, when they were not reacting to an immediate external stimulus and were not attempting to direct their thoughts. The severely depressed patients often experienced long, uninterrupted sequences of depressive associations, completely independent of the external situation.

Low self-regard. Low self-evaluation formed a prominent part of the depressed patients' ideation. This generally consisted of an unrealistic downgrading of themselves in areas that were of particular importance to them. A brilliant academician questioned her basic intelligence, an attractive society leader insisted she had become repulsive looking, and a successful business executive believed he had no real business acumen and was headed for bankruptcy.

The low self-appraisal was applied to personal attributes such as ability, virtue, attractiveness, and health; to acquisitions of tangibles or intangibles (such as love or friendship); or to past performance in one's career or in one's role as a spouse or parent. In making these self-appraisals, the depressed patient was prone to magnify any failures or defects and minimize or ignore any favorable characteristics.

A common feature of many of the self-evaluations was the patients' unfavorable comparisons with other people, particularly in their own social or occupational group. Almost uniformly, in making comparisons, depressed patients rated themselves as inferior: less intelligent, less productive, less attractive, less financially secure, or less successful as a spouse or parent than those in their comparison groups. These types of self-ratings comprise the feeling of inferiority, which has been noted in the literature on depressives.

Ideas of deprivation. Allied to the low self-appraisals are the ideas of destitution seen in certain depressed patients. These ideas were noted in the patient's verbalized thoughts that he or she is alone, unwanted, and unlovable, often in the face of overt demonstrations of friendship and affection. The sense of deprivation was also applied to material possessions, despite obvious contrary evidence.

Self-criticisms and self-blame. Another prominent theme in the reported thoughts of the depressed patients was concerned with self-criticism and self-condemnation. These themes should be differentiated from the low self-evaluation already described. The low self-evaluation refers simply to the appraisal of themselves relative either to their comparison group or to their own standards, but the self-criticism represents the reproaches they leveled against themselves for their perceived shortcomings. It should be pointed out, however, that not all patients with low self-evaluation showed self-criticism.

The self-criticisms, just as the low self-evaluations, were usually applied to the specific attributes or behaviors most highly valued by the individual. A depressed woman, for example, condemned herself for not having breakfast ready for her husband one morning when it was her turn to make it. She reported a sexual affair with one of his colleagues, however, without any evidence of regret, self-criticism, or guilt. Competence as a cook was one of her expectations of herself but marital fidelity was not.

Patients' tendency to blame themselves for their mistakes or shortcomings generally had no logical basis. This was demonstrated by a woman who took her children on a picnic. When a thunderstorm suddenly appeared, she blamed herself for not having picked a better day.

Overwhelming problems and duties. The patients consistently magnified problems or responsibilities that they considered minor or insignificant when not depressed. A depressed woman, confronted with the necessity of sewing name tags on her children's clothes in preparation for camp, perceived this as a gigantic undertaking that would take weeks to complete. When she finally got to work at it she finished in less than a day.

Self-commands and injunctions. Self-coercive cognitions, although not prominently mentioned in the literature on depression, seemed to form a substantial proportion of the verbalized thoughts of the patients in the sample. These cognitions consisted of constant nagging or prodding to do things. The prodding would persist even when it was impractical, undesirable, or impossible for the person to implement these self-instructions.

The "shoulds" and "musts" were often applied to an enormous range of activities, many of them mutually exclusive. A married woman reported that in a period of a few minutes, she had compelling thoughts to clean the house, lose some weight, visit a sick friend, be a den mother, get a full-time job, plan the week's menus, return to college for a degree, spend more time with her children, take a memory course, be more active in women's organizations, and start putting away her winter clothes.

Escapist and suicidal wishes. Thoughts about escaping from the problems of life were frequent among all the patients. Some had daydreams of being a hobo, or of going to a tropical paradise. It was unusual, however, that evading the tasks brought any relief. Even when a temporary respite was taken on the advice of the psychiatrist, the patients were prone to blame themselves for shirking responsibilities.

The desire to escape seemed to be related to the patients' viewing themselves at an impasse. They saw themselves as incapable, incompetent, and helpless, and their tasks as ponderous and formidable. Their response was a wish to withdraw from the "unsolvable" problems. Several patients spent considerable time in bed, some hiding under the covers.

Suicidal preoccupations seemed similarly related to the patients' conceptualization of the situation as untenable or hopeless. They believed they could not tolerate a continuation of suffering, and could see no solution to the problem. The psychiatrist could not help, the symptoms could not be alleviated, and the problems could not be solved. The suicidal patients generally stated that they regarded suicide as the only possible solution for their desperate or hopeless situations.

Typology of Cognitive Distortions

A crucial characteristic of these cognitions is that they represent varying degrees of reality distortion. Although some degree of inaccuracy and inconsistency is expected in the cognitions of any individual, the distinguishing characteristic of the cognitions of the depressed patients is that they show a *systematic error*, a bias against themselves. Systematic errors were also noted in the idiosyncratic ideation of the other nosological groups.

The typical depressive cognitions can be categorized according to the ways in which they deviate from logical or realistic thinking. The processes may be classified as paralogical (arbitrary inference, selective abstraction, and over-generalization), stylistic (exaggeration), or semantic (inexact labeling). These cognitive distortions were observed at all levels of depression, from the mild neurotic depression to the severe psychotic. Although the thinking disorder was most obvious in the psychotic depressions, it was observable in more subtle ways among all the neurotic depressed.

Arbitrary inference is defined as the process of drawing a conclusion from a situation, event, or experience when there is no evidence to support the conclusion or when the conclusion is contrary to the evidence.

A patient riding on an elevator had the thought, "He [the elevator operator] thinks I'm a nobody." The patient then felt sad. On being questioned by the psychiatrist, he realized there was no factual basis for this thought.

Such misconstructions are particularly prone to occur when the cues are ambiguous. An intern became quite discouraged, for example, when he received an announcement that all patients worked up by the interns should be examined subsequently by the resident physicians. His thought on reading the announcement was, "The chief doesn't have faith in my work." In this instance, he personalized the event, although there was no reason to suspect that his performance had anything to do with the policy decision.

Intrinsic to this thinking is the lack of consideration of alternative explanations that are more plausible and more probable. The intern, when questioned about other possible explanations for the policy decision, then recalled a previous statement by her chief that he wanted the residents to have more contact with the patients as part of their training. The idea that this explicitly stated objective was the basis for the new policy had not previously occurred to her.

Selective abstraction refers to the process of focusing on a detail taken out of context, ignoring other more salient features of the situation, and conceptualizing the whole experience on the basis of this element.

A patient was praised by her employer about aspects of her work. At one point, the employer asked her to discontinue making extra carbon copies of his letters, and her immediate thought was, "He is dissatisfied with my work." This idea became paramount despite all his positive statements.

Overgeneralization is the patients' pattern of drawing a general conclusion about their ability, their performance, or their worth on the basis of a single incident.

A patient reported the following sequence of events occurring within a period of half an hour: His wife was upset because the children were slow in getting dressed. He thought, "I'm a poor father because the children are not better disciplined." He then noticed a leaky faucet and thought that this showed he was also a poor husband. While driving to work, he thought, "I must be a poor driver or other cars would not be passing me." As he arrived at work, he noticed some other personnel had already arrived. He thought, "I can't be very dedicated or I would have come earlier." When he noticed folders and papers piled up on his desk, he concluded, "I'm a poor organizer because I have so much work to do."

Magnification and minimization refer to errors in evaluations so gross as to constitute distortions. As described in the section on thematic content, these processes were manifested by underestimation of the individuals' performance, achievement, or ability and inflation of the magnitude of their problems and tasks. Other examples were exaggeration of the intensity or significance of a traumatic event. It was frequently observed that the patients' initial reaction to an unpleasant event was to regard it as a catastrophe. It was generally found on further inquiry that the perceived disaster was often a relatively minor problem.

A man reported that he had been upset because of damage to his house as the result of a storm. When he first discovered the damage, his thought sequence was, "The side of the house is wrecked. . . . It will cost a fortune to fix it." His immediate reaction was that the repair bill would be several thousand dollars. After the initial shock had dissipated, he realized that the damage was minor and that the repairs would cost around fifty dollars.

Inexact labeling often seems to contribute to this kind of distortion. The affective reaction is proportional to the descriptive labeling of the event, rather than to the actual intensity of a traumatic situation.

A man reported during his therapy hour that he was very upset because he had been "clobbered" by his superior. On further reflection, he realized that he had magnified the incident and that a more adequate description was that his supervisor "corrected an error" he had made. After reevaluating the event, he felt better. He also realized that whenever he was corrected or criticized by a person in authority he was prone to describe this as being "clobbered."

Formal Characteristics of Depressive Cognitions

One of the striking features of the typical depressive cognitions is that they were generally experienced by the patients as arising as though they were *automatic* responses, that is, without any apparent antecedent reflection or reasoning. For example, a patient observed that when he was in a situation in which somebody else was receiving praise, he would automatically have the thought, "I'm nobody. . . . I'm not good enough." Later, when he reflected on his response, he would then regard it as inappropriate. Nonetheless, his immediate response to such situations continued to be self-devaluation.

The depressive thoughts not only appeared to be automatic, in the sense just described, but they seemed, also, to have an *involuntary* quality. The patients frequently reported that these thoughts would occur even when they had resolved "not to have them" or were actively trying to avoid them. This involuntary characteristic was clearly exemplified by repetitive thoughts of suicide, but was found in a less dramatic way in other types of depressive cognitions. A number of patients were able to anticipate the kind of depressive thoughts that would occur in certain specific situations and would prepare themselves in advance to make a more realistic judgment of the situation. Nevertheless, despite the intention to ward off or control these thoughts, they would continue to preempt a more rational response.

Another characteristic of depressive thoughts is their *plausibility* to the patient. At the beginning of therapy the patients tended to accept the validity of the cognitions uncritically. It often required considerable experience in observing these thoughts and attempting to judge them rationally for the patients to recognize them as distortions. It was noted that the more plausible the cognitions seemed (or the more uncritically the patient regarded them), the stronger the affective reaction. It was also observed that when the patient was able to question the validity of the thoughts, the affective reaction was generally reduced. The converse of this also seemed to be true: When the affective reaction to a thought was particularly strong, its plausibility became enhanced, and the patient found it more difficult to appraise its validity. Furthermore, once a strong affect was aroused in response to a distorted cognition, any subsequent distortions seemed to have an increased plausibility. This characteristic appeared to be present irrespective of whether the affect was sadness, anger, anxiety, or euphoria. Once the affective response was dissipated, however, the patient could then appraise these cognitions critically and recognize the distortions.

A final characteristic of depressive cognitions is their *perseveration*. Despite the multiplicity and complexity of life situations, the depressed patient was prone to interpret a wide range of experiences in terms of a few stereotyped ideas. The same type of cognition would be elicited by highly heterogeneous experiences. In addition, these idiosyncratic cognitions tended to occur repetitively in the patients' ruminations and stream of associations.

Relationship of Depressive Thoughts to Affect

As part of psychotherapy, the author encouraged the patients to attempt to specify as precisely as possible their feelings and their thoughts in relation to these feelings.

A number of problems were presented in the attempt to obtain precise descriptions and labeling of the feelings. Patients had no difficulty in designating their feelings as pleasant or unpleasant, and they were readily able to specify whether they felt depressed (or sad), anxious, angry, and embarrassed. When they were asked to discriminate further among the depressed feelings, there was considerable variability. Most patients were able to differentiate with a reasonable degree of certainty among the following: sad, discouraged, hurt, humiliated, guilty, empty, and lonely.

To determine the relationship of specific feelings to a specific thought, the patients were advised to develop the routine of trying to focus their attention on their thoughts whenever they had an unpleasant feeling or whenever the feeling became intensified. This often meant thinking back after they were aware of the unpleasant feeling to recall the content of the preceding thought. They frequently observed that an unpleasant thought preceded the unpleasant affect.

The most noteworthy finding was that when the thoughts associated with the depressive affects were identified, they were generally found to contain the type of conceptual distortions or errors already described, as well as the typical depressive thematic content. Similarly, when the affect was anxiety, anger, or elation, the associated cognitions had a content congruent with these feelings.

An effort was made to classify the cognitions, to ascertain whether there were any specific features that could distinguish among the types of cognitions associated respectively with depression, anger, or elation. We found, as might be expected, that the typical thoughts associated with the depressive affect centered around the idea that the individual was deficient in some way. Furthermore, the specific types of depressive affect were generally consistent with the specific thought content. Thus, thoughts of being deserted, inferior, or derelict were associated respectively with feelings of loneliness, humiliation, or guilt.

In the nondepressed group, the thoughts associated with the affect of anxiety had the theme of anticipating some unpleasant event. Thoughts associated with anger had an element of blame directed against some other person or agency. Finally, feelings of euphoria were associated with thoughts that were self-inflating in some way.

Discussion

The material in this section is reprinted in its entirety from the first edition.

It has been noted that "the schizophrenic excels in his tendency to misconstrue the world that is presented."[57] Although the validity of this statement has been supported by numerous clinical and experimental studies, it has not generally been acknowledged that misconstructions of reality may also be a characteristic feature of other psychiatric disorders. The present study indicates that, even in mild phases of depression, systematic deviations from realistic and logical thinking occur. A crucial feature of these cognitive distortions is that they appeared consistently only in the ideational material that had a typically depressive content, for example themes of being deficient in some way. The other ideational material reported by the depressed patients did not show any systematic errors.

The thinking-disorder typology outlined here is similar to that described in studies of schizophrenia. Although some of the most flagrant schizophrenic signs (such as word-salad, metaphorical speech, neologisms, and condensations) were not observed, the kinds of paralogical processes in the depressed patients resembled those described in schizophrenics.[59] Moreover, the same kind of paralogical thinking was observed in the nondepressed patients in the control group.

Although each nosological category showed a distinctive thought *content*, the differences in terms of the *processes* involved in the deviant thinking appeared to be quantitative rather than qualitative. These findings suggest that a thinking disorder may be common to all types of psychopathology. By applying this concept to psychiatric classification, it would be possible to characterize the specific nosological categories in terms of the degree of cognitive impairment and the particular content of the idiosyncratic cognitions.

The failure of various psychological tests to reflect a thinking disorder in depression warrants consideration. It is suggested that the tests employed are not specifically designed for detecting the thinking deviations in depression. Since clinical observation indicates that the typical cognitive distortions in depression are limited to particular content areas (such as self-devaluations), the various object-sorting, proverb-interpreting, and projective tests may miss the essential pathology. Even in studies of schizophrenia, the demonstration of a thinking disorder is dependent on the type of test administered and the characteristics of the experimental group. Cohen and his coworkers,[57] for example, found that the only instrument eliciting abnormal responses in acute schizophrenics was the Rorschach test, whereas chronic schizophrenics showed abnormalities on a Gestalt completion test as well as on the Rorschach.

The clinical finding of a thinking disorder at all levels of depression should focus attention on the problem of defining the precise relationship of the cognitive distortions to the characteristic affective state in depression. The [1952] diagnostic manual of the American Psychiatric Association[54] defines the psychotic affective reactions in terms of "a primary, severe disorder of mood with resultant disturbance of thought and behavior, in consonance with the affect." Although this is a widely accepted concept, the converse would appear to be at least as plausible, namely, that there is primary disorder of thought with resultant disturbance of affect and behavior in consonance with the cognitive distortions. This latter thesis is consistent with the conception that the way individuals structure an experience determine their affective response to it. If, for example, they perceive a situation as dangerous, they may be expected to respond with a consonant affect, such as anxiety.

It is proposed, therefore, that the typical depressive affects are evoked by the erroneous conceptualizations. If patients incorrectly perceive themselves as inadequate, deserted, or sinful, they will experience corresponding affects such as sadness, loneliness, or guilt. However,, the possibility that the evoked affect may, in turn, influence the thinking should also be considered. It is conceivable that once a depressive affect has been aroused, it will facilitate the emergence of further depressive-type cognitions. A continuous interaction between cognition and affect may, consequently, be produced and, thus, lead to the typical downward spiral observed in depression. (The theoretical implications of this study are discussed more fully in Chapter 13.) Since it seems likely that this interaction would be highly complex, appropriately designed experiments would be warranted to clarify the relationships.

A few methodological problems should be mentioned. A question could be raised, for example, regarding the generalizing of the observations. Since the sample consisted largely of psychotherapy patients of a relatively narrow range of intelligence and social index, there may be some uncertainty as to whether the findings are applicable to the general population of depressed patients. In view of the obvious problems associated with using data from handwritten notes of psychotherapy sessions, it is apparent that the findings of the present study will have to be subjected to verification by more refined and systematic studies. One promising approach has been developed by Gottschalk, Gleser, and Springer,[60] who utilized verbatim recordings of five-minute periods of free association by depressed patients, and subjected this material to blind scoring by trained judges. Such a procedure circumvents the hazards of therapist bias and suggestion associated with verbal material recorded in psychotherapy interviews.

In summary, a group of 50 depressed patients in psychotherapy and a control group of 31 nondepressed patients were studied to determine the prevalence and types of cognitive abnormalities. Evidence of deviation from logical and realistic thinking was found at every level of depression from mild neurotic to severe psychotic.

The ideation of the depressed patients differed from that of the nondepressed patients in the prominence of certain typical themes, namely, low self-evaluation, ideas of deprivation, exaggeration of problems and difficulties, self-criticism and self-commands, and wishes to escape or die. Similarly, each of the nondepressed nosological groups could be differentiated on the basis of their idiosyncratic thought content.

Abnormalities were detected consistently only in those verbalized thoughts that had the typical thematic content of the depressed groups. The other kinds of ideation did not show any consistent distortion. Among the deviations in thinking, the following processes were identified: arbitrary inference, selective abstraction, overgeneralization, and magnification and minimization.

Afterword

The above studies summarize Beck's original tests of Freud's theory. They are most relevant to the initial development of the cognitive theory of depression. As articulated in the chapters to follow, the "anomalous finding" of the dream studies (Beck 2006) eventually generated a new system of treatment, cognitive therapy. Since the first edition of the present volume,[4] numerous cognitive models have been proposed,[61] and more elaborated reviews presented elsewhere (e.g., Clark et al.;[62] Haaga et al.;[63] Scher et al.[64]). Part III, Theoretical Aspects of Depression, includes many more recent developments, such as the psychological studies on reactivity, vulnerability (diathesis), genetic findings, the empirical support of the theory, and the integrative theory that now underpins the cognitive system of therapy.

Part III
Theoretical Aspects of Depression

Chapter 11
Theories of Depression

The theories of depression that have been most tested and applied to the psychotherapeutic treatment of the mood disorders include the interpersonal and cognitive behavioral formulations.[1] Other theories include Freud's psychoanalytic theory, evolutionary theories, existentialism, neurological and neuropsychological perspectives, biochemical theory, and animal models.

Behavioral Theories

Several behavioral theories of depression have been advanced. Among the early theorists in this area were Ferster,[2] Seligman,[3,4] and Lewisohn.[5]

Seligman suggested that the phenomenon of "learned helplessness" in animal models might be meaningfully analogous to clinical depression in humans. Briefly, Seligman found that when a normal dog receives escape-avoidance training, it quickly learns to avoid a shock by moving to the safe side of a shuttle box. However, dogs given inescapable shocks before avoidance training were found to act quite differently. Instead of attempting to escape, such dogs would give up and passively accept the shock.

Seligman reviewed similar studies with a variety of animals and concluded that learned helplessness is found in "rats, cats, dogs, fish, mice, and men" (p. 86).[4] Based on this generalization, he theorized a specific arrangement of reinforcement contingency, that is, inescapable punishment, could be a causative factor in the lives of those who become clinically depressed.

Ferster and Lewisohn likewise referred to basic behavioral principles to account for clinical depression. Ferster theorized that depression may be a reduced frequency of "adjustive behavior," or behavior that maximizes reinforcing outcomes. Put simply, the depressed person increases avoidance and escape behavior in situations where it is possible to obtain positive reinforcement, and conversely develops a passive behavioral repertoire in circumstances where escape would be reinforcing, thus (as in the "learned helplessness" model) failing to escape punishment.

Like Ferster, Lewinsohn[5] suggested that operant behavioral theoretical concept "reinforcement" was sufficient to explicate the origins of clinical depression. He advanced the idea that depression is due to (or constituted by) "low rate response-contingent positive reinforcement." He used this basic construct to explain the other aspects of clinical depression, such as low rates of behavior.

A major limitation of the behavioral theories is that behavioral factors alone have not been shown to induce clinical depression. In addition, pure behavioral interventions have not been found to be effective treatments for clinically significant depression.[6] Consistent with this, comprehensive volumes on depression no longer include pure behavioral theories among the significant approaches to etiology and treatment (e.g., Gotlib and Hammen[7]).

When more purely behavioral interventions have been evaluated (and they have not been extensively tested), they typically have done well in controlled trials.[8] In components analysis research, one element of cognitive therapy for depression, "behavioral activation," has generated some renewed theoretical interest. However, problems remain in trying to disentangle the cognitive from the noncognitive processes (for a review, see Hollon et al.[8]).

Cognitive and Evolutionary Theories

Contemporary cognitive[9] and evolutionary[10,11] theories of depression have conceptual commonalities, including emphasis on continuity of normal and abnormal mechanisms. Cognitive theory is independently considered in more detail in Chapter 12.

The evolutionary perspective is closely aligned with the behavioral and cognitive theories. The behavioral theories of Ferster,[2] Seligman,[3] and Lewinsohn[5] are derived from the instrumental (operant) behavioral concepts of B. F. Skinner.[12] Skinner[13] drew explicit analogies between the selection of species' characteristics and selection of individual behavior by its consequences, or "contingencies of reinforcement."

Similar to Skinner's emphasis on both individual and ethological consequences, Beck[9] has theorized the nature of clinical depression (and mania) to be an atavistic mechanism or program that may have been adaptive in earlier environments but is generally less so today. The distinct and prolonged negative cognitive biases implicated in clinical depression (selective abstraction, overgeneralization, negative self-attributions) are theorized to have evolved within contexts where these cognitive configurations were useful for survival. Thus, the evolutionary perspective can help explain the distal causes of the nature of the depressive phenomena.

However, in addition to the evolutionary aspects of depression, cognitive theory posits several interrelated theoretical constructs, including cross-sectional models, in which negativity is a necessary (but not sufficient) component of depression; a structural model in which biased schemas become hypervalent in depression; the stressor-vulnerability model in which stress impinges upon specific cognitive vulnerabilities; the reciprocal-interaction model that focuses on interaction with key figures; and the psychobiological model that integrates genetic, neurochemical, and cognitive processes as different sides of the same coin.[9] Through articulating the interrelationship of the various systems or levels of analysis, cognitive theory integrates diverse levels, including the incorporation of evolutionary principles (pp. 27-30).[14]

Nesse[11] considered the adaptive nature and functions of low mood and clinical depression from an evolutionary viewpoint. The possible survival functions include (1) communicating a need for help; (2) signaling one's place in a hierarchy conflict; (3) promoting disengagement from unreachable goals; and (4) regulating patterns of investment of energy. Ongoing theorizing on evolutionary advantages of depression has focused on identifying how low mood may increase an organism's ability to cope with the adaptive challenges within unpropitious environments. Such environments would include those in which effort to pursue a goal is counterproductive, perhaps resulting in danger, loss, or wasted effort. In this manner, depression and its related phenomena may serve adaptive survival functions within environments where it is advantageous to be "pessimistic," thus inhibiting certain actions.[11] Manic symptoms (see Chapter 6) are explained by the presence of natural selective pressures within contrasting environmental contexts, for example, those that reward risk-taking.

Psychoanalytic Theories

In his papers of 1911 and 1916, Abraham discussed the significance of hostility and orality in depression. Ungratified sexual aims bring about feelings of hatred and hostility that reduce the depressed patient's capacity for love. The patient projects this hatred externally, and the repressed hostility manifests itself in dreams and abnormal behavior, in a desire for revenge, in a tendency to annoy other people, in ideas of guilt, and in emotional impoverishment.

Abraham's 1924 paper, "A Short Study of the Development of the Libido," discussed the relationship between manic-depressive psychosis and obsessional neurosis. Anal eroticism and sadistic impulses, he wrote, exhibit opposite tendencies to expel or destroy and to retain or control what is perceived as personal property—the feces or the loved object. Abraham concluded that an inherited predisposition toward oral eroticism fixed the melancholic's psychosexual development at the oral stage. Childhood disappointments in love, especially when occurring before the Oedipal wishes have been resolved, and the repetition of these disappointments in later life were further factors in the origins of melancholia.

In *Mourning and Melancholia* (1917), Freud compared melancholia to normal grief. While both may occur as a reaction to loss of a loved object, melancholia may occur in specially predisposed people in reaction to an imaginary or vaguely perceived loss that deprives the ego. The melancholic's self-accusations were seen as manifestations of hostility toward the lost loved object. Freud explained this phenomenon as the narcissistic identification of the ego with the object through introjection, a regression to the oral stage of erotic development. (In his further consideration of psychic introjection, Freud referred to the "self-criticizing faculty" of the ego, the foundation for his later concept of superego. He hesitated to generalize too widely in this regard, because of his uncertainty as to the somatic aspects of melancholia.)

Rado,[15] considering predispositional factors in depression, stated that depressives are people with intense narcissistic needs and precarious self-esteem who, when they lose their love object, react with angry rebellion and then try to restore their self-esteem by the punishment of their ego (which includes the introjected bad part of the object) by the superego.

Gero[16] outlined in great detail his therapeutic work with two cases of neurotic depression. Gero disagreed with former writers concerning the universality of the obsessional character structure in depression; neither of his depressives used an obsessive character defense, but both demonstrated an underlying narcissistic hunger, intolerance of frustration, and introjection of the love objects.

Melanie Klein[17] believed that the predisposition to depression depended not on a series of traumatic incidents but on the mother-child relationship in the first year of life. Her contribution pushed psychoanalytic speculations back to the infant's first year to explain the effects of introjection and projection on psychic development. Klein felt that the child, as a defensive technique, denies the complexity of his or her love object and sees it as either all good or all bad. This tendency is a characteristic of the adult manic depressive.

Bibring[18] departed from classical theory and allied himself with those who viewed depression as an affective state characterized by a loss of self-esteem. Like the earlier writers, he felt that a predisposition to depression stemmed from early childhood traumatic experiences. However, he added that self-esteem may be decreased, not only by frustration of need for love and affection, but also by frustration of other aspirations. He indicated that all depressive reactions have something in common, although they exhibit a multiplicity of forms.

As did Bibring, Jacobson[19] proposed that the loss of self-esteem is the central psychological problem in depression. She postulated the goals of the development of self-esteem, superego, and ego ideal as the firm establishment of one's own identity, the differentiation of one's self from others, the maintenance of self-esteem, and the capacity to form satisfactory object-relationships. She considered that self-esteem "represents the degree of discrepancy or harmony between the self-representations and the wished-for concept of the self." She regarded all the determinants of self-esteem as having relevance for depression.

Jacobson distinguished between neurotic and psychotic depressions and attempted to clarify the nature of ego regression in psychotic depression. She proposed that the premature and excessive disappointment in the parents with the accompanying devaluation of them—and the self—occurs in the early life of depressive patients. The prepsychotic manic depressive exhibits an unusual degree of dependency and an extreme intolerance to hurt, frustration, or disappointment.

Hammerman[20] differentiated between depression in which the role of "sadistic superego" is prominent and self-esteem collapses due to guilt in transgressing superego standards and the depression due to defective ego organization. The sadism of the superego presupposes the existence of a comparatively well-developed ego organization and psychic structure formation; faulty ego development due to very early trauma, early loss, or defective relationships results in a distorted self-image and lack of self-esteem because of failure to measure up to a narcissistic ego ideal.

According to Zetzel,[21] psychological maturity consists in passively accepting the limitations of reality and actively working toward realistic goals. In view of the reality principle, the recognition, tolerance, and mastery of depression, like that of anxiety, must be regarded as a developmental challenge in preparation for the stress of normal adult life. Failure in this respect may lead to symptom formation, inhibition, and adaptive failures and may be caused by mechanisms such as projection and denial, which prevent the subjective experience of threat, loss, and personal limitations. Such failure may also predispose an individual to chronic and psychotic depressions.

Aggression in Depression

Psychoanalysts since Abraham[22] have ascribed a central role to aggression in the development of depression. Four writers have challenged the universality of this association. Balint[23] considered the depressive's feelings of bitterness and resentment as reactions to, rather than essential elements of, depression. Bibring[18] also regarded aggression as a secondary phenomenon due to the breakdown of self-esteem. Cohen and her group[24] posited that the hostility exhibited by the patient is due to his or her "annoying impact upon others, rather than the primary motivation to do injury to them." Gero[16] also challenged the view that self-devaluation can be considered self-directed aggression.

Orality in Depression

Since Abraham[25] theorized that oral eroticism in neurotic depressives has the function of preventing episodes of depression, other authors have broadened the concept of orality and concluded that depressives, because of their excessive dependence upon external supplies of love, affection, and attention to maintain self-esteem, are orally dependent people who lack these vital supplies.

Bibring[18] first questioned the universality of oral fixation in depression. He called attention to the clinical fact that while one person may depend upon the attainment of narcissistic supplies from an outside source, another's equilibrium may depend upon supplies from an internalized source, that is, by the fulfillment of certain aspirations and ideals.

Jacobson[26] conceived of the mechanism in depression not as an identification achieved through oral means, but as a regressive breakdown of ego identifications in which reality testing is lost and the self-images are confused with object representations. The object representations no longer adequately reflect the actual objects.

Psychodynamic and Psychological Theories

Cohen et al.[24] studied the family backgrounds of 12 manic-depressive patients (see Chapter 10 for a review of the systematic research related to this study). The authors described the typical family situation as one in which the mother was the stronger and more stable parent and tended to deprecate her husband. The typical parent-child relationship was one in which the parent's approval of the children was contingent on the children's accomplishments in the form of grades and other prestige symbols. The child destined to be a manic depressive was often selected as the family's standard bearer in the battle for social status.

The writers delineated a typical personality structure characterized by denying the complexity of people and seeing them as "either all white or all black." This inability to view people as complex, multifaceted individuals was viewed as a distinguishing characteristic of the adult manic depressive's interpersonal relationships. Cohen and her group regarded this denial of the complexity of people as a defense and attributed it to the difficulty these patients had as children in integrating the different aspects of their mothers into a unified picture.

Cohen et al. asserted that manic depressives' hostility has been overstressed as a dynamic factor in their illness; the patients' hostile feelings do not arise primarily from the frustration of their needs, but are the result of the annoyance they arouse in others by their demanding behavior. The manic depressive does not suffer genuine guilt or feelings of regret but expresses feelings of guilt and self-reproach as an exploitive technique "to placate authority."

According to Lichtenberg,[27] depression results when a person feels responsible for his or her hopelessness in regard to the attainment of goals. The author distinguishes three forms of depression, which vary with the kind of goal—a specific situation, a behavior style, or a generalized goal—to which vulnerable people direct their expectancy. This conceptualization of depression is particularly well-suited to further clinical and experimental research.

Schwartz[28] attempted to construct a unitary formulation of manic-depressive reactions. He suggested that manic-depressive reactions occur when a person with excessive, unsatisfied narcissistic needs introjects the attitudes of those responsible for his or her "deprivation." In adult life, increased stress creates a sense of loss that is identified with the earlier deprivation. Retaliatory aggression is then directed against the introjected parental figures, but the ego defends against this. In mania, ceaseless activity blocks the perception of hostility and deprivation. In depression, inhibition and immobilization are a denial of the capacity to carry out the aggressive impulses.

Existential Theories

In 1959, Arieti[29] published a summary of the existential theories of depression. He pointed out that according to the existentialists, the ambivalence of the manic-depressive patient is different from that of the schizophrenic. Whereas the schizophrenic may hate and love at the same time, the manic depressive alternates between love and hate. According to Arieti, Henry Ey considered the depressed state to be an arrest or insufficiency of all the vital activities. Ey viewed depression as a "pathetic immobility, a suspension of existence, a syncope of time." As a result, the patient experiences a sense of incompleteness, impotence, and unreality.

The question of depressed patients' attitude toward time has occupied the attention of many existential writers. They emphasized that time seems to have slowed down for depressed patients. In their subjective experience, only the past matters. Painful memories dominate their thinking and remind them of their unworthiness and inability to accomplish.

Hubert Tellenbach in his book *Melancholie*[30] (Dr. Egbert H. Mueller was of great help translating this book from the German) offered a thorough analysis of depression that in many respects is representative of existential thinking. Tellenbach presented an analysis of the case histories of 140 melancholics. He asserted that they all have a relatively uniform premorbid personality structure. Their life and work are dominated by a strict order: orderliness in dealing with things, conscientiousness in work, and an overriding need to do right to those close to them. They have a great sensitivity to the dos and don'ts, the shoulds and should nots. At the same time, they have a great sensitivity to guilt. Melancholics devote their lives to fulfilling their sense of order and avoiding situations of guilt. They prefer the security of steady employment to the risk involved in free, self-propelled work.

Tellenbach described a series of specific situations in which the melancholic sense of orderliness and guilt is threatened. The interplay of these situations and the melancholics' personality results in their getting increasingly tangled. The basic paradox is this. On the one hand, they are so sensitive to guilt that they will do everything to keep abreast of obligations, while on the other hand, they make such an exacting interpretation of their obligations that they are close to the brink of getting behind in their own aspirations. In such a precariously balanced way of living, any accidental situation may throw them over the brink into being behind in obligations or in sense of fulfillment. In the depressive psychosis, the distance between being and aspiration becomes an abyss.

Schulte[31] considered the inability to be sad as the crux of the melancholic experience. According to the author, a person who can still be sad is not really melancholic, and the improvement in the state of melancholy starts when the individual can experience sadness. Schulte stated that melancholics have lost the ability to sympathize and be moved. They experience a need for an emotion that is tormenting to them. The author cautioned that the use of the word *sad* by the patients should be regarded as a metaphor by which they try to make some sense out of something that cannot really be expressed and explained and that is not comparable to other things.

Neurological Theory

Kraines[32] wrote extensively on the possible biological explanations of depression. He based his theory on the following assumptions. There is frequently a history of "hereditary susceptibility," especially in identical twins. He inferred that the occurrence of postpartum depressions, premenstrual depressions, and greater frequency of manic attacks in youth and depressive attacks later in life are due to hormonal changes (for a critique of the hereditary and endocrine studies, see Chapter 9).

Neuropsychological Theories

Much more recently, Shenal et al.[33] reviewed the literature on the neuropsychological theories of depression. They speculated that dysfunction in any of three neuroanatomical divisions (left frontal, right frontal, and right posterior) is associated with depression.

Their review included the prominent neuropsychological theories, including those on cerebral asymmetries in emotional processing. Combining theories of arousal, lateralization, and functional cerebral space, they advanced a research model suggesting that (1) left frontal dysfunction is said to result in sparsity of positive affect; (2) right frontal dysfunction is posited to cause lability and emotional disregulation; and (3) right posterior dysfunction is theorized to result in bland affect, or indifference.

In suggesting the promise of neuropsychological assessment and research to better understand clinical depression, they proposed the possible utility of

testing predictions of different qualities of depressive symptoms corresponding to the abovementioned specific regions of brain dysfunction.[33]

Biochemical Theory

The effectiveness of the MAO inhibitors and tricyclic compounds has led to
research on their biochemical effects. The evidence resulted in an interesting
supposition called "the catecholamine hypothesis of affective disorders." The
strength of this hypothesis received an excellent discussion in Schildkraut's
1965 review.[34] He concluded that the hypothesis could be neither definitely
accepted nor eliminated, given data available at the time, but that it was useful
as a guide to further experimentation.

The essential idea of the catecholamine hypothesis is that in depression the
supply of active norepinephrine (at central adrenergic receptor sites) is
depleted. The major evidence for this statement came from the study of drug
effects on experimental animals. In these earlier studies, researchers hypothesized that both the MAO inhibitors and imipramine might serve to increase the
availability of active norepinephrine. According to them, the MAO inhibitors
probably act by directly inhibiting the enzymatic oxidative deamination of
norepinephrine. Imipramine, on the other hand, might act by decreasing mem-
brane permeability that blocks the intracellular release (and hence deamination) of the storage norepinephrine, and by increasing cellular reuptake, thus
diminishing the inactivation of free extracellular norepinephrine. Furthermore,
reserpine-induced sedation in animals might be associated with catecholamine
depletion, though some investigators believed that other amines, most impor-
tantly serotonin, are critical here. In any case, the probable increase of active
norepinephrine following antidepressant administration and the decrease in
reserpine sedation (both in animals) would be consistent with the catecholamine hypothesis.

The hypothesis thus had a definite quantity of consistent evidence supporting it. However, this evidence in general came not from studies of depressed
patients but from other sources. The hypothesis, of course, did not contain an
explanation for the large number of patients in whom the drugs do not work.
Schildkraut stated, "It must be stressed, however, that this hypothesis is
undoubtedly, at best, a reductionistic over-simplification of a very complex
biological state." This did not deny the usefulness of the supposition in guiding investigators in the search for a more sophisticated biochemical basis for
depressive disorders.

Thirty years later, citing Schildkraut's[34] influential theorizing in this area,
Dubovsky and Buzan[6] stated that subsequent research has not confirmed the
monoamine depletion hypothesis.

Indeed, increasing synaptic availability of monoamines does not explain the
effects of antidepressants. Several findings support this conclusion, including

the following: (1) precursors to monoamine taken alone, such as tyrosine and tryptophan, do not improve mood; (2) monoamine depletion does not typically cause depression; (3) in cases when monoamine depletion does cause it, the depression is transient; (4) monoamine reuptake inhibitors do not have reliable antidepressant properties; (5) certain antidepressants are effective without having any effect on monoamine reuptake; (6) when monoamine reuptake inhibitors are effective antidepressants, inhibition of reuptake is immediate, but antidepressant effect does not occur until a month or more later.[6] However, Dubovsky and Buzan conclude that neurotransmitter reuptake inhibition does predict side effects.

Animal Models

In 1994, Willner[35] reviewed studies of the effects of stress in animal models of depression. In such models, exposure to stress over time results in a generalized insensitivity to reward, such as reducing the reinforcing properties of food. This effect is then shown to be reversible through the use of a variety of antidepressant medications, including tricyclic antidepressants and fluoxetine.

Animal models of depression have focused largely on models of anhedonia. The creation of anhedonia in laboratory animals has been found to have multiple causal influences and can be produced in a variety of ways. For example, causal influences are genetic, such as strain differences in effects of uncontrolled shock on stress reactions, or epigenetic, such as neonatal antidepressant treatment. Anhedonia may be produced through acute severe stress, chronic mild stress, and psychostimulant withdrawal.

In considering the future of animal models, Wilner[35] identified their substantial limitations. They continue to enjoy little face or construct validity. The experimental initiation of "anhedonia" is merely suggestive of depression, rather than demonstrably parallel to actual clinical phenomena experienced by humans. However, he concluded by speculating that the primary contribution of the continued use of animal models might be to better elucidate the mechanisms of action of the antidepressant drugs.[35]

Expressed Emotion

Though not derived from the animal models, one stress theory of depression relapse has been advanced.[36] The effects of interpersonal stress over time were subjected to empirical scrutiny in a clinical population.

Hayhurst et al.[36] noted that of the four studies on the effects of "expressed emotion" (criticism by significant others within the family), two found a positive association between expressed emotion (EE) and relapse during acute depressive illness. In their longer-term study, 39 depressed patients and their partners were interviewed individually at three-month intervals for about one year.

Patients who fully recovered had partners who were consistently uncritical. Those with residual symptoms during remission had more continuously critical partners. However, the causal sequence of events was questioned. Rather than criticism leading to depression, Hayhurst et al.[36] concluded that "continuing criticism was a result of continuing depression" (p. 442). As in discussing the development of depression, the idea of a "circular feedback model" might fit here (see Chapter 13).[37]

The interaction between the negative effects of depressed mood on significant others, and in turn increased criticism from those significant others directed toward the patient, may be the best model of the interpersonal interactions identified in this study. Thus, the interaction would be depressed symptoms ↔ increased EE (criticism) by family members.

Chapter 12
Cognition and Psychopathology

Historically, most writers on the psychological aspects of depression used a motivational or adaptational model. Some authors viewed depressive symptomatology in terms of the gratification or discharge of certain needs or drives.[1,2] Others emphasized the role of the defenses against these drives.[3] Still others emphasized the adaptive aspects of the symptomatology.[2,4]

Most early attempts to explain the symptoms of depression in psychological terms had introduced troublesome conceptual or empirical problems. First, many writers had a tendency to ascribe some purpose to the symptoms. Rather than looking upon the symptoms simply as a manifestation of the psychological or physiological disorder, these writers viewed the symptoms as serving an important intrapsychic or interpersonal function. The sadness of the depressed person, for example, was explained by some writers (e.g., Rado and Adler) as an attempt to manipulate other people. Although such functionalist interpretations sometimes seemed to fit a particular case, they had strong teleological overtones. As the history of science demonstrates, theories that ascribe some design or purpose to natural phenomena have generally been superseded as basic knowledge increased.

Second, in attempting to account for paradoxical aspects of depression, some writers presented formulations that are so elaborate or abstract that they cannot be correlated with clinical material. Freud's conceptualization of depression in terms of the attack of the sadistic part of the ego on the incorporated loved-object within the ego is so remote from any observables in clinical data that it defies systematic validation. Similarly, Melanie Klein's[5] formulation of adult depression as a reactivation of an early infantile depression does not provide any bridge to observable behavior.

Third, most writers skirted the problem of the specificity of their formulations. Many of the most popular psychodynamic formulations of depression, such as the concepts of increased orality or repressed hostility, have also been attributed to a multiplicity of other psychiatric and psychosomatic disorders. Hence, the particular formulations, if valid, might be characteristic of psychiatric disorders in general and not exclusively applicable to depression.

Finally, the various theories offered, at best, explanations for only circumscribed aspects of the diversified clinical picture of depression. Explanations that seem to fit certain specific groups of phenomena often seem irrelevant or incongruous when applied to other phenomena.

In undertaking a conceptualization of the psychological processes in depression, writers must account for a wide variety of psychopathological phenomena.[6] As described in Chapter 2, we found 21 different symptom categories that occurred significantly more frequently in depressed than in nondepressed patients. The various symptoms of depression fell into certain clusters and were grouped under the following headings. The *affective* group includes the various adjectives and phrases employed by patients to describe their feelings: sad, lonely, empty, bored, and hopeless. The *motivational* group includes intensified wishes for help, yearning to escape, desire to commit suicide, and the phenomenon of loss of spontaneous motivation (paralysis of the will). The *cognitive* group includes negative self-concept, pessimism, and negative interpretations of experience. The *physical and vegetative* symptoms include retardation, fatigability, loss of appetite, loss of libido, and sleep disturbance.

These groupings of symptoms may not seem to bear much relationship to each other. Many previous writers have attempted to present a unifying theory that would establish understandable connections among these groupings. Freud's theory of retroflected hostility, for instance, may be used to interrelate negative self-concept, self-criticism, and suicidal wishes but falls short in providing plausible connections with the other symptoms. His complimentary concept of depression as a grief reaction provides a thread between affects (especially sadness and loneliness), loss of outside interests, and loss of appetite but does not offer a rational explanation for other major symptoms such as loss of self-esteem and suicidal wishes. The concept of depression as an attempt to gain love (Rado) does not explain such behaviors as seclusiveness or the physical and vegetative symptoms. The theories of autonomic or hypothalamic dysfunction[7,8] may provide a possible explanation of the physical and vegetative phenomena but offer no plausible explanations of the other symptoms.

In an attempt to find some alternative explanations for the behavioral characteristics of depression, Beck reviewed the clinical material of 50 depressed patients in psychotherapy and selected those themes that differentiated these patients from a control psychotherapy group (Chapter 10). These themes were regarded as derivatives of certain basic cognitive patterns that are activated in depression. Similar thematic contents were observed in the dreams, early memories, and responses to projective tests in several systematic studies of depression (Chapter 10).

The Primary Triad in Depression

The paradigm of the primary triad shows the connections between the cognitive aspects described previously and the affective, motivational, and physical

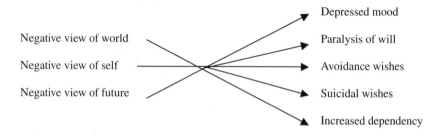

Figure 12-1. The effect of cognitive patterns on affects and motivations in depression.

phenomena of depression. They are applicable to the various types of depression.

The disturbances in depression may be viewed in terms of the activation of a set of three major cognitive patterns that force the individual to view self, world, and future in an idiosyncratic way. The progressive dominance of these cognitive patterns leads to the other phenomena that are associated with the depressive state.

The first component of the triad is the pattern of construing experiences in a negative way. Patients consistently interpret their interactions with their environment 'as representing defeat, deprivation, or disparagement. They see their lives as filled with a succession of burdens, obstacles, or traumatic situations, all of which detract from them in significant ways.

The second component is the pattern of viewing oneself in a negative way. Patients regard themselves as deficient, inadequate, or unworthy, and tend to attribute their unpleasant experiences to physical, mental, or moral defects in themselves. Furthermore, they regard themselves as undesirable and worthless because of the presumed defect and tend to reject themselves because of it.

The third component consists of viewing the future in a negative way. Patients anticipate that their current difficulties or suffering will continue indefinitely. As they look ahead, they see a life of unremitting hardship, frustration, and deprivation.

The relationship between the cognitive patterns and the affective and motivational symptoms is illustrated in Figure 12-1. This relationship will be described in detail in later sections.

Negative Interpretation of Experience

Depressed patients selectively or inappropriately interpret their experiences as detracting from them in some substantive way. Whereas the manic sees neutral or ambiguous life situations as self-enhancing, the depressive regards them as self-deflating. The manic, for instance, may interpret a neutral attitude on the part of a friend as indicating overwhelming approval; the depressive may regard the same attitude as a rejection. This is particularly evident in patients with manic-depressive cycles who show completely opposite reactions to the same set of external conditions when they are in different phases of the cycle.

As was pointed out in Chapter 10, the distorted conceptualizations may range from mild inaccuracies to total misinterpretations. The typical cognitions show a variety of deviations from logical thinking, including arbitrary inferences, selective abstractions, overgeneralizations, and magnifications. The patient automatically makes a negative interpretation of a situation even though more obvious and more plausible explanations exist. He or she tailors the facts to fit preformed negative conclusions, and may, furthermore, exaggerate the significance of any actual loss, thwarting, or deprecation encountered.

Thwarting or Defeat

Depressed patients are peculiarly sensitive to any impediments to their goal-directed activity. An obstacle is regarded as an impossible barrier; difficulty in dealing with a problem is interpreted as a total failure. Their cognitive response to a problem or difficulty is likely to be an idea such as "I'm licked," "I'll never be able to do this," or "I'm blocked no matter what I do."

A depressed woman, for example, having some difficulty finding a pencil she knew she had placed in her purse, had the thought, "I'll never be able to find it." She experienced a strong sense of frustration, even though she was able to find it in a few seconds. Any problem seemed insoluble, and any delay in reaching a goal seemed interminable. Similarly, a depressed man discovered that his car had a flat tire. Although he was a good mechanic, he was overwhelmed by the idea that there was nothing he could do about the tire. In consonance with his sense of defeat, he abandoned the car.

In achievement-oriented situations, depressed patients are particularly prone to react with a sense of failure. As shown in certain controlled experiments (Chapter 10), they tend to underestimate their actual performance. Furthermore, if their actual performance falls short of the high standards they set for themselves, they are likely to regard their work as a total failure. A mildly depressed student, for example, barely missed making the honor roll at school. He looked upon this as a complete defeat and considered dropping out of school.

Deprivation

Depressed patients are apt to interpret relatively trivial events as constituting a substantial loss. A patient on the way to see his psychiatrist reacted to a large number of incidents as though he had lost something of value. First, he had to wait about 30 seconds for the elevator and thought, "I'm losing valuable time." As he rode up alone on the elevator, he regretted having no one to ride with and thought, "I'm missing out on the companionship of other people." When he discovered that another patient had an earlier appointment, he regretted that he was not the first patient the psychiatrist would see that day. When he had to wait a few minutes in the waiting room, he had the thought that the psychiatrist did not care for him. He started to read a magazine and when he had to put it down to start his appointment he felt deprived of the opportunity to finish the magazine.

The sense of loss often centers around money. Many depressed patients regard any expenditure of money as a loss; for example, a very wealthy man felt deprived when he had to pay fifteen cents to ride on the subway. The opposite reaction is sometimes observed. One man felt deprived whenever he was prevented from spending money. This occurred when the stores were closed or when a store did not have a particular item he wanted to buy. The act of buying tended to ward off the sense of deprivation. When he wasn't able to make purchases, he felt sad and empty.

Making comparisons with other people is especially likely to activate feelings of deprivation. Many depressed patients reported having thoughts such as "I don't have anything" when one of their friends acquired something new. A well-to-do businessman was prone to regard himself as poor whenever he heard that someone made more money than he. A wealthy woman regarded herself as deprived whenever one of her friends made a new acquisition, whether it was an entertainment system, a third car, or a house.

Deprecation

Depressed patients are prone to read insults, ridicule, or disparagement into what other people say to them. They often interpret neutral remarks as directed against them in some way. They may even twist a favorable comment so that it seems unfavorable. An employer, for instance, praised an employee for her work. The entire time he was talking, she had the repetitive thought, "He's criticizing me."

Often patients believe that other people have derogatory ideas about them (negative attributions). They may attribute such negative judgments to others only in certain limited situations, or in severe cases may succumb to them in every personal contact. One woman, for example, regarded practically every statement, change of facial expression, or movement by the psychiatrist as indicating a criticism of her. Even when he asked her questions, she thought he was criticizing her. While she was talking and he was listening, she also attributed negative judgments to him, such as "He thinks I'm a bore," or "He must think I'm awfully childish."

Some patients tend to make negative attributions whenever they are in a competitive situation. One patient had the highest standing in class, but whenever the teacher called on another student to answer a question, the patient thought, "He doesn't really think I'm smart or he would have called on me." If the professor complimented other students, she would have the thought that the professor had a low opinion of her. Another patient would make a characteristic negative attribution while driving. If another driver passed him, he would think, "He thinks I'm the kind of person who can be pushed around." He would have the same thought if he was kept waiting by a salesperson or a server in a restaurant.

Similar negative attributions are often aroused in group situations. One patient participating in group therapy thought, "They must think I'm an awful dunce because I don't talk more." When somebody told a joke, he thought, "They must think I am not amusing because I didn't tell a joke." When he did speak, he had the thought, "They think I talk too much." When a group member agreed with another patient's opinion, he thought, "They think I'm not worth listening to because nobody agrees with me."

Negative View of Self

Depressed patients not only interpret their experiences as detracting from themselves in some way, but also concurrently devalue themselves. If she does not do as well as she expected on a test or a business venture, she regards herself as socially undesirable. If his children seem boisterous, he views himself as a poor parent.

To sharpen the distinction between negative interpretation of experience and negative view of the self, we can compare the paranoid with the depressed patient. Like depressed patients, paranoid patients may see others as thwarting or rejecting them, but unlike depressed patients, paranoid patients maintain a positive self-concept. They tend to blame others for fantasized thwarting, deprecation, or deprivation; depressed patients tend to blame themselves.

A striking feature of depressed patients is the tendency to generalize from a particular behavior to a character trait. Any single deviation from a high level of performance is assumed to represent a major shortcoming. If they do not do as well as somebody else financially, socially, or academically, they tend to regard themselves as generally inferior. A male student, for example, who had difficulty getting a date on a single occasion thought, "I must be repulsive to girls." A highly successful businesswoman who made one transaction that lost money became obsessed by the idea that she was stupid. A mother whose child was untidy on one occasion thought, "I'm a terrible parent."

The supposed deficiency becomes so magnified that it occupies the individual's total self-concept. The patient seems incapable of viewing him- or herself in any way other than in terms of this deficiency. A woman who thought she was losing her beauty could describe herself only as unattractive and automatically excluded any other traits or characteristics. She tended to equate herself with her superficial physical characteristics.

The negative self-concept is associated with self-rejection. Patients not only see themselves as inferior, but dislike themselves for it. They criticize, reproach, and castigate themselves for being so inferior. If they recognize that they are depressed, they criticize themselves for being ill. They regard it as an inexcusable weakness to "let themselves" become ill.

Negative Expectations

Depressed patients generally show considerable preoccupation with ideas of the future. Their expectations usually have a negative cast and may occur in the form of pictorial fantasies or as obsessive ruminations. Their anticipations of the future are generally an extension of what they view as their present state. If they regard themselves as currently deprived, immobilized, or rejected, they visualize a future in which they are continually deprived, immobilized, or rejected. They seem to be unable to view their current state as having any time limits or to consider the possibility of any improvement.

Not only are the patients' long-range forecasts of a negative nature, but their short-term predictions are similarly negative. When they awaken in the morning, they anticipate that every experience during the day will pose great difficulties. When they contemplate undertaking a task, they predict they will make a mess of it. When a suggestion is made to engage in an activity they ordinarily enjoy when not depressed, they automatically assume they will not have a good time. One patient frequently had an elaborate fantasy before engaging in any activity. When she thought of driving to the psychiatrist's office for an appointment, she pictured herself making a wrong turn and getting lost. When she considered calling a friend on the phone, she had a daydream of getting no answer or a busy signal. If she decided to go shopping, she imagined herself losing her purse or making the wrong purchases. When the doorbell rang, she would have a fantasy of receiving a telegram or special delivery letter with bad news.

It is useful to distinguish between the negative predictions of the depressed patient and the fears of the anxious patient. This may be illustrated by the following example. A student preparing for an examination experienced continual thoughts that he might fail. Each time he thought of failing, he experienced anxiety. Questioned as to what he thought would happen if he failed, he responded that everybody would think he was stupid. His apprehension continued until he completed the examination. Up to this point, his thinking was similar to that observed in an anxiety neurotic. He was reacting to a situation that he perceived as a source of harm. The threatening situation was distinct from him—it had not yet inflicted its damage, and his concept of himself was still intact.

After taking the examination, the student thought he had performed poorly and concluded that he had failed. He no longer felt anxious—he felt depressed. The change in his feeling may be explained as being consonant with a change in his conceptualizations. Before he took the examination the harm to his self-esteem was only potential; now it was actual. Once the injury had been inflicted, he suffered from the psychic pain it had produced. Before the examination, he could see himself as a person with many attributes, some positive and some negative. Now he could see himself in only one way: as a failure. When he looked ahead to the future, he could foresee a procession of future failures: this prospect did not produce apprehension because he did not expect them to make him feel any worse than he now felt. The anticipated failures merely represented to him the impossibility of ever feeling better and the futility of trying.

The difference between the fears of the anxious patient and the gloomy outlook of the depressed patient may be summarized as follows: The anxious patient is concerned with the possibility of being hurt (either physically or emotionally) but sees the trauma as something in the future. The depressed patient perceives him- or herself as already damaged (defeated, deprived, or deprecated). When such a patient thinks of the future, it is in terms of a continuation of present pain. There is no alarm stimulus because the dreaded event has already occurred. The patient anticipates future failures in terms of a replication of the failure already experienced.

The Affective Response

The affective state can be regarded as the consequence of the way individuals view themselves or their environment. We have noted that there is a predictable relationship between an antecedent event and the affective response (Chapter 10). Depressed patients who were rejected would experience a negative affect. If they simply *thought* they were rejected, they would experience the same negative affect. We concluded that the way individuals structure their experiences determines their mood. Since depressed persons consistently make negative conceptualizations, they are prone to consistently negative moods.

We also noted that there was a similar consistency between the ideation and the affect in patients' free associations. If a patient had the thought that he was a social outcast, he would feel lonely. If she had the thought that she would never get well, she would feel sad and hopeless.

The conception that the mood disorder in depression is secondary to the cognitive disorder is not new. Robert Burton, writing in the seventeenth century, quoted a number of writers from antiquity to the seventeenth century who held that the "afflictions of the mind" produced the affective disturbance. In 1602, Felix Platter described melancholia as "a kind of mental alienation, in which imagination and judgment are so perverted that without any cause the victims become very sad and fearful."[9] He emphasized that the whole illness "rests upon a foundation of false conceptions."[10]

Cognitive Primacy

The 1950s and early 1960s saw an increasing emphasis on the role of cognitive processes in psychiatric disorders.[11,12,13,14] Ellis, in 1963 and again in 1993, within the framework of his concept of psychotherapy, stressed the primacy of irrational thinking in depression, anxiety reactions, and other neuroses.[13,15]

In the moderate and severe depressions, in which the depressive feeling is constantly present, there may be some argument as to which comes first: the cognition or the affect. In one sense, cognitive aspects of depression are probably best understood as *part of* the depressive episode (or clinical syndrome), rather than "causes" of it. Still, studies of the concurrent relationship between affect and cognition have shown interesting correlations (e.g., Rholes et al.[16]).

In a causal (temporal primacy) study of nonclinical levels of depressive symptoms, hierarchical multiple regression analyses showed negative view of the future (hopelessness) to be related 4 weeks later to depressive symptoms, but not to anxiety.[17] However, it should be noted that the 36 (out of 156) subjects who experienced increases in symptoms from time 1 to time 2 had scores on the Beck Depression Inventory that are best described only as dysphoric, rather than obtaining a *DSM* diagnosis of clinical depression (see Kendall et al.[18]).

Beck reviewed several additional studies supportive of cognitive primacy.[19] These studies suggested that (1) cognitive changes come before affective changes;[20] (2) reducing negative thought content leads to the greatest reduction of negative affect;[21] and (3) the cognitive variable hopelessness in prospective studies confirms its crucial role in the prediction of suicide.[22,23,24]

Rush et al.[25] studied the temporal order of patients' improvement in response to cognitive therapy. Using data from Rush et al.,[26] they determined that patients improved first on measures of hopelessness, followed by improvement in self-view, motivation, mood, and vegetative symptoms. This was not found to be true for drug treatment.

Roseman and Evdokas[27] found experimental evidence that appraisals cause emotions. Their study included several strengths: Multiple appraisals were manipulated, several different emotions were measured, subjects' ongoing emotions were used, and the emotions that were measured were in response to situations actually confronted. They concluded that appraisals do cause experienced emotions.

In clinical studies, Beck noted that changes in the intensity of the depressed feeling followed changes in the patient's cognition. This principle was borne out in a controlled experimental manipulation. We found that we were able to reduce or accentuate patients' negative affect by exposing them to situations in which they were induced to regard themselves as having succeeded or failed, respectively, in a task.[28]

The following example is presented to illustrate the interplay of cognition and affect. A student was informed by a classmate that he had failed the final examination in one of his courses. He realized that he would fail the course as a consequence, and he felt discouraged and hopeless. Later, he checked his grade on the bulletin board and discovered that he had actually passed the examination. He verified that the initial information was incorrect, and his mood changed from sadness to jubilation. In this example, the relationship between the conceptualization of the experience and the consequent affect is clear-cut.

In the case of depressed patients a similar consistency is found between conceptualization and affect. They perceive that they have failed or lost something of value, and consequently feel sad or apathetic. Clinically depressed patients differ from the the student who received false information about his grade—and this difference is crucial in distinguishing between normal and abnormal reactions—in that the source of the error is internal rather than external. The depressive's reaction is based on a faulty interpretation of available data rather than on incorrect data. Sometimes, an event that precipitates a depression may indeed be noxious, but once the depressive machinery is in operation, neutral or even favorable events are processed in such a way as to produce a negative conclusion. The presentation of new information to correct this erroneous conclusion is subjected to the same distorting procedure, and consequently it frequently fails to change the patient's conceptualization. As the erroneous conceptualizations become more refractory to modification by external information, the negative mood becomes more intractable.

A wide range of unpleasant feelings has been reported by patients diagnosed as depressed. A careful scrutiny of the detailed descriptions of the feeling states indicates that these are not the same for all patients. Some complain of a sad feeling, which they liken to grief; some describe feelings of shame or humiliation; some emphasize a feeling of being bored. It is possible to establish a plausible connection between the experienced affect and the predominant cognitive pattern. A patient, for example, who believes he has lost his friends complains of feeling lonely. The patient who sees the future as bleak and hopeless emphasizes feelings of discouragement. The patient who perceives herself as constantly thwarted complains of feeling frustrated. The patient who believes he appears stupid or inept feels humiliated. The patient who regards her life as devoid of any possibility of gratification complains of feeling apathetic or bored.

Changes in Motivation

The motivational changes in depressed patients may be considered under four groupings: paralysis of the will, escapist and avoidance wishes, suicidal wishes, and intensified dependency wishes. The sequential relationship between cognition and motivation may be observed under two conditions. First, by knowing an individual's cognitions one can predict his or her motivation or lack of motivation. Second, by changing the cognition one can change the motivation.

The loss of spontaneous motivation, or paralysis of the will, has been considered a symptom par excellence of depression in the classical literature. The loss of motivation may be viewed as the result of the patient's hopelessness and pessimism: as long as he or she expects a negative outcome from any course of action, he or she is stripped of any internal stimulation to do anything. Conversely, when the patient is persuaded that a positive outcome may result from a particular endeavor, he or she may then experience an internal stimulus to pursue it.

An example may illustrate this point. I was searching for some way to induce a woman with psychomotor retardation and depression to go to occupational therapy. When I first recommended this activity, she remained immobile. Then I suggested that she could make something pretty for her granddaughter, and that this would please her granddaughter. At this point, she became more animated and expressed a desire to start the project. She got up from her chair with some vigor. All at once, she slumped back, an expression of despair on her face. Questioned about her reaction, she told me that the following sequence had occurred: At first when she thought of pleasing her grandchild, she experienced a desire to work on the project. Then, she pictured herself making a mess of it. She then had an image of herself feeling humiliated and disappointed at the failure. Interestingly, she actually experienced the humiliated feeling while she was having the fantasy. Once she had fantasized this unfavorable outcome, she lost all desire to start the project and returned to her immobile position in the chair. Further questioning brought out her deep sense of futility: She felt that nothing she did could turn out right or could give her any satisfaction.

Avoidance and escapist wishes are similarly related to expectations of a negative outcome. A moderately depressed student had a strong desire to avoid studying. He felt that he would find the material dull and boring. I pointed out to him that he had always enjoyed studying this particular material once he became absorbed in it. When he could see the possibility of some gratification, he experienced a desire to study. With the change in his expectancy came a consequent change in his motivation.

Another patient wanted to stay home from work. He gave as his reason that the responsibilities at work were too great and that he would not be able to cope with them. As he thought of the things he had to do, he envisioned himself failing at each task. I suggested that we examine the specific responsibilities he had to encounter that day and some of the problems that might arise. As we reviewed the responsibilities, the patient acknowledged that he had taken care of these many times in the past. We then discussed the difficult problems that might arise, and I induced the patient to verbalize the steps he would take to solve them. Following this discussion, the patient changed from an expectation of being overwhelmed to an expectation that he would probably be able to handle things adequately. At this point his desire to escape from work was superseded by a desire to go to work.

Suicidal wishes may be regarded as an extreme expression of the desire to escape. Suicidal patients see the future as filled with suffering. They cannot visualize any way of improving things and do not believe it is possible to get better. Suicide under these conditions seems to such patients to be a rational solution. It promises an end to their own suffering and a relief of the supposed burden on their family. Once suicide appears as a reasonable alternative to living, the patient feels attracted to it. The more hopeless and painful life seems, the stronger the desire to escape from that life.

The wish to escape from life via suicide because of suffering and hopelessness is illustrated in the following quotation from a patient who had been rejected by her boyfriend. "There's no sense in living. There's nothing here for me. I need love and I don't have it any more. I can't be happy without love—only miserable. It will just be the same misery, day in and day out. It's senseless to go on."

The desire to escape from the apparent futility of his existence was expressed by another patient. "Life is just to go through another day. It doesn't make any sense. There's nothing here that can give me any satisfaction. The future isn't there. I just don't want life any more. I want to get out of here. It's stupid just to go on living."

Another false premise that underlies suicidal wishes is patients' belief that everybody would be better off it they were dead. Since they see themselves as worthless and a burden, arguments that their family would be hurt if they died seem hollow. How can they suffer from losing a burden? One patient envisioned killing herself as doing her parents a favor. She would not only end her own suffering but relieve them of psychological and financial responsibilities. "I'm just taking money from my parents. They could use it to better advantage. They wouldn't have to support me. My father wouldn't have to work so hard and they could travel. I'm unhappy taking their money and they could be happy with it."

In a number of cases, the suicidal wishes were ameliorated by examining the underlying premises and considering alternative solutions. A patient became depressed because he had lost his job. He said, "I want to shoot myself. Nobody thinks I'm capable of doing anything. I don't think so either.

I'll never get another job. I don't have any friends or dates. I'm isolated. I'm just completely stuck for all time. If I shot myself, it could solve all my problems."

In this case, I had a detailed discussion with the patient about all the job opportunities available to him. His professional training was in high demand, and in the course of the discussions he was able to see many means of getting another position, for example, through a placement bureau or an employment agency. His attitude that it would be impossible to get further employment changed to an expectation that he probably would get a job. Concurrently, his suicidal wishes disappeared.

The increased dependency that is so characteristic of many depressions may be attributed to a number of factors. Patients see themselves in negative terms—as being inept, inadequate, and undesirable. Furthermore, they tend to overestimate the complexity and difficulty of the normal details of living. In addition, they expect everything to turn out badly. Under these conditions, many depressed patients yearn for somebody strong to take care of them and to help them with their problems. They often tend to magnify the strength of the person on whom they are dependent. One woman who generally disparaged her husband when she was not depressed regarded him as a kind of superman when she was depressed.

As with the other motivations, I have found that the dependency wishes may be attenuated if patients can view themselves and their problems more objectively. As their self-esteem improves and they see ways of coping with their problems, they feel less driven to seek help from others.

The relationship between cognition and motivation has also been demonstrated in a controlled experimental situation. We found that patients who (as a result of the experimenter's manipulation of the degree of difficulty of an assigned task) viewed their performance on a task as inferior were less motivated to volunteer for a new experiment than those who believed their performance was superior.

Physical Symptoms

The explanation of the physical and vegetative symptoms of depression in the framework of a psychological model presents certain difficulties. The introduction of physiological variables requires the mixing of different conceptual levels and entails the risk of confounding rather than clarifying the problem. Furthermore, whereas the patients' verbal material has been a rich source of information for establishing meaningful connections among the psychological variables, it has provided scanty data for determining psychophysiological relationships.

With these reservations in mind, Beck attempted to relate the cognitive patterns to some of the physical correlates of depression—retardation, fatigability, and agitation. The retarded patients Beck observed generally expressed attitudes of passive resignation to their supposedly terrible fate. The attitude is expressed in such statements as "There's nothing I can do to save myself." In the most severe cases, such as the benign stupors, patients may believe they are already dead. In any event, the profound motor inhibition appears to be congruent with the patients' negative view of themselves, sense of futility, and loss of spontaneous motivation. When Beck was able to stimulate the patient's desire to do something (as described in the section on motivation), he found that the retardation became reduced or temporarily disappeared. Moreover, when the patient could entertain the idea of gaining some gratification from what they were doing, there was a reduction in the subjective sense of fatigue.

The influence of psychological factors on inertia, retardation, and fatigability in depression has been confirmed by several systematic studies. We found that when depressed patients are given a concrete task, such as the Digit-Symbol Substitution Test, they mobilize sufficient motivation to perform as well as nondepressed patients with similar severity of illness (Chapter 10). Since this test is essentially a speed test, it should be particularly sensitive to psychomotor retardation. Similarly, Friedman[29] found that depressed patients showed either no impairment or only minimal impairment when engaged in a variety of psychological tests.

The thought content of the agitated depressive is congruent with the overt behavior. Unlike retarded patients, agitated patients do not accept their fate passively and do not believe it is futile to try to save themselves. They desperately seek some way to ease the distress or escape from the problems. Since there is no apparent method for achieving this, their frantic search drives them into aimless motor activity such as pacing the floor, scratching their skin, or tearing their clothes. These behaviors reflect ideas such as "I can't stand this;" "I've got to do something;" or "I can't go on any longer this way." They also manifest these attitudes in frenzied entreaties for help.

Cognition in Mania and Other Disorders

Psychiatric disorders other than depression also show an idiosyncratic thought content that is specific for the particular disorder. This holds true for the neuroses as well as the psychoses.[30] The cognitive patterns peculiar to the manic phase of the manic-depressive reaction have a content that is directly opposite to that observed in depression. It is possible, in fact, to delineate a *manic triad* that corresponds to the depressive triad. The manic triad consists of an unrealistically *positive* view of the world, of the self, and of the future. The affective and motivational characteristics of the manic phase may be viewed as a consequence of the operation of these cognitive patterns.

The relationship between the depressive and manic phases may be illustrated by the following case history. A 40-year-old man was admitted to the hospital following a serious suicide attempt. At the time of admission, he thought that his friends and relatives had contempt for him and that everybody in the hospital disliked him. He attributed their low opinion of him to his personal deficiencies and worthlessness. He considered himself lacking in character and ability. He anticipated that nothing would ever improve for him and that he would fail miserably in anything he undertook. He felt sad, discouraged, and fatigued and had no spontaneous desire to do anything. Continuous observation indicated that he appeared generally retarded in his speech and movements.

On the tenth day of hospitalization, there was a dramatic change in his behavior. He began to show typical manic symptoms—excessive volubility, overactivity, and excessive cheerfulness. His thought content showed the following themes. He believed that he was popular among the patients and that the ward personnel admired him for his helpfulness, ability, and wit. He believed that he had an unusual insight into other patients' problems that enabled him to cure them. He expressed the opinion that he was a deeply religious man who could inspire others by his example. He planned to devote his life to helping psychiatric patients and foresaw a future of happiness from being of service to others.

The various affective and motivational reactions of this patient may be attributed to the change in his cognitive patterning. His euphoria stemmed from his positive evaluations of himself and his expectations of future achievement and happiness. His greatly increased drive, energy, and activity may similarly be attributed to his positive view of himself and his expectations of success.

When the specific cognitive content of depression is compared with that of other disorders, it is found that although there are some similarities, there are important differences. For instance, typical paranoid patients may believe that other people dislike them (negative view of the world). They tend, however, to blame others for those negative reactions and maintain a favorable view of themselves. They regard the others as unfair and unjustified in their supposed mistreatment of them. Their affect is in accord with this conceptualization—anger.

In anxiety reactions, there is an anticipation of future unpleasantness that is similar to that seen in depressions (negative expectations of the future). As was pointed out previously, however, depressed patients see themselves as already damaged, and their view of the future is essentially a reproduction of their image of the present. Anxious patients, on the other hand, anticipate certain potentially harmful experiences but are able to maintain a positive self-regard. Also, unlike depressed patients, they are capable of anticipating that certain experiences in the future might be pleasant, and that at least some endeavors might have a favorable outcome.

Some patients may show two components of the depressive triad but not the third. They consequently may experience a few of the typical symptoms of depression but not enough to warrant the diagnosis of clinical depression. One woman, ordinarily energetic and optimistic, complained of an overwhelming feeling of lassitude and fatigability of many months' duration. She felt so exhausted that she spent most of the day in bed and engaged in minimal physical activity. On interview, the following data were elicited. She saw herself as burdened with insoluble problems: an egocentric husband, who made great demands on her but was insensitive to her needs, and a variety of household difficulties (negative view of the world). She could not see any way out of this difficult situation (negative view of the future). She was able, however, to maintain a positive view of herself, and in fact attributed her difficulties to shortcomings in her husband. In the course of her brief psychotherapy some of the household problems were solved, and she was able to establish a more effective working relationship with her husband. At this point, her negative view of her home and her marriage dissolved, and with it went her extreme feelings of fatigue. She once again was outgoing, cheerful, and energetic.

Other patients may manifest a negative self-concept and may tend to interpret their current experiences negatively but still maintain a positive view of the future. These patients feel sad but at the same time look forward to an improvement in their lot and consequently are motivated to keep trying. In other words, they show some of the affective symptoms but do not experience the motivational or physical symptoms associated with depression. Hence, they would not be diagnosed as depressed.

The psychiatric conditions described above show distorted conceptualizations. These distortions constitute one aspect of a thinking disorder. The term *thinking disorder*, as commonly used, generally encompasses, in addition to cognitive distortions, the broad areas of impairment Bleuler described under the term "loosening of associations." Factor analytic studies of the verbal behavior of patients have indicated the presence of two independent factors.[31] One factor, related to disruption of the formal thought processes, includes such characteristics as irrelevant responses, disconnected ideas, vagueness, and peculiar word usage or syntax. The factor, which could be labeled "conceptual disorganization," is characteristic of schizophrenia. The other factor appears to be related to a distortion of thought content rather than to the disorganization of thought. This second factor appears to be characteristic of neuroses as well as psychoses and is related to the cognitive triad described in this chapter.

A Cognitive Classification of Psychiatric Disorders

A thinking disorder is by no means limited to depression but is a general characteristic of psychopathology. A sharp delineation of the specific content of

TABLE 12-1. Neurotic and Allied Disorders Differentiated According to Cognitive
            Content

Reaction	Idiosyncratic ideational content
Depressive	Negative concept of self, world, and future
Hypomanic	Exaggerated positive concept of self, world, and future
Anxiety	Concept of personal danger
Phobic	Danger connected with specific, avoidable situations
Conversion (hysterical)	Concept of motor or sensory abnormality
Paranoid	Concept of abuse, persecution, injustice
Obsessive	Repetitive thought, usually a warning or doubting
Compulsive	Self-command to perform a specific act to allay obsessive doubting

the thinking disorder can help in making a differential diagnosis among the various psychiatric disorders. In addition, a careful assessment of the degree of cognitive impairment can help distinguish neurosis from psychosis.

Neuroses

For the most part, the neuroses may be differentiated on the basis of the thought content. In some cases, additional characteristics are important; for example, whether a specific situation is necessary to produce a symptom, as in the case of phobic reaction, or whether abnormal behavior is a basic criterion, as in the compulsions (see Table 12-1).

Depressive

The thought content is concerned with ideas of personal deficiency, impossible environmental demands and obstacles, and nihilistic expectations. As a result, the patient experiences sadness, loss of motivation, suicidal wishes, and agitation or retardation.

Hypomanic

The thought content is opposite that of depression. The dominant cognitive patterns are exaggerated ideas of personal abilities, minimization of external obstacles, and overly optimistic expectations. These patterns lead to euphoria, increased drive, and overactivity.

Anxious

The ideational content is dominated by themes of personal danger. In contrast to the phobic, who experiences a sense of danger only in specific, avoidable situations, the anxiety neurotic perceives danger continuously and, consequently, is continuously anxious.

The danger may be perceived as internal: A patient with an irritable colon had unremitting anxiety because of his idea that he might have cancer. The stimuli may be external: A patient interpreted every loud sound as a signal of catastrophe. A siren meant her house was on fire, an automobile backfiring indicated somebody shooting at her, and the noise of an airplane suggested an atomic attack. Another patient was constantly in dread of being rejected by members of her family, friends, and even strangers; she consequently had continuous anxiety.

Phobic

Phobic patients expect some physical or psychological injury in certain defined situations. If they avoid these situations, the danger is averted and they are tranquil. When exposed to the stimulus situation, they react with all the typical signs and symptoms of the anxiety neurotic.

The cognitive reaction to the phobic situation may be expressed in purely verbal form or in the form of imagery. A patient with a bridge phobia would have the thought, "The bridge is going to collapse." Another patient would get a visual image of the bridge collapsing and of himself drowning.

Some of the typical cognitions in the common phobic situations are: elevators—"I am starting to suffocate"; high places—"I might jump off," "I may fall off," or "It may collapse"; tunnels—"The walls may cave in," or "I don't have enough air"; boats—"It is starting to sink and I'll drown."

Somatization

In conversion (hysterical) reactions, patients erroneously believe that they have a particular physical disorder. As a result of this belief, they experience sensory and/or motor abnormalities consistent with the faulty conception of organic pathology. Their symptoms are manifestations of the particular idea and are often at variance with those produced by an actual lesion.

Charcot[32] cited the case of a patient involved in a street accident who believed (erroneously) that a carriage had run over both legs. He subsequently developed hysterical paralysis of both legs. Sometimes, the symptom is based on an incorrect diagnosis by the patient of an actual lesion. A soldier sustained a bullet wound in his leg and subsequently developed "stocking" anesthesia: He believed the bullet had severed a nerve in his leg. When it was demonstrated to him that the nerve was intact, his anesthesia began to disappear. Patients with hysterical motor paralyses believe that a part of the body is paralyzed and therefore do not try to move it: The patient, in fact, often resists attempts by the examiner to move the "paralyzed" part.

It is possible to demonstrate that not only the hysterical sensory and motor paralyses but also the hyperalgesias and hyperkinetic reactions are based on an erroneous idea of physical pathology. When the erroneous idea is undermined through suggestion, hypnosis, or reeducation, the symptom disappears.

Paranoid

The cardinal feature of the paranoid reaction is misinterpretation of experience in terms of mistreatment, abuse, or persecution: A patient hears people whispering and has the thought that they are jealous of him and are saying degrading things about him. A student gets a low grade on an exam and immediately thinks the teacher was biased.

Anxious paranoids do not feel capable of coping with the sinister behavior of others. They feel the threat is too overwhelming and want to flee. Hostile paranoids experience anger rather than anxiety because they do not feel helpless in the face of the apparent discrimination or injustice. They want to fight back against the persecutors and protect their rights.

Obsessive and Compulsive

The obsessions may be defined as recurrent thoughts having the same or similar content. The content is usually concerned with some risk or danger expressed in the form of a doubt or a warning: "Did I turn off the gas in the oven?" "Will I be able to speak?" "Perhaps I got some disease from the dirt," "My eyeglasses are on crooked," "I may get a speck in my eye."

Compulsions are based on obsessions and represent attempts to allay the obsessive doubts or worries through action. A patient with a handwashing compulsion would get the thought after each handwashing ritual, "I didn't get all the dirt off." Another patient with the obsession that he looked odd to other people would compulsively turn his head away when anybody approached. Another patient would count to nine each time she had a thought that something terrible would happen to her family; the number represented a magical device for averting disaster.

Salkovskis et al.[33] tested the effects of the way intrusive cognitions are interpreted. They assessed responsibility beliefs in patients suffering from Obsessive Compulsive Disorder, other anxiety disorders, and nonclinical controls. They found that people suffering from obsessions have an exaggerated sense of personal responsibility for causing or preventing possible harm.[33]

Psychoses

The thought content of the psychoses is similar to that of the neuroses. The themes in the cognitive distortions of psychotic depressive reaction parallel those of neurotic depressive disorder; manic disorder parallels hypomanic; paranoia or paranoid schizophrenic disorder parallels the paranoid state. Although the general themes in neuroses and psychoses may be similar, the specific content is often more extreme or more improbable in the psychoses. A neurotic depressive may view himself as a sinner or as socially undesirable; a psychotic depressive may believe she is the devil or emanates disgusting odors.

The major difference between neurosis as a class and psychosis as a class is the presence of more pronounced cognitive impairment in the latter. The erroneous ideas are more intense, more compelling, and more impermeable. The conceptual errors (arbitrary inference, selective abstraction, and over-generalization) are more frequent and more extreme. On the one hand, the distortions are more fixed; on the other, the patient's ability to view them objectively is impaired. In short, the patient has a delusion.

Schizophrenic disorder may be distinguished from the other psychoses by the disruption of formal thought processes. As mentioned previously, Overall and Gorham[31] attached the label "conceptual disorganization" to the factor characterized by irrelevant, vague, disconnected, or peculiarly formed verbal responses. On the basis of the content of the cognitive distortions, a patient is diagnosed as having psychotic depressive disorder reaction, manic disorder, or paranoia; if conceptual disorganization is present, the diagnosis is schizo-affective disorder or paranoid schizophrenic disorder. If there is conceptual disorganization without any consistent distortion, then the diagnosis is schizo-phrenic disorder, simple type.

Conclusions

We have attempted to clarify the relationships among the variegated phenomena of depression—cognitive, affective, motivational, and physical. A primary factor appears to be the activation of idiosyncratic cognitive patterns that divert thinking into specific channels that deviate from reality. As a result, the patient perseveres in making negative judgments and misinterpretations. These distortions may be categorized within the triad of negative interpretations of experience; negative evaluations of the self; and negative expectations of the future.

The cognitive distortions lead to the affective and motivational symptoms that are characteristic of depression. The misinterpretation of experience in terms of deprivation leads to sadness, just as in the case of an actual deprivation. Unrealistic negative expectations lead to hopelessness, just as do reality-based expectations. Similarly, the negative view of the world, the self, and the future strips the patient of any positive desires and stimulates desires to avoid the apparent unpleasantness, intensifies dependency wishes, and evoke wishes to find an escape route via suicide.

Some of the physical symptoms of depressed patients may be ascribed to the way they structure their experiences. Retardation may be regarded as the outcome of passive resignation, sense of futility, and loss of spontaneous motivation. Agitation, on the other hand, appears to be related to the frantic desire to fight the way out of a situation the patient regards as desperate.

The differential diagnosis of the psychiatric disorders may be sharpened by using the cognitive content and the degree of impairment as diagnostic criteria. Depression, mania, anxiety reaction, conversion reaction, and paranoid reaction may be diagnosed, respectively, according to themes of self-deflation, self-enhancement, danger, motor or sensory abnormality, and persecution. Psychosis is distinguished from neurosis on the basis of more severe cognitive impairment. Schizophrenic reaction is distinguished from other psychotic reactions on the basis of conceptual disorganization.

Although theoretical progress is evident, many questions remain for future research. Several of these were identified by Beck,[19] including the following. (1) Can depression be prevented? (2) What factors produce and maintain the negative thinking bias? (3) Do interactions between stress and personality predict vulnerability to depression in specific individuals? (4) Do the various types of effective treatments (e.g., cognitive therapy, drugs, ECT) have a "final common pathway" that can explain how improvement takes place? (5) Does one type of treatment compared to another produce a more durable effect (Beck, p. 371).[19] Preliminary answers to some of these questions will be addressed in the chapters in Part IV, "Treatment of Depression."

Chapter 13
Development of Depression

PREDISPOSITION TO DEPRESSION

Formation of Permanent Concepts

Early in life, individuals develop a wide variety of concepts and attitudes about themselves and their world. Some of these concepts are anchored to reality and form the basis for a healthy personal adjustment. Others deviate from reality and produce vulnerability to possible psychological disorders.

People's concepts—realistic as well as unrealistic—are drawn from experiences, from the attitudes and opinions communicated to by others, and from identifications. Among the concepts that are central in the pathogenesis of depression are people's attitudes toward self, environment, and future. Since the formulation of all three types of concept is similar, that of the self-concepts can serve as a pattern for the other two.

People's self-concepts are clusters of attitudes about themselves, some favorable and others unfavorable. These clusters consist of generalizations they have made on the basis of interactions with the environment. They derive their self-concepts from personal experiences, from others' judgments, and from identifications with key figures such as parents, siblings, and friends.

Once a particular attitude or concept has been formed, it can influence subsequent judgments and become more firmly set. For instance, a child who gets the notion that he or she is inept, as a result of either a failure or being called inept by somebody else, may interpret subsequent experiences according to this notion. Each time thereafter that difficulties are encountered in manual tasks he or she may have a tendency to judge him- or herself as inept. Each negative judgment tends to reinforce the negative concept or self-image. Thus, a cycle is set up: Each negative judgment fortifies the negative self-image, which in turn facilitates a negative interpretation of subsequent experiences, which further consolidates the negative self-concept. Unless this negative image is extinguished, it becomes structuralized, that is, it becomes a permanent formation in the cognitive organization. Once a concept is structuralized, it remains permanently with the individual even though it may be dormant; it becomes a cognitive structure, or *schema*.

Among the positive (or self-enhancing) self-concepts are such attitudes as "I am capable," "I am attractive," "I can get what I want," "I can understand problems and solve them." Examples of negative (or self-diminishing) self-concepts are "I am weak," "I am inferior," "I am unlovable," and "I can't do anything right." These negative self-concepts emerge with great force in depression.

The nuclei of positive and negative self-concepts determine the direction of an individual's self-esteem. When the positive self-concepts are activated, individuals regard themselves more favorably that is, they experience an increase in the self-esteem. Activation of the negative self-concepts lowers the self-esteem. The role of an individual's self-esteem is regarded by Jacobson[1] and Bibring[2] as of central importance in depression.

Value Judgments and Affect

Of pertinence in the predisposition to depression are the value judgments or connotations attached to the self-concepts. When people make negative generalizations about themselves, such as that they are inept, unpopular, or dull, they are prone to regard these attributes as bad, unworthy, or undesirable. They may extend their dislike for the particular trait to a dislike of themselves, and move from specific rejection of the trait to global rejection of themselves.

Concepts such as good and bad are "superordinate constructs."[3] A specific attribute may not be regarded initially as either good or bad but may, as the result of social learning, be organized under such a superordinate construct. Subsequently, when people judge themselves as "inept," the connotation "bad" automatically accompanies the judgment.

Constructs such as "bad" or "undesirable" can become closely linked to affective responses. When individuals perceive themselves as bad or undesirable, they are likely to experience an unpleasant feeling such as sadness. But when they view themselves positively as admirable or desirable, they experience a pleasant affect. Once the pathways between a certain concept such as "I am inept" and the negative affect have been established, the person experiences the unpleasant affect each time he or she makes the negative judgment. Similar interconnections are established between cognitions such as "Things never work out for me" or "I will never get what I want" and affects such as discouragement and hopelessness. In this manner, cognitive learning takes place.

Specific Vulnerability

The vulnerability of the depression-prone person is attributable to the constellation of enduring negative attitudes about self, world, and future. Even though these attitudes (or concepts) may not be prominent or even discernible at a given time, they persist in a latent state like an explosive charge ready to be detonated by an appropriate set of conditions. Once activated, these concepts dominate the person's thinking and lead to the typical depressive symptomatology.

The specific depressive constellation is composed of a network of interrelated negative attitudes. One group of attitudes consists of negative generalizations about the self such as "I am dumb," "People don't like me," "I'm a weakling," and "I don't have any personality." These generalizations are connected to negative attitudes about the attributes, such as "It's terrible to be stupid" or "It's disgusting to be weak." Hence, the linkage of the self-concept to the negative value judgment produces attitudes such as "I'm no good because I'm weak," or "I'm nothing because I'm unattractive."

In order for a negative self-concept to be pathogenic, it must be associated with a negative value judgment. Not all people who regard themselves as physically, mentally, or socially deficient consider these traits bad nor are repelled by them. I have interviewed several intellectually and physically handicapped people who do not attach a negative value to their disabilities and who have never shown any depressive tendencies. Furthermore, some individuals with traits that are distasteful to most people may admire themselves for that trait, for example, a juvenile delinquent who takes pride in being bad.

The concept of self-blame is another component of the predepressive constellation. According to a primitive notion of causality, individuals hold themselves responsible for their defects and presumed deficiencies. This attitude is expressed as follows: "It's my own fault I always make mistakes. I'm to blame for being so weak."

Another group of attitudes in the predepressive constellation revolves around the theme of negative expectations. The pessimistic view of the future is expressed in attitudes such as "Things will never get any better for me." "I will always be weak and get pushed around." "I'm basically unlucky and always will be." When these attitudes are mobilized, they produce the feeling of hopelessness characteristic of depression. Many individuals confronted with adversity face the future with equanimity and are not gripped by negative attitudes about the future. Many patients with chronic or fatal medical illnesses are optimistic about the future, in contrast to manic-depressive patients, who have a good prognosis for recovery but who uniformly expect to remain ill.[4]

When all the components of the depressive constellation are activated, a sequence such as the following occurs. Individuals interpret an experience as representing a personal defeat or thwarting; they attribute this defeat to some defect in themselves; they regard themselves as worthless for having this trait; they blame themselves for having acquired the trait and dislike themselves for it; and since they regard the trait as an intrinsic part of themselves, they see no hope of changing and view the future as devoid of any satisfaction or filled with pain.

Precipitation of Depression

An individual who has incorporated the cognitive constellation of attitudes just described has the necessary predisposition for the development of clinical depression in adolescence or adulthood. Whether he or she will ever become depressed depends on whether the necessary conditions are present at a given time to activate the depressive constellation.

Specific Stress

In the first edition of this volume,[5] the following theoretical statement appeared:

> In childhood and adolescence, the depression-prone individual becomes sensitized to certain types of life situations. The traumatic situations initially responsible for embedding or reinforcing the negative attitudes that comprise the depressive constellation are the prototypes of the specific stresses that may later activate these constellations. When a person is subjected to situations reminiscent of the original traumatic experiences, she may then become depressed. The process may be likened to conditioning in which a particular response is linked to a specific stimulus; once the chain has been formed, stimuli similar to the original stimulus may evoke the conditioned response. (p. 278)

The above has proven to be a testable theory, and it has now been largely confirmed through properly designed empirical studies. In 2005, Scher et al.[6]—citing the above statement (p. 505)—presented a comprehensive narrative review of all the studies to date that have been generated by this theory. They found 18 studies that used priming designs, that is, studies of vulnerable persons under conditions of schema activation. The priming design studies included Teasdale & Dent,[7] Miranda & Persons,[8] Miranda et al.,[9] Ingram et al.,[10] Hedlund & Rude,[11] Roberts & Kassel,[12] Dykman,[13] Gilboa & Gotlib,[14] Miranda et al.,[15] Solomon et al.,[16] Brosse et al.,[17] Segal et al.,[18] Taylor & Ingram,[19] Ingram & Ritter,[20] McCabe et al.,[21] Gemar et al.,[22] Murray et al.,[23] and Timbremont & Braet.[24]

In addition to the 18 priming design studies, 11 additional studies have used longitudinal designs. Such designs follow people over time to determine whether cognitive vulnerability interacts with life events to predict depression. Scher et al.[6] evaluated the following longitudinal studies that provided tests of Beck's[5] theory: Barnett & Gotlib,[25] Barnett & Gotlib,[26] Kwon & Oei,[27] Brown et al.,[28] Dykman & Johll,[29] Shirk et al.,[30] Joiner et al.,[31] Lewinsohn et al.,[32] Abela & D'Alessandro,[33] Beevers & Carver,[34] and Hankin et al.[35] The conclusions of Scher et al.[6] were that cognitive priming studies and studies utilizing longitudinal designs now support the theory of cognitive vulnerability in adults, and evidence is emerging for children as well.

To elaborate by examples, the association of stimulus situation and response may be illustrated by the following: A successful businesswoman stated that she had always felt inferior to her classmates who came from prosperous families because she was from a poor family. She always felt distinctly different and unacceptable. When, as an adult, she was with people wealthier than she, this caused her to have thoughts that she did not belong, that she wasn't as good as the others, and that she was a social outcast. These ideas were associated with transient feelings of sadness. At one point in her career, she was elected to the board of directors of a corporation. She viewed the other directors as coming from the "right side of the tracks" and herself as from "the wrong side." She felt she could not measure up to the other directors and slipped into a depression lasting several days.

Situations that might be expected to lower an individual's self-esteem are frequent precipitators of depression. Some that have been observed in clinical practice include failing an examination, being jilted by a lover, being rejected by a fraternity or sorority, and being fired from a job.

Another type of situation that may precipitate a depression is one involving a thwarting of important goals or posing an insoluble dilemma. A woman became depressed when her summons to military service forced her to relinquish her plans to enter medical school. A male soldier assigned to duty in a remote portion of Canada, confronted with the prospect of an unlimited period of time devoid of any satisfactions, slipped into a depression. A man was trapped between his fiancée, who insisted that they get married or break the engagement, and his parents, who adamantly refused to give their permission for the marriage; he reacted by feeling hopeless and suicidal.

Sometimes the precipitating event is a physical disease or an abnormality that activates ideas of physical deterioration and death. A woman observed a red coloration in her urine and developed the idea that she had cancer. Despite reassurances by her physicians after an exhaustive series of tests, she became more convinced that she had cancer and became increasingly depressed. She anticipated steady deterioration and felt she was worthless and a burden to everyone.

A man developed mild arthritis. He saw it as a disabling illness and visualized himself as completely bedridden. He predicted a hemmed-in, pleasureless existence for himself and became increasingly hopeless and agitated.

These circumstances might produce feelings of pain or frustration in most people, but they would not cause a depression. A person must be peculiarly sensitive to the situation and must have a predepressive constellation to react with a clinical depression. A nondepressive person who has experienced a trauma such as a financial reversal or the news that he or she has a chronic illness may still be able to maintain interest in all aspects of life. The depression-prone person, on the other hand, experiences a *constriction of his or her cognitive field* and is bombarded by negative self-judgments and negative ideas about the future.

Depression often seems to arise from a *series* of stressful situations that impinge on the specific vulnerability rather than from a single situation. A number of blows in rapid succession to the sensitive areas may be sufficient to exceed the patient's tolerance, although he or she might be able to absorb a single trauma.

One of the problems in assessing the contribution of external factors to the precipitation of depression is that these factors are often insidious. The patient may not be aware of their operation and may pass through several depressive episodes without identifying the pairing of the depression with a recurrent set of traumatic conditions. One woman experienced depressions during three consecutive summers. These started in July and August and did not begin to subside until the end of September. It was not until the third episode that Beck ascertained that each depression began about five weeks after her son came home from college for a summer vacation. It was then established that her son had a contemptuous attitude toward her and that, without her realization, he constantly undermined her self-esteem. His incessant but subtle grinding away at her slid her into a depression that persisted until he returned to school.

Genetic Moderation of the Stress-Depression Link

In addition to the presence of a specific stress relevant to the cognitive constellation, researchers have studied genetic influences to account for why only some people become depressed in response to stressful experiences. The idea that genetic makeup interacts with stressful life events is an example of the "diathesis-stress theory" of depression.[36,37,38] Consider an epidemiological study that tested the presence of a gene-by-environment interaction, in which a person's response to stressful events is determined by his or her genetic makeup.[39]

The study was designed as a prospective-longitudinal study with 1,037 children (52 percent male) assessed at ages 3, 5, 7, 9, 11, 13, 15, 18, and 21. At age 26, 96 percent of the cohort was intact. Participants were divided into three groups based on the 5-HTTLPR genotype. A life history calendar was used in assessing stressful life events, such as employment, financial, health, and relationship stressors. No evidence was found to suggest that genotype influenced number of stressful life events, since the three genotype groups did not differ in number of such events. At age 26, the Diagnostic Interview Scale was used to determine the presence of depression over the past year.[39]

The influence of stressful life events in predicting depression was moderated (affected) by a functional polymorphism in the promoter region of the serotonin transporter (5-HTT) gene. Those with one or two copies of the short allelle of the polymorphism differed from individuals homozygous for the long allele. Specifically, the short allele was associated with more depression and suicide attempts or thoughts in response to stress compared to individuals homozygous for the long allele. However, the authors recognized that their study does not provide unequivocal evidence for a gene by stress interaction, since it is possible that frequent exposure to stressful life events could itself be mediated by the genetic variation.

Along the same lines of speculation, Penza et al.[38] suggested that developmental neurobiological mechanisms may help explain the observation of increased vulnerability to depression following childhood abuse (e.g., physical, sexual, or psychological abuse) or stress in adulthood (e.g., death of a spouse). Early life stress, during a time of neuronal plasticity, may cause relatively enduring hypersensitivity in neuroendocrine stress response systems, which may lead to supersensitivity to subsequent exposure to additional stress.[38]

Nemeroff and Vale[37] pointed out that most psychiatric disorders, including mood and anxiety disorders, are polygenetic in nature rather than determined by traditional autosomal-dominant Mendelian genetics. Neural circuits containing corticotropin-releasing factor (CRF) have been identified as an important mediator of the stress response. Early-life adversity, such as physical or sexual abuse during childhood, results in long-lasting changes in the CRF-mediated stress response and a greatly increased risk of depression in genetically predisposed persons.[37]

Heim et al.[36] reviewed preliminary animal and human studies on how emotional trauma during development permanently shapes brain circuits involved in the regulation of stress and emotion, leaving "biological scars" that may increase the likelihood of adult psychopathology (also see Chapter 9).

Nonspecific Stress

An individual may develop some form of psychological disturbance when exposed to any overwhelming stress, even if it does not strike at the specific sensitivity. A woman became depressed when her husband and all her children were killed in an automobile accident. A man was precipitated into a depression when he was wrongfully accused of a crime and discharged from his job as a result of the notoriety.

Sometimes a depression is precipitated, not by a single overwhelming incident, but by a series of traumatic events. A law professor was able to maintain her equilibrium even after being passed over for a promotion she felt she deserved and after losing her most important court case, but when she discovered that her husband was having an affair she was unable to ward off her feelings of despair and slipped into a depression.

These nonspecific stress situations do not necessarily produce depression.

Other types of pathological reaction may be produced, depending on the specific predispositions of a particular person. Other individuals subjected to the same traumatic situations might have totally different disturbances such as paranoid reactions, anxiety reactions, or psychosomatic disorders—or no psychiatric disorder at all.

Other Contributing Factors

The predispositional and precipitating factors probably do not include all the conditions necessary for the development of depression. It is likely that there are other, not readily identifiable contributing factors.

One such factor I call *psychological strain*. I have observed that a number of patients who have been overtaxed or overstimulated for long periods are especially susceptible to specific stress. The same patients, however, can sustain the same stress if it comes at a time when they have not been strained.

Developmental Studies of Effects of Chronic Stress

A study by Hayden and Klein[40] supports the thesis of psychological strain. In attempting to predict the course and outcome of depression, 86 outpatients were included in a prospective 5-year follow-up study. Patients were all diagnosed with early-onset (before age 21) dysthymic disorder. The variables assessed at baseline included family history of psychopathology, early home environment, axis I and II comorbidity, social support, and chronic stress. Chronic stress was associated with higher levels of depression at follow-up, as were other variables, including family history of psychopathology, early adversity, and axis I and II comorbidity.

Extending the analysis of this same data set to 7 $\frac{1}{2}$ year follow-up, Dougherty et al.[41] examined the effects of chronic stress, adverse parent-child relationships, and family history. Depression severity was predicted by higher levels of chronic stress in the 6 months prior to each assessment. This association was moderated by adverse parent-child relationships and family history of dysthymic disorder. In those with a history of poorer parent-child relationships, chronic stress was related to increased depression severity at follow-up. In patients with a higher familial loading for dysthymic disorder, chronic stress over time was less predictive of higher levels of depressive symptoms.

Genetic Risk, Previous Episodes, and Chronic Stress

As is often the case in clinical depression, the complexities do not end there. An interesting study by Kendler et al.[42] evaluated two other variables that must be considered in predicting the relation between stress and depression onset: genetic risk and number of previous depressive episodes. Multiple studies have documented that as the number of depressive episodes increases, the association between reports of stressful life events and the onset of depression decreases. In other words, the ability to predict the onset of a depressive episode from life stressors goes down as the number of previous episodes experienced by the individual goes up.

Kendler et al.[42] examined the interaction between genetic risk, frequency of previous depressive episodes, and reported stressful events. In people with high genetic risk for depression, depression was frequently experienced in the absence of prior depressive episodes and without reported environmental stressors. For those people with low genetic risk, as the number of previous depressive episodes increased, there was a decline in the association between stress and onset of depression. Thus, depressive episodes that occur in the absence of stress may be explained by two pathways, genetic risk and previous depressive episodes.

Personality Organization in Depression

In the preceding discussion, the characteristics of depression were described primarily in terms of phenomena introspectively identified by the patient and reported to the investigator. Constructs such as self-concept and specific sensitivities are *close to the data*, that is, they are easily inferred from the clinical material and do not represent a high level of abstraction.

There are a number of questions still unanswered. How does the peculiar depressive thinking become dominant? Why does the depressed patient cling so tenaciously to painful ideas, even when confronted with contradictory evidence? What is the relationship between thinking and affect?

To answer these questions it is necessary to provide more abstract and more speculative formulations. The theory in this section deals with entities (hypothetical constructs) not experienced by the patient as such but whose existence is postulated to account for the regularities and predictabilities in her or his behavior. These hypothetical constructs include cognitive structures and energy. The formulations are not intended to present a comprehensive explanation of depression but will be limited to a few broad areas in which the relevant clinical material was adequate to warrant a formal theoretical exposition.

Literature on Cognitive Organizations

The study of cognitive systems began receiving increasing attention in the 1950s. The relevant psychoanalytic literature, particularly in the area of ego psychology, was systematically reviewed and integrated by Rapaport.[43] The early psychological literature on cognition was more diverse, as indicated by the disparate approaches of writers such as Allport,[44] Bruner et al.,[45] Festinger,[46] Osgood,[47] Sarbin et al.,[48] Harvey et al.,[49] and Ellis.[50]

There was a notable lag in applying the structural concepts generated by studies of normal thinking to the thinking disorder associated with various psychiatric syndromes. There were few attempts to formulate the particular cognitive organizations in these syndromes. A number of clinicians, however, provided constructs that, although not explicitly defined as such, had the earmarks of cognitive structures. Among these are Freud's conceptualizations of the primary and secondary processes,[51] Horney's concept of the self-image,[52] Rogers's formulation of the self-concept,[53] Kelly's theory of personal constructs,[3] and Ellis's concept of self-verbalizations.[50] Harvey et al.[49] presented the most complete model of the conceptual systems in specific forms of psychopathology, including depression.

Definition of Schemas

In conceptualizing any life situation composed of a kaleidoscopic array of stimuli, individuals have a number of alternatives as to which aspects of the situation they extract and how they combine them into a coherent pattern. Different people react differently to specific complex situations and may reach quite dissimilar conclusions.

A particular individual, moreover, tends to show consistencies in the way he or she responds to similar types of events. In many instances these habitual responses may be a general characteristic of individuals in the culture; in others they may represent a relatively idiosyncratic type of response derived from experiences peculiar to the individual. In any event, stereotyped or repetitive patterns of conceptualizing may be regarded as manifestations of cognitive organizations or structures.

A cognitive *structure* is a relatively enduring component of the cognitive organization, in contrast to a cognitive *process*, which is transient. Cognitive structures were postulated by a number of earlier writers to account for the observed regularities in cognitive behavior. Piaget's "schemas,"[54] Rapaport's "conceptual tools,"[43] Postman's "categories,"[55] Kelly's "personal constructs,"[3] Bruner's "coding systems,"[45] Sarbin's "modules,"[48] and Harvey's "concepts"[49] are examples of such postulated structures.

In this text we use the term *schema* to designate a cognitive structure because of its relatively greater usage and familiarity than other terms. English and English[56] defined a cognitive schema as "the complex pattern, inferred as having been imprinted in the organismic structure by experience, that combines with the properties of the presented stimulus object or of the presented idea to determine how the object or idea is to be perceived and conceptualized." The term is broad and has been applied both to small patterns involved in relatively discrete and concrete conceptualizations, such as identifying a shoe, and to large, global patterns such as ethnocentric prejudice (which causes one to regard the behavior of persons from another social group in an unfavorable way). In this discussion, we focus on the broader, more complex schemas such as the self-concepts and constellations described earlier in this chapter.

A schema is a structure for screening, coding, and evaluating the stimuli that impinge on the organism. It is the mode by which the environment is broken down and organized into its many psychologically relevant facets. On the basis of the matrix of schemas, the individual is able to orient him- or herself in relation to time and space and to categorize and interpret experiences in a meaningful way.[49] The schemas channel thought processes irrespective of whether they are stimulated by the immediate environmental situation. When a particular set of stimuli impinge on the individual, a schema relevant to these stimuli is activated. The schema condenses and molds the raw data into cognitions. A cognition, in our usage, refers to any mental activity that has a verbal content; hence, it includes not only ideas and judgments but also self-instructions, self-criticisms, and verbally articulated wishes. In the formation of a cognition, the schema provides the conceptual framework and the particular details are filled in by the external stimuli.

Cognitive activity may proceed independently of immediate external events. The schemas pattern the stream of associations and ruminations as well as the cognitive responses to external stimuli. Hence, the notion of schemas is utilized to account for the repetitive themes in free associations, daydreams, ruminations, and dreams, as well as in the immediate reactions to environmental events.

When a verbal response consists of labeling a discrete configuration such as a shoe, the particular schema utilized may be a simple linguistic category. A more abstract conceptualization, such as an individual's judgment of other people's attitudes toward him or her, involves a more complicated schema. Schemas include not only complex taxonomic systems for classifying stimuli, but also structuralized logical elements consisting of premises, assumptions, and even fully developed syllogisms. An individual who, for example, has the notion that everybody hates him will tend to interpret other people's reactions on the basis of this premise. Schemas such as these are involved in the inaccuracies, misinterpretations, and distortions associated with all kinds of psychopathology.

The schemas have a content that corresponds to the constellations previously described. But since schemas are structures, they are also characterized by other qualities, such as flexibility-inflexibility, openness-closedness, permeability-impermeability, and concreteness-abstractness. They may be inactive at a given time and have no effect on the thought process, but they become active when energized and they remain active as long as they carry a specific quantity of energy. A specific schema can be energized or deenergized rapidly as a result of changes in the type of input from the environment.

Identification of Schemas

The most striking characteristic of the schemas is their content. The content is usually in the form of a generalization corresponding to the individual's attitudes, goals, values, and conceptions. The content of the idiosyncratic schemas found in psychopathology is reflected in the typical chronic misconceptions, distorted attitudes, invalid premises, and unrealistic goals and expectations.

Their content may be inferred from an analysis of the individual's characteristic ways of structuring specific kinds of experiences; from the recurrent themes in free associations, ruminations, and reveries; from the characteristic thematic content of dreams; from direct questioning about attitudes, prejudices, superstitions, and expectations; and from responses to psychological tests designed to pinpoint stereotyped conceptions of self and world.

How the clinician may obtain an idea of the content of a schema is illustrated in the following example. A highly intelligent patient reported that whenever she was given a problem to solve her immediate thought was, "I'm not smart enough to do it." During psychotherapy interviews, she frequently experienced the same type of reaction, as, for example, when she was asked for associations to a dream. Her free associations showed the same theme, that is, of not being smart. A scrutiny of her history revealed that her self-devaluation was a pattern occurring repeatedly throughout her life. Its incongruity was borne out by the fact that she was unusually successful in solving problems. When asked directly about her concept of her own intelligence, she replied that, although all the evidence indicated she was very bright, she "really believed" she was stupid. In the manifest content of her dreams she frequently appeared as stupid, inept, and unsuccessful.

In analyzing this clinical material, it may be concluded that one of the patient's characteristic modes of organizing her experiences was in terms of the notion "I am stupid." This idea corresponds to a specific schema, which was evoked repetitively and inappropriately in response to situations relevant to her intellectual ability.

Schemas in Depression

Depressed people's ideation is tinged with certain typically depressive themes. Their interpretation of experiences, explanation for their occurrence, and outlook for the future show, respectively, themes of personal deficiency, self-blame, and negative expectations. These idiosyncratic themes pervade not only their interpretations of immediate environmental situations but also their free associations, ruminations, and reflections.

As the depression deepens, their thought content becomes increasingly saturated with depressive ideas. Almost any external stimulus is capable of evoking a depressive thought. There may be no logical connection between the interpretation and the actual situation. Patients reach negative conclusions about themselves based on the most scanty data and shape their judgments and interpretations according to their idiosyncratic preconceptions. As distortion and misinterpretation of reality increases, self-objectivity decreases.

This cognitive impairment may be analyzed in terms of the proposition that in depression specific idiosyncratic schemas assume a dominant role in shaping the thought processes. These schemas, relatively inactive during the nondepressed period, become progressively more potent as the depression develops. Their influence is reflected in characteristic disturbances in the patient's thinking.

Modes and Psychopathology

Psychological disorders like depression show evidence of broad systematic cognitive biases that influence several psychological domains.[57,58,59] Several theorists have concluded that a global or broader perspective is needed to account for the cognitive basis of emotional disorders.[60,61,62,63,64] In this section, we advance and clarify the concept of "modes" and how it is useful in understanding psychopathology.

In cognitive theory, the structural aspect of a clinical syndrome is composed of schemas, as discussed above. Schemas provide the "structure" for both phenomenological experience and interrelated cognition, affect, and behavior. In the general statement of cognitive theory, the various types of schemas constitute the explanatory terms for the organization of psychological activity and of phenomenological experiences. One metatheoretical implication of the foregoing is that a schema is correctly understood to be more like a force than an object. These cognitive structures influence the emotional, behavioral, and physiological aspects of the various psychological disorders. The manner in which schemas interrelate in coordinating the various psychological systems is referred to as the *mode*.[58]

Modes and schemas can be differentiated in terms of the time frame of their operation, and the degree of "complexity" or diversity of levels of analysis subsumed by the respective terms. Temporally, schemas are the structural determinants of reactions to events, such as loss. They are the relatively permanent or habitual ways in which an individual interprets or reacts to the environment. By contrast, the mode is the activation of clusters of schemas and will vary according to the person's context and perception of events.

As noted earlier in this chapter, a cognitive structure (schema) is a relatively enduring component of the cognitive organization, in contrast to a cognitive process, which is transient. Analogous to this formulation, in *DSM-IV* there is a distinction between episodes and syndromes. The primary distinction is between the contemporaneous display of the various symptoms (episode) and the enduring nature of such (clinical syndrome). In terms of complexity, the mode includes the various systems (behavioral, affective, physiological) in an activated state. In the cognitive model of depression, the concept of mode incorporates the various components that are activated in response to environmental demands. It is the integrated operation of the respective psychological systems. For a more detailed discussion of the various modes (e.g., primal, constructive, minor) and their characteristics, see Beck.[58]

Distortion and Misinterpretation

The depressed patient shows certain patterns of illogical thought. The systematic errors, leading to distortions of reality, include arbitrary interpretation, selective abstraction, overgeneralization, exaggeration, and incorrect labeling (see Chapter 10). The deviant thinking may be understood in terms of the hyperactivity of the idiosyncratic schemas.

When one attempts to predict the response to a stimulus situation, it is apparent that there are a variety of ways in which the situation may be construed. Which construction is made depends on which schema is selected to provide the framework for the conceptualization. The specific steps of abstraction, synthesis, and interpretation of the stimuli depend on the specific schemas activated. Normally, a matching process occurs, so that a schema evoked by a particular external configuration is congruent with it. In such a case, although a certain amount of variation may occur from one individual to another, the cognition resulting from the interaction of the schema with the stimuli may be expected to be a reasonably accurate (veridical) representation of reality. In depression and in other types of psychopathology, however, the orderly matching of stimulus and schema is upset by the intrusion of the hyperactive idiosyncratic schemas. Because of their greater strength, these schemas displace the more appropriate schemas, and the resulting interpretations deviate from reality to a degree corresponding with the incongruity of the schema to the stimulus situation.

As these schemas become more active, they are capable of being evoked by stimuli less congruent with them ("stimulus generalization"). Only those details of the stimulus situation compatible with the schema are abstracted, and these are reorganized in such a way as to make them congruent with the schema. In other words, instead of a schema being selected to fit the external details, the details are selectively extracted and molded to fit the schema.

Perseveration (Rumination)

The moderately or severely depressed patient has a tendency to brood or ruminate over a few characteristic ideas such as "I'm a failure," or "my bowels are blocked up." These repetitive ideas are generally the same as those cognitive responses to external situations described in the previous section. The idiosyncratic schemas continually grind out the depressive cognitions that crowd out the nondepressive cognitions.[5]

As the depression progresses, patients lose control over their thinking processes; that is, even when they try to focus on other subjects the depressive cognitions continue to intrude and occupy a central position. Furthermore, they are unable to suppress these thoughts or be more than momentarily distracted from them. The depressive schema is so potent that the patients are unable to energize other schemas sufficiently to offset its dominance.

There has been increasing attention to testing the above theory of perseveration (or rumination) as an important factor in depression.[65,66] Nolen-Hoeksema et al.[67] hypothesized that women are more vulnerable to depressive symptoms than men in part because of such increased rumination. They studied approximately 1,100 community-based adults and found rumination (along with greater negative circumstances and low mastery) more common in women and mediated the gender difference in depressive symptoms. In addition, (1) chronic strain and rumination had reciprocal effects, (2) low mastery contributed to rumination, and (3) depressive symptoms contributed to rumination and less mastery over time.[67] Rumination about depressive symptoms has also been found to predict new onsets of depressive episodes and may be particularly characteristic of people with mixed anxiety/depressive symptoms.[68]

Loss of Objectivity

In the milder stages of depression, patients are able to regard their negative thoughts with objectivity and, if not able to reject them completely, they are able to modify them. They can, for instance, change the idea, "I'm a complete failure" to "I may have failed at a lot of things but I've also succeeded at a lot of things."

In the more severe stages, patients have difficulty in even considering the possibility that their ideas or interpretations might be erroneous. They find it difficult or impossible to consider contradictory evidence or alternative explanations. The idiosyncratic schema may be so strong as to interfere with recalling any events that might be inconsistent with it.

A highly successful research scientist had a chronic attitude, "I am a complete failure." Her free associations were largely concerned with thoughts of how inferior, inadequate, and unsuccessful she was. When questioned regarding past performance, she was unable to recall a *single experience* that did not constitute a failure to her.

In this case, a schema with a content such as "I am a failure" worked over the raw material of her experiences and distorted the data to make them compatible with this content. Whether the particular cognitive process was recollection, or evaluation of her current status, or prediction of the future, her thoughts bore the imprint of this schema.

The loss of objectivity and reality testing perhaps may be understood in terms of the hyperactivity of the depressive schemas. The energy attached to those schemas is substantially greater than that possessed by other structures in the cognitive organization. Hence, the idiosyncratic schemas tend to interfere with the operation of the cognitive structures involved in reasoning and reality testing.

The cognitions produced by the hyperactive idiosyncratic schema are exceptionally compelling, vivid, and plausible. The nondepressive cognitions tend to be relatively faint in comparison with the depressive cognitions. In scanning the various possible interpretations of a situation, the individual is affected by the idea with greatest intensity rather than by that which is most realistic.

In severe cases, the cognitive processes may be likened to the situation during dreaming. When individuals are dreaming, the imagery of the dream totally occupies the phenomenal field and is accepted as reality. If they attempt to assess the reality of the dream while asleep, they are generally forced to accept that it is real.

Affects and Cognition

Chapter 12 summarized the characteristic thoughts and affects of depressed patients and indicated that there is a definite temporal contiguity of thought and affect. We noted, furthermore, that there is a logical consistency between them, that is, the specific affect is congruent with the specific thought content.

The thesis derived from these clinical observations is *The affective response is determined by the way an individual structures his or her experience.* Thus, if an individual's conceptualization of a situation has an unpleasant content, he or she will experience a corresponding unpleasant affective response.

The cognitive structuring or conceptualization of a situation is dependent on the schema elicited. The specific schema, consequently, has a direct bearing on the affective response to a situation. It is postulated, therefore, that the schema determines the specific type of affective response. If the schema is concerned with self-deprecation, a feeling of sadness will be associated with it; if the schema is concerned with the anticipation of harm to the individual, anxiety will be produced. An analogous relationship between the content of the schema and the corresponding feeling holds for the other affects, such as anger and elation. Roseman and Evdokas[69] have provided experimental evidence on this relationship between appraisals and experienced emotions.

In clinical syndromes such as depression, this relationship between cognitive process and affective response is easily identified. When the affective response seems inappropriate to a particular stimulus situation, the incongruity may be attributed to the particular schema evoked. Thus, the paradoxical gloom in depression results from the idiosyncratic schemas that are operative. This may be illustrated by the example of a depressed patient who wept bitterly whenever she was praised. Her predominant attitude (schema) was that she was a fraud. Any praise or other favorable comment activated this idea about herself. Receiving praise was interpreted by her as confirmatory evidence of how she consistently deceived people.

The specific types of depressive affects are related to the specific types of thought patterns. Thus, schemas that have content relevant to being deserted, thwarted, undesirable, or derelict in one's duties will produce, respectively, feelings of loneliness, frustration, humiliation, or guilt. The relative absence of anger among the more severely depressed patients, particularly in situations that uniformly arouse anger in other people, may be attributed to their tendency to conceptualize situations in terms of their own supposed inadequacies. One currently popular explanation for the relative absence of overt anger in depression is that this affect is present and, in fact, intensified in depression but is repressed or inverted. The present explanation seems to be closer to the data. The theme of the dominant schemas is that the depressed patient is deficient or blameworthy. Proceeding from this assumption, the patient is forced to the conclusion that insults, abuse, and deprivation are justifiable because of his or her own supposed shortcomings or mistakes. Remorse rather than anger stems from these conceptualizations.

In other clinical syndromes characterized by an abnormal intensity of a particular affect, there is a dominance of the cognitive patterns corresponding to that affect. The anxiety neurotic demonstrates the dominance and inappropriate use of schemas relevant to personal danger. The hostile paranoid is dominated by schemas concerned with blaming or accusing other individuals (or external agencies) for their perceived abuse. The manic patient is influenced by schemas of positive self-evaluation.

It could be speculated that once these idiosyncratic schemas have been mobilized and have produced an affective reaction, the schemas are in turn affected by the affects. It is possible that a circular mechanism is set up, with the schemas stimulating the affects and the affects reinforcing the activity of the schemas.[5] For example, some evidence suggests that endorsement of negative beliefs is influenced by mood state.[8,9]

A Feedback Model

The discussion so far has viewed the connection between cognitive structure and affect as a kind of one-way street, that is, the direction has been from cognition to emotion. But it is conceivable that there is an interaction between these, and that feelings may also influence thought content. The formulation of a mutually reinforcing system[70] can provide a more complete explanation for the phenomena observed in depression. The operation of this system can be presented as follows: Let us assume that an unpleasant life situation triggers schemas relevant to loss, self-blame, and negative expectations. As they become activated, these schemas produce a stimulation of the affective structures connected to them. The activation of the affective structures is responsible for the subjective feeling of depression. These affective structures in turn, further innervate the schemas to which they are connected and consequently reinforce the activity of these schemas. The interaction, thus, consists of schemas ↔ affective structures. This model could explain the downward spiral in depression: the more negatively patients think, the worse they feel; the worse they feel, the more negatively they think.

It is possible to travel into still more speculative areas by incorporating the concept of energy into this formation. In discussing structure and process it is difficult to avoid the introduction of energy concepts. Such concepts are often vague and elusive and their utility and validity in personality theory have been strongly challenged. At a 1962 symposium sponsored by the American Psychoanalytic Association there was sharp disagreement regarding the advisability of retaining energy concepts in psychoanalytic theory. Still, the concept is employed by many disparate schools of psychological theory. Floyd Allport,[44] for example, utilizes energy concepts extensively in his formulation of the processes of perception and cognition. Let us assume that initially the schema is energized as the result of some psychological trauma. The activation of this cognitive structure leads to the stimulation of the affective structure. The activation of the affective structure produces a burst of energy, which is experienced subjectively as a painful emotion. The energy then flows back to the cognitive structure and increases the quantity of energy attached to it. This then produces further innervation of the affective structure.

Further data are certainly required to remove this discussion from the realm of speculation and to determine whether there is any utility in the formulation.

During the developmental period depression-prone individuals acquire certain negative attitudes regarding themselves, the outside world, and the future. As a result of these attitudes, they become especially sensitive to certain specific stresses such as being deprived, thwarted, or rejected. When exposed to such stresses they respond disproportionately with ideas of personal deficiency, self-blame, and pessimism.

The idiosyncratic attitudes represent persistent cognitive patterns, designated as schemas. The schemas influence the way an individual orients to a situation, recognizes and labels the salient features, and conceptualizes the experience.

The idiosyncratic schemas in depression consist of negative conceptions of the individual's worth, personal characteristics, and performance or health, and include nihilistic expectations. When these schemas are evoked they mold the thought content and lead to the typical depressive feelings of sadness, guilt, loneliness, and pessimism. The schemas may be largely inactive during the asymptomatic periods but become activated with the onset of depression. As the depression deepens, these schemas increasingly dominate the cognitive processes and not only displace the more appropriate schemas but also disrupt the cognitive processes involved in attaining self-objectivity and reality testing.

We suggest that the affective reactions may facilitate the activity of these idiosyncratic schemas and, consequently, enhance the downward spiral in depression. The relative absence of anger in depression may be due to the displacement of schemas relevant to blaming others by schemas of self-blame.

Part IV
Treatment of Depression

Chapter 14
Somatic Therapies

This chapter provides an overview of the development and status of the somatic treatments of mood disorders. We delineate conclusions and key questions, rather than providing a comprehensive guide to treatment. This overview may supplement other sources that are designed to provide more direct clinical guidance to the practicing psychiatrist.[1,2,3]

The main topics covered here include (1) history and development of pharmacotherapy, (2) methodological problems and scientific controversies, (3) switching and augmentation strategies for treatment-resistant depression, and (4) early development and contemporary status of electroconvulsive therapy (ECT). We note several of the common pharmacological agents, past to present, such as tricyclics and MAO inhibitors. More recent drugs, the selective serotonin reuptake inhibitors (SSRIs), are also included, along with pharmacological issues and controversies.

We delineate the methodological problems in evaluating antidepressant drugs, such as controversies regarding placebo controls. Adverse effects (side effects) are reviewed. The greater clinical safety of newer drug classes, like SSRIs, is highlighted, along with questions about the relative efficacy of these substances with the more severe depressions. Finally, we consider the most promising innovations and future directions, such as transcranial magnetic stimulation (TCMS), and pharmacogenomics.

Pharmacotherapy

Pharmacotherapy for depression is at least as old as Homer, being mentioned in *The Odyssey* when Penelope takes a drug to dull her grief for her long-absent husband. Historically, two classes of drugs were originally tested in schizophrenic patients but, as in the case of electroconvulsive therapy, were found to be more effective in treating apathy and depression than other clinical symptoms.[4,5.] Iproniazid, in the first major class, was shown to prevent sedation in mice given reserpine; this drug had also been used in the treatment of

TABLE 14-1. DRUGS USED IN TREATMENT OF DEPRESSION

Generic name	Trade name
Tricyclic compounds	
imipramine	Tofranil
desipramine	Norpramin
	Pertofrane
amitriptyline	Elavil
nortriptyline	Aventyl
Monoamine oxidase (MAO) inhibitors	
phenelzine	Nardil
isocarboxazid	Marplan
nialamide	Niamid
tranylcypromine	Parnate
iproniazid*	Marsilid
Psychomotor stimulants	
amphetamines	
amphetamine	Benzedrine
dextroamphetamine	Dexedrine
methamphetamine	Methedrine, etc.
methylphenidate	Ritalin

*Withdrawn from use.

tuberculosis in 1955 and was observed to produce a euphoric effect. Interest in imipramine and certain of its derivatives was stimulated because of their structural resemblance to the phenothiazines, which had been used successfully in schizophrenia. Iproniazid seemed to be effective in its first tests as an antidepressant, and imipramine given to a large group of patients seemed, to the surprise of investigators, to work far better with predominantly depressive than with predominantly schizophrenic patients.

The tricyclic antidepressants and the monoamine oxidase inhibitors (MAO inhibitors) were introduced in 1957. These drugs are listed in Table 14-1 along with a number of other compounds whose effectiveness in treating depression has been studied.

The Tricyclic Drugs

Early Studies

The methodological issues involved in the early studies remain with us today and will be treated in detail below. The early studies presented here provide a history of the development of the pharmacological approach to treating the mood disorders. The main question was whether there could be found pharmacological substances superior to placebo effects in their impact upon the symptoms, course, and recurrence of clinical depression. In cases where the subsequent findings depart from or converge with the early studies cited here, and the early studies are specifically cited, this fact will be noted parenthetically.

Imipramine was the first thoroughly studied antidepressant drug. Its effectiveness in comparison with placebo in double-blind studies was initially reviewed by Brady,[6] Cole,[7] Klerman and Cole,[8] and Friedman et al.[9] Brady's review of inpatient and outpatient studies and the review by Friedman et al. of inpatient studies found an essentially even distribution of positive and negative results.[6,9] The reviews by Cole and by Klerman and Cole, in contrast, found a definite weighting in favor of positive results.[7,8]

The differences in the findings reported by Klerman and Cole as compared with Brady were explained partly on the basis of two factors. First, Klerman and Cole missed three negative studies included by Brady; also, Klerman and Cole included seven studies published in 1964 after Brady completed his review. Second, Klerman and Cole counted as positive results many studies in which the superiority of imipramine was slight and fell short of statistical significance, but Brady used the 5 percent level of significance to designate a study as positive.[6,8]

(Note: Thirty-five years after the publication of the Klerman and Cole review, Quitkin et al.[10] documented extensive converging findings to support the conclusion that antidepressants are effective above placebo effect: "These overviews approximate the global advantage of imipramine versus placebo reported by Klerman and Cole[8] more than 30 years earlier" (p. 328).)

Cole found 15 studies on hospitalized inpatients. Friedman et al. found 21 studies on hospitalized psychotic depressives. This was an important difference, for Friedman et al. found four more negative studies. This was in addition to their own study, which indicated that imipramine was no more effective than placebo in hospitalized psychotic depressives.[7,9]

All the reviewers attempted to evaluate the methodological adequacy of the studies they reviewed. Cole and Brady criticized the negative studies and Friedman et al. and Wechsler et al., whose conclusions on imipramine are negative, criticized the positive studies.[6,7,9,11] Cole and Brady stated that samples in the negative studies were too small and Friedman et al. leveled the same criticism against the positive studies. In a review of both controlled and uncontrolled studies, Wechsler et al. found no significant correlation of result with sample size.[11] Furthermore, Davis charged that the negative studies often used dosages that were too small; Klerman and Cole stated that the effect of dosage was unknown; and Wechsler and his coworkers claimed no correlation of result with dosage size. Davis asserted that the patient populations in the negative studies were too chronic, while Brady said that they were too heterogeneous.[12,8,11,6]

Wechsler and his coworkers, examining controlled and uncontrolled studies, found a clearly superior response with depressions of recent onset.[11] Klerman and Cole, who looked only at controlled, double-blind studies, did find a significant recent versus chronic difference.[8] Friedman et al. suggested that perhaps the improvement observed in so many studies is actually only an acceleration of spontaneous remissions during the first two or three weeks.[9]

MAO Inhibitors

The early reviews compared the effectiveness of MAO inhibitors to placebo. There was more agreement here of both fact and opinion than with imipramine. The authors in general found at least one of the MAO inhibitors to be effective, but differed about which one it was. Hordern concluded that iproniazid, withdrawn from the market in the United States, was the best MAO inhibitor and phenelzine the best then available. Davis agreed that phenelzine was best, but Cole asserted that tranylcypromine was best. Wechsler showed an equal range of improvement on all the MAO inhibitors mentioned in his review with the exception of nialamide, for which the improvement range was a little narrower.[5,12,7,11]

As in the case of the tricyclic antidepressants, Fiedorowicz and Swartz suggested in 2004 that the use of MAOIs by psychiatrists had declined over the past several decades.[13] They attributed the decline to several factors, including (1) the development of the newer medications, such as the SSRIs (below), (2) side effects, (3) food and drug interactions, and (4) decreased physician experience with MAOIs. Nevertheless, Fiedorowicz and Schwartz suggested that there remains a place for this class of antidepressant drugs, since research has expanded the MAOI diet, and the specific symptoms that are indicative of response are now better known.[13]

Selective Serotonin-Reuptake Inhibitors (SSRIs)

In a 1991 review of pharmacologic treatment of depression, Potter et al.[14] stated that the original tricyclic antidepressants (TCAs) were still best for patients with major depressive disorders. At least through 1996, data from the Department of Health in England showed no decrease in TCAs following the introduction of SSRIs, but total antidepressant prescribing rates had increased.[15] (Note: As reviewed below, Stafford et al.[16] found higher rates of SSRI prescriptions and much lower use of TCAs in the USA, based on a nationally representative survey of office-based physicians through 2001.)

Summarizing two reviews available at the time, Potter et al. characterized the newer SSRI antidepressant agents, such as fluoxetine (Prozac), as less useful in treating of severe melancholic depression. They further concluded that, based on data available at the time, SSRIs were indicated for initial therapy only in certain special cases. These were said to be known intolerance to a tricyclic agent, or concern over side effects that might be expected to adversely impact an identified physical illness. Also, they suggested that the newer antidepressant agents might be prescribed in cases where inhibition of serotonin uptake would generate a concurrent therapeutic response in another psychiatric disorder, such as obsessive-compulsive disorder.[14]

Masand and Gupta[17] reviewed the double-blind, placebo-controlled studies of five SSRIs—fluoxetine, sertraline, paroxetine, fluvoxamine, and citalopram—published from 1990 to 1998. The studies included were those intended to evaluate efficacy and side effects.

Contrary to Potter et al., Masand and Gupta believed SSRIs were the treatment of choice for depression and related disorders. Noting that they are chemically unrelated to tricyclic, heterocyclic, and other first-generation antidepressants, the authors noted several advantages of SSRIs over first-generation antidepressants, including (1) better side-effect profile, (2) safety in overdose, (3) tolerability, and (4) patient compliance.[17]

In their review, Masand and cited several studies that show SSRIs to be more cost effective than tricyclic antidepressants (TCAs). This finding was attributed to a smaller chance of discontinuation of treatment and greater probability of receiving an adequate dose. They said that SSRIs are comparable in efficacy to TCAs, and can be augmented with lithium, psychostimulants, and a variety of other agents in treatment-resistant depression.

Antidepressant Prescribing Patterns

Studies in the United States by Stafford et al., Pirraglia et al. and Ma et al. identified trends in number of physician visits for depression, and in the prescribing patterns for the various classes of antidepressant drugs.[16,18,19]

Stafford et al. analyzed data from the National Disease and Therapeutic Index, a survey of U.S. office-based physicians, during 1987–2001. They found that annualized visits by patients with depression increased from 14.4 million in 1987 to 24.5 million in 2001. Antidepressant medication for depressed patients was used in 70 percent of cases in 1987, and increased to 89 percent of presenting cases in 2001.[16]

Among those patients receiving pharmacological treatment, tricyclic antidepressants were used in treating 47 percent of patients in 1987, the most common being amitriptyline (14 percent), trazodone (12 percent), doxepin (8 percent), and desipramine (6 percent). One year after becoming available, Prozac (fluoxetine) was prescribed to 21 percent of patients. Total SSRI use grew to 38 percent in 1992, 60 percent in 1996, and 69 percent in 2000. The leading antidepressants were sertraline (18 percent), paroxetine (16 percent), fluoxetine (14 percent), citalopram (13 percent), and bupropion (9 percent). Among the office-based physicians surveyed, by the year 2001 tricyclics were used in

TABLE 14-2. Comparison of Side-Effect Profiles of SSRIs

SSRI	Orthostatic hypotension	Anticholinergic effects	Sedation	Gastrointestinal effects*	Sexual effects
Citalopram	0	0	+	+ +	+ + +
Fluoxetine	0	0	0	+ +	+ + +
Fluvoxamine	0	0	+	+ +	+ + +
Paroxetine	0	+	+	+ +	+ + +
Sertraline	0	0	0	+ +	+ + +

Adapted from Masand & Gupta 1999.
0 = minimal to none; + = low; + + = moderate; + + + = high. *Excluded constipations due to anticholinergic side effects.

only 2 percent of patients in these settings, and benzodiazepines in only 8 percent of cases.[16]

Pirraglia et al.[18] studied prescribing rates for the SSRIs and other newer non-SSRI drugs in adult primary care settings. Their database was U.S. adult primary care visits, as recorded in the National Ambulatory Medical Care Survey between 1989 and 2000. The SSRIs included citalopram, fluoxetine, fluvoxamine, paroxetine, and sertraline. Non-SSRI antidepressants included bupropion, mirtazapine, nefazodone, and venlafaxine. The data included 89,424 adult primary care visits. They found that antidepressant drug use increased in this setting from 2.6 percent of visits in 1989 to 7.1 percent of visits in 2000. The increase in antidepressant use was attributed to the availability of newer agents, which made up 13.5 percent of all antidepressant use in 1989, and increased to 82.3 percent of antidepressant prescriptions in 2000.

In treating depression in children and adolescents, similar trends are observed. Ma et al.[19] studied antidepressant drug therapy in the 7–17 age group between 1995 and 2002. The number of outpatient visits for problems with depression doubled from 1.44 million in 1995–96 to 3.22 million visits in 2001–2. Selective serotonin reuptake inhibitors (SSRIs) represented 76 percent of all antidepressants prescribed in 1995–96, and increased to 81 percent in 2001–2. The authors concluded that the observed trend raises concerns regarding off-label use of antidepressants that have not been sufficiently tested for safety and efficacy in this age group.

Side Effects

Side effects include the potential lethal drug-drug interaction between SSRIs and MAOIs. Side-effect profiles of SSRIs are shown in Table 14-2. The most frequent unintended effects include gastrointestinal disturbances, nausea, and somnolence, but these usually dissipate within 2–4 weeks. Masand and Gupta include a number of practical clinical interventions that can be used to manage most of these, including the mitigation of sexual dysfunction, which affects 60 percent of patients.[15]

Stimulants

Satel and Nelson reviewed the 10 placebo-controlled studies of stimulant drugs in the treatment of primary depression. Although the studies reviewed were described as methodologically unsophisticated in several cases, they were judged to be as good as those studies conducted during the same period that established the usefulness of imipramine.[20]

Stimulant drugs were found to be inferior to antidepressants. However, the studies in lethargic or depressed geriatric patients were more positive, with some partial improvement in symptoms. They did not find evidence to support concerns about possible hazards of the use of stimulants. Side effects were found to be minimal, and these drugs may pose less of a danger than tricyclics in the medically ill or elderly. Moreover, stimulants appear to be "reasonably safe" even in cardiac patients (p. 248). Though habituation was suspected, no placebo-controlled studies were available to confirm this.[20]

Numerous isolated single studies support the effectiveness in depression of various miscellaneous drugs or combinations of known drugs. According to Cole, the evidence supporting the usefulness of Deaner is meager and that regarding the efficacy of Deprol is equivocal.

Lithium

Johnson[21] reviewed 19 controlled studies of the therapeutic effects of lithium. The 1968–84 studies in his review evaluated lithium for treatment of acute depressive episodes and refractory depression, and as a prophylactic treatment in recurrent depression. The acute antidepressant effect of lithium alone was described as "neither as impressive nor as predictable as its antimanic action" (p. 356). It was found inferior to the tricyclic antidepressants.

However, Johnson concluded that the addition of lithium results in better antidepressant response in patients whose depression has not improved with tricyclics or monoamine oxidase inhibitors, or "refractory" depression. (Table 14-3 shows results from the six studies of lithium use in refractory depression.) Moreover, the studies in his review showed lithium to be an effective prophylactic drug for both unipolar and bipolar mood disorder, and the drug of choice for bipolar disorder.[21]

Johnson's[21] observation that adding lithium improves response in treatment-resistant depression is consistent with findings of Sharma et al.,[22] who found a bipolar diathesis in such cases. In a diagnostic reevaluation study of 61 refractory "unipolar" patients, the Structured Clinical Interview for *DSM-IV* was used along with supplemental information from family members. They

TABLE 14-3. Lithium Treatment of "Refractory" Depression

Study	Diagnosis	Patient (n)	Medication	Outcome	Comment
Worral et al. 1979	MDP	29	Lithium + tryptophan (15), tryptophan (14)	Lithium + tryptophan > tryptophan	Effect of combination equivocal
De Montigny et al. 1981	UP	8	Lithium + TCA	100 percent marked improvement in 48 hours	Relapse: 1/6 following lithium discontinuation
De Montigny et al. 1983	UP	34	Lithium + TCA	74 percent responders in 48 hours (50 percent decrease in Hamilton rating scale)	Relapse 5/9
Heninger et al. 1983	Major Depression	15	Lithium + TCA Placebo + TCA	Lithium > placebo	Gradual improvement 2–3 weeks
De Montigny et al. 1985	UP	7	Lithium + iprindole	68 percent improvement in 48 hours	Selective 5HT effect proposed
Price et al. 1985	UP (10) BP (2)	12	Lithium + tranylcypromine	8 responders	Refractory to lithium augmentation of TCAs

Adapted from Johnson 1987.
UP = unipolar depression; BP = bipolar mood disorder; MDP = manic depressive psychosis; TCA = tricyclic

found that 80 percent of these patients actually suffered from bipolar disorders. The most common diagnosis was bipolar II disorder, followed by bipolar spectrum disorder. This finding was attributed to the use of extended and systematic follow-up, expert questioning to uncover symptoms of hypomania, and routine interviews of family. By changing medication to mood stabilizers, significant improvement in functioning was observed from the time of initial consultation. However, limitations of the study were acknowledged, including the fact that it was a naturalistic study, and researchers were aware of the data as they were being collected.[22]

Kessing et al.[23] provided data comparing 13,186 patients who purchased at least one prescription of lithium to 1.2 million people from the general population in Denmark. They found that those who purchased lithium had a higher suicide rate then those who did not purchase it, and that those who purchased at least twice experienced a 44 percent reduced rate of suicide compared to those who purchased only once. Moreover, suicide rate decreased as number of prescriptions of lithium increased. The authors discussed (but dismissed) the possibility of selection bias accounting for the observed differences. In other words, perhaps persons who are inclined to continue with lithium treatment commit suicide less frequently because of positive attributes independent of the effects of lithium, such as personality strengths that lead both to treatment adherence as well as reduced risk for suicide.[23]

A comprehensive review by Baldessarini et al.[24] reported that at least five placebo-controlled studies showed lithium to produce short-term recovery rates twice as high as the 25–35 percent found with placebo and nonspecific management. In bipolar disorder, a review of 28 studies with a total of 2,985 participants found recurrence risk to be 3.2-fold lower during lithium treatment. None of the clinical factors thought to contradict the utility of lithium were supported, including (1) mixed manic-depressive states, (2) multiple episodes, (3) long history of untreated disorder, and (3) rapid cycling. Table 14-4 summarizes situations in which lithium may be effective, according to the studies reviewed by Baldessarini et al.[24]

Current Use of Tricyclics and MAOIs

For subtypes of clinical depression, the question of the comparative effectiveness of SSRIs versus tricyclic antidepressants remains unresolved. The American Psychiatric Association (2000) practice guidelines suggest that SSRIs might be relatively ineffective in cases of major depression with melancholic features.[2] Because of this, Parker[25] makes a case for the need to "revisit the utility of the older antidepressants" compared to SSRIs in the treatment of depressive subtypes. He at the same time points out in general that from a cost-benefit analysis the greater adherence and side-effect profile clearly favor the newer drugs.

TABLE 14-4. Situations in Which Lithium May Be Effective

Effective
- Prevention of recurrence of mania* and depression in bipolar I disorder
- Reduction of suicidal risk in recurrent major affective disorders

Probably effective
- Treatment of mania or bipolar disorder variants in children and the elderly
- Long-term treatment (alone or with valprate) of rapid-cycling bipolar disorder
- Long-term treatment after delay or following multiple bipolar episodes
- Long-term retreatment after discontinuation
- Prevention of recurrences of depression (and hypomania) in bipolar II disorder
- Prevention of recurrences in unipolar or pseudounipolar major depression
- Supplementation of antidepressants in major depression

Possibly effective or insufficiently investigated
- Treatment of acute major depression (particularly bipolar I or II or pseudounipolar)
- Long-term treatment of schizoaffective psychosis
- Treatment of personality disorders involving cyclothymia or emotional instability
- Treatment of episodic impulsive-aggressive behavior in adults or children (including those with developmental delay or brain damage)
- Treatment of stimulant-induced euphoria

Adapted from Baldessarinia et al. 2002.
*Conditions for which lithium is approved by the Food and Drug Administration and recommended by manufacturers. Empirical clinical use for other conditions is not unusual, especially when alternatives prove unsuccessful

Due to the side-effect profile of MAOIs compared to tricycics and especially SSRIs, the use of this drug class for the treatment of clinical depression has fallen into disfavor among clinical practitioners. Not a small part of the reduction in prescribing is undoubtedly due to the well-known risk of severe reactions, such as hypertensive crisis when dietary restrictions are violated. Nevertheless, some research and clinical interest does persist, given the relatively good antidepressant effects of these drugs. This is especially true of cases where people are not responding to the other, safer drugs. For example, Fava found a 67 percent response rate in switching from tricyclics to MAOIs. A 41 percent rate of improvement was found in switching from MAOIs to tricyclics.[26]

Treatment Resistance

Augmenting Versus Switching Antidepressants

Rush et al.[27] suggest that augmenting and switching strategies are essential, since "only 30–40 percent of depressed outpatients who begin a medication or psychotherapy will remit" (p. 47). Likewise, Marangell[28] notes that a sizeable proportion of patients suffering from major depression fail to respond to appropriate monotherapy treatment. In Thase et al.'s[29] review of 10 studies, the overall response rate from switching was found to be about 50 percent. This review included the largest double-blind study of switching antidepressants conducted to date. Consistent with the other 9 studies reviewed, Thase et al. found that more than 50 percent of chronically depressed antidepressant nonresponders improved following the medication switch.

If side effects are intolerable, or if an adequate dose and duration of antidepressant medication has yielded no response, switching to a different monotherapy is an option. Switching medications rather than adding a second one has these advantages: (1) reduced costs, (2) fewer interactions, and (3) superior treatment adherence.[28]

However, some discord exists among reviewers with respect to the question of response rates obtained by augmenting (combining) versus switching antidepressants in treatment resistant cases. Marangell's review[28] suggested response rates of 50 percent by switching rather than combining drugs. However, a review by Lam et al.[30] suggests an advantage to combining antidepressants in cases of treatment-resistant depression. Combining drugs might capitalize on multiple therapeutic mechanisms of action.

The review by Lam et al.[30] included studies obtained through a MEDLINE search over 15 years (to June 2001). They identified studies that combined any 2 antidepressants. The 27 studies (total $n = 667$) included 5 randomized controlled trials and 22 open-label trials. In 24 studies (total $n = 601$) reporting response rates, the overall rate of 62.2 percent is superior to the 50 percent rate reported for switching.[28] However, the authors listed several methodological limitations, including variability in definitions of treatment-resistance and response to treatment, and inconsistency in drug dosing. They suggested further randomized controlled trials with larger sample sizes to show the value of a combination antidepressant strategy.

Placebo-Controlled Studies of Drug Combinations

Coryell[31] pointed out that the open studies reviewed above are prone to false-positive results for these reasons: depression tends to spontaneously remit, and patients who have yet to respond to an antidepressant trial may show a placebo response to the addition or substitution of another drug. In a review of seven placebo-controlled studies, a significant advantage was found for lithium supplementation added to tricyclic antidepressants or serotonin reuptake inhibitors.[31] Four positive studies added lithium to tricyclic antidepressants and two to an SSRI. Lithium doses of at least 750 mg daily and adjusted doses in the traditional antimanic range were used in the trials that favored the addition of lithium.[31] Augmentation with triiodothyronine, pindolol and dehydroepiandrosterone (DHEA) was also promising.

Medication, Psychotherapy, and Prescriptive Indices

Hollon et al.[32] reviewed studies cited in MEDLINE and PsychINFO from January 1980 to October 2004 that used random assignment of patients to either combined treatments or a single treatment. They concluded that medication generally produces a rapid and substantial effect, but for the prevention of relapse or recurrence, adding a psychotherapeutic approach could be useful (see Chapter 16 for a detailed description and review of the randomized controlled trials comparing pharmacological and psychological treatments).

Hollon et al.[32] suggested that it may be advisable to combine medication with either interpersonal therapy or cognitive behavior therapy, especially with chronic depressions. They found little prescriptive information to predict which specific treatment would work best, but with respect to pharmacotherapy the authors cited research suggesting that some types of depression are more responsive to certain medications than to others. For example, patients with atypical depression have been found to respond best to the MAOIs compared to the TCAs or the SSRIs. In cases of chronic depression, women until menopause may respond somewhat better to SSRIs, and men are more responsive to TCAs (p. 457). Given the variation of response in an individual case, augmenting and switching strategies (described above) are typically recommended after 6 to 8 weeks of nonresponse while taking an adequate dose of a given medication.[32]

Clinical Considerations

Mendlewicz[33] provides several practical suggestions on the selection of pharmacotherapy agents in the treatment of clinical depression. In addition to efficacy, safety, and tolerability, he suggested that "real-world efficacy" and economic value should also be taken into account.

Undertreatment is a major problem. Patient attitudes, inadequate antidepressant prescribing, and limited health insurance coverage add to such undertreatment. Only about one-third of people with depression seek treatment. In primary care or outpatient settings, pharmaceuticals are the treatment of choice about 75 percent of the time. However, only about 25 percent of patients in clinical practice are adequately treated when they are prescribed antidepressants even with the better-tolerated SSRIs.[33]

To better realize the promise of effective treatment implied by clinical trial efficacy rates, Mendlewicz suggested that clinicians take into account specific variables that impact how antidepressants are actually used in the real world. These include "need for titration, ease of use, frequency of dosing, compliance, medication availability, insurance coverage, length of treatment, prior experience with specific drugs or drug classes, and side effects" (p. s2).[33]

Treatment After Age 60

There is a need for more attention to depression in older adults, according to Freudenstein et al.[34] They reviewed the trials of treatments for depression for those over 60 years of age, including a search of MEDLINE, Embase, Cinahl, the Cochrane Library, Psyclit, BIDS-Social Science, and BIDS-Science Citation Indices for English, French, or German articles published between the years 1980 and June 1999.

They included studies of drug treatment, interpersonal psychotherapy, cognitive behavioral psychotherapy, counseling, and social interventions. Limiting their analysis to primary care and population samples (effectiveness studies), they found only two were of patients over 60 years of age and met all inclusion criteria for content and quality. These two studies found better results using a community psychiatric team (40–50 percent of patients improved) rather than routine treatment in primary care (25–30 percent improved). In studies restricted to those over age 60, the authors found studies of drug treatment to be short and to exclude patients with other illnesses, raising questions of whether efficacy studies can be translated into conclusions about effectiveness, or how drug treatment would work under everyday health service conditions.[34]

Studies of nonpharmacological interventions (such as psychotherapies) are needed for older patients in primary care settings. Also, the studies comparing SSRIs and the older antidepressants have all been efficacy studies. Pharmacological studies of older patients with minimal exclusions are clearly needed.[34]

Another important issue with respect to elderly patients is how to approach failure to respond to treatment. According to Baldwin,[35] studies of mixed aged and elderly patients in psychiatric settings show poor response to pharmacological treatment in one-third of patients. After reviewing the possible strategies used by clinicians in cases of nonresponse, Baldwin suggested specific prospective evaluation of the following approaches in elderly depressed patients: (1) maintain nonresponders on the same antidepressant for at least 12 weeks, (2) change to another drug class after six weeks and no response, and (3) in a third group give lithium augmentation after six weeks of treatment without full recovery.[35]

Finally, Satel and Nelson[36] suggested the need for placebo studies of stimulants in treating depression. Their review showed that controlled studies were more likely to be positive in geriatric patients, and that stimulants were less likely to pose a risk to the elderly, who frequently suffer concurrent medical illnesses.

Research Problems and Controversies

In this section, we provide an overview of select problems and controversies in conducting outcome research on treating the mood disorders. This is not intended to provide a comprehensive review of all methodological approaches and issues but rather to convey a sense of the complexities of ascertaining the relative effects of a given treatment in both research and clinical settings. In Chapter 16, "Evaluating Depression Treatments: The Randomized Controlled Trials," the studies discussed were selected according to criteria such as a convincing basis for the diagnosis of major depression, a comparison to clinical pharmacotherapy, the source of patients treated, the length of therapy, completion rates, and inclusion of the percentage of patients that recovered and experienced no relapse or recurrence following treatment.

Rater Bias

Before any drug is subjected to controlled experimentation, its clinical value must first be estimated in a series of uncontrolled tests. These generally give a much more rosy picture of the effectiveness of the drug than do the eventual controlled studies. Thus, before any controlled investigations are conducted, a clinical consensus on the efficacy of the antidepressant already exists. It is possible that this favorable attitude biases future controlled research; for example, if researchers use an inactive placebo they can distinguish some drug subjects by the side-effects, and ratings may be influenced toward a positive result. Or if investigators get a negative result, they may doubt its validity and, consequently, may look very closely for faults in research design. If they find them, they may fail to publish the data at all.

To control side effects, atropine, which has similar autonomic affects to imipramine, was used in early studies as an active placebo. When low or moderate doses of atropine were used, however, few imipramine-placebo differences were observed.[8] This suggested the possibility that the raters were unable to distinguish between the patients receiving imipramine and atropine, and consequently that there was no bias in rating. Such a hypothesis suggested that imipramine was no more effective than atropine. Alternatively, it is possible that the side effects of atropine may work on patients' suggestibility to give a very high rate of placebo response.

Placebo Response

The rate of placebo response is radically different in different studies, and has ranged from 0 to 77 percent.[11,9] In the earliest imipramine studies cited by Klerman and Cole,[6] the placebo response rate was 21 percent in outpatients, 46 percent in the newly hospitalized, and only 16 percent in the chronic inpatients. In the initial studies that showed imipramine to be efficacious the rate of placebo response was 27 percent. Where studies showed it to be ineffective it was 41 percent. The rate of response to imipramine was respectively 70 percent and 58 percent for the positive and negative studies. The difference between the two kinds of study does not depend solely on the placebo response rate.

The question of placebo response is connected with still another factor. Various experiments may not be directly comparable because of differing time intervals between initiation of the treatment and evaluation. Take the example where the range between studies is, say, 2 weeks to 2 1/2 months. In the longer time periods, under conditions of high spontaneous remission, drug-placebo differences may be obscured.

Several other factors should be considered in evaluating the placebo response. (1) The improvement in the placebo group may reflect the natural history of the illness, that is, spontaneous remission. (2) Nondrug factors such as hospital milieu and psychotherapy may produce improvement in the placebo group. (3) The placebo effect itself may be therapeutic. It is possible that merely receiving medication may help to break the vise of hopelessness that grips the depressed patients. It is also possible that the patients report subjective improvement in order to please the rater even though the basic disorder has not improved. Studies that use no placebo in the control group should therefore be conducted.

Nonrandom Distribution of Variables

The rate of placebo response may be connected with another problem that affects not only each individual study but any comparisons of them. Each study must decide how to limit its patient sample. Studies of depression can have very broad or very narrow sample groups. Since it is unknown what variables in the patient are related to the efficacy of the antidepressants, nonrandom distribution of patient characteristics into experimental and control groups may well occur.[37] Some variables not often considered crucial, for example, socioeconomic status, may be important.[38,39] Also, a variable such as age, which may well be controlled for, may be important. Grosser and Freeman,[40] for example, produced data indicating that patients under 40 show a high placebo response rate. In a different setting, Friedman et al.[9] showed that inpatients of average age 60, with psychotic depressions, respond at an unusually high rate to placebo.

Variability of Measures

A variety of measures have been used to evaluate the results of treatment, and the results seem to depend somewhat on the measure utilized. Klerman and Cole[8] made the following observations on the measures used in the imipramine studies. Eleven of 12 studies that used global ratings showed an imipramine-placebo difference, but only half the studies using total morbidity scores demonstrated such a difference. Seven studies showed differences on some factor scores representing aspects of psychopathology or on certain single measures of psychopathology. Two studies did not show either of these differences. It has long been known that in studies in which two different measures have been used the results may seem contradictory.[37]

Other Problems

Many authors have claimed that a high or low dosage is responsible for a particular positive or negative result.[5,12] Others have denied this, and the problems of identifying the maximum safe dosage and individualized prescriptive dosages remain.[8,11] A number of other factors that play a role in pharmacological studies have long been recognized. These factors include aspects of the researcher and research team other than bias, subject-researcher relations, the physical environment, and the social setting.[41]

Issues of Risk Versus Benefit

Even after a pharmacological agent has been proven relatively "safe and efficacious" and effective in real-life patient populations with concomitant disorders and diverse variables, the risk versus benefit calculation remains a salient factor in prescribing for an individual patient. As one example, consider the older and newer medications. Despite advances in the development of new antidepressant drugs, such as the selective serotonin reuptake inhibitors (SSRIs), they are not always effective for a given case. The relative utility of the older classes of antidepressants, despite generally greater risks, remains under discussion.

Bolwig[42] cites studies that suggest the newer antidepressants are inferior to the tricyclic antidepressants. He notes that the most serious risk associated with depression is suicide, and that melancholic depression is especially associated with this risk. He believes that TCAs are superior to SSRIs for treatment of melancholic depression and concludes that "not starting treatment with TCA at an early stage deprives melancholic patients of the possibility of successful treatment" (p. 1236).

A commentary in *The Lancet* by Summerfield[43] questions even the commonly held belief that patients can best be treated through prescribing antidepressants. He suggests instead that there has been a "medicalisation of unhappiness," that the outcome in primary care settings is not substantially improved, and that the clinical problem of discontinuation reactions to antidepressants should be given greater weight.

Controversy About Placebo Effect

Not only is the assessment of risk problematic—and complicated by possible long-term side effects not detectable during the course of the initial studies—

but also the assessment of benefit is not straightforward. One complexity in depression outcome research is the fact that this disorder seems particularly prone to influence by "nonspecific" or placebo factors, at least short-term. Moreover, the magnitude of this effect appears variable. Early double-blind studies comparing imipramine with a placebo yielded differences in placebo effect size. These debates have persisted.[44,45,46,10]

Greenberg et al.[44] conducted a metaanalysis of 22 studies of antidepressant outcome. They included only studies that compared a newer antidepressant (amoxapine, maprotiline, or trazodone) with older or traditional antidepressants (imipramine or amitriptyline) and placebo control groups. Effect sizes based on clinician ratings were found to show less antidepressant effect than outcome effect sizes based on patient ratings. They concluded the antidepressant effect of drugs to be "quite modest," and for the patient-rated measures not much greater than the placebo effect.

Ten years later, Moncrieff et al.[45] reviewed the metaanalytic trials comparing antidepressants with "active" placebos, which are designed to mimic the side effects of actual drugs. The use of inert placebos has been thought to bias drug trials in favor of antidepressant drugs, since side effects of real medications may result in a stronger placebo effect. Moncrieff et al. found nine active placebo trials, and in only two of these were improvement effects in favor of the active antidepressant drug. This metaanalysis was said to provide a more rigorous test of the efficacy of antidepressants. Taken together, studies such as these have raised questions about whether (or to what extent) standard antidepressants are more effective than placebo and suggested that active placebo is a better methodological control compared to an inert or inactive placebo.

Contrary to the above studies (Greenberg et al.; Moncrieff et al.), in 2000, Quitkin et al.[10] provided arguments in support of the adequacy of the design of antidepressant studies and suggested that antidepressants enjoy unequivocal proof of superiority over placebo. They reviewed several metaanalyses, and found that antidepressant efficacy above placebo rates of improvement to be consistent across the well-controlled studies. They concluded that the standard antidepressants are at least twice as effective in alleviating clinical depression compared to placebo.

Adverse Effects of Antidepressant Drugs

There has been a relatively strong consensus on the adverse effects of the tricyclic and MAO-inhibiting compounds.[47,7,5,8]

Klerman and Cole[8] pointed out a general problem in the assessment of side effects: It is necessary to have a control group and careful reporting of somatic complaints *prior* to the beginning of drug therapy. Otherwise, many of the symptoms noted as side effects may represent complaints that already exist or that would arise without the use of the drug.

SSRIs

Hu et al.[48] studied the incidence and duration of the side effects of the selective reuptake inhibitors (SSRIs). Their study was based on patient and physician reports in a real-world setting, rather than controlled clinical trials.

Participants were patients who had received an SSRI for a new or recurrent case of depression (ICD-9 code 296.2 or 311) between December 15, 1999 and May 31, 2000. Between 75 and 105 days after initiation of the SSRI therapy, patients participated in a telephone interview that used closed-ended questions. Interviewers asked patients directly about the presence of 17 specific side effects commonly associated with SSRIs. Questioning also focused on duration and how bothersome the side effects were.

Patient responses were then compared to a written survey of prescribing physicians, in which the physicians predicted frequency and degree of severity of SSRI side effects. Results showed that 344 of 401 patients who completed the interview (86 percent) reported at least 1 side effect, and 219 (55 percent) experienced 1 or more troubling side effects. The most bothersome were drowsiness and sexual dysfunction. The physician survey ($n = 137$) underestimated the occurrence and degree of the 17 side effects, compared to patient reports. Side effects typically began within the first 2 weeks of treatment, and continued throughout the first three months, especially blurred vision (85 percent) and sexual dysfunction (83 percent).

Culpepper et al.[49] provided a discussion of the issues surrounding the US Food and Drug Administration (FDA) public health advisory that antidepressants might be associated with an increase in suicidal thoughts and behavior. The advisory contained warnings relevant to 10 popular antidepressant agents, though a definitive causal link between the drugs and suicide has yet to be established.

Tricyclic Drugs

One of the more serious complications that can arise from the use of imipramine is jaundice. The hepatitis resulting from the tricyclics is obstructive in type and does not primarily involve parenchymal tissue. It generally clears up fairly quickly when drug administration is suspended.

Imipramine can also cause agranulocytosis, although this type of hypersensitivity has appeared rarely. Leukopenia, leukocytosis, and occasional low-grade eosinophilis have also been observed. Ayd states that amitriptyline has proved safer than imipramine in producing less frequent hepatitis and agranulocytosis.

Imipramine and amitriptyline also produce various autonomic effects and cardiovascular complications. The most frequent autonomic effects are dry mouth, increased sweating, difficulties with visual accommodation, and constipation (Klerman and Cole[8]). These are "annoying rather than serious," according to Cole.

Cardiovascular problems represent a greater danger. Postural hypotension and tachycardia are relatively frequent. Klerman and Cole[8] include coronary thrombosis, congestive heart failure, and pulmonary emboli. Other tricyclics—desipramine, protriptyline, and nortriptyline—have been said to produce fewer autonomic and cardiovascular side effects (Hordern[3]), but they may yield other side effects. Finally, tricyclic compounds can be toxic.

MAO Inhibitors

The possible undesirable side effects of the MAO inhibitors have been discussed thoroughly by Ayd.[47] These effects are similar to those produced by the tricyclic drugs but are more numerous and more severe. Iproniazid is not now available in the United States because of the severity of certain side reactions.

The first major problem is cephalgia. Headache can be caused by all the antidepressants, but in some cases the MAO inhibitors have caused severe cephalgia with hypertension. Accompanying symptoms may include apprehension, restlessness, muscle twitchings, dizziness, pallor, sweating, nausea, tachycardia or bradycardia, precordial pain, elevated blood pressure, and photophobia. Body temperature may change. The crisis may be acute for only a few hours, but several days can pass before complete recovery. The most serious consequence of such an episode is intracranial hemorrhage, sometimes resulting in death.

There is no way of identifying the patients who will suffer such a hypertensive crisis. As with other adverse effects of the MAO inhibitors, there is wide individual variation in sensitivity to the drug. There is some indication that women and the elderly may be more prone to side reactions. These crises can occur at any time during the administration of the drug, although they seem very often to be concomitant with the ingestion of other pharmacological agents. In particular, the concurrent consumption of hypertensive sympathomimetics or certain types of aged cheese (containing significant concentrations of pressor amines) may bring on hypertension with severe cephalgia or a cerebrovascular accident.

The hydrazine derivatives (isocarboxazid, nialamide, and phenelzine) may also cause hepatitis. Two other dangers are widely agreed upon. One cannot use tricyclic and MAO inhibitors simultaneously or switch from one to the other without waiting at least a week. Reports of cases in which this precaution has not been taken describe "severe dizziness, tremor, restlessness, hallucinations, profuse sweating, vascular collapse, and extreme hyperpyrexia" (Klerman and Cole[8]). Such consequences are less likely if the switch is from a tricyclic to an MAO inhibitor than if it is the reverse.

The last danger is that a severely depressed patient may try to commit suicide with any of the drugs he or she may be taking. In patients who have taken large doses of imipramine severe symptoms of various kinds have been present for two or three days, followed by complete recovery.

Despite the advances in the development of newer antidepressants, such as the SSRIs, they are not always effective. Rush et al [27] suggested that augmenting and switching strategies are essential, since "only 30–40% of depressed outpatients who begin a medication or psychotherapy will remit" (p. 47).

The treatment of clinical depression remains controversial on several other points. The relative utility of the other classes of antidepressants remains under discussion. Bolwig[42] has suggested that newer antidepressants are inferior to the tricyclic antidepressants, noting that the most serious risk associated with depression is suicide, and that melancholic depression is especially associated with this risk. He writes that TCAs are superior to SSRIs for melancholic depression, and concludes "not starting treatment with TCA at an early stage deprives melancholic patients of the possibility of successful treatment" (p. 1236).

Both tricyclics and MAO inhibitors remain under investigation. Some studies have suggested that switching between these older medications can be an effective strategy. For example, Fava[26] found a 67 percent response rate in switching from tricyclics to MAOIs, and a 41 percent response rate from MAOIs to tricyclics.

Finally, dissenting voices remain concerning the wisdom of using the pharmaceutical approach to help resolve the mood disorders. Summerfield's *Lancet* commentary[43] questions that patients need antidepressants. He suggested instead that there has been a "medicalisation of unhappiness," that the outcome in primary-care settings is not substantially improved, and that the clinical problem of discontinuation reactions to antidepressants should be given greater weight. However, this view is held only by a very small minority of experts on the mood disorders.

Electroconvulsive Therapy

Convulsions induced by substantial doses of camphor were used in the treatment of mental disorders as long ago as 1785. The treatment was revived in 1933 by Meduna who used camphor in the treatment of schizophrenic patients. Camphor was gradually replaced by more effective drugs such as Metrazol. In 1938, Cerletti and Bini refined the technique of producing convulsions when they introduced the technique of passing an electric current through two electrodes placed on the forehead. Consequently, a relatively safe, convenient, and painless method of convulsive therapy could be used in the

treatment of mental disorders. Electroconvulsive therapy (ECT) was introduced into the United States by Kalinowski in 1939.

Physiological Effects

The physiological effects of ECT were first summarized by Holmberg in
1963.[50] Electroconvulsive therapy, when not modified by muscle-relaxing
agents, produces a grand mal seizure. Initially there is a tension or jerk produced by direct cortical stimulation. This is followed by a latent period and
then by tonic and clonic convulsions. The electroencephalogram during the
tonic phase is characterized by a generalized, intensive spike activity. During
the clonic phase the EEG shows spike-wave activity that is not synchronous
with the clonic movements. Immediately following the convulsion, the EEG
shows a brief period of electrical silence followed by a gradual return of activity until the preconvulsive pattern is resumed.

Holmberg[50] listed a variety of physiological changes that occur during the
convulsion. Respiration is suspended as a result of spasm of the respiratory
muscles and glottis. There is an elevation of the blood carbon dioxide tension
and a substantial reduction of the oxygen tension. Although the cerebral circulation is markedly increased during the convulsion, the increased blood supply
does not meet the demand of the tremendously increased brain metabolism.
The discrepancy between the available cerebral circulation and the increased
brain metabolism is the main reason for the spontaneous termination of the
convulsion.

Anoxia is readily counteracted by the insufflation of oxygen prior to ECT.
The heart rate is frequently rapid and irregular, and there may be extreme
fluctuations in blood pressure. The irregularity of the heart rate may be neu-
tralized by premedication. Muscle relaxants may be used to reduce the
increase in arterial pressure.

The immediate effects on the EEG following ECT are brief and reversible.
The effects tend to be cumulative, however, over a series of treatments. They
do not persist in general for more than a month following a course of treatment. Some investigators have reported an association between the severity of
memory defects and the degree of EEG change. In other studies, however, no
such correlation has been found. In general, the EEG changes are correlated
more highly with memory defects than with the antidepressive effects.

ECT produces a variety of autonomic changes that are attributable to the
excitation of the autonomic regulatory centers. One of the most prominent
effects is psychomotor restlessness. A number of cholenergic effects such as
transient arrhythmias may occur, but these are easily controlled by the use of
anticholenergic drugs. The increase in salivary and bronchial secretions may
similarly be counteracted by preliminary atropinization.

Biochemical Effects

A number of biochemical and hormonal changes have been reported in conjunction with ECT. Hyperglycemia of one to several hours duration is a constant phenomenon. There is also an increase in nitrogen compounds, potassium, calcium, phosphorus, and steroids in the blood. Several investigators have demonstrated an increase in the catecholamines and serotonin of the blood, but there is no evidence that this effect has anything to do with the therapeutic action of ECT.[50]

Psychological Effects

Some impairment of memory occurs almost constantly with ECT. This impairment may range from a mild tendency to forget names or dates to a severe confusion. The amnesia may be both anterograde and retrograde. It is often disturbing to the patient and may continue for several weeks following the conclusion of treatment. The impairment of memory usually disappears within a month (Cronholm and Molander[51]). There is no lasting impairment of memory even after as many as 250 treatments. Most authors believe that the efficacy of ECT in depression bears no relationship to the memory defects.

Complications

Cardiovascular accidents are most likely to occur if there is preexisting pathology. Transient cardiac arrhythmias may occur but their incidence may be reduced by premedication with acetycholine-blocking agents. In earlier studies, the mortality risk for a specific patient was approximately 3 in 1,000. With the more modern modifications of ECT, the fatality rate has been reduced even more. Holmberg reported that several thousand electroconvulsive treatments with pentobarbital-succinlycholine relaxation over a 10-year period had resulted in no complications.

Mechanism of Action

Kalinowsky and Hoch[52] described a wide variety of theories of the mode of action of ECT. While the mechanism of action has still not been established, it has been possible to eliminate many factors previously considered to be of major importance in producing therapeutic effects. Among the factors that can be discarded as therapeutically important are anoxia, hypercapnia, muscular exertion, adrenal reactions, peripheral excretion of catecholamines, and other biochemical changes in the blood (Holmberg[50]).

The effectiveness of ECT is dependent on the production of seizure activity in the brain. Subconvulsive treatment and nonconvulsive electrostimulation of the diencephalon have been shown to be of no therapeutic value. Moreover it has been reported that reducing the convulsive activity by premedication with anticonvulsive drugs reduces the therapeutic effect of ECT. Intensification of the convulsive activity by the use of muscular relaxants and oxygenation increases the therapeutic effects (Holmberg[50]).

Consistent with the early perspectives described above, a more contemporary review by Holden[53] notes that the effects of ECT are broad, and the active ingredients not yet clear. ECT not only induces seizures, but also increases serotonin levels, mitigates the effects of stress hormones, and stimulates neurogenesis in the hippocampus.

Efficacy

Although still the focus of some criticism (Sterling), modern ECT quickly and more consistently resolves depression compared to other antidepressant treatments (Fink).[54,55] A wide-ranging systematic review and metaanalysis of the efficacy and safety of ECT in depressive disorders was completed by the UK ECT Review Group.[56] In the course of the review, they obtained 624 reports altogether and identified 73 randomized trials and observational studies published since 1962 that met inclusion criteria. Sources included the Cochrane Collaboration Depressive Anxiety and Neurosis and Schizophrenia Group Controlled trial registers, MEDLINE, PsychINFO, and SIGLE, reference lists, and specialist textbooks.

The main outcome measures were depressive symptoms, cognitive function, and mortality. Metaanalysis of data of short-term efficacy compared ECT with simulated ECT, ECT versus pharmacotherapy, and diverse forms of ECT for patients with depressive illness. Real ECT was more effective than simulated (six trials, 256 patients), ECT was significantly more effective than pharmacotherapy (18 trials, 1,144 participants), and bilateral ECT was more effective than unipolar ECT (22 trials, 1,208 participants).

The UK ECT Review Group noted that in the 1970s the concern with ECT was with efficacy, but now the issues are dose and site of shock administration. They concluded that ECT remains an important treatment for severe depression. It was found to be "probably more effective" than drug therapy, bilateral ECT "moderately more effective" than unilateral, and high dose ECT more effective than low dose.[56]

Kho et al.[57] provided a metaanalysis of ECT efficacy in depression limited to the fifteen controlled trials published since 1978. They calculated 20 effect sizes of ECT and found an absence of publication bias. There was no amplification of effect size in the lower quality trials. Consistent with findings of Carney et al.[56], ECT was shown to be superior to medication and simulated ECT. In addition, they found some evidence that better response to ECT was predicted by the presence of psychosis.

This finding is consistent with suggestions by Potter, Rudorfer, and Manji, who concluded that ECT is highly effective in treating delusional depression. Potter et al.[14] also recommended it for those with severe melancholic depression who are nonresponsive to tricyclic drugs. They noted that ECT should generally be considered sooner the more severe the depression.

Future Directions

Transcranial Magnetic Stimulation

Several studies have tested transcranial magnetic stimulation as an innovative treatment (Pridmore[58]; Pridmore et al.[59]; Grunhaus et al. [60,61]).

Pridmore[58] used a randomized, single-blind, controlled study of 22 patients and found that it was possible to substitute TMS treatments for ECT treatments in a course of ECT without loss of antidepressant effect. Pridmore et al.[59] compared TMS to ECT in 32 patients with major depressive episode. The participants in their study had failed to respond to at least one course of pharmacological treatment. They found that ECT patients improved somewhat more on measures of depression overall, but TMS produced comparable results on a number of measures. They concluded that further studies are indicated. Grunhaus et al.[60] randomly assigned 40 patients with major depressive disorder to either ECT or repetitive TMS. While overall patients responded best to ECT, those with major depressive disorder without psychosis responded similarly to both treatments. Finally, Grunhaus et al.[61] reported a controlled randomized comparison of ECT and TMS in severe and resistant nonpsychotic major depression. Response rate was 58 percent (23 out of 40 patients responded to treatment). For ECT, 12 responded and 8 did not. In the TMS group, 11 responded and 9 did not. Their conclusions were that, in this study, patients responded as well to either ECT or TMS.

Pharmacogenomics

Several studies have tested whether genetic markers can predict differential drug response, thus leading to the possibility of individualized pharmacological treatment of depression. Smeraldi et al.[62] advanced the following line of reasoning: (1) depression with psychotic features has been shown responsive to SSRIs, (2) the 5-HTT gene is a prime target for SSRIs, and (3) a polymorphism within 5-HTT has been found to lead to variations in transcriptional efficiency; therefore (4) perhaps allelic variation of the 5-HTT promoter may relate to antidepressant response. Their study design included 102 inpatients with major depression with psychotic features. Patients were randomly assigned to treatment with fluvoxamine and placebo or pindolol for 6 weeks. Homozygotes for the long variant (*l/l*) of the 5-HTT promoter and heterozygotes (*l/s*) showed a better response to fluvoxamine than homozygotes for the short variant (*s/s*). They concluded that fluvoxamine efficacy in delusional depression is related to variation within the promoter of the 5-HTT gene.

Pollock et al.[63] studied response to paroxetine in relation to the serotonin transporter gene polymorphism (5-HTTLPR). Reductions in HRSD were more rapid for those with the *ll* genotype than for those possessing an *s* allele, despite equivalent paroxetine concentrations. Response to nortriptyline was not affected, suggesting that allelic variation of 5-HTTLPR may contribute to the initial response of patients treated with SSRIs.

Rausch et al.[64] conducted the first study on the antidepressant dose-response relationship to 5-HTT kinetics and genetics. Fifty-one patients with major depression were classified for 5-HTT promoter region polymorphism and platelet 5-HTT. They found that the long allele group responded more to both placebo and drug dose, compared to the short allele group. The authors noted previous studies suggesting the long allele is associated with lower neuroticism or anxiety, but it remains unclear why the long allele might be linked to faster improvement. Future pharmacogenomic studies will continue to identify genetic markers in hopes of better predicting individual drug response, and the reasons for such.

Chapter 15
Psychotherapy

In this chapter, we consider the major psychotherapeutic approaches to the mood disorders, including supportive and psychoanalytic psychotherapy, interpersonal therapy, behavioral treatments, and cognitive therapy. We also consider the psychotherapeutic treatment of bipolar disorder, the prevention of suicide, relapse prevention, and psychotherapy change processes. The greater focus is on the treatments that have been utilized in studies of major depressive disorder and those with comparatively convincing empirical support.[1,2] In the concluding chapter, Chapter 16, we provide a specific comparison of pharmacotherapy to psychotherapy and review the relapse prevention studies that have compared the relative effects of drugs and psychotherapy.

Early Approaches

Prior to the use of treatment manuals (for example, Beck et al.[3]) to guide clinical practice, the psychotherapy of depression was usually described in a relatively vague and poorly focused manner. However, there were exceptions: among the more structured approaches, Campbell's *Manic-Depressive Disease* (1953)[4] suggested a number of steps in the psychological therapy of manic depressives, including proper diagnosis, explaining somatic symptoms to the patient, removing precipitating or aggravating environmental factors, combat conscientiousness, psychotherapy, advising family and friends as to the patient's needs, rest and relaxation, occupational therapy, and bibliotherapy.

Other initial writings on the dynamics and psychotherapy of depression include those of Wilson,[5] Kraines,[6] Ayd,[7] Arieti,[8] Gibson,[9] Regan,[10] and Bonime.[11]

Wilson[5] pointed out that when the necessary state of personality equilibrium is disrupted, a "need-satisfaction sequence" is set up. Kraines, in *Mental Depressions and Their Treatment*,[6] stressed, as did Campbell, the physical basis of manic-depressive illness, but considered psychotherapy essential to shorten the illness, alleviate the patient's suffering, and prevent complications. Ayd, in *Recognizing the Depressed Patient*,[7] also stressed (as did Campbell and Kraines) that the physician start by telling the patient that the illness has a physical basis and that she or he will improve. He felt that encouragement is important and that the physician should dissuade the patient from trying what is likely to be difficult since failure only reinforces the sense of inadequacy and guilt.

Arieti[8] stated that "Depression is . . . a reaction to the loss of a normal ingredient of psychological life." The patient must reorganize his or her thinking "into different constellations which do not bring about sadness." Depression changes the thought processes, apparently to decrease the quantity of thoughts "in order to decrease the quantity of suffering." In cases of moderate intensity, Arieti suggested that the therapist alter the environment, especially the relationship to the dominant other; relieve the patient's feeling of guilt, responsibility, lack of accomplishment, and loss; and disallow depressive thoughts to expand into general mood of depression.

In an article on psychotherapy of manic-depressive states, Gibson[9] singled out the patient's difficulty in establishing a relationship with the therapist in which meaningful communication can take place. The patient tends to recast the therapist's remarks and interpretations into his or her own predetermined way of perceiving relationships. It may help for the therapist to challenge the patient's view in order to introduce a new point of view.

In an article entitled, "Brief Psychotherapy of Depression," Regan[10] was concerned with "tactics," a "circumscribed set of procedures aimed at a specific tactical goal." He advocated a number of tactical approaches in psychotherapy of depression: (1) protecting the patient, (2) the need for preparatory exploration, (3) interrupting the ruminative cycle, (4) using physical therapy, and (5) initiating attitudinal change.

Bonime[11] stated that depression is a sick way of relating to other human beings. Characteristically, the depressive makes inordinate demands on others. Depressive living has a basic consistency pervading all its variations from neurotic sulking to psychotic mania, the elements of which are manipulativeness, aversion to influence, unwillingness to give gratification, hostility, and anxiety. Bonime suggested that the therapist must foster both patients' recognition of their role in bringing about their pain and the personal resources they have for altering their practices.

Supportive Psychotherapy

Reassurance

Kraines[6] gives his patients lengthy explanations, both of the factors involved in depression and of the course of the illness, and concludes, "The thing for you to remember is that this exhaustion can and will be overcome. You will need patience and you will need to cooperate. It won't be easy; it will take time; but you will recover" (p. 409).

Optimistic statements about the outcome may encourage the patient to become more active and may help to neutralize the all-pervasive pessimism. In mild or moderate depressions such positive predictions may have a noticeable ameliorating effect, but severely depressed patients may view these optimistic statements with skepticism and may fail to be influenced by them.

Another technique that is often helpful in countering patients' low self-esteem and hopeless feeling is a discussion of their positive achievements. If allowed to follow their inclinations, patients are likely to dwell on past failures and traumatic experiences. The therapist can foster a more realistic appraisal of the past and can raise the patients' self-evaluation by skillfully guiding them into describing their successes in detail.

Ventilation and Catharsis

Some depressed patients experience considerable relief after ventilating their feelings and concerns to the therapist. The emotional release produced by crying occasionally produces a notable alleviation of the symptoms. Severely depressed patients, however, may react adversely to ventilation. After a discussion of their problems, they may not only feel more overwhelmed and helpless but also feel humiliated over having exposed themselves.

Guidance and Environmental Change

The need for some change in patients' activities is often obvious, and the therapist may draw on the therapeutic relationship to induce the patient to modify his or her routine. For instance, the therapist may act as a catalyst to redirect the patient from self-preoccupation to an interest in the outside world and might suggest appropriate forms of recreational, manual, intellectual, or aesthetic activities.

In recommending activities to a depressed patient, the therapist should attempt to gauge both the patient's tolerance for the stress involved and the probabilities of success. The particular task should not be too difficult or too time consuming. We have found that the successful completion of a task by depressed patients significantly increases optimism, level of aspiration, and performance on subsequent tasks.[12]

Psychoanalysis and Psychoanalytic Psychotherapy

Many of the early strategies noted above have been incorporated into the contemporary treatments of the mood disorders, the empirically validated psychotherapies for depression, described below. Other approaches, including psychoanalysis and psychoanalytic psychotherapy, are well-known therapies but are targeted more toward global personality reconstruction, and focused on the resolution of childhood neurosis.[13]

The theorized time frame for improvement in psychoanalysis is four to five sessions per week for three to six years average duration. There are evident problems in conducting clinical outcome studies on such a lengthy therapeutic approach. In most cases of mood disorder, there is complete remission of symptoms, and functioning returns to the premorbid level. The time frame for improvement in psychoanalysis (3–6 years) may be compared to that of the typical course of a major depressive episode (90–95 percent of individuals experience at least partial remission within two years of onset).[14] Thus, therapy length prohibits a determination of efficacy or effectiveness, since it is impossible to disentangle the natural course of improvement from therapeutic effects. Of course, studies of relapse prevention would be possible.

In any case, such research has yet to be completed. In a review of psychoanalysis, psychoanalytic psychotherapy, and supportive psychotherapy, Ursano and Silberman[13] noted that there are no studies comparing well-defined psychodynamic psychotherapies with medication in the treatment of depression. Similarly, they suggested that a better delineation of the specific techniques that define supportive psychotherapy is required before controlled research can be conducted on this approach.

Dewald[15] suggested the following theoretical point concerning the short-term derivations from the practice of psychoanalysis: "In my opinion, it (psychoanalytic psychotherapy) is a form of treatment based on the psychoanalytic theory of mental functioning" (p. 542). As such, the process of change would be theoretically equivalent to that advanced by Freud. This would be expected to take some time.[16]

In a contemporary overview of the psychotherapies,[17] psychoanalytic or psychodynamic psychotherapy is not included among the 12 current psychotherapy systems. Psychoanalysis is included,[18] but the author concludes that "no adequate study exists evaluating the results of psychoanalytic therapy" (p. 40).

Depression-Focused Psychotherapies

Thase et al.[19] reviewed the psychosocial factors that may adversely impact treatment of depression, along with the psychotherapeutic principles found to be helpful in short- and long-term therapy. They focused on the interpersonal, cognitive, and behavioral treatments that have been utilized in studies of major depressive disorder.[2]

Many of the relevant psychosocial factors that predict poor response to pharmacological interventions are at least somewhat amenable to psychotherapeutic solutions. These include cognitive or personality factors like neuroticism or pessimism. Other aspects may also be ameliorated through psychological therapies, but to a much smaller degree. These would include factors like low social support, life stress, and chronic adversity.

Treatment observance is necessary to the successful treatment of chronic mood disorders. Thase et al.[19] suggested that the inability to adhere to treatment is responsible for as many as one-third of antidepressant nonresponders. Thus, enhancing medication adherence (e.g., behavior change mediated through cognitive therapy) is a major contribution of psychological therapies.

Better medication compliance has been found in patients receiving CT.[20] Of course, this observation does not preclude the need for further process studies to partial out the relative contribution of the modification of depressogenic cognitive process as such versus improvements mediated through behavioral modificaton.

Thase et al.[19] suggested several guidelines for psychotherapeutic intervention, based on their review of depression-focused therapies. These psychotherapies include cognitive, interpersonal, and behavior therapy. Among their suggested guidelines are the following: (1) use a collaborative therapy relationship centered on the goal of developing new coping skills; (2) incorporate from other medical models examples of treating chronic disorders; (3) elicit feedback about what has failed to work in the past while remaining cautiously optimistic about the possibility of improvement; (4) establish stepwise, short-term goals with graded task assignments; (5) have frequent meetings with short sessions, if necessary; (6) use homework and rehearsal to develop skills; (7) meet with and involve significant others in order to enhance alliance and provide psychoeducation; (8) as short-term goals are reached, establish intermediate and long-term ones; and (9) keep the patient in therapy for 4–6 months following therapeutic response.

Their review concluded that the depression-oriented psychotherapies are more effective than wait-list controls, that response rates are comparable to antidepressant meds in randomized clinical trials, that cognitive therapy may have more enduring effects long-term, and that treatment-resistant depression responds best to combined psychotherapy and pharmacotherapy.[19]

Interpersonal Therapy (IPT)

The two "pure-form" systems of psychotherapy that have been compared to pharmacotherapy in the treatment of depression include interpersonal psychotherapy and cognitive therapy.

In discussing the development of depression in Chapter 13, we advanced the idea of a "circular feedback model" between thoughts and emotions.[21] In this model, an unpleasant life situation triggers schemas relevant to loss and negative expectancies. Such expectancies, in turn, become activated and stimulate affective structures that are responsible for the subjective feeling of depression. The affective structures further innervate the schemas to which they are connected, reinforcing the activity of such. Thus, the interaction schemas ↔ affective structures constitutes a reciprocal determinism in generating the depressive syndrome (Beck 1967).[21]

Similar to this formulation, Interpersonal Psychotherapy is based on the idea that negative life events can lead to disturbed mood, and vice versa.[22] An interpersonal history is taken (using the interpersonal inventory), and the therapist explains the depressive episode in one of two ways: (1) connecting a recent life event to the acute depressive episode or (2) linking a mood episode to a negative impact on the person's interpersonal competence, thus generating problems and distressing life events.[22,23,24]

Manualized treatment consists of 12 to 16 weekly sessions that center on solving an interpersonal crisis, such as complicated bereavement, role dispute, role transition, or deficits in relationship skills. The sessions discuss associations between the patient's depressive mood state and relevant life events. The therapist provides social approval for incidents where the patient succeeds in interpersonal encounters. If such an encounter goes badly, the therapist explores with the patient alternative ways to handle future similar interpersonal situations.[22]

IPT for Chronic Depression

Markowitz[23] suggests the adaptation of IPT to chronic forms of unipolar depression. To do so, the identification of recent interpersonal life events is replaced by the recognition and resolution of chronic social skills deficits. The emphasis is on building interpersonal function.

However, according to the few studies conducted to date, the advantages of such an adaptation of interpersonal therapy appear modest.[23] This is consistent with the opinion of other experts. For example, Eugene S. Paykel, one of the key participants in the original Yale-Boston collaborative trial, reported that the precursor of IPT did not prevent relapse, though continuation antidepressants did.[25]

A study on the prophylaxis of future depressive episodes using IPT was conducted by Frank et al.[26] They studied 128 patients with recurrent depression in a randomized 3-year maintenance trial. The study site was a specialty clinic with over 10 years experience in treating recurrent affective disorders.

All participants had previously responded to combined treatment with imipramine and IPT. Active imipramine at an average dose of 200 mg reduced recurrence to only about 22 percent over the following 3-year period. A maintenance form of IPT alone resulted in a recurrence rate of about 61 percent over the subsequent three-year period. Combined active imipramine and maintenance IPT resulted in a recurrence rate of about 24 percent over three years.

For patients who did not receive active medication, continued monthly IPT maintenance sessions extended "survival time," or time without recurrence, to greater than one year. Frank et al. concluded that there is a highly significant prophylactic effect for active imipramine therapy and a modest preventative effect for monthly interpersonal psychotherapy.[26]

IPT for Elderly Populations

Hinrichsen[27] described how psychiatric illness strains family relations and noted that interpersonal factors can influence remission and relapse rates. He suggested that IPT holds promise as a treatment for late-life depression.

Elaborating a treatment rationale for the use of IPT in elderly patient populations, Hinrichsen[27] cited findings of a strong association between expressed emotion (EE) (e.g., expressions of criticism) and psychiatric outcome. Specifically, he noted that sociologists focus on the "rolelessness" and "normlessness" often associated with late life. This is said to parallel IPT's attention to role transitions. In his geriatric psychiatry clinic, IPT is used to focus on role transitions and interpersonal difficulties. Hinrichsen reported reductions in depressive symptoms in several patients treated with this adaptation of IPT for the elderly.

Cognitive Therapy

Formulation and Conceptualization

As described in Chapter 10, the dominant theory of depression prior to Beck's[21] test of it was the psychoanalytic idea of "retroflected hostility,"[28] what might be thought of as "motivated misery." Cognitive symptoms were interpreted as expressions of taboo but unconscious wishes. The distorted thinking in itself was not recognized as the core formulation.

The psychoanalytic meaning was to be found through interpretation by a trained analyst, and the proper interpretations were to be consistent with the notion of anger turned inward. The content of a patient's negative bias about self, experience, and the future was missed.

Guided by the anomalous findings described in Chapter 10, Beck's new formulation posited a simpler solution. There is no universal symbolic meaning. Rather, the cognition itself—the negative way in which depressed patients see themselves—is the basic process.[29] This cognitive process was found to be highly unique to each individual. "Automatic thoughts" were idiosyncratic in the manner and situations in which the negative cognitive bias was expressed.

By removing the idiosyncratic thoughts as such and substituting universal symbolic interpretation, Freud's formulation had resulted in the loss of personal meanings that were found to be specific to each disorder. The difference between Freud's and Beck's formulation of depression suggested a new clinical approach in how to treat it.

Structure and Strategy

Cognitive psychotherapy is based on the theory elaborated in Chapters 12 and 13. In brief, the theory postulates that the depressed or depression-prone individual has certain idiosyncratic cognitive patterns (schemas), which may become activated either by specific stresses impinging on specific vulnerabilities or by overwhelming, nonspecific stresses. When the cognitive patterns are activated, they tend to dominate the individual's thinking and to produce the affective and motivational phenomena associated with depression. Cognitive psychotherapy may be used symptomatically during depressions to help the patient gain objectivity toward his or her automatic reactions and counteract them. During nondepressed periods, the therapy is designed to modify the idiosyncratic cognitive patterns to reduce the patient's vulnerability to future depressions.

The purpose of the cognitive therapy session is to facilitate the transfer (from the therapist) and internalization (by the patient) of the cognitive perspective. This process is characterized by a Socratic—rather than disputational—dialogue. The patient is sensitively guided to reflect critically on the evidence (or dearth of evidence) that confirms or disconfirms psychopathogenic thoughts and beliefs. One defining feature of cognitive therapy is this collaborative empirical process of examining thoughts and beliefs in a supportive-directive manner. Consequently, the therapist uses an active didactic stance to communicate with the patient. Nontechnical terms are used to educate patients on the cognitive formulation of psychological disorders.

The cognitive process in clinical depression is relatively undifferentiated. Beck et al.[3] observed that, in depression, the cognitive mode of organizing reality is "primitive." Judgments of life events are broad and global. Meanings are extreme, negative, categorical, absolute, and judgmental, leading to an emotional response that is negative and extreme.

By contrast, more mature thinking harmonizes life situations into many dimensions or qualities rather than a single category. Mature processing is generally quantitative, rather than exclusively in qualitative terms, and standards are relative rather than absolute. Adaptive thinking is characterized by its greater complexity and variability, whereas primal thinking reduces the diversity of human experiences into a few crude categories (p. 15).[3]

Ideas are seen as "facts" more so in clinical depression than in the nondepressed state. The negative bias becomes exacerbated when the patient behaves in a manner that conforms with the biased thinking. In modifying the negative cognitive processing, the patient learns relevant attentional and recording skills, and comes to recognize the links among certain cognitions and painful affects.

Basic Elements

Cognitive therapy is the application of cognitive theory to the individual case. In general, the cognitive therapist modifies current thinking in order to reduce symptoms, and corrects beliefs in order to prevent relapse.

There are many related conceptual ingredients in cognitive therapy, including the breakdown of problems into resolvable units of analysis. The Socratic method and problem definition facilitate the achievement of therapeutic goals, including (1) identifying negative attitudes, (2) pinpointing the most urgent and accessible problem, (3) developing homework strategies, (4) monitoring (recording) homework strategies between therapy sessions, and (5) reviewing problems and accomplishments since the previous session (pp. 409–411).[3]

Structure of Sessions

After obtaining cognitive and standard assessments for baseline information concerning the disorder, empathy is established and a "therapeutic, supportive relationship" formed, from which to collaborate with the patient on resolving problems.[3] The structure of cognitive therapy sessions then consists of the following elements.

(1) Mood checks are obtained to provide information on the patient's current emotional state. (2) An agenda is set, based on case formulation, including understanding of the historical antecedents related to the current dysfunction. (3) Problems and treatment goals are developed and prioritized in collaboration with the patient. Attention is given to the dual aims of both building realistic confidence through graded task assignments and taking on the most pressing concerns first. (5) Socialization of the patient to cognitive theory and therapy is a focus of each session. Educating the patient is an essential component of treatment. (6) Negative automatic thoughts and beliefs are identified and tested. (7) Homework from the previous week is reviewed, and new assignments developed, typically using a Daily Record of Dysfunctional Thoughts (DRDT). Experiments are designed to test/examine specific negative automatic thoughts identified through DRDT recordings. (8) Sessions are summarized to facilitate consolidation of the salient points learned from (a) homework review and (b) evaluation of the results of the "cognitive experiments." (9) Feedback is garnered from the patient concerning reactions to the therapy session and to the treatment approach in general. The extent to which the patient is learning to independently apply the procedures of cognitive therapy is assessed. Treatment evaluation occurs during and following cognitive

therapy through the use of standardized tests such as the Beck Depression/ Hopelessness Scales and a variety of other psychometric devices.

Behavioral Aspects

From its beginning, cognitive therapy incorporated the established behavioral principles of operant and classical conditioning (e.g., Beck[30]). This is probably most apparent in the use of clinical techniques to facilitate engagement with the environment, such as activity schedules and graded task assignment.

One of the core processes of clinical depression is negative perspectives of self. The depressed person is often quick to accept blame or responsibility for adverse events and to blame negative events on imagined lack of effort, talent, or abilities. The technique of reattribution focuses the depressed person's attention on alternative explanations for failure experiences, and tests the negative formulations both through homework assignments ("behavioral" tests) and prior and subsequent logical analysis.

Activity scheduling. There are many techniques available to increase behavioral activation and modify the negative self-concept. Early in therapy, negative cognition content can be modified through encouraging the patient to become involved in constructive activities. Activity schedules counter the patient's loss of motivation, fixation on depressive ideas, and negative concepts regarding personal capability.

The specific technique of scheduling the patient's time can facilitate momentum and prevent slipping back into inactivity. The activity schedule focuses on specific goal-directed tasks and furnishes the patient and therapist with specific data on which to realistically evaluate the patient's functional abilities.[3]

Prior to utilizing activity scheduling, several principles should be clear to the patient. These include (1) the idea that no one can accomplish all his or her plans; (2) one's goals should be in terms of what kind of actions to take rather than on how much should be accomplished; (3) acceptance of the fact that external uncontrollable factors (interruptions, computer/mechanical failures) and subjective factors (fatigue, motivation) can interfere with progress; and (4) the need to set aside time to plan for the next day. These ideas are intended to counteract negative thoughts about attempting the scheduling task. In scheduling activities, "the therapist clearly states that the initial purpose of the program is to observe and not to evaluate how well or how much the patient does each day" (pp. 123–124).[3]

Graded task assignment. Activities are categorized as either "mastery" (accomplishment) or "pleasure" (pleasant feelings). These dimensions are rated on a 5-point scale with 0 being no mastery (pleasure), and 5 maximum mastery (pleasure). Graded Task Assignment modifies schematic content by inducing the patient to recognize partial successes and small degrees of plea-sure and counteracts dichotomous (all-or-nothing) thinking (p. 128).[3]

As with activity scheduling, there are several principles of graded task assignment, including (1) problem definition; (2) formulation of a task; (3) stepwise assignment of activities from simpler to more complex; (4) immedi-ate and direct observation of success experiences; (5) verbalization of the patient's doubts, negative reactions, and minimization of achievements; (6) encouragement of realistic evaluation of performance; (7) emphasis on goal achievement as a result of the patient's own efforts; and (8) the collaborative development of new, more complex goals (p. 132).[3] All these procedures weaken the patient's beliefs regarding personal inadequacies by providing cor-rective experiences that, with the therapist's assistance, can form the basis for more realistic interpretations on the part of the patient.

Interpersonal Aspects of Change

The therapeutic interactions (cognitive, behavioral, emotional exchanges) between the therapist and the patient is the "therapeutic relationship."[31] The idiosyncratic, relatively autonomous nature of the depressed person's biased cognitions can make establishing a therapeutic relationship difficult. Beck et al.[3] explained this disengagement by comparing the depressed person to a purely "cerebral" being seeing the point of a joke but not being amused; describing positive aspects of significant others without a sense of satisfaction; detecting the appeal of a favored food or music, but with no sense of enjoy-ment (p. 34).

In order to better penetrate the biases, Beck et al. (p. 61)[3] suggested that the therapist keep certain principles in mind during treatment. One of these is that the depressed patient's personal world view (negative ideas and beliefs) appears sensible to the patient, though it may be quite unbelievable to the ther-apist.

The radically different constructions of personal meaning of the therapist and patient can place considerable strain on the interpersonal interactions, making it difficult to establish a collaborative, trusting, and empathic thera-peutic context. Thus, before an effective psychological intervention can be introduced, the therapist must nurture a healthy therapeutic relationship, despite holding an opposing perspective to that of the patient.

Maintaining a Therapeutic Relationship

Safran and Segal[32] used the term "ruptures" in the therapeutic relationship, referring to problems in working collaboratively with patients in therapy. There are a number of ways in which the working alliance may go awry.[33]

Ruptures in the therapeutic relationship are times in therapy when therapist and patient are not working together on common therapeutic goals. This failure can be caused by several factors, such as (1) lapses in effective communication, (2) differences in interpretations or values between therapist and patient concerning the nature of the presenting problems and the actions that might correct such problems, and/or (3) dysfunctional personality strategies (or disorders) that frequently are present along with the depressed mood.

One source is the patient not understanding the rationale of therapy and/or thinking that the therapist does not understand his or her perspective. In such cases, the therapist must demonstrate an understanding of the patient's perspective. Using the patient's own words can sometimes assist in this regard. The therapist must go back and review any aspects that have been misunderstood, in order to repair the relationship.

Another potential problem stems from the patient's emotional turmoil associated with the depressed state. If the patient is overwhelmed by affect and can focus only on how bad she or he feels, then the therapist will have difficulty in educating the patient and in providing the other components of effective cognitive therapy. If the therapist suspects that emotions are so overwhelming that the therapeutic relationship has been damaged, or that establishing such a relationship is problematic, then this issue must be directly discussed with the patient in order to properly understand the cause(s) of the rupture.

Some patients do not carry out the homework assignments that are necessary to obtain information on their negative interpretations. Other patients are very sensitive to criticism and prone to interpret the therapist's focus as blaming them for their problems. Others fail to self-disclose, keep therapy at a distance, and treat it as an intellectual exercise. Still others may have a hidden agenda (e.g., the patient is in therapy to please someone else, perhaps a spouse or employer), and really do not believe therapy is needed. In all these cases, the therapist must utilize effective listening skills and empathic response to repair the interpersonal difficulties.

A Collaborative Context

Patient and therapist must assume responsibilities in the development of a therapeutic relationship.[31] To facilitate this relationship, the respective responsibilities must be made clear. The patient's expectations must be articulated and corrected as needed.

Among the essential areas of agreement are the patient's candid reactions (positive or negative) to treatment. The therapist's responsibilities are (1) to provide the best treatment possible, and to help the patient apply the principles of therapy; (2) to make an authentic attempt to understand the patient from the patient's viewpoint; (3) to help develop homework assignments that are agreeable to the patient (i.e., that the patient agrees to carry out), and (4) to take the initiative to direct and guide the development of interventions.

Parallel to the therapist's responsibilities, the patient must agree (1) to provide a good faith effort to master the strategies of clinical treatment; (2) to be candid in revealing symptoms, thoughts, and reasons for seeking cognitive therapy; (3) to fulfill the homework exercises that are necessary for understanding specific problems and that are essential for the successful implementation of therapy; and (4) to follow the therapist's lead in problem solving by cooperating and assisting with the development of homework experiences. In addition, the patient must accept that effort and personal risk are often required in order to correct long-standing problems.

Teaching Independent Problem-Solving

All three of the empirically tested therapies for depression are directive, focused, structured approaches.[19] A large part of such guidance by the therapist involves educating the patient regarding the nature and treatment of depression. Thus, part of the interpersonal relationship between the therapist and the patient will include the therapist playing the role of educator concerning the application of therapy.

The therapeutic relationship in the treatment of depression is highly structured, and specific responsibilities are assumed by therapist and patient.[31] One primary responsibility of the therapist is to develop an accurate understanding of the patient and of unique aspects of the particular therapeutic relationship. The therapist must understand the patient's view of the therapist and of therapy and how this changes over time. Also, the therapist must apprehend any errors in the patient's idea of the collaborative therapy process. To take one example of a common misconception, homework is to be taken not as "directions from an expert," but rather as a structured opportunity to test one's thoughts and beliefs.

Homework empowers the patient, since only the patient can determine (and report on) the impact of the various therapeutic techniques utilized outside the therapy sessions. By collaboratively developing homework assignments and by discussing the outcomes of these activities, the patient learns skills that can be generalized to new problem situations that will inevitably arise in the future. This equips the patient to resolve problems independently by applying principles that are learned through repeated applications in homework.

Dependency in psychotherapy can be categorized as either therapeutic or nontherapeutic. Therapeutic dependency has been described as an interpersonal position of the patient toward the therapist in which the patient endeavors to learn the cognitive theory (and techniques) as explained by the therapist. Nontherapeutic dependency designates an interpersonal stance in which the patient resists the collaborative empirical approach and persists in relying completely on the therapist (rather than his or her own experience) as an arbiter or source of information.[31]

Modification of Interpersonal Dysfunctions

Thase et al.[19] reviewed the psychosocial factors that may adversely impact treatment of depression. They noted that many of the relevant psychosocial factors that predict poor response to pharmacological interventions are amenable to psychotherapeutic solutions. These include cognitive or personality factors like neuroticism or pessimism. Other aspects may also be ameliorated through psychological therapies, but to a smaller degree: factors like low social support, life stress, and chronic adversity.[19]

Interpersonal behaviors associated with a transient dysthymic mood can potentially escalate in a vicious cycle. Beck (p. 269)[34] cited Bandura's work and the concept of reciprocal determinism in explicating this phenomenon.

A person's behavior can influences others' behavior toward that person. Negative actions associated with the onset of depression can result in negative interpersonal interactions that then exacerbate the depressed mood.

The first link in the chain leading to depression can be either negative reactions from others, such as rejection, or negative actions on the part of the depressed person toward others, such as withdrawal from social interaction with significant others.

To take the latter as an example, one natural consequence of a depressed person withdrawing from friends and relatives is criticism or rejection by those significant other people. This may exacerbate the depressed person's self-criticism and negative conceptualizations of others, thus leading to further impairment in interpersonal functioning and thereby to additional negative cognitive processing. This vicious interpersonal-cognitive cycle can deepen the person's depression to the point that intervention by significant others becomes fruitless, thereby necessitating professional treatment.

Of course, such a negative cycle probably accounts for only some cases of clinical depression, since there is individual variation in the impact of interpersonal factors on functioning. Also, for many individuals, precipitating social-environmental events appear to play a minimal role in the development and maintenance of depression.[34]

When the individual case formulation suggests a significant role for behavioral/interpersonal dysfunctions, the cognitive therapist works with the patient to (1) increase the patient's cognizance of this phenomenon, (2) incorporate tests of this conceptualization into homework assignments, and (3) provide guidance in the development of more functional conceptualizations as to the meanings attributed to the interpersonal difficulties experienced by the depressed patient. Homework can consist, for example, of relatively simple "behavioral" experiments, such as approaching others and engaging in brief conversations.

As in the standard practice of cognitive therapy, such exercises are posed as graded tasks so that the likelihood of success is maximized. If the therapist is careful to explain and convey the conceptualization, as elaborated above, then the depressed individual will be better able to understand the treatment rationale and thereby have reason to persist in correcting the "vicious interpersonal cycle" that can exacerbate the depression. Thus, the cognitive therapist utilizes behavioral and interpersonal techniques in cases that suggest that social factors are implicated in the disorder.

Behavioral Activation

Jacobson et al.[35] found that using only one component of cognitive therapy, "behavioral activation," was as effective as their application of all the other techniques of cognitive therapy in terms of altering negative thinking, as well as modifying dysfunctional attributional styles. A follow-up study by Dimidjian et al.[36] was consistent with this preliminary study.

This would seem to be an important finding, one that deserves theoretical comment. Two brief points in response to these findings are these. First, since the time of the "cognitive revolution," behavioral processes have been understood to be cognitively mediated. Thousands of basic and applied studies were conducted to demonstrate this. Thus, it is a bit puzzling now to suggest a dichotomy between processes shown previously to be identical.

Second, the concept *schema*—covered in detail in Chapters 12 and 13—is consilient with and an elaboration of the term as used by Piaget and other cognitive theorists. In these systems, schema change requires behavioral action to modify cognitive structure, so these "behavioral activation" studies are consistent with these cognitive theoretical formulations. Aside from these two clarifications, we here limit discussion to that which is relevant to therapeutic intervention.

A process closely related to facilitating coping, success, and mastery is to reactivate the person's interest in prior intrinsic life goals (or to develop such goals, if absent). One central aspect of clinical depression is its negative effect on goal-relevant actions. It attenuates motivation to achieve previously valued goals and ambitions.

In order to reactivate the depressed person's interest in persisting toward goals, the therapist and patient list and discuss those actions that were previously reinforcing (or valued) but are now latent due to the depressive state. The myriad goals that are typically no longer salient are then arranged in order of priority. These interactions between therapist and patient help to refocus on positive goal-directed activities that the depressed person may (incorrectly) believe are no longer possible. Concrete methods to hypothesis-test the negative predictions in this regard—along with between-session practice of such skills—can help develop a sense of hope and resourcefulness in overcoming one's depressive state.

At times and with certain patients it may be possible, through the influence of the therapeutic relationship, to make specific suggestions for activity scheduling that patients may carry out, even though they may not yet be convinced such actions will lead to alleviation of depression. In such cases, the process of therapeutic change may properly be conceptualized as an interpersonal influence process whereby the patient agrees to test the cognitive model as suggested by the therapist.

In other words, to facilitate (or activate) a depressed person's goal-directed behaviors, the therapist in some cases must engage in a collaborative interpersonal influence process with the patient. If the patient agrees to carry out actions that have in the past brought satisfaction and pride in accomplishment, then the consequences may serve to disconfirm (or deactivate) the negative schematic processing, and thus facilitate the remission of the depressed mode.

An analogy to the scientific method as such provides an effective model of behavioral activation as a method to facilitate empirical tests of thoughts/beliefs in cognitive therapy. In the initial sessions of cognitive therapy, a conceptualization of the patient's presenting problem(s) is developed. The most salient questions and focus must be identified. At this point in therapy—as in the "Introduction" sections of scientific reports—clear and operational questions are developed.

Operationalization of relevant hypotheses may be brief, a few minutes only, or may take much longer. In either case, the stage is being set to devise appropriate methods to test out specific hypotheses. The actual test requires something similar to what Jacobson et al.[35] call behavioral activation.

In the case of the scientific investigator, as well as in the collaborative relationship between cognitive therapist and patient, the crucial test of successful process at this stage is whether reasonable hypotheses are developed that may be tested through the next logical process to be carried out, that is, developing appropriate methods to evaluate the questions.

In summary, to test beliefs or hypotheses, behavioral actions ("experiments") are required.[30] The patient must understand that hypotheses are taken to be neither "true" nor "false," and that, in the absence of proof, it is advantageous to doubt one's preconceived ideas. In this manner, the value of maintaining openness to observation is imparted to the patient. The adaptive value of leaving oneself open to the accommodation of new information (rather than fitting observations exclusively into preexisting molds) is discussed. The patient learns that behavioral experiments are necessary to test ideas.

Cognitive Techniques

Cognitive techniques consist of: a macroscopic or longitudinal approach, aimed at mapping out the patient's sensitivities, exaggerated or inappropriate reactions, and the cause-effect relationships between external events and internal discomfort; a microscopic or cross-sectional approach, focused on recognizing and evaluating specific cognitions; and the identification and modification of the misconceptions, superstitions, and syllogisms that lead to maladaptive reactions.

There is a special application for cognitive therapy during the postdepressed period. During this period, patients may have transient periods of feeling blue but for the most part are functioning well enough to be able to examine objectively their life patterns, automatic thoughts, and basic misconceptions. This approach is designed to produce changes in the cognitive organization to reduce the patient's vulnerability to future depressions.

Two standard cognitive therapy techniques have been designed to increase the patient's objectivity. These involve *reattribution* and *alternative conceptualization*. These techniques teach skills of empirical hypothesis testing so that the patient learns to distance from thoughts, or to see thoughts as psychological events.[3] The initial focus is on correcting the present thinking in order to provide immediate relief from symptoms. Then the therapist works with the patient to reexamine dysfunctional beliefs in order to prevent relapse.

Delineating the Major Maladaptive Patterns

One of the first steps in the cognitive psychotherapy of depressed patients is a survey of life history data. In reviewing a patient's history of difficulties, the therapist tries to identify the major patterns and sequences in the patient's life. It is generally possible to demonstrate to patients that they respond selectively to certain types of experiences; that is, they do not overreact to every type of difficult or unpleasant situation but have a predilection to react excessively to certain events.

The therapist should attempt to reconstruct with patients the stages in the development of their depression (Chapter 13). These include the formation of maladaptive attitudes as the result of early experiences, the sensitization to particular types of stresses, and the precipitation of the depression as the result of a gross traumatic event or of more insidious influences. By reviewing their history in this way, patients are able to see their psychological disturbance in terms of specific problems rather than in terms of symptoms. The increased objectivity and understanding removes the mystery and may then provide a measure of mastery of the problems.

A patient suffering from intermittent depression reported that he had been feeling blue all day. At first he had no idea what had initiated his depressed feeling; he recalled that when he awoke he felt quite good. As he reported this he remembered that he started to feel somewhat below par when his wife did not respond immediately to his cheerful conversation at breakfast. In recounting this episode he became visibly upset. He then realized that he had felt rejected by his wife's silence—even though he knew that she was very tired because it had been her turn to get up at night with their colicky baby, and she had been up most of the night.

Tracing back his patterns of reaction, the patient recognized that he generally responded adversely whenever he did not get much attention. In grade school, for instance, where he was the teacher's pet, he felt hurt whenever the teacher praised another student or did not pay him a compliment. That he got more praise than any other student in the class did not relieve his feelings on the few occasions when he did not get praise. He recalled that later he felt similarly rejected when any of his close friends did not show the usual amount of warmth or camaraderie. Both his parents were very warm and indulgent people, and he was aware of always wanting their approval (which he usually got) as well as that of almost everybody else he met.

In reviewing the cause-and-effect sequences, the patient recognized that he had a pattern of reading rejection into any situation in which he did not get preferential treatment. He could see the inappropriateness of this reaction. He realized, furthermore, that he depended on getting constant approval to maintain his sense of worthwhileness. When the approval was not forthcoming, he was prone to react with hurt feelings. In applying this formulation to his reaction to his wife that morning, he realized that he had misinterpreted her behavior. As he said, "I guess I got it all wrong. She wasn't rejecting me. She simply was too tired to talk to me. I took it though as a sign of her not liking me and I felt bad about it."

Among the more common situations that produce disproportionate or inappropriate reactions in the depression-prone patient are failing to reach a particular goal, being excluded from a group, being rejected by another person, receiving criticism, and not receiving expected approval, encouragement, or guidance. Although such situations might be expected to produce transient unpleasant reactions in the average person, they may produce prolonged feelings of disappointment or hopelessness in the depression-prone person.

By being primed in advance to recognize his or her typical overreaction, the patient is fortified when the specific stress occurs and is less likely to be overwhelmed by it. It is generally possible for the therapist to point out the precise characteristics of the exaggerated reaction, namely, that the patient is reacting according to a repetitive pattern rather than to the specific features of the reality situation. The patient feels overwhelmed or hopeless, for example, not because the situation is overwhelming or insoluble but because he or she construes it that way. By referring to the past history, the therapist can demonstrate how the maladaptive pattern got started and was repeated on various occasions.

One woman, for instance, felt sad and unwanted whenever a friend or acquaintance had a party and did not invite her. Intense and prolonged feelings of rejection were aroused, although she was very popular and was, in truth, invited to more parties than she had time to attend. We were able to date the onset of this rejection pattern to early adolescence when she entered junior high school. At that time she was excluded from various cliques that the other girls formed. She vividly remembered sitting alone in the cafeteria and thinking that she was socially undesirable and inferior to the other girls. In therapy, she was able to recognize that the rejection pattern was mobilized inappropriately in her adult life. Her concept, "I have no friends and nobody wants me," was no longer valid. Until it was pointed out that she was simply reliving a past experience, in a sense, she tended to believe that not being invited to a party indicated that she did not really have any friends.

Neutralizing Automatic Thoughts

The second approach in insight therapy consists of the patient's focusing on his or her specific sadness-generating cognitions. In the mild or moderately ill depressed patient, these thoughts are often at the periphery of awareness and require special focusing in order for the patient to recognize them. In psychoanalytical terminology, they would probably be regarded as preconscious. In the more severely ill depressed patient, however, these thoughts are at the center of the patient's phenomenal field and tend to dominate the thought content.

This kind of depression-generating cognition seems to be a highly condensed representation of more elaborate ideas. The ideas are apparently compressed into a kind of shorthand, and a rather complicated thought occurs within a split second. Albert Ellis[37] referred to these thoughts as "self-statements" or "internalized verbalizations." He explained these thoughts as "things that the patient tells himself."

Although both the psychoanalysts and Ellis were correct in their respective observations, a new term was needed to convey the dual nature (preconscious to conscious) of such ideation. These types of cognitions were labeled automatic thoughts in the first edition of this book.[21]

As pointed out in Chapter 10, these self-statements or cognitions reflect the distortions that occur in the depressed state. As a result of these distortions, patients experience dysphoria. But when they can identify the distorted cognitions and can acquire objectivity toward them and correct them, they can neutralize some of their pathogenic quality.

Pinpointing Depressive Cognitions

At the beginning of therapy the patient is generally aware only of the following sequence: event or stimulus→affect. He must be trained to fill in the link between the stimulus and the affect: stimulus→cognition→affect.

A patient, for example, reported that he felt blue every time he made a mistake, and he could not understand why he should feel this way. He fully accepted the notion that there was nothing wrong in making mistakes and that it was an inevitable part of living. He was instructed to focus on his thoughts the next time he felt an unpleasant affect in connection with making a mistake. At the next interview he reported the observation that whenever he made a mistake he would think, "I'm a dope," or "I never do anything right," or "How can anybody be so dumb." After having one of these thoughts he would become depressed. By becoming aware of the self-criticisms, however, he was able to recognize how unreasonable they were. This recognition seemed to remove the sting from his blue reactions.

The automatic thoughts bear a relationship not only to unpleasant affect but also to many of the other phenomena of depression. Loss of motivation, for example, is based on such ideas as "I won't be able to do it," or "If I do this, I will only feel worse." Examples of the influence of the depressive thinking on motivation are found in Chapter 12.

As patients become more adept at recognizing the precise wording of their automatic thoughts, they are less influenced by them. They can view them as though from a distance and can assess their validity. The processes of recognition and distancing—metacognitive or "mindfulness" processes—are the initial steps in neutralizing the automatic thoughts.

Identifying Idiosyncratic Content

As patients gain experience in recognizing their cognitions, they become ready to identify the common themes among the cognitions that produce unpleasant feelings. In order to help them to categorize their cognitions, the therapist generally points out the major depressive themes, such as deprivation, self-reproach, or sense of inferiority. It is important to emphasize that of the innumerable ways in which they can interpret their life experiences they tend to perseverate in a few stereotyped interpretations or explanations; they may, for example, repeatedly interpret any interpersonal difficulty or dissension as indicating their own deficiency. It is also important to point out to them how these depressive cognitions actually represent distortions of reality.

It is often difficult for patients to accept the idea that their interpretations are incorrect, or at least inaccurate. In fact, the more depressed a patient is, the more difficult it is for him or her to regard the depressive cognitions with any degree of objectivity.

Recognizing Formal Characteristics of Cognitions

To increase depressed patients' objectivity toward their cognitions and to help them evaluate them, it is often helpful to point out some of the characteristics of the cognitions. This not only helps patients to identify them, but also gives them a chance to question their authenticity.

It is often valuable to make a distinction for the patient between "two types of thinking." The first type is the higher-level type of thinking that involves judgment, weighing the evidence, and considering alternative explanations (secondary process). The lower-level form of cognition, in contrast, tends to be relatively rapid and does not seem to involve any complicated logical processes (primary process).

One of the characteristics of the lower-level cognitions is that they tend to be automatic. They arise as if by reflex and are generally not the result of deliberation or careful reasoning. A patient observed that when she approached a task (preparing a meal, writing a letter, phoning a client) she immediately had the thought, "I can't do it." When she focused her attention on this thought, she recognized its arbitrariness and was able to assume some detachment toward it. A patient who has been successful in specifying the idiosyncratic cognitions generated by certain specific situations is in a better position to prepare to deal with them when they arise.

Another important characteristic of the depressive cognitions is their *involuntary* quality. In the more severe cases, particularly, it is apparent that these cognitions continuously invade the phenomenal field, and that the patient has little power to ward them off or to focus attention on something else. Even when severely depressed patients are determined to think rationally about a situation and make an objective judgment, they are apt to be diverted by the relentless intrusion of the depressive cognitions. This perseverating and compelling quality of the depressive cognitions may be so strong as to make any form of insight therapy fruitless at this stage.

In less severely ill patients, the recognition of the involuntary aspect of the cognitions helps to drive home that they are not the result of any deliberation or reasoning. The patients are able to look on them as a kind of obsession that intrudes into their more rational thinking but does not have to be given any particular truth value.

One of the crucial characteristics of these cognitions in terms of psychotherapy is that they seem plausible to the patient. Even normal people tend to accept the validity of their thoughts without subjecting them to any kind of careful scrutiny. The problem is compounded for the depressed patient because the idiosyncratic cognitions seem especially plausible or real. At times, the more incongruous these cognitions may appear to the therapist, the more plausible they may seem to the patient. The more reasonable the thought seems to be, the greater is the affective reaction. The converse also seems to be true: the more intense the affective state, the more credible the depressive cognitions are to the patient. When the intensity of the affect is reduced through antidepressant drugs, there is a diminution in the compelling quality of the cognitions. This seems to indicate an interaction between cognition and affect.

Distinguishing "Ideas" from "Facts"

After patients become experienced in recognizing the idiosyncratic content and other characteristics of the cognitions, the therapeutic work consists of training them to evaluate their validity or accuracy. This procedure consists essentially of the application of the rules of evidence and logic to the cognitions and the consideration of alternative explanations or interpretations by the patient.

In examining the validity of a cognition, patients first must learn to distinguish between thinking and believing; that is, simply because they think something is so does not, ipso facto, mean they should believe it. Despite the often apparent sophistication of a patient, it is necessary to point out that thoughts are not equivalent to external reality, and, no matter how convincing they may seem, they should not be accepted unless validated by some objective procedure.

A patient, for instance, had the thought that his girlfriend no longer liked him. Instead of treating this notion as a hypothesis, he accepted it as an actuality. He then used this notion to explain recent differences in his girlfriend's behavior and thus fortified his acceptance of the idea. The goal of therapy is to help patients shift from this type of deductive analysis of experience to more inductive procedures. By checking their observations, by taking into account all the data, and by considering other hypotheses to explain the events, they are less prone to equate automatic thoughts with reality.

Checking Observations

The validation of patients' interpretations and judgments depends on checking the accuracy and completeness of the initial observations. On reflection, patients frequently discover that their original impression of a situation was distorted or that they jumped to a conclusion too quickly and thus ignored or rejected salient details that were not compatible with that conclusion. A professor, for example, was downcast and complained that he was "slipping" because "nobody showed up" for a lecture. On reexamining the evidence, he realized that this was his initial impression, but that in actuality most of the seats in the lecture hall were filled. Having made an incorrect preliminary judgment, he had failed to correct it until he was helped to reexamine the evidence.

A woman told me she had "made a fool out of myself" in a job interview the day before. She felt humiliated and downcast up to the time of our appointment. I then inquired, "What actually happened in the interview?" As she recounted the details of the interview, she realized that she had handled it rather well and that her negative judgment was based on only one short portion of the interview.

Responding to Depressive Cognitions

Once the patient has established that a particular cognition is invalid, it is important for him or her (or the therapist) to neutralize its effects by stating precisely why it is inaccurate, inappropriate, or invalid. By verbalizing the reasons that the idea was erroneous, the patient is able to reduce the intensity and frequency of the idea as well as of the accompanying affect.

A depressed patient, for instance, found that no matter how fastidiously she cleaned a drawer or closet, she thought that it was still dirty. This made her feel discouraged until she began to counter the thought with the following rebuttal: "I'm a good housekeeper—which I know and other people have told me. There's absolutely no sign of dirt. It's just as clean as it ever is when I'm not depressed. There may be a few specks of dust but that's not dirt." On another occasion, when she started to prepare a roast, she had the thought, "I won't be able to do it." She reasoned the problem through and verbalized to herself, "I've done this many times before. I may be a little slower than usual because I'm depressed but I know what to do and if I think it out step-by-step there's no reason why I can't do it." She felt heartened after this and finished preparing the meal.

It is often helpful for patients to label the particular paralogical mechanisms involved in the depressive cognition, for example, overgeneralization, arbitrary inference, selective abstraction, or magnification (Chapter 12). If they can say to themselves, "I'm taking this out of context," or "I'm jumping to conclusions," or "I'm exaggerating," they may be able to reduce the power of the depressive cognition.

Weighing Alternative Explanations

Another method of neutralizing the inaccurate negative interpretations is to consider alternative explanations. For instance, a patient who was exceptionally personable and popular would characteristically interpret any reduction of enthusiasm toward her as a sign of rejection and also as evidence that she was unlikable. After some training in dealing with her idiosyncratic cognitions, she reported the following incident. She was conversing on the telephone with an old friend when the friend said she had to hang up because she had an appointment for a haircut. The patient's immediate thought was, "She doesn't like me," and she felt sad and disappointed. Applying the technique of alternative explanations, she countered with the following: "Marjorie has been my friend for many years. She has always shown that she likes me. I know she has an appointment today, and that is obviously the reason why she had to hang up." Her initial interpretation was part of a stereotyped pattern and excluded the proffered explanation. When the patient reviewed the episode and considered the possible explanations she was able to accept her friend's explanation as more probable than her automatic interpretations.

Validating Basic Premises

Although the technique just described deals directly with the specific cognitions, the operation to be described in this section is directed toward patients' underlying chronic misconceptions, prejudices, and superstitions about themselves and their world. Allied to these are the assumptions basic to the way individuals set goals, assess and modify behavior, and explain adverse occurrences; these assumptions underlie the injunctions, debasements, criticisms, punitiveness, and blame patients direct to themselves. The aim to modify these chronic attitudes and patterns (schemas) is based on the thesis that they partly determine the content of the individual's cognitions. It should follow that a basic modification or attenuation of these schemas would modify the way a person organizes and interprets specific experiences, sets goals, and goes about achieving them.

The content of the chronic attitudes may be readily inferred by examining the recurrent themes in patients' cognitive responses to particular situations and in their free associations (themes of personal deficiency, debility, and hopelessness). Further information about their basic premises and assumptions may be obtained by asking either what they base a particular conclusion on or their reasons for a specific judgment. An inquiry into their values, opinions, and beliefs will yield additional data. Some idea of the schemas used in approaching their problems or in attaining goals may be obtained by an examination of their self-instructions and self-reproaches. One of the useful features of this approach is that it attempts to correct the major premises or assumptions that form the basis for deductive thinking. Since the predominance of deductive (as opposed to inductive) thinking is an important determinant of the cognitive distortions in depression, any correction of the invalid major premises will tend to reduce the erroneous conclusions.

Ideas such as the following illustrate the typical assumptions and premises underlying the cognitive distortions in depression: "It is very bad to make a mistake"; "If anything goes wrong, it's my fault"; "I'm basically unlucky and bring bad luck to myself and everybody else"; "If I don't continue to make a lot of money, I will go bankrupt"; "I really am quite stupid and my academic success is the result of clever faking"; "Trouble with constipation is a sign of disintegration."

Let us say that a patient reports, "Everything I did today was wrong" or "Everybody has been pushing me around" or "I'm getting uglier every day." The therapist may review with the patient the evidence for these conclusions and may attempt to demonstrate that the ideas are exaggerations or frank misinterpretations. Often, however, the ideas are so strong that the patient cannot even contemplate the possibility that they could be inaccurate. In such cases, the force of the ideas may be weakened by dissecting the network of underlying assumptions.

A depressed woman of 40 had strong suicidal wishes. She justified these as follows: "What's the use of living? I've got to die some time anyhow. I'm just prolonging something that's deteriorating. It's a losing battle, so I might as well get out now before I've deteriorated completely." Rebuttals to the effect that she was still relatively young, attractive, and healthy and that she still had many potential years of happiness did not influence her thinking. She clung to the notion that she was decaying and that, if she lived, she would soon experience the horror of physical disintegration.

One day, in looking in the mirror, she observed that the image appeared to be that of her mother during her terminal illness. She turned her head in disgust and felt more depressed. Although she realized that the reflection was hers, not her mother's, she could not shake the belief that she had already deteriorated so much that she now looked like her dying mother.

Drawing on this information, the therapist said to the patient, "Your whole idea of quitting life is based on one premise: you believe that you are following in your mother's footsteps. You got the notion when she was dying that when you reached her age [40 years] you would start to have strokes and would go to pieces. The truth of the matter is that all our tests have shown that your physical health is perfect. Your mother had severe diabetes since childhood and she became blind and had her strokes as a complication of the diabetes. However, you don't have diabetes and, in fact, you don't have any physical disease."

The therapist then explained to the patient how she had identified herself with her mother and how this formed the basis for the premise that she was starting to deteriorate. She had, without fully realizing it, adopted the formula: getting old (more than 40) equals becoming deteriorated and ugly. By pinpointing this formula, we were able to discuss its validity. As she was able to see the arbitrariness of this equation, her ideas that she was ugly and deteriorating started to fade, as did her suicidal wishes.

Sometimes the patient can see the fallacy of his or her basic assumptions without any difficulty. However, the simple acknowledgment of their irrationality may not change them. They may continue to be manifest in repetitive automatic thoughts. It is often necessary to examine the invalid assumptions repeatedly and to encourage the patient to state the reasons they are invalid. Sometimes, the patient may be directed to specify the argument in favor of the invalid assumption and then the argument against it. At other times the argument supporting an invalid assumption may be suggested, and the patient induced to supply the rebuttal.

A scientist felt sad and empty whenever she failed to get recognition for her performance. We were able to establish that she had a set of interlocking premises: "It is of utmost importance that I become famous. The only gratification I can get out of life is by being acclaimed by everybody. If I do not achieve fame, then my life is worthless and meaningless." If these premises were correct, then it would be inevitable that she would feel ungratified and empty when she missed out on recognition. If they were invalid, then they could be modified and she would be less subject to feelings of desolation when she failed to get recognition.

To test the validity of these assumptions, the therapist presented the following argument. "If these premises are true, we would expect the following to happen. One, that you never obtain gratification from anything except recognition. Two, that recognition has brought you gratification. Three, that nothing in life means anything or is worth anything to you except fame."

Upon hearing this argument, the patient was quick to provide a rebuttal. "I have gotten pleasure from lots of things that don't involve recognition. I enjoy my family and friends. I get a lot of satisfaction from reading and listening to classical records and going to concerts. Also I really do enjoy my work and would like what I'm doing even if I did not get any recognition at all. Besides, when I do get recognition, I don't get much feeling of satisfaction from it. Actually, I find that personal relationships are more satisfying than getting an article published."

Modifying Mood by Induced Fantasies

Some depressed patients report spontaneous fantasies (daydreams) that have a gloomy content such as deprivation, personal inadequacy, and thwarting. When they contemplate an event in the near or distant future, they have a pictorial image of a negative outcome.

A depressed man sat down to prepare his list of items to be purchased at a grocery store. He then experienced the following fantasy, which he later reported to me: "I went into the supermarket with my grocery list. I went from counter to counter and I couldn't find what I wanted. I then noticed that people were looking at me peculiarly as though they thought I was crazy. I felt so humiliated I had to leave without buying anything." As a result he did not go to the supermarket that day.

It is noteworthy that while he was having this fantasy, the patient experienced intense humiliation as though the fantasized event was occurring in reality. In an attempt to help him deal with the expectation of frustration and humiliation, he was asked to imagine the scene in the supermarket again. This time he felt less humiliation. After imagining the same scene three more times, he no longer felt any unpleasant affect in association with the fantasy. He remarked, "I can see that I was really exaggerating the problem in my daydream." Following this interview, the patient was able to do his shopping without any difficulty.

This example illustrates that patients may react to their fantasies in much the same way that they react to their automatic thoughts. Patients may be trained to deal therapeutically with their fantasies in much the same way as they can deal with maladaptive ideas of a verbal nature.

By having patients repeat the depressive fantasy during the therapy session, the therapist can help them gain greater objectivity toward the actual real life situation. This kind of rehearsal may enable them to undertake a task that they had previously avoided.

Sometimes spontaneous modification of the content of the fantasy may be achieved by simple repetition of the fantasy. A patient was feeling pessimistic about his job and had a fantasy on the way to the office: "I went into my superior's office with a suggestion. He got very angry with me. I felt I had stepped beyond the proper bounds." The feeling that accompanied this fantasy was discouragement and humiliation. When asked to imagine the scene again, he experienced a repetition of the same unpleasant affects.

The patient was then asked to imagine the scene once more. This time the fantasy was as follows: "My boss was interested in what I had to say. He wanted more information. I felt that there was a mutual interchange between two professionals." The affect accompanying this fantasy was pleasant. Concomitantly, the patient's generally pessimistic mood about the anticipated events of the day lifted, and he went to work feeling more optimistic and self-confident. The actual outcome of his interaction with his superior was similar to that in the pleasant fantasy.

In other cases it is possible to alleviate pessimism by inducing the patient to have more realistic fantasies about anticipated events. Another technique of combating the sense of inadequacy or deprivation is to suggest that the patient recall in pictorial form certain past successes or gratifications. Upon revivifying the past memories, the patients often experience a sense of gratification that persists for the rest of the day.

The technique of fantasy induction serves much the same purpose as examining maladaptive self-verbalizations. By examining their gloomy fantasies, patients are able to loosen their grip, reality test them, and consider more favorable outcomes. Moreover, the induction of pleasant fantasies helps to neutralize sadness and pessimism.

Case Illustration

A case illustration provides an example of the typical structure and flow of cognitive therapy. K.M. was an attractive, pleasant young woman who had been unsuccessfully treated for ongoing dysthymic disorder by an "eclectic," nondirective therapist. One presenting concern was that the new sales management position she had recently accepted was "an impossible situation," since, in her view, "nobody could ever manage all these people."

Two prominent thoughts were found to recur, both outside therapy and in session. First, she thought that persons under her supervision were grossly inadequate to handle job responsibilities. Second, she viewed herself as unable to change the situation, calling it "completely impossible and hopeless."

In educating K.M. to cognitive treatment, we considered examples of her current thinking in order to identify automatic thoughts and beliefs. The dual and repetitive thoughts "they're incompetent" and "the situation is impossible" were shown to be interrelated. Because she thought of the people she supervised as intractable, she assumed change to be unlikely. She was able to link these perceptions to her recently exacerbated depressed mood and negative ruminations, as well as to her avoidance of certain administrative duties, such as providing job performance evaluations in a timely manner.

After reviewing therapist and patient responsibilities in therapy, the therapist focused the cognitive therapy sessions on teaching K.M. concrete methods to hypothesis-test the negative predictions, and developed specific between-session homework. The therapist discussed with K.M. the dysfunctional and harmful recurrent cognitions, noted above, and suggested homework to monitor thoughts, especially to note mood changes that might correlate with increases/decreases in specific cognitions. The patient was also taught to identify the relationship between negative thoughts ("it is impossible") and core beliefs ("they are all incompetent").

In order to gain a more complete picture of the presenting problems, the therapist employed a variety of instruments, including cognition checklists and self-report inventories of depression and hopelessness. Individual responses on the standard self-report inventories were discussed in therapy and were individualized for K.M., and her own idiosyncratic automatic thoughts (e.g., "they're incompetent" and "the situation is impossible"), were examined.

Empirical hypothesis testing, or "cognitive experiments," was used. She was encouraged to break down the work assignments of employees into manageable units, and thereby to facilitate their success experiences. Her experience with this method helped disconfirm her core negative beliefs about her employees' abilities, and her negative evaluations and ruminations were mitigated. She changed her viewpoint concerning her employees through reviewing actual accomplishments, such as sales reports of individual employees and profits.

Case Illustration: Relapse Prevention

After K.M.'s mood was stabilized, the therapist suggested (and K.M. agreed) a focus on "chronic beliefs." A time frame of 3 months was suggested for this work. Sessions during this time period focused on K.M.'s past history in a family with several accomplished siblings. One sibling was described as "extremely cynical" concerning other people's abilities and intelligence, including those of K.M. There was a considerable age difference between

K.M. and this sibling, and questions revealed the tendency to take this sibling's word as absolute. Thus, the dual beliefs about her employees' incompetence and her own inadequacies seemed parallel to—and perhaps incorporated from—a significant person in the patient's life. K. M. readily recognized these possible origins of the core maladaptive belief. This realization served as the focus for relapse prevention.

The therapist and patient then collaborated to examine the links between core beliefs and dysfunctional thinking, and arranged creative ways to test the content of the dysfunctional conceptualizations. In general, she was taught to question and test her dysfunctional beliefs about herself, other people, and her main strategies of relating to others.

Treating Bipolar Disorder: Drugs and Psychotherapy

Since the time of Campbell's *Manic-Depressive Disease,*[4] the treatment of bipolar disorder has undergone great innovation (e.g., Newman et al.[38]). This is especially true in the last two decades.[39]

The question of the possible utility of psychotherapies for relapse prevention is especially relevant, given the natural course of bipolar affective disorder. Despite the value of lithium in long-term prevention of relapse, full protection (zero recurrences) over one year is obtained in only about one-third of patients.[39] A randomized trial in bipolar patients by Colom et al.[40] tested whether psychological-educational intervention can reduce relapse when added to standard pharmacotherapy. Study participants included 120 bipolar outpatients matched for age and sex (Young Mania Rating Scale score <6, Hamilton Depression Rating Scale-17 score <8). All had been in remission for at least 6 months prior to the study, and all were receiving standard pharmacologic treatment. Subjects received standard psychiatric care, plus either 21 sessions of group psychoeducation or 21 nonstructured group meetings. Assessment was conducted monthly during the treatment period and throughout 2-year follow-up.

Using group psychoeducational procedures, they found that only 38 percent of those in the educational group relapsed, compared to 60 percent in the control group, during the 21-week treatment period. At the end of a 2-year follow-up period, 92 percent of those receiving only standard psychiatric care (pharmacologic treatment) had experienced relapse compared to 67 percent of those for whom a psychoeducational component had been added. By excluding mild episodes (hypomania) from the data analysis, they found recurrence rates to be 87 percent for standard drug therapy versus 63 percent in the psychoeducational group approach.[40]

Citing two promising pilot studies, Lam et al.[20] used a randomized controlled design to study the effects of cognitive therapy in relapse prevention for bipolar affective disorder. They hypothesized that cognitive therapy, in conjunction with mood stabilizers, might be well suited to teaching patients to cope with bipolar illness.

Treatment-manual-based cognitive therapy was devised, which added to the standard approach used in treating depression. New elements included (1) teaching the diathesis-stress model and the need for combining psychological and medical approaches; (2) monitoring mood, especially prodromal symptoms, and developing skills to obviate expansion of the full-blown syndrome; (3) addressing the value of sleep and routine to avoid sleep deprivation acting as a trigger for a bipolar episode; and (4) treatment of compensatory behaviors, or extreme striving, which patients sometimes use to make up for time perceived to have been lost during previous periods of illness.

The study design included 103 patients with bipolar I disorder. All had relapsed frequently, despite being treated with mood stabilizers. Subjects were randomized into a CT group or a control group, with both groups receiving mood stabilizers and regular psychiatric follow-up. The CT group received an average of 14 sessions of CT during the first 6 months and 2 booster sessions in the second 6 months.

Results found an overall relapse rate of 53 percent during the 12-month treatment period. Relapse rate for the CT group was 28 percent at month 6, and 44 percent at month 12. Relapse rate for the control group was 50 percent at month 6, and 75 percent at month 12. In addition, the CT group had significantly fewer days in a bipolar episode, and fewer admissions for bipolar episode. Moreover, they showed significantly higher social functioning, fewer mood symptoms on the monthly mood questionnaires, and significantly less fluctuation in manic symptoms.

Compared to the use of psychoeducational procedures, reviewed above,[40] it might be noted that CT produced a lower relapse rate (28 percent) compared to educational therapy (38 percent) at a comparable time in treatment (month 6). Moreover, the CT group relapse rate of only 44 percent at month 12 (versus 75 percent for the control group) appears substantially less than the 67 percent rate found using lithium alone for long-term relapse prevention.[39] Limitations of this study were said to include the absence of controls for sleep routine and better medication compliance in the patients receiving CT.[20]

Prevention of Suicide

By focusing on core beliefs, cognitive therapy aims to engender more enduring change. Brown et al.[41] tested the effects of cognitive therapy in the prevention of repeat suicide attempts. In a randomized controlled trial, a 10-session cognitive therapy intervention was applied to adults who recently had attempted suicide. They were followed for 18 months. Those who received cognitive therapy had a significantly lower reattempt rate and were 50 percent less likely to reattempt suicide than participants in the usual care group, which included tracking and referral services. The cognitive therapy group reported lower depression severity at 6 months, 12 months, and 18 months, and less hopelessness than the usual care group at 6 months.

Prevention of Relapse

A study by Klein et al.[42] tested the efficacy of the cognitive-behavioral analysis system of psychotherapy (CBASP) as a maintenance treatment for chronic forms of MDD. This approach is said to combine "elements of behavioral, cognitive, interpersonal, and psychodynamic psychotherapy" (p. 682).

Strengths of this study include rigorous diagnosis of the sample, inclusion of a no-treatment control condition, blinded raters to assess MDD symptoms, both self-report and interview assessment of depression, and random assignment to monthly CBASP or assessment only for 1 year. The study included 82 patients who had responded to acute and continuation phase CBASP. Results found that fewer patients in the CBASP condition experienced a recurrence.[42]

Limitations in the Klein et al.[42] study include the fact that the group that was compared to CBASP received no treatment, but rather assessment only. This absence of a treatment control group means that factors such as placebo effects could account for the observed differences in relapse. Moreover, even had such controls been utilized, the mixture of diverse treatment elements that constitute CBASP would allow no theoretical conclusions concerning the reasons for the prevention of relapse, had such findings been unequivocally demonstrated. Thus, the efficacy of classic behavior therapy remains undetermined.

A study by Bockting et al.[43] provided a randomized controlled trial of relapse/recurrence prevention using group cognitive therapy. The study compared treatment as usual, including continuation of pharmacotherapy, to treatment as usual plus brief cognitive therapy. Patients ($n = 187$) were at high risk for recurrent depression.

Cognitive therapy was shown to provide a significant protective effect for relapse/recurrence to major depression over the two-year assessment period. The protective effect was especially pronounced in those patients with 5 or more previous episodes (41 percent of the sample). In this group, cognitive therapy reduced relapse/recurrence by 26 percent (from 72 percent to 46 percent).

Psychotherapeutic Change Processes

Theoretically, the correction of distressful or dysfunctional emotional states and syndromes occurs through the distancing (metacognitive) process, which may be activated through diverse routes (e.g., cognitive, behavioral, pharmacological). One distinguishing characteristic of the examination of one's beliefs is the active versus passive monitoring of conscious experience. The "intentional," deliberative control function of conscious experience is accentuated (Beck,[44] pp. 242–245; Moore;[45] Reisberg,[46] p. 363).

This mode of information processing is characterized by an increased cognizance of one's experiences and of the manner in which experience is organized, or conceptually structured, and it stands in contrast to the automatic level, in which the person acts with less conscious mediation. Thus, the automatic and controlled processing of information (meaning) is corrected through cognitive therapy.

Regardless of the approach taken, cognitive theory predicts that the degree of symptomatic improvement depends on the magnitude of change in the information processing system. Sustained recovery will occur when the underlying beliefs are corrected, rather than only the negative thinking. Theoretically, then, the modification of dysfunctional information processing is the final pathway to correct emotional disorders. Changes in cognition may be essential for (a central part of) the symptomatic improvement observed during recovery from depression.

Several studies have addressed the process of cognitive therapy. (For a review of the tests of psychotherapy—compared specifically to pharmacotherapy in randomized clinical trials—see Chapter 16.) Simons et al.[47] tested the lasting benefit of cognitive therapy compared to a 3-month treatment of antidepressant medication (without medication continuation). The authors, based on their findings, concluded that cognitive therapy and pharmacotherapy may differ in how they lead patients to consider their depressive symptoms. In cognitive therapy, patients come to view their symptoms as "cues for hope," or as reminders to strive to use the various cognitive and behavioral strategies they have learned from their therapist. Such learned coping skills may account for the differential effects between cognitive therapy and pharmacotherapy that were observed in this study.[47]

Robins and Hayes[48] concluded that several studies support specific components of cognitive therapy to be associated with change: "interventions designed to identify, reality test, and correct distorted conceptualizations and the dysfunctional schemata that underlie them" (p. 207). Teaching hypothesis-testing by means of concrete methods and between-session practice of such skills appear to be active ingredients of CT, but "further research is clearly warranted" (p. 207).

Rush et al.[49] conducted an analysis of the data collected by Rush et al.[50] which compared 35 patients treated with cognitive therapy ($n = 18$) or pharmacotherapy (imipramine HCL) ($n = 17$). Patients were unipolar depressed outpatients. Rush et al.[49] used cross-lagged panel analyses to evaluate the temporal order of changes in views of the self, hopelessness, mood, motivation and vegetative symptoms. They found that, during weeks 1–2 of treatment, patients improved first on measures of hopelessness, followed by improvement in self-view, motivation, mood, and vegetative symptoms. During weeks 2–3, hopelessness preceded improvement in mood. Finally, from weeks 3–4 self-view and mood improved before motivation, and mood changed prior to vegetative symptoms. Overall conclusions were that cognitive therapy may lead to therapeutic changes in cognitive factors (view of self and future), and thereafter to improvements in other symptoms. This was not found to be true for drug treatment. Findings are consistent with the hypothesis that alterations in negative thinking and mood lead to improvements in other depressive symptoms.

For relapse prevention, change may be necessary at the "structural" or schematic level. If a schema is sufficiently permeable, then it should be possible to modify its content, or "beliefs." For example, a schema—that is, its content—can be modified from dysfunctional to functional. A person may have a low-level schema "I am a failure," or even more dysfunctional, "Since I am a failure, I am worthless." These beliefs could be modified to the following, "I have failed at some things and succeeded at others, so it's a trade-off"; "Even if I am a failure, it does not mean I am worthless."

The dysfunctional schemas become prepotent when they are activated, usually through a congruent external stimulus but possibly also through some internal, endocrine, or other biological derangement. Consistent with this, Segal & Ingram[51] reviewed the issue of the activation of schemas and concluded that studies that ensured that the cognitive constructs to be tested were activated have supported cognitive theory. They suggestd that future studies must do a better job of triggering diathesis-stress processes in order to test the causal role of theorized constructs. More recent preliminary evidence from prospective studies has identified cognitive style not only in unipolar depressive disorder—but also in bipolar disorder—as an important variable in need of further investigation.[52,53]

Oei and Free[54] reviewed 44 outcome or process studies of therapy with depression. The categories of treatment included cognitive therapy, drug therapy, other psychological therapy, and wait-list controls. They concluded that cognitive change occurs in all treatments, and that the relationship between cognitive change and depression is not unique to cognitive therapy. Cognitive change may be the final pathway to change across diverse systems of therapy.

Chapter 16
Evaluating Depression Treatments: Randomized Controlled Trials

Outcome and Follow-Up Data

In this chapter we focus on outcome studies comparing psychological to pharmacological treatments. Understanding the relative merits of these respective approaches has obvious clinical implications. We consider studies from more recent to earlier trials, recognizing that (in general) the more recent studies offer more rigorous experimental design and controls.

Although there have been skeptics,[1] previous meta-analyses[2,3] and reviews[4,5] have supported the efficacy of psychological treatments of depression. Bailar[6] suggested that conventional narrative literature reviews have special advantages, and pointed out that in no case in medicine have metaanalyses alone led to a major change in treatment policy. We have limited this *narrative* review to those studies that provide (1) a convincing basis for the diagnosis of major depression, (2) a comparison to clinical pharmacotherapy, (3) the source of patients treated, (4) the length of therapy, (5) completion rates, and (6) the percentage of patients that recovered following treatment.

Randomized Clinical Trials

Table 16-1 summarizes the randomized controlled trials. In a placebo-controlled trial, DeRubeis et al.[7] compared cognitive therapy to medications in treating moderate to severe depression. The study was conducted at the University of Pennsylvania and Vanderbilt University research clinics, with 240 patients (120 at each site) randomly assigned to treatments. The sample of patients in this study was described as "highly chronic or recurrent, with early onsets and a substantial rate of prior hospitalizations" (p. 412).[7] Comorbidity rates were found to be 72 percent for a concurrent Axis I disorder, and 48 percent for at least one Axis II disorder.

Of the 240 patients, 120 received 16 weeks of paroxetine (Paxil), up to 50

TABLE 16-1. Trials Compare Psychotherapy and Pharmacotherapy Depression

Study	Overall conclusions	Patients entering treatment	Source(s) of patients	Basis for depression diagnosis	Length of therapy	Treatment comparisons	Treatment completion rates	% recovered	% remaining well after recovery
DeRubeis et al. (2005)	CT is as effective as drug therapy	240 F = 59% M = 41%	(1) referrals (2) advertisement	Structured Clinical interview and modified HRSD	16 weeks	(1) CT (n = 51) (2) PH (n - 101) (3) P-P (n - 52)	(1) CT-85% (2) PH-84% (3) P-P-87%	(1) CT-40.0% (2) PH-45.8% (3) P-P-25%	Not reported
Jarrett et al. (1999)	CT is an effective alternative to drug treatment	142 F = 68% M = 32%	(1) media (2) printed announcements (3) referrals	DSM-II-R, HRSD	10 weeks	(1) CT (n = 36) (2) PH (n = 36) (3) P-P (n = 36)	(1) CT-86% (2) PH-75% (3) P-P-36%	(1) CT-58% (2) PH-58% (3) P-P-28	Not reported
Hollon et al. (1992)	CT is as effective as drugs or combined cognitive-drug treatment	107 M = 20% F = 80%	(1) psychiatric treatment facility (2) mental health center	Research Diagnostic Criteria, BDI, GAS, HRSD, MMPI, MMPI-D, RDS	12 weeks	(1) CT (n = 16) (2) PH (n = 32) (3) CT + PH (n = 16)	(1) CT = 64% (2) PH = 56% (3) CT + PH = 64%	(1) CT = 50% (2) PH = 53% (3) CT + PH = 75%	Not reported
Bowers (1990)	CT + drugs is more effective than drugs alone or drugs and relaxation	33 M = 20% F = 80%	psychiatric hospital inpatients	ATQ, BDI, DAS, HRSD, HS	(1) CT + PH = 29 days (2) PH = 32 days (3) PH + relaxation = 27 days	(1) CT + PH (n = 10) (2) PH (n = 10) (3) PH + relaxation (n = 10)	(1) CT + PH = 91% (2) PH = 91% (3) PH + relaxation = 91%	(1) CT + PH = 80% (2) PH = 20% (3) PH + relaxation = 10%	Not reported

Study	Finding	N / Gender	Source	Measures	Duration	Groups (n)	Results	Results	Follow-up
Elkin et al. (1989)	CT is as effective drug treatment	239 M=30% F=70%	(1) psychiatric outpatients (2) self-referrals (3) mental health facilities	Research Diagnostic Criteria, BDI, GAS, HRSD, HSCL	16 weeks	(1) CT (n=37) (2) IPT (n=47) (3) IMI-CM (n=37) (4) PLA-CM (n=34)	(1) CT=68% (2) IPT=77% (3) IMI-CM=67% (4) PLA-CM=60%	(1) CT = 51% (2) IPT = 55% (3) IMI-CM=57% (4) PLA-CM=29%	Not reported
Miller et al. (1989)	CT adds to the effectiveness of pharmacotherapy for severely depressed patients	46 M=26% F=74%	psychiatric hospital inpatients	Diagnostic Interview Schedule, BDI, HRSD	During hospitalization + 20 weeks	(1) CT (n=15) (2) PH (n=17) (3) Social skills training n=14	(1) CT=67% (2) PH=59% (3) Social skills training=86%	(1) CT=80% (2) PH=41% (3) Social skills training=50%	Not reported
Covi & Lipman (1987)	CT and CT+PH are more effective than traditional therapy	70 M=40% F=60%	newspaper ads	Research Diagnostic Criteria, BDI, HRSD	14 weeks of individual and group therapy	(1) CT (n=27) (2) CT+PH (n=23) (3) Traditional group psychotherapy (n=20)	(1) CT=84% (2) CT+IMI=68% (3) TRAD=83%	(1) CT=52% (2) CT+IMI=61 (3) Traditional therapy=5	Not reported
Beck et al. (1985)	CT alone is as effective as combined cognitive-drug treatment.	33 M=27% F=73%	(1) self-referrals (2) professional referrals	Feighner's Diagnostic Criteria, BDI, HRSD	12 weeks 20 sessions	(1) CT (n=18) (2) CT+PH (n=15)	(1) CT=78% (2) CT+PH=73%	(1) CT=71% (2) CT+PH=36%	(1) CT=58% (2) CT+PH=82%

TABLE 16-1. (Continued)

Study	Overall conclusions	Patients entering treatment	Source(s) of patients	Basis for depression diagnosis	Length of therapy	Treatment comparisons	Treatment completion rates	% recovered	% remaining well after recovery
Murphy et al. (1984)	CT alone is as effective as combined cognitive-drug treatment.	87 M = 26% F = 74%	psychiatric outpatient hospital	Research Diagnostic Criteria, BDI, HRSD	12 weeks	(1) CT (n = 24) (2) PH (n = 24) (3) CT + PH (n = 22) (4) CT + Active placebo (n = 17)	(1) CT = 79% (2) PH = 67% (3) CT + PH = 82% (4) CT + Active Placebo = 100%	(1) CT = 53% (2) PH = 56% (3) CT + PH = 78% (4) CT + Active Placebo = 65%	Not reported
Blackburn et al. (1981)	While CT + drugs was most effective, CT alone was more effective than drugs alone	88 M = 28% F = 72%	(1) hospital outpatient clinics (2) a general practice clinic	Research Diagnostic Criteria, BDI	12–15 weeks	(1) CT (n = 22) (2) PH (n = 20) (3) CT + PH (n = 22)	(1) CT = 73% (2) PH = 71% (3) CT + PH = 73%	(1) CT = 77% (2) PH = 60% (3) CT + PH = 86%	Not reported
Rush et al. (1977)	CT was more effective than drugs	41 M = 37% F = 63%	Moderate and severe hospital outpatients	Feighner's Diagnostic Criteria, BDI, HRSD	12 weeks 20 sessions	(1) CT (n = 19) (2) PH (n = 22)	(1) CT = 95% (2) PH = 64%	(1) CT = 79% (2) PH = 22%	(1) CT = 67% (2) PH = 38%

Abbreviations: 1. Measures used—ATQ = automatic thoughts questionnaire; BDI = Beck depression inventory; CRT = cognitive response test; DAS = dysfunctional attitudes scale; GAS = global assessment scale; HRSD = Hamilton rating scale for depression; IDA = irritability, depression & anxiety (mood rating scale); LIFE-II-II = longitudinal interval follow-up evaluation II; MADS = Montgomery & Asberg depression scale; PSR = psychiatric status ratings; RDS = Raskin depression scale; SCL-90 = Hopkins symptom checklist; VAS = visual analogue scale. 2. Treatment comparisons—CT = cognitive therapy; PH = pharmacotherapy; IPT = interpersonal therapy; PLA-CM = placebo + clinical management; IMI-CM = IMI-CM + clinical management; TAU = treatment as usual.

milligrams daily; 60 patients were given pill-placebo; 60 received 16 weeks of cognitive therapy. For the 120 patients in the medication (paroxetine) group, augmentation with lithium or desipramine (Norpramine, Pertofrane) was initiated if positive clinical response was not achieved after 8 weeks.

Treatment completion rates were comparable between cognitive therapy and medication groups (see Table 16-1). After 16 weeks of therapy, 85 percent of the cognitive therapy group and 84 percent of the medication group remained in treatment. No significant differences in attrition rates were found between sites, or across conditions, after 8 weeks or after 16 weeks. Results at 8 weeks show the percentage recovered (Hamilton Rating Scale for Depression score of 12 or below) to be 50 percent for medications, 43 percent for cognitive therapy, and 25 percent for placebo. At 16 weeks, response rates were 58 percent in each of the active conditions: medications and cognitive therapy. "Remission" was defined in the same way as "response," but with the added stipulation of final Hamilton Rating Scale for Depression score of 7 or less. Remission rates were 46 percent for medications and 40 percent for cognitive therapy. A site-by-treatment interaction was found only at Vanderbilt, where medications were superior to cognitive therapy. Differing patient characteristics and experience levels of the cognitive therapists contributed to this interaction. The authors concluded that, with a high level of therapist experience or expertise, cognitive therapy is as effective as medications in initial treatment of moderate to severe major depression.[7]

Hollon et al.[8] reported on a comparison between cognitive therapy and imipramine hydrochloride tricyclic pharmacotherapy, singly and in combination. Patients were 107 nonpsychotic, nonbipolar depressed outpatients who were randomly assigned to treatment. Sixty-four percent of patients met criteria for recurrent depression. Of these, 27 percent had no previous major depressive episodes, whereas 37 percent did. Of the 107 patients assigned to treatment conditions, 43 (40 percent) dropped out before completing the 12 week protocol; 38 (35 percent) began but did not complete treatment; and 5 (5 percent) failed to begin treatment. These dropout rates did not differ significantly across the treatments, but medications were more likely to result in problematic reactions that prevented continuation. Two participants died by suicide, using study medication (p. 300; pp. 776-778).[4,8]

The Hollon et al.[8] study found no differences of symptom measures between the treatment groups (cognitive therapy versus drugs). Also, the sample as a whole was rated to be at least as severely depressed as the sample groups in the NIMH TDCRP[9] and other comparable studies. Results found that all three groups (drug, cognitive therapy, and combined drug and cognitive therapy) improved substantially from pretreatment to midtreatment (first six weeks). Greater than 90 percent of clinical improvement was found to occur within the first six weeks of treatment compared to the next six weeks, and only the combined cognitive therapy + drugs group continued to improve between six weeks (midtreatment) and 12 weeks (posttreatment).

Bowers[10] evaluated the treatment of 33 inpatients who were divided into three groups, including (1) cognitive therapy plus medication, (2) medication (nortriptyline) alone, and (3) relaxation therapy plus medication. All patients received "ward milieu" therapy. At sessions 1, 6, 12, and discharge, symptoms of depression and related cognitive variables (automatic thoughts and dysfunctional attitudes) were assessed. It was found that, in all groups, depressed symptoms and cognitive variables improved as a result of treatment. However, the group receiving cognitive therapy plus ward milieu therapy improved the most by the time of discharge.

The National Institute of Mental Health Collaborative study[9] is among the many that have addressed the question of effectiveness. Elkin et al.[9] compared the effectiveness of cognitive therapy to that of interpersonal therapy, imipramine hydrochloride plus "clinical management," and placebo plus "clinical management" (see Table 16-1). The experimenters randomly assigned 250 patients to the respective treatments. Of this number, 239 patients ($m = 30$ percent; $F = 70$ percent) actually entered treatment. The diagnosis of major depression was obtained by using Research Diagnostic Criteria. The overall conclusions of Elkin et al.[9] were stated as follows: "In analyses carried out on the total samples without regard to initial severity of illness (the primary analyses), there was no evidence of greater effectiveness of one of the psychotherapies as compared with the other and no evidence that either of the psychotherapies was significantly less effective than the standard reference treatment, imipramine plus clinical management" (p. 971). Patients showed significant reduction in measures of depression across treatments. Table 16-1 shows completion rates and percentage of patients recovering for each of the four treatment comparisons.

Among the group of patients in Elkin et al.[9] whose intake Hamilton Depression scores were 20 or greater, differences in favor of drug treatment (compared to both placebo and cognitive therapy) were found on a minority of relevant comparisons (p. 980). However, research site differences were found in the more severely depressed patients.[11] More specifically, differential effects of specific treatments were observed between sites. The authors concluded: "Until we unravel these findings, final judgment must be withheld about the specific effectiveness of the two psychotherapies with more severely depressed and impaired patients" (p. 980).[9] (Several other important issues concerning this study were reviewed by Jacobson and Hollon,[11] and interested readers may refer directly to their critique.)

Miller et al.[12] were interested in whether cognitive therapy might produce additional improvement in patients who were provided a standard regime of "hospital milieu," pharmacotherapy, and brief supportive psychotherapy (Table 16-1). Patients were recruited from the inpatient units at Butler Hospital, a private psychiatric hospital in Rhode Island. To study the possible incremental efficacy of cognitive therapy, 47 depressed inpatients were randomly assigned to one of three conditions. (Of these 47 patients, 46 actually entered treatment.) The patients in this study generally had an early onset and chronic course (mean of 6.7 previous depressive episodes), and 44 percent had a concurrent diagnosis of dysthymia. Treatments included (1) a "standard treatment" of hospital milieu, pharmacotherapy, medication, and management sessions; (2) cognitive therapy + standard treatment; and (3) social skills training + standard treatment. The "hospital milieu" treatment component consisted of several hospital activities that were standard treatment for all inpatients, such as meetings with nurses, occupational therapy, and social work evaluations. In order to provide the best possible pharmacotherapy, the usual procedure of increasing dosages of a single medication was replaced by utilizing at least 150 mg/day of two different medications thought to work through modification of different neurotransmitters. The medication protocol allowed much flexibility on the part of treating physicians, including the use of other types of agents such as neuroleptics and antianxiety drugs.

Both the cognitive therapy and social skills training treatments began after the second week of hospitalization and continued for a 20-week outpatient period. In both therapies, flexibility was allowed in the frequency of sessions provided. The three treatments began during hospitalization and continued after discharge for 20 weeks. Categorical analyses of outcomes defined "responders" in three ways: (1) a BDI score of 9 or less; (2) a modified HRSD score of less than 7; and (3) a SCl-90 General Symptom Index of at least 50 percent improvement from pretreatment symptom levels. Results across the three definitions were fairly consistent. Table 16-1 shows the percentage of responders as defined by HRSD scores at the end of outpatient treatment to be 80 percent response rate for cognitive therapy, 41 percent response rate for standard treatment, and 50 percent response rate for social skills training. The cognitive therapy and social skills training group scores significantly lower than the standard treatment group at the end of outpatient treatment, but not at the time of discharge from the hospital. Compared to pretreatment symptom levels, all treatment groups showed significant improvement both at the time of discharge from the hospital and at the end of outpatient treatment.

Covi and Lipman[13] evaluated whether the addition of drug treatment to cognitive therapy would result in greater clinical improvement than cognitive therapy alone (Table 16-1). Participants were 70 individuals (m = 40 percent, F = 60 percent) recruited from ads in daily newspapers. Participants met criteria for primary major depression based on Research Diagnostic Criteria. Those selected had depression of at least 1 month duration and cutoff scores of 20 on the BDI and 14 on the HRSD. These criteria were reviewed by an independent evaluator, a highly experienced psychiatrist who did not have access to the initial ratings. The independent evaluator was blind to the treatment conditions throughout treatment, and provided follow-up evaluations.

Treatment was conducted both in individual sessions and in group sessions, 15 patients per group. Therapists were a psychiatrist and a psychologist who had 2 years training in cognitive therapy. The treatment comparisons were cognitive therapy ($n = 27$), cognitive therapy + imipramine treatment ($n = 23$), and traditional psychotherapy ($n = 20$), which was based on "interpersonal-psychoanalytic" theories and provided a credible (placebo) control treatment. Results showed that end-point remission rates were 52 percent for cognitive therapy alone, 61 percent for cognitive therapy plus imipramine treatment, and 5 percent for interpersonal-psychoanalytic (traditional) psychotherapy. These differences were statistically significant at the end of therapy and at 3- and 9-month follow-up, both for the independent physician-rated Global Improvement Scale and the Beck Depression Inventory. Data were not reported on the percentage of each group remaining well after recovery.

Beck et al.[14] tested whether the combination of drugs and cognitive therapy improve the efficacy of either treatment alone in outpatients with nonbipolar depression (see Table 16-1). Prior knowledge of cognitive therapy and potential expectation biases were similar for the two groups. The research protocol was 20 sessions over a 12-week period. Therapists were three psychiatrists and six psychologists who had at least six months of experience prior to seeing their first study patient. Results showed comparable therapy completion rates for the two groups, both groups improved substantially during therapy, and there were no differences between the two groups in the magnitude of the improvement of depressive symptoms. During the short-term treatment phase, the use of tricyclic antidepressant medication along with cognitive therapy did not improve the response rate obtained by cognitive therapy alone. Of the patients treated with cognitive therapy, 71 percent completely recovered compared to 36 percent of those treated with cognitive therapy plus pharmacotherapy.

At 12 months following treatment, the findings were that 58 percent remained well for the group that received cognitive therapy alone, and 82 percent for the group that received the combined treatment. This might suggest a nonsignificant trend of greater stability of gains for the combined treatment. However, this difference at 12 months is probably the result of the patients in the combined group receiving more therapy during the follow-up period compared to the cognitive therapy group alone: 91 percent of patients in the combined group received additional therapy during the 12-month follow-up period, whereas only 71 percent of those who received cognitive therapy alone sought additional treatment. Those receiving combined treatment had more cognitive therapy sessions (14.81 additional sessions) during follow-up period compared to the cognitive therapy alone group (5.93 sessions).[14]

Murphy et al.[15] assigned 87 moderately to severely depressed psychiatric outpatients to 12 weeks of cognitive therapy (CT) ($n = 24$), pharmacotherapy ($n = 24$), CT plus pharmacotherapy ($n = 22$), or CT plus active placebo ($n = 17$) (Table 16-1). The Diagnostic Interview Schedule, BDI, and HRSD were among the instruments used as the basis for the depression diagnosis. Seventy patients (18 males, 52 females) completed the 12 week treatment protocol. Cognitive therapy consisted of 50-minute sessions twice weekly for eight weeks, then weekly for the remaining four weeks. Those receiving combined cognitive and pharmacotherapy were seen on this same schedule, but for 60 minutes per session. The group that received pharmacotherapy alone was seen for 20 minutes weekly. The cognitive therapy plus active placebo group was given placebo capsules that had a mild sedative and anticholinergic effects similar to actual medication. The completion rates were 79 percent for cognitive therapy, 67 percent for pharmacotherapy, 82 percent for combined treatment, and 100 percent for cognitive therapy plus active placebo. Thus, 70 of the original group of 87 patients continued in therapy to the end of treatment, and dropout rates did not differ statistically among the four treatment groups.

Those participants who completed treatment showed significant improvement from initial evaluation to termination on the Beck Depression Inventory and the Hamilton Rating Scale for Depression. The different treatments did not produce significantly different improvement rates. The percentage of patients who recovered in each treatment modality was calculated using diverse cutoff scores of the BDI and HRSD. Using BDI scores of ≤ 9, the percentages of each group that recovered were 53 percent for cognitive therapy, 56 percent for drugs, 78 percent for cognitive therapy plus drugs, and 65 percent for cognitive therapy plus active placebo. Overall conclusions were that cognitive therapy alone is as effective as combined cognitive-drug treatment. Either cognitive therapy or antidepressant drug treatment was effective with nonbipolar moderate to severe depression. Gains in all groups were continued 1 month after treatment termination.

Blackburn et al.[16] found cognitive therapy alone to be more effective than drugs alone, while cognitive therapy plus drugs was most effective (Table 16-1). There were two selection criteria for the study participants: Research Diagnostic Criteria and at least mild depressive symptoms as measured by BDI scores (14 according to British norms). Of 140 patients screened, 88 were selected, from teaching hospital outpatient clinics and a general practice clinic. They were randomly assigned to cognitive therapy, antidepressant drugs and a combination of these two treatments. Of the 88, 64 completed the trial. Attrition rates were equal across the three groups, with completion rates 73 percent for cognitive therapy, 71 percent for antidepressant drugs, and 73 percent for the combination of both treatments.

Overall recovery rates were 73 percent for patients treated with cognitive therapy, 55 percent for pharmacotherapy, and 82 percent for combined cognitive therapy and drugs. The antidepressant drug group (typically 150 mg daily of amitriptyline or clomipramine) responded more poorly in both hospital and general practice. In both settings, the combination treatment was superior on seven mood measures to drug treatment alone. In general practice, cognitive therapy alone was superior to drug treatment alone. The response of endogenous and non-endogenous subgroups was equivalent across treatments.

Rush et al. [17] randomly assigned a sample of 15 males and 26 females to either cognitive therapy or antidepressant medication (imipramine hydrochloride) (see Table 16-1). The patients were moderately to severely depressed hospital outpatients, the majority of whom had previously been treated with psychotherapy and/or antidepressant medications; 22 percent had been previously hospitalized, 12 percent had a previous suicide attempt, and 755 reported suicidal ideation. The sample had a median of 2 previous therapists and 2.9 previous episodes of depression; 39 percent had been depressed for longer than one year at the time of the study.

Both cognitive therapy and drugs were provided over a 12-week period, with a maximum of 20 sessions for cognitive therapy or 12 sessions of pharmacotherapy. Completion rates were significantly lower for pharmacotherapy (64 percent) compared with cognitive therapy (95 percent). On both clinical ratings and self-report measures, cognitive therapy was found to be more effective than pharmacotherapy. This finding was true both for patients who completed treatment and for the entire sample admitted to treatment. Recovery rates (BDI < 10) were 79 percent for cognitive therapy and 22 percent for pharmacological treatment. However, DeRubeis et al.[7] noted two limitations of this study: relatively low levels of antidepressant medication were used, and medications were tapered 2 weeks before the final assessment outcome.

Ecological Validity and Randomized Clinical Trials

The use of randomized controlled trials (RCTs) to determine the empirically validated (supported) therapies has generated much attention.[18] Chambless and Hollon[19] noted that the term *empirically validated* may suggest that the results of research are definitive in cases where this may not be true, and that using the term *empirically supported* is probably better. Also, randomized clinical trials may differ in several ways from clinical practice.[20] Jonas[21] has identified and responded to several issues in the use of clinical trials: (1) limited numbers and homogeneous groups, (2) short duration, (3) no individualization of therapy, (4) use of surrogate endpoints, (5) significance and usefulness, (6) relevance, (7) data interpretation, and (8) adverse effects.

Chambless and Hollon[19] used the term *efficacy* to refer to the performance of a psychological treatment in a randomized trial, and *effectiveness* to designate the utility of the treatment in actual clinical practice. For example, a study by Persons et al.[22] provided empirical support for the clinical *effectiveness* of cognitive therapy for depression. They compared the outcome of 45 depressed patients treated in a private practice to patients in two randomized controlled trials. They found that the private practice patients had more psychiatric and medical comorbidities and a wider range of initial depression severity, but that BDI scores at posttreatment did not differ in the private practice and research settings.[22]

As concluded by the Task Force on Promotion and Dissemination of Psychological Procedures,[23] cognitive therapy for depression has been found to be an effective treatment for clinical depression. Chambless and Hollon[19] have suggested that a more appropriate term is "empirically supported" to make clear the point that research continues, rather than being entirely conclusive. For example, one important unresolved issue in need of further research is whether the combination of cognitive therapy with pharmacotherapy is better than either alone. Three of the randomized controlled trials reviewed here[16,10,12] suggested that there might be an advantage to the combined treatments (see Table 16-1). Also, a metaanalysis by Thase et al.[24] suggests that combined therapy may be superior to either cognitive therapy alone or interpersonal therapy alone in treating more severe recurrent depressions. Their data analysis included 595 patients with major depressive disorder who were treated in 6 standardized protocols.[24]

Cognitive therapy has generally proven to be a superior treatment for depression when compared to minimal treatment controls and alternative interventions.[25] Studies have demonstrated its efficacy in comparisons with no treatment or wait-list in college students, adult outpatients, community volunteers, and geriatric populations.[25] In addition, it has been found effective compared with behavioral interventions, and dynamic, interpersonal, and nondirective therapies.[3,25]

Using the Beck Depression Inventory (BDI) in computing effect sizes, a meta-analysis of 56 studies (all studies published before January 1991) found cognitive therapy to be at least as effective as drug therapy, combined therapies, or other diverse psychotherapies in the treatment of depression.[3,26] Greater efficacy for cognitive therapy is found on the BDI but not on the Hamilton Rating Scale for Depression (HSRD) (perhaps because the BDI is more sensitive in detecting levels of depression, or maybe because the BDI detects cognitive changes specifically). At the same time, the follow-up BDI scores in Dobson et al.[26] showed that cognitive therapy was no better than pharmacotherapy, combination therapy, or "other" therapies. This was said to be equivocal, however, because (1) subjects who relapse were usually not included in follow-up data, which give more favorable results than may actually be the case; (2) variables between treatment termination and follow-up may account for differences between groups; and (3) follow-up varied among studies.[26]

Aspects of the NIMH Treatment of Depression Collaborative Research Project study remain puzzling. The "clinical management" plus placebo condition showed as much improvement as active treatments in previous studies. Clinical management included provision of support, encouragement, and direct advice that perhaps resulted in greater engagement in activities and a sense of mastery and pleasure.[27] Concerning the treatment of more severe depression, research site differences were found.[11] McLean and Taylor[28] examined treatment-by-severity interactions with depressed outpatients, and concluded the NIMH trial findings could not be replicated, and that this failure to replicate was not due to treatment differences, populations or statistical power.[28] Ahmed et al.[29] critiqued the status of randomized controlled trials in the psychiatric literature, and suggest that a single such trial is not sufficient to guide clinical practice.

The TDCRP is also inconsistent with findings of Jarrett et al.[30] They conducted a 10-week, double-blind, randomized controlled trial comparing cognitive therapy or clinical management plus either phenelzine or placebo. Response rates on the 21-item Hamilton Rating Scale for Depression were 58 percent for cognitive therapy, 58 percent for phenelzine, and 28 percent for placebo. This study suggests that cognitive therapy may offer an effective alternative to standard acute-phase treatment with a monoamine oxidase inhibitor in the treatment of major depressive disorder and atypical features.

Given all these questions and anomalies, we agree with the following conclusion about the TDCRP: "Until we unravel these findings, final judgment must be withheld about the specific effectiveness of the two psychotherapies with more severely depressed and impaired patients" (p. 980).[9]

Relapse Prevention

Major depressive disorders are now understood to be chronic rather than acute.[31] There are reasons to believe that specific psychological intervention—and cognitive therapy in particular—prevents relapse.[32] Table 16-2 summarizes the randomized clinical trials that provide data on prevention of relapse and recurrence.

To review individual studies, we first considered Hollon et al.[33] They examined differential relapse rates for the 104 patients who met response criteria (i.e., completed and responded positively to treatment) in a study that compared the treatment efficacy of antidepressant medication to cognitive therapy. These patients were a subset of those who participated in the randomized placebo-controlled clinical trial by DeRubeis et al.[7] (see above section, "Randomized Clinical Trials").

12-month continuation phase. The patients in the 12-month continuation phase included 35 of 60 (58.3 percent) who met response criteria following acute treatment with cognitive therapy, and 69 of 120 (57.5 percent) who responded positively to acute treatment with antidepressant medication. For patients who responded positively to antidepressant medication(s), 34 were

TABLE 16-2. Percentage of Patients Remaining Well

Study	Source(s) of patients	Treatment comparisons	% recovered	% remaining well after recovery	Definition of "remaining well"	Follow-up period	Follow-up conclusions
Hollon et al. (2005) [follow up on DeRubeis et al (2005)]	(1) referrals (2) advertisement	(1) CT (n=60) (2) PH (n=120)	(1) CT=58.3 (2) PH=57.5	(1) CT=69% (2) Placebo Continuation 24% (3) PH Continuation =53%	HDRS<14 for at least two weeks	12 months	CT is as effective as continuation medication
Evans et al. (1992) [follow-up on Hollon et al. (1992)]	(1) psychiatric treatment facility (2) mental health center	(1) CT (n=10) (2) PH (n=10) (3) CT+PH (n=13) (4) PH Continuation (n=11)	(1) CT=70% (2) PH=20% (3) CT+PH=55% (4) PH Continuation =77%	(1) CT=79% (2) PH=50% (3) CT+PH=85% (4) PH Continuation 68%	No two consecutive BDI scores of 16 or above	4, 8, 12, 16, 20 and 24 months	CT alone or with drugs reduces relapse rates by >50%
Shea et al. (1992) [follow-up on Elkin et al. (1989)]	(1) psychiatric outpatients (2) self-referrals (3) mental health facilities	(1) CT (n=59) (2) IPT (n=61) (3) IMI-CM (n=57) (4) PLA-CM (n=62)	(1) CT=49% (2) IPT=40% (3) IMI-CM=38% (4) PLA-CM=31%	(1) CT=28% (2) IPT=17% (3) IMI-CM=15% (4) PLA-CM=18%	Absence of MDDD criteria and receiving no treatment	6, 12, and 18 months	Though not statistically significant, the results favored cognitive therapy

TABLE 16-2. (Continued)

Study	Source(s) of patients	Treatment comparisons	% recovered	% remaining well after recovery	Definition of "remaining well"	Follow-up period	Follow-up conclusions
Blackburn et al. (1986) [follow-up on Blackburn et al. (1981)]	(1) hospital outpatient clinics (2) a general practice clinic	(1) CT (n=22) (2) PH (n=20) (3) CT+PH (n=22)	(1) CT=77% (2) PH=60% (3) CT+PH=86%	(1) CT=77% (2) PH=22% (3) CT+PH=79%	BDI of 8 or less *and* HRSD of 7 or less	Two years	CT alone or with PH was more effective than drugs alone
Simons et al. (1986) [follow-up on Murphy et al. (1984)]	psychiatric outpatient hospital	(1) CT (n=24) (2) PH (n=24) (3) CT+PH (n=22) (4) CT+Active placebo (n=17)	(1) CT=53% (2) PH=56% (3) CT+PH=78% (4) CT+Active Placebo=65%	(1) CT=100% (2) PH=33% (3) CT+PH=83% (4) CT+Active placebo=100%	BDI of 15 or lower *and* not reentering treatment	One year	CT is more effective for preventing relapse than drugs
Kovacs et al. (1981) [follow-up on Rush et al. (1977)]	moderate and severe hospital outpatients	(1) CT (n=19) (2) PH (n=25)	(1) CT=83% (2) PH=29%	(1) CT=67% (2) PH=35%	BDI of 9 or lower	One year	CT is more effective than drugs

Abbreviations: 1. Measures used—ATQ = automatic thoughts questionnaire; BDI = Beck depression inventory; CRT = cognitive response test; DAS = dysfunctional attitudes scale; GAS = global assessment scale; HRSD = Hamilton rating scale for depression; IDA = irritability, depression & anxiety (mood rating scale); LIFE-II-II = longitudinal interval follow-up evaluation II; MADS = Montgomery & Asberg depression scale; PSR = psychiatric status ratings; RDS = Raskin depression scale; SCL-90 = Hopkins symptom checklist; VAS = visual analogue scale. 2. Treatment comparisons—CT = cognitive therapy; PH = pharmacotherapy; IPT = interpersonal therapy; PLA-CM = placebo + clinical management; IMI-CM = IMI-CM + clinical management; TAU = treatment as usual.

randomly assigned to stay on medications at full dosage levels during the one-year follow-up, and 35 were withdrawn onto pill-placebo, phased in over a 4–6-week period. Patients, psychiatrists, and evaluators were all kept blind as to which patients were still on medications, and which on placebo.

These 69 responders to antidepressant medications were all provided with follow-up sessions held every two weeks for one month with the same psychiatrist they had seen for treatment. Sessions were then reduced to once monthly thereafter, and lasted 15–30 minutes. The focus of these continuation follow-up sessions was on symptoms, side effects, limited advice giving, and therapeutic support.

Patients who responded to acute cognitive therapy treatment, and were therefore withdrawn from cognitive therapy, were allowed 3 cognitive therapy booster sessions during the one-year follow-up period. Sessions could be scheduled at any time, including at regular intervals or "as needed." Session content was allowed to vary and could include "crisis intervention," relapse prevention, or any other standard practice within the domain of cognitive therapy.

Results of the 12-month continuation phase included complete information on 88 of the 104 treatment responders (85 percent). These patients experienced high levels of comorbidity and chronic depression, with over 80 percent meeting criteria for at least one supplementary disorder, including 69 percent meeting criteria for another axis I disorder, and 49 percent for an axis II (personality) disorder. Relapse rates among these patients were found to be 31 percent for cognitive therapy, 47 percent for continuation antidepressant medication, and 76 percent for pill-placebo. The relapse rate of 31 percent for cognitive therapy in this study is consistent with an earlier study that found continuation phase cognitive therapy relapse or recurrence rates of only 27 percent at 12 months, compared to 50 percent relapse or recurrence at 12 months without continuation phase cognitive therapy.[34]

12-month recurrence follow-up. Using the 40 patients who completed the 12-month continuation phase with no relapse, a naturalistic 12-month follow-up was conducted to compare recurrence rates. Conceptually, these would be rates of the onset of entirely new depressive episodes. Cognitive therapy patients were allowed no additional booster sessions, and antidepressant medication patients were withdrawn from all pills (active and placebo).

Results of the 12-month recurrence evaluation phase showed that 5 of 20 (25 percent) of patients treated with cognitive therapy had a recurrence, compared to 7 of 14 (50 percent) of the patients who were withdrawn from antidepressant medication. Thus, the effect of CT in this study included prevention of recurrence. This effect was as strong as keeping patients on medication.[7]

Evans et al.,[35] a follow-up on Hollon et al.,[8] monitored patients who were successfully treated during a 3-month period with either imipramine hydrochloride pharmacotherapy, cognitive therapy, or combined cognitive-pharmacotherapy. The initial sample included 107 nonbipolar, nonpsychotic outpatients from a psychiatric treatment facility and a mental health center. To be included in the follow-up, patients had to both complete and respond to treatment. Of the 64 patients who completed treatment, 50 showed at least partial treatment response and were sufficiently remitted to be considered as part of the posttreatment follow-up. Of these, 44 participated in the follow-up. Participants were observed during a 2-year posttreatment follow-up period, during which half of the patients treated with pharmacotherapy alone were continued on study medications for the first year. This medication-continuation condition included 11 participants, 10 in the medication, no continuation group, 10 in the cognitive therapy group, and 13 in the combined cognitive-pharmacotherapy group. Except for the medication continuation participants, patients continued treatment only through the termination of the acute treatment phase. Findings showed that those treated with cognitive therapy (alone or in combination with drugs) were only half as likely to relapse as those patients placed in the "medication no continuation" condition. Moreover the rate of relapse for those treated with cognitive therapy was no greater than patients who were provided with continuation medication. Conclusions were that relapse may be prevented by using cognitive therapy during acute treatment.

Similar findings come from Shea et al.,[36] who conducted a naturalistic 18-month follow-up of outpatients with Major Depressive Disorder treated in the National Institute of Mental Health Treatment of Depression Collaborative Research Program (NIMH-TDCRP) (see Table 16-2). The treatments tested in the NIMH-TDCRP included 16 weeks of cognitive therapy, interpersonal therapy, imipramine hydrochloride plus clinical management (CM), or placebo plus CM. The follow-up assessments were conducted at 6, 12, and 18 months. With relapse defined as either major depressive disorder or additional treatment, the following rates of "recovery and remained well" were found for each of the four treatments: 28 percent (13 patients out of 46) for cognitive therapy group, 17 percent (9 of 53) for interpersonal therapy, 15 percent (7 of 48) for imipramine plus CM group, and 18 percent (9 of 51) for placebo plus CM. Though not reaching statistical significance, as in Evans et al.[35] the results favored cognitive therapy.

Blackburn, Eunson, and Bishop[37] addressed the question of the prophylactic effect of cognitive therapy using a naturalistic follow-up period of two years (see Table 2). Participants were those patients who had responded to cognitive therapy, pharmacotherapy, or combined cognitive therapy plus drug therapy.[16] The researchers adopted Klerman's definition for relapse, which is the return of symptoms within 6–9 months of treatment. A naturalistic methodology was adopted, meaning that in the follow-up period (as in the treatment period, Blackburn et al.[16]) physicians followed their normal practice with regard to the medications prescribed. Maintenance medications were stipulated to continue for at least 6 months. Sixty-four patients who had completed and responded to treatment were included in the study. Positive response rates were 77 percent for cognitive therapy (across referral sources), 60 percent for pharmacotherapy, and 86 percent for combined cognitive therapy and drugs. Patients in the pharmacotherapy treatment group experienced greater relapse rates at 6 months, and more recurrences over the two year follow-up, compared to the combined or cognitive therapy treatment groups. Recurrence rates were 17 percent for cognitive therapy; 75 percent for pharmacotherapy, and 33 percent for combined cognitive therapy and drugs. Thus, the percentage of patients who remained well over follow-up differed substantially between the cognitive therapy groups and those receiving pharmacotherapy alone (see Table 16-1).

Simons et al.[38] compared the relapse rates of 70 patients with nonbipolar affective disorder who had previously completed a 12-week course of either cognitive therapy (CT), pharmacotherapy, CT plus active placebo, or CT plus pharmacotherapy.[15] Assessment was conducted 1 month, 6 months, and 1 year after termination of active treatment. In the original study,[15] 70 patients completed treatment, and 44 responded as defined by BDI scores ≤ 10 at termination of therapy. Of these 44, 28 remained well and 16 relapsed. When the researchers defined "responders" as patients who had BDI scores <4 at termination, 26 remained well.[38] Using these 26 patients, statistical tests of remission rates between groups found that CT and CT + active placebo were significantly more likely to remain well for the 1-year follow-up period (CT vs. PH: generalized Wilcoxon $= 4.12, p = .04$; CT + active placebo vs. PH: generalized Wilcoxon $= 5.42, p = .02$].[38] The percentage of patients remaining well was 100 percent for CT, 100 percent for CT + active placebo, 33 percent for pharmacotherapy, and 83 percent for CT + pharmacotherapy. Patients who had relatively high levels of remaining depressive symptoms following treatment relapsed more often than those who showed no residual depression (BDI scores <10 following treatment). Relapse was also related to higher scores on a measure of dysfunctional attitudes.

Kovacs et al.[39] provided a follow-up of Rush et al.[17] (see Table 16-2). This study used Feighner's Diagnostic Criteria, the Hamilton Rating Scale, and the Beck Depression Inventory to select 44 hospital clinic outpatients suffering from at least a moderate level of clinical depression. Seventeen men and 27 women were assigned randomly to either cognitive therapy or imipramine hydrochloride. The average length of treatment was 11 weeks and 20 sessions. Completion rates were 95 percent for the cognitive therapy patients and 64 percent for the pharmacotherapy group. The clinical status was compared between groups at 1 year posttreatment. Results showed no significant between-groups differences, although the trends favored cognitive therapy. Self-ratings of depressive symptoms on the BDI showed that 67 percent of those treated with cognitive therapy remained free of symptoms at one year follow-up, compared to 35 percent of those treated with imipramine.

Averaging across studies, the patients treated with cognitive therapy had a relapse rate of only 30 percent compared to 69 percent for patients treated with pharmacotherapy alone. The definition of "relapse" differed across these five studies (see Table 16-2). Also, note that the percentages reported here differ slightly from those cited in Hollon et al.[8] This is because here we are including Shea et al.,[36] which was not available earlier. Hollon et al. (p. 90)[8] reported a relapse rate of 26 percent for patients treated to remission with cognitive therapy, versus 64 percent for pharmacotherapy. Thus, data so far indicate that, compared to drug therapy, there may be a relapse preventive effect resulting from the application of cognitive therapy to clinical depression.

Consistent with the cognitive primacy hypothesis, there is some evidence to support the possibility that modifying cognition is followed by control over other symptoms. Rush et al.[40] conducted an analysis of the data collected by Rush et al.[17] to evaluate the temporal order of changes in views of the self, hopelessness, mood, motivation, and vegetative symptoms. They found that patients improved first on measures of hopelessness, followed by improvement in self-view, motivation, mood, and vegetative symptoms. This was not found to be true for drug treatment.

A number of other methodological issues remain. Therapy outcomes are better when conducted by therapists who are committed to a particular approach to treatment, but the mechanisms of this effect are not known.[11] Treatment integrity is also an issue for future research. The effective application of cognitive therapy depends upon considering unique patient characteristics, the context of the depressive episode, and the case formulation. Outcome measures must be designed to detect treatment effects, such as the modification of cognitive structures that may relate to the relapse preventive effect of cognitive therapy. Individual subject experimental designs are needed in order to better identify individual differences in the speed of response, course of response, direction of response (improved or deterioration), and degree of endpoint improvement. Drop-out rates must be understood both in terms of the interpersonal processes that may be implicated in such outcomes, as well as in terms of patient characteristics that may predict dropout.

Overall Conclusions

Based on the above review, we now address the question how major depression should be treated. People who seek treatment for depression want to know which approach is most likely to work. Between drug classes, selective serotonin reuptake inhibitors (SSRIs) have fewer side effects compared to tricyclic antidepressants, and with mild to moderate depression the two drug classes are equivalent in outcome, so it would seem most reasonable to try

SSRIs first (see Chapter 14). Between psychotherapy and drugs, cognitive behavior therapy has fewer side effects compared to SSRIs, and in many studies prevents relapse better than pharmacotherapy. So the case could be made to try cognitive therapy first, if a trained therapist is available.

In addition to these general considerations, a study on optimizing treatment strategies was completed by Vos et al.[41] They presented an analysis that supports the routine use of maintenance treatment for depression. Even assuming treatment adherence rates of only 60 percent, they suggest half of all depression during the five years following a major depressive episode can be averted by using maintenance treatment in all cases of depression, either cognitive behavior therapy or antidepressants. From the review of the studies presented above, it might better be suggested that therapists use maintenance cognitive behavior therapy if available, or, as an alternative, antidepressants. Combining medication and interpersonal psychotherapy or cognitive behavior therapy should also be considered in cases of chronic depression.

Issues for Further Study

One of the most important questions for continuing research is the preventative effect of cognitive and other psychotherapies. For example, cognitive therapy is theorized to achieve a prophylactic action through modification of the depressotypic schemas.[42] As a collaborative endeavor, cognitive therapy enhances self-knowledge and personal responsibility. The depressed individual views self, world, and future as bleak, hopeless, and without personal meaning or control. Through cognitive therapy, personal control is restored, and the negativity is undermined. The patient learns to be "realistically optimistic" that, regardless of the perceived and/or objective difficulties, some degree of personal control over symptoms can be achieved.

Another important question is that of combining medication with cognitive behavior therapy. Hollon et al.[43] cite meta-analyses suggesting that combining medication with cognitive behavior therapy "is associated with a modest increment in overall response" (p. 463). They conclude that medication generally produces a rapid and substantial effect, but for the prevention of relapse or recurrence, adding a psychotherapeutic approach could be useful, especially with chronic depressions.[33]

Hollon et al.[43] also noted that preliminary support for combining treatments came from a trial in which a "cognitive behavioral-analysis" intervention was added to nefazodone. The combination was better than either treatment alone, thus renewing interest in combined therapies. Further work in different settings will be needed to determine whether the finding is robust and replicable. If so, then the study also supports (and perhaps extends) the earlier recommendations in *Cognitive Therapy of Depression* (Beck et al. 1979) emphasizing direct action in the treatment of severe depression.

DeRubeis et al.[44] studied whether pharmacotherapy or cognitive therapy works better for severe depression. They compared the outcomes of antidepressant medication and cognitive behavior therapy in the severely depressed outpatient subgroups of four major randomized trials. Also, they evaluated the results obtained in the National Institute of Mental Heath Treatment of Depression Collaborative Research Program with the other three studies. Their analysis of effect sizes showed no advantage of antidepressant medication over cognitive therapy with severely depressed outpatients.[44] This is consistent with the findings reported by DeRubeis et al. that compared cognitive therapy to medications in patients with moderate to severe depression.[7]

A report by John Rush [45] summarizes findings and questions from the STAR*D study ("Sequenced Treatment Alternatives to Relieve Depression"), a 7-year study funded by the National Institute of Mental Health that involved hundreds of researchers and thousands of patients. Some specific findings conceptually related to that project were described in Chapter 14 (see "Treatment Resistance" section). However, several key issues need further investigation. Research is needed to determine the best strategies for combination (two antidepressants) and augmentation (one antidepressant plus a second drug to augment its effect). It is an open question whether additive approaches will prove better than sequenced therapy with single medications.

Rush [45] suggested that studies are needed to test whether cognitive therapy prevents relapse better than medication if used as a switch or augmentation strategy. He also noted the need to "enhance the delivery and convenience of obtaining cognitive therapy" (p. 202).

Overall, the psychological and pharmacological theories and treatments continue their evolution and refinement. There are countless important questions for further study. We have highlighted some here, and anticipate more to originate as these give way to new advances in the cognitive and biological perspectives.

Afterword

Although the cognitive model of depression and its application in cognitive therapy has rested primarily on clinical observation and psychological theory and experiments in the past, several exciting and recent developments suggest that an integration with findings from neuroscience is now possible. This development promises to broaden the scope of both cognitive theory and therapy. Perhaps of most significance, gene mapping and imaging techniques provide new possibilities for clarifying the cognitive neurobiology of depression. Current studies have been testing cognitive theory by examining physiological structure and function.[1,2,3] This approach elucidates the causes and treatments of depression from the perspective of brain science, and is a natural progression (and expansion) of the scientific foundations of cognitive therapy.[4]

In the first edition of this volume, the cognitive model of depression was described along with original research that led to a number of testable hypotheses. The basic model included cognitive bias and the relation of specific cognition to behavioral, emotional, and physiological symptoms. The cognitive profile of depression was identified through clinical observation and research and an analysis of basic psychological research. The approach, grounded in the concept "levels of analysis," is known today as the biopsychosocial model. Today, we see this formulation supported at the neurobiological level, something impossible to detect at the time of its original construction.

In the next few pages, we consider basic research that links the cognitive and neurobiological levels: genetic vulnerability, cognitive vulnerability, and physiological hyperreactivity. In addition, we articulate an expanded cognitive model of depression.

The New Developmental Cognitive Model

To fully account for the development of depression, a new formulation is required. A complete account incorporates the genetic and the neurobiological vulnerabilities that predispose people to depression. Cognitive theory as originally formulated included the following specific components and sequence of events. (1) Depression-prone individuals react selectively to negative experiences and gradually construct a negative attitude (schema) about themselves, their future, and their personal world (cognitive vulnerability). (2) A major negative experience or a series of smaller traumas activate these schemas to the point that they become prepotent in information processing. (3) This results in continual negatively biased cognitions leading to the typical symptoms of depression.

The constellation of enduring negative attitudes may not be prominent or even discernible at a given time, but may persist in a latent state ready to be ignited by an appropriate set of conditions. Once activated, these concepts dominate the person's thinking (cognitive distortion) and lead to a *negative mental set*. This negative cognitive set is characterized by a more profound cognitive bias, or shift in information processing, that simultaneously induces hopelessness and *suppresses coping skills*. This structuralized mental set (schema system) is characterized by a negative cognitive bias toward events, selective focus on and exaggeration of negative events, and a relative blocking out of positive events and positive meanings. This dual action of the negative processing system is then manifest or expressed as *clinical depression*.

Missing from the original formulation was an explanation of why certain individuals are predisposed to become depressed after traumatic events and others exposed to the same stressors do not become depressed. Here we consider basic research on the cognitive neurobiology of depression, consistent with the above formulation.

Cognitive Vulnerability

At the psychological level, hundreds of basic and applied research studies have tested cognitive theory and therapy of depression.[5,6,7] Experimental investigations and longitudinal studies have supported the theory of cognitive vulnerability in adults and children.[5] Researchers have found that tests of cognitive variables (such as dysfunctional attitudes) demonstrate sensitivity, specificity, and stability. These variables are present in depressed individuals (sensitivity), are found more frequently in depression than in other psychiatric samples (specificity), and are present and accessible when activated experimentally (stability).[6] Moreover, there is evidence to support the hypothesis that they mediate improvement in treatment interventions.[7]

Genetic Links to Cognitive Vulnerability

Recent genetic research provides clues regarding why some individuals have a cognitive vulnerability and others do not. These studies have evaluated the relation between genetic variations and reactions to stress. Caspi et al.[8] found that a functional polymorphism (variant) in the promoter region of the serotonin transporter gene (the short allele) was associated with depression and suicide in response to stress. The serotonin transporter protein is a regulator substance implicated in the removal of serotonin from the synaptic cleft. Based on the Caspi[8] study (supported by two studies that replicated Caspi's findings), Canli[9] noted that carriers of the short variant of this gene are up to twice as likely to experience depression after stressful events compared to those without this genetic link. Of relevance to the cognitive model, this genetic variant is associated with stronger activation in brain regions critical for processing emotional stimuli, including differences in attentional biases for emotional (anxious words) stimuli.[10] Preliminary studies also have found that children who have the short gene show an overgeneralizing bias in response to experimental stimuli.[11]

The amydala seems to be especially interactive with genetic influences. A review[9] and a meta-analysis[12] of amygdala activation studies of the short-variant carriers complement the findings of Caspi[8] by clarifying the neurobiological events at the genetic level. Physiological hyper-reactivity is implicated in the interactions among genetic vulnerability, stress or "hassles," and depression.

Physiological Hyperreactivity

Based on a review of studies, Canli[9] concluded that a chronic level of hyper-reactivity of the amygdala (and other brain regions) in short variant carriers could predispose these individuals to more rapid acquisition of negative emotional memories, greater maintenance of these memories, increased vigilance, and other characteristics that may increase their physiological vulnerability to depression.[9] Canli[9] reviewed seven imaging studies[13,14,15,16,17,18,19] to evaluate the relation between short-variant carriers and amygdala behavior. This review found greater sensitivity (detection) at this level compared to association studies based on self-report. Canli's review indicated that short variant carriers show greater activation during (a) passive viewing of negative pictures, (b) implicit processing of negative words, and (c) visuospatial matching of emotional faces. These studies taken together provide convergent evidence that increased amygdala activation in response to emotional stimuli is a robust effect.[9] There is also some evidence for a relationship between amygdala hyperactivity and negative bias in the processing of emotions.[20]

Cognitive Neurobiology

A new area of research is emerging, *cognitive neurobiology* (CN) of depression. This discipline includes the study of the stress-activated physiological substrates[21–24] that are dysfunctional in clinical depression, and that are corrected through the effective application of cognitive therapy.[25,26] This larger focus will provide a more unified framework for theory and research. The cognitive model will be understood more completely through studies that relate psychological phenomena (e.g., cognitive vulnerabilities and coping capacities) to their neurobiological correlates.

By theorizing at multiple levels, cognitive theory can subsume structure and function at the "biological" level. Biological structure and function in depression must manifest consistency (theoretical accord) with cognitive theory and therapy. In this way, the theoretical axioms of cognitive therapy are elaborated through neuroscience. Functional MRI studies are already exploring the neuroanatomy of biased reasoning in tasks performed under various cognitive demands, as well as higher control and reasoning related to specific brain centers.[27] It is not hard to envision a time when depressive thinking and beliefs are routinely correlated with basic corresponding physiological dysfunctions. By having this more complete information, specific risk of depression relapse or recurrence will be known, and better treated.[28]

Appendix: Scoring Instructions for Negative Dreams

Definition

The term "negative dream" designates a class of unpleasant dreams characterized by a specific thematic content. The image of the dreamer has negative characteristics and/or the outcome of the dream sequence is essentially a negative one. The dreamer is either represented as less fortunate or less attractive than he is in reality (such as defective, ugly, or sick) or he is subjected to an unpleasant experience (such as thwarting, rejection, or deprivation). The description of the dreamer, the action, the setting, or the outcome of the dream suggests that the dream is unpleasant.

Scoring

The dream is designated as negative if it contains any of the elements listed below. The scoring is dichotomous: Each dream is scored + if it contains one or more of these elements; 0 if it does not.

Negative Representation of the Self

The dreamer is portrayed in a negative way. He or she has unpleasant attributes that are not present in reality or are exaggerated in the dream. He or she is deficient or defective in some way. His or her appearance has changed so as to be less attractive.

Examples: "I was a bum."
"I was mentally defective."
"I had pus oozing out of all my pores."
"I was a cripple."
"I was blind."
"I was too weak to move."
"I had become old and ugly."

"I had a disgusting odor."
"I had tuberculosis."
"My hair fell out."
"I was very dirty."

The negative representation may be in terms of deficiencies in mental functioning or personality.

Examples: "Somebody gave me directions. My mind was all messed up and I didn't know what he was talking about."
"I had a repulsive personality and people shunned me."

When the dream is scored blindly, there may be no basis for deciding whether the negative characteristics are a correct portrayal or a distortion of reality. In such a case, the rule is to score the dream as negative since our experience has shown that the negative self-representations are almost always distortions or exaggerations of reality.

Physical Discomfort and Injury

Discomfort, suffering, or pathological changes are explicitly stated or are reasonable inferences from the dream content. Sometimes, this category overlaps the previous category.

Examples: "Leeches were crawling all over me."
"Blood was coming out of my nose."
"I was strapped down to a table."
"I was buried alive."
"I hurt myself."
"Our auto crashed. We were all taken to the hospital."
"A horse kicked me in the head."
"I was burned in a fire."

Thwarting

The dreamer does something or tries to do something but the outcome is unsatisfactory. The actions have an obvious goal and the dreamer is prevented from attaining it by an external factor. The thwarting must be something the dreamer does not deliberately bring on her- or himself. It should be likely from the context or wording that this kind of thwarting would produce distress if it happened in actuality (in waking life).

Examples: "I rushed to get to my analytic session. When I got there, the door was locked."

"I made some toast. The popper did not work and the toast burned."

"I drove over to visit some old friends but ended up at the wrong house."

"I took careful aim and fired at the deer, but my gun didn't go off."

"I tried to save my daughter but my feet got stuck in the mud."

"I looked and looked and looked, but I couldn't find my notes."

"I got into a fight but my blows did not touch my opponent."

The following do not score because there is no indication that the goal is important to the dreamer or that thwarting occurs.

Examples: "I suggested lunch to the men but they weren't hungry. So we just sat around."

"I went into town to see a movie. I saw a parade and I followed it. I never did get to the movie."

"I was on my way to class. Then the scene shifted and I was skiing."

Deprivation

Disappointment: The patient wants or requests something but what he or she gets is less than what was wanted or expected. Or the patient may receive something not explicitly sought but which is obviously unsatisfactory. (This category sometimes overlaps the previous category.)

Examples: "I ordered rye and ginger. The bartender gave me warm beer and liquor, mixed."

"I bought some shoes but they were both for the left foot."

"I was in a restaurant but the waitress would not serve me."

"I put a dime in the coke machine. All that came out was fizz."

"My husband bought me furniture but it was in bad shape and the colors were horrible."

"My father gave me my allowance for the week. It was only a penny."

Loss: The dreamer has sustained the loss of something or someone.

Examples: "All my friends had died."

"A robber stole my watch."

"I lost all my money."

Lack: The key factor is the lack of something important to the dreamer such as friendship, affection, food, or material possessions.

Examples: "I was single again. I had no friends, nobody to go to."
"I was all alone. I felt very lonely."
"I had nothing to eat."
"I was in a foreign country. I had nobody to turn to for help."
"I didn't have a cent to my name."

Physical Attack

Another person deliberately attacks (and presumably hurts) the dreamer. The attack is completed and not simply threatened. If the injury is not inflicted deliberately, the dream element is scored under Category 2.

Examples: "A man fired a shot at me and it hit me in the arm."
"A gang of bullies beat me up."
"He beat me over the head."

The following do not score because the element of injury is absent.

Examples: "He kept hitting me but I didn't feel the blows."
"Somebody fired at me but missed."
"A man chased me."

Nonphysical Attack

The patient is ridiculed, criticized, scolded, blamed, or mistreated.

Examples: "He called me a crybaby."
"My wife said she was disgusted with me."
"I made a fool of myself. Everybody laughed at me."
"They accused me of the crime."
"He cheated me."

Exclusions: Self-blame and self-criticism do not score +.
"It was all my fault."
"I felt I was a crybaby."

Simply being in an argument does not score. It is necessary that the dreamer is getting the worst of it. "He said I should shut up. I said he should shut up" does not score, but "He demolished everything I said" does score.

Excluded, Superseded, or Abandoned

The dreamer is left out, rejected, or displaced by another person.

Examples: "I was the only one not invited to the party."
"My analyst said he didn't want to see me any more."
"My wife married another man."
"My mother gave my brother a ticket but not me."

Lost

The dreamer is lost.

Examples: "I was in a strange house and couldn't find my way out."
"I kept running through tunnels and I couldn't find the exit."
"I was in a city. I didn't know which way to go to get home."

Punishment

The dreamer receives punishment from a legal agency or an authority figure.

Examples: "I was in jail."
"My mother spanked me."
"I was expelled from school."
"I got a parking ticket."

Failure

The dreamer fails in a specific activity. There is no evidence in the dream that the lack of success is due to an external agent (as in Category 3).

Examples: "I flunked the exam."
"I came in last in the race."
"I aimed at the target and missed."
"I tried to solve the problem but I couldn't do it."
"I got up to make a speech and I couldn't think of anything to say."

Exclusions

No score is given for the following dream actions:

(1) When somebody else is the recipient of the unpleasant experience (even though the dreamer may be identified in some way with the other person).

Examples: "My father was hit by a car."
              "A little girl, who looked like me, was lost."

(2) When there is doubt whether the experience is unpleasant.

(3) When the accompanying affect or other statement denies unpleasantness or when the damage is undone.

Examples: "I was shot through the stomach but I did not feel anything."
              "I fell into a sewer. It did not bother me at all."
              "My hair was messed up but I didn't care."
              "Somebody stole my books but returned them to me."
              "There was a plot against me but I foiled them."
              "I lost my hat but I found it again."

Threat Dreams

These *do not score* as negative dreams unless one of the specific elements or themes listed in Section II is present. It is possible for a dream to score both as threat and negative if both kinds of themes are present. Threat dreams are frequently associated with anxiety states and have the following characteristics:

1. The *affect* is described as fright, fear, apprehension, or a synonym of these. In negative dreams, on the other hand, the affect is stated to be sadness, loneliness, or frustration.

2. There is a danger or threat but no harm, injury, or loss occurs in the dream sequence. In the negative dream, in contrast, the negative experience occurs before the dream is terminated.

Examples: "A man was chasing me."
              "I was falling into a pit."
              "There was some dangerous force in the building."

The negative dreams corresponding to these themes would be:

              "A man caught me and beat me."
              "I fell into a pit and hit bottom."
              "A dangerous force was crushing me."

References

Preface

1. Beck AT. How an anomalous finding led to a new system of psychotherapy. *Nature Med.* 2006;12(10):xii–xv.

Chapter 1. The Definition of Depression

1. Kline N. Practical management of depression. *J. Amer. Med. Ass.* 1964; 190:732–740.
2. Dunlop E. Use of antidepressants and stimulants. *Mod. Treat.* 1965; 2:543–568.
3. Murray CJL, Lopez AD (Eds.). *The Global Burden of Disease: A Comprehensive Assessment of Mortality and Disability from Diseases, Injuries, and Risk Factors in 1990 and Projected to 2020.* Cambridge, MA, Harvard School of Public Health; 1996.
4. Sørenson A, Strömgren E. Frequency of depressive states within geographically delimited population groups. *Acta Psychiat. Scand. Suppl.* 1961;162:62–68.
5. American Psychiatric Association. *Diagnostic and Statistical Manual of Mental Disorders (DSM-IV-TR)* (4th ed., textual revisions). Washington, DC, APA; 2000.
6. Piccinelli M. Gender differences in depression: a critical review. *Brit. J. Psychiat.* 2000;177:486–492.
7. National Institute of Mental Health. The numbers count (NIH Publication No. NIH 99-4584). http://www.nimh.nih.gov/health/publications/the-numbers-count -mental-disorders-in-america.shtml. CFM;1999.
8. Kessler RC, Chiu WT, Demler O, Walters EE. Prevalence, severity, and comorbidity of 12-month DSM-IV disorders in the National Comorbidity Survey Replication. *Arch. Gen. Psychiat.* 2005; 62:616–627.
9. Kessler RC, Berglund P, Demler O, Jin R, Walters EE. Lifetime prevalence and age-of-onset distributions of DSM-IV disorders in the National Comorbidity Survey Replication. *Arch. Gen. Psychiat.* 2005; 62:593–602.
10. Jelliffe SE. Some historical phases of the manic-depressive synthesis. *Ass. Res. Nerv. Ment. Proc.* 1931; 11:3–47.
11. Zilboorg G. *A History of Medical Psychology.* New York, Norton, 1941. 67.
12. Beers CW. *A Mind that Found Itself; an Autobiography.* Garden City, NY, Doubleday;1928.
13. Burton R. *The Anatomy of Melancholy* (1621), ed. Dell F, Jordan-Smith P. New York, Tudor;1927.
14. Hinsie L, Campbell R. *Psychiatric Dictionary* (3rd ed.). London, Oxford Univ. Press;1960.
15. Wessman AE, Ricks EF. *Mood and Personality.* New York, Holt;1966.

16. Hankin BL, Fraley RC, Lahey BB, Waldman ID. Is depression best viewed as a continuum or discrete category? a taxometric analysis of childhood and adolescent depression in a population-based sample. *J. Abnorm. Psych.* 2005; 114:96–110.

17. Meehl PE. Bootstraps taxometrics: Solving the classification problem in psychopathology. *Amer. Psychologist* 1995; 50:266–275.

18. Haslam N, Beck AT. Subtyping major depression: a taxometric analysis. *J. Abnorm. Psych.* 1994; 103:686–692.

Chapter 2. Symptomatology of Depression

1. Campbell JD. *Manic-Depressive Disease*. Philadelphia, Lippincott;1953.

2. Cassidy WL, Flanagan NB, Spellman M. Clinical observations in manic-depressive disease: a quantitative study of 100 manic-depressive patients and 50 medically sick controls. *J. Amer. Med. Ass.* 1957; 164:1535–1546.

3. Grinker R, Miller J, Sabshin M, Nunn R, Nunnally J. *The Phenomena of Depressions*. New York, Hoeber;1961.

4. Friedman AS, Cowitz B, Cohen HW, Granick S. Syndromes and themes of psychotic depression: a factor analysis. *Arch. Gen. Psychiat. (Chicago)*. 1963; 9:504–509.

5. Lewis A. Melancholia: a clinical survey of depressive states. *J. Ment. Sci.* 1934; 80:277–378.

6. Watts CA. The mild endogenous depression. *Brit. Med.* J. 1957;1:4–8.

7. Bradley JJ. Severe localized pain associated with the depressive syndrome. *Brit. J. Psychiat.* 1963; 109:741–745.

8. Kennedy F. The neuroses: related to the manic-depressive constitution. *Med. Clin. N. Amer.* 1944; 28:452–466.

9. VonHagen KO. Chronic intolerable pain; discussion of its mechanism and report of 8 cases treated with electroshock. *J. Amer. Med. Ass.* 1957; 165:773–777.

10. Saul LJ. *Emotional Maturity*. Philadelphia, Lippincott;1947.

11. Nussbaum K, Michaux WW. Response to humor in depression: a prediction and evaluation of patient change? *Psychiat. Quart.* 1963; 37:527–539.

12. Stenstedt A. A study in manic-depressive psychosis: clinical, social, and genetic investigations. *Acta Psychiat. Scand. Suppl.* 1952; 79.

13. Rennie T. Prognosis in manic-depressive psychoses. *Amer. J. Psychiat.* 1942; 98:801–814.

14. Abraham K. "Notes on the Psychoanalytic Investigation and Treatment of Manic-Depressive Insanity and Allied Conditions" (1911), in *Selected Papers on Psychoanalysis*. New York, Basic Books; 1960. 137–156.

15. Rado S. The problem of melancholia. *Int. J. Psychoanal.* 1928; 9:420–438.

16. Kraines SH. *Mental Depressions and Their Treatment*. New York, Macmillan; 1957.

17. Oswald I, Berger RJ, Jaramillo RA, Keddie KMG, Olley PC, Plunkett GB. Melancholia and barbiturates: a controlled EEG, body and eye movement study of sleep. *Brit. J. Psychiat.* 1963; 109:66–78.

18. Lehmann HE. Psychiatric concepts of depression: nomenclature and classification. *Canad. Psychiat. Ass. J. Suppl.* 1959; 4:S1–S12.

19. Hoch A. *Benign Stupors: A Study of a New Manic-Depressive Reaction Type*. New York, Macmillan; 1921.

20. Bleuler E. *Dementia Praecox or the Group of Schizophrenia* (1911), trans. Zinken J. New York, Internat. Univ. Press; 1950.

21. Weiss B, Garber J. Developmental differences in the phenomenology of depression. *Development and Psychopathology* 2003; 15:403–430.

22. American Psychiatric Association. *Diagnostic and Statistical Manual of Mental Disorders (DSM-IV)* (4th ed., textual revisions). Washington, DC, APA; 2000.

Chapter 3. Course and Prognosis

1. Kraepelin E. "Manic-Depressive Insanity and Paranoia," in *Textbook of Psychiatry*, trans. Barclay RM. Edinburgh, Livingstone;1913.

2. Paskind HA. Brief attacks of manic-depression. *Arch. Neurol. Psychiat.* 1929; 22:123–134.

3. Paskind HA. Manic-depressive psychosis as seen in private practice: sex and age incidence of first attacks. *Arch. Neurol. Psychiat.* 1930a; 23:152–158.

4. Paskind HA. Manic-depressive psychosis in private practice: length of attack and length of interval. *Arch. Neurol. Psychiat.* 1930b; 23:789–794.

5. Rennie T. Prognosis in manic-depressive psychoses. *Amer. J. Psychiat.* 1942; 98:801–814.

6. Lundquist G. Prognosis and course in manic-depressive psychoses. *Acta Psychiat. Neurol. Suppl.* 1945; 35.

7. Hopkinson G. Onset of affective illness. *Psychiat. Neurol. (Basel)* 1963; 146:133–140.

8. Hopkinson G. The prodromal phase of the depressive psychosis. *Psychiat. Neurol. (Basel)* 1965;149:1–6.

9. Steen R. Prognosis in manic-depressive psychoses: with report of factors studied in 493 patients. *Psychiat. Quart.* 1933; 7:419–429.

10. Strecker EA, Appel KE, Eyman EV, Farr CB, LaMar NC, et al. The prognosis in manic-depressive psychosis. *Res. Publ. Ass. Res. Nerv. Ment. Dis.* 1931; 11:471–538.

11. Astrup C, Fossum A, Holmboe F. A follow-up study of 270 patients with acute affective psychoses. *Acta Psychiat. Scand. Suppl.* 1959; 135.

12. Stenstedt A. A study in manic-depressive psychosis: clinical, social, and genetic investigations. *Acta Psychiat. Scand. Suppl.* 1952; 79.

13. Cassidy WL, Flanagan NB, Spellman M. Clinical observations in manic-depressive disease: a quantitative study of 100 manic-depressive patients and 50 medically sick controls. *J. Amer. Med. Ass.* 1957; 164:1535–1546.

14. Ayd FJ Jr. *Recognizing the Depressed Patient*. New York, Grune & Stratton; 1961.

15. Klein DK, Schwartz JE, Rose S, Leader JB. Five-year course outcome of dysthymic disorder: a prospective, naturalistic follow-up study. *Amer. J. Psychiat.* 2000; 157:931–939.

16. Buist-Bouwman MA, Ormel J, deGraaf R, Vollebergh WAM. Functioning after a major depressive episode: complete or incomplete recovery? *J. Aff. Disord.* 2004; 82:363–371.

17. Pollack HM. Prevalence of manic-depressive psychosis in relation to sex, age, environment, nativity, and race. *Res. Publ. Ass. Res. Nerv. Ment. Dis.* 1931; 11:655–667.

18. Kraines SH. *Mental Depressions and Their Treatment*. New York, Macmillan; 1957.

19. Belsher G, Costello CG. Relapse after recovery from unipolar depression: a critical review. *Psych. Bull.* 1988; 104:84–96.

20. Kiloh LG, Andrews G, Neilson M. The long-term outcome of depressive illness. *Brit. J. Psychiat.* 1988; 153:752–757.

21. Hoch PH, Rachlin HL. An evaluation of manic-depressive psychosis in the light of follow-up studies. *Amer. J. Psychiat.* 1941; 97:831–843.

22. Lewis NDC, Piotrowski ZS. "Clinical Diagnosis of Manic-Depressive Psychosis," in *Depression*, ed. Hoch PH, Zubin J. New York, Grune & Stratton; 1954. 25–38.

23. Farberow NL, Schneidman ES. *The Cry for Help*. New York, McGraw-Hill; 1961.

24. Meerloo JAM. *Suicide and Mass Suicide*. New York, Grune & Stratton;1962.

25. Vital Statistics of the United States; 1960.

26. Pokorny AD. Suicide rates in various psychiatric disorders. *J. Nerv. Ment. Dis.* 1964; 139:499–506.

27. Temoche A, Pugh TF, MacMahon B. Suicide rates among current and former mental institution patients. *J. Nerv. Ment. Dis.* 1964; 136:124–130.

28. Moss LM, Hamilton DM. The psychotherapy of the suicidal patient. *Amer. J. Psychiat.* 1956; 112:814–820.

29. Robins E, Gassner S, Kayes J, Wilkinson RH, Murphy EG. The communication of suicidal intent: a study of 134 consecutive cases of successful (completed) suicide. *Amer. J. Psychiat.* 1959; 115:724–733.

30. Wheat WD. Motivational aspects of suicide in patients during and after psychiatric treatment. *Southern Med. J.* 1960; 53:273–278.

31. Wendel HF, Wendel CS. (Eds.). *Vital Statistics of the United States: Births, deaths, and Selected Health Data.* Lanham, MD, Bernan Press; 2004.

32. MacDonald JM. Suicide and homicide by automobile. *Amer. J. Psychiat.* 1964; 121:366–370.

33. Stengel E. Recent research into suicide and attempted suicide. *Amer. J. Psychiat.* 1962; 118:725–727.

34. Campbell JD. *Manic-Depressive Disease*. Philadelphia, Lippincott; 1953.

35. American Psychiatric Association. *Diagnostic and Statistical Manual of Mental Disorders (DSM-IV)* (4th ed., textual revisions). Washington, DC, APA; 2000.

36. Brown GK, Beck AT, Steer RA, Grisham JR. Risk factors for suicide in psychiatric outpatients: a 20-year prospective study. *J. Consult. Clin. Psych.* 2000; 68:371–377.

37. Motto JA. Suicide attempts: a longitudinal view. *Arch. Gen. Psychiat. (Chicago)* 1965; 13:516–520.

38. Brown GK, Have TT, Henriques GR, Xie SX, Hollander JE, Beck AT. Cognitive therapy for the prevention of suicide attempts: a randomized controlled trial. *J. Amer. Med. Assoc.* 2005; 294:563–570.

39. Pichot P, Lemperière T. Analyse factorielle d'un questionnaire d'autoévaluation des symptoms dépressifs. *Rev. Psychol. Appl.* 1964; 14:15–29.

40. Fagiolini A, Kupfer DJ, Rucci P, Scott JA, Novick DM, Frank E. Suicide attempts and ideation in patients with bipolar I disorder. *J. Clin. Psychiat.* 2004; 65:509–514.

41. Riso LP, Miyatake RK, Thase ME. The search for determinants of chronic depression: a review of six factors. *J. Aff. Disord.* 2002; 70:103–115.

42. Riso LP, Blandino JA, Penna S, Dacey S, Grant MM, Toit PL, et al. Cognitive aspects of chronic depression. *J. Abnorm. Psych.* 2003; 112:72–80.

Chapter 4. Classifying Mood Disorders

1. American Psychiatric Association. *Diagnostic and Statistical Manual of Mental Disorders (DSM-IV)* (4th ed., textual revisions). Washington, DC, APA; 2000.

2. American Psychiatric Association. Diagnostic and Statistical Manual: Mental Disorders. Washington, DC, APA; 1952.

3. American Psychiatric Association. *Diagnostic and Statistical Manual of Mental Disorders (DSM-III)* (2nd ed.). Washington, DC, APA; 1968.

4. American Psychiatric Association. *Diagnostic and Statistical Manual of Mental Disorders (DSM-III)* (3rd ed.). Washington, DC, APA; 1980.

5. American Psychiatric Association. *Diagnostic and Statistical Manual of Mental Disorders (DSM-III)* (3rd ed. revised). Washington, DC, APA; 1987.

6. American Psychiatric Association. *Diagnostic and Statistical Manual of Mental Disorders (DSM-IV)* (4th ed.). Washington, DC, APA; 1994.

7. Fleming GW. The revision of the classification of mental disorders. *J. Ment. Sci.* 1933; 79:753.

8. Wakefield JC. Disorder as harmful dysfunction: A conceptual critique of *DSM-III-R*'s definition of mental disorder. *Psych. Rev.* 1992; 99:232–247.

9. Wakefield JC. The concept of mental disorder: On the boundary between biological facts and social values. *American Psychologist* 1992; 47:373–388.

10. Wakefield JC. Limits of operationalization: A critique of Spitzer and Endicott's (1978) proposed operational criteria for mental disorder. *J. Abnorm. Psych.* 1993; 102:160-172.

11. Kreitman N, Sainsbury P, Morrissey J, Towers J, Schrivener J. The reliability of psychiatric assessment: an analysis. *Brit. J. Psychiat.* 1961; 107:887–908.

12. Beck AT, Ward CH, Mendelson M, Mock JE, Erbaugh JK. Reliability of psychiatric diagnoses: 2. A study of consistency of clinical judgments and ratings. *Amer. J. Psychiat.* 1962; 119:351–357.

13. Ward CH, Beck AT, Mendelson M, Mock JE, Erbaugh JK. The psychiatric nomenclature: reasons for diagnostic disagreement. *Arch. Gen. Psychiat. (Chicago)* 1962; 7:198–205.

14. Clark JA, Mallet BA. Follow-up study of schizophrenia and depression in young adults. *Brit. J. Psychiat.* 1963; 109:491–499.

15. Lewis NDC, Piotrowski ZS. "Clinical Diagnosis of Manic-Depressive Psychosis," in *Depression*, ed. Hoch PH, Zubin J. New York, Grune & Stratton; 1954. 25–38.

16. Lewis A. States of depression: their clinical and aetiological differentiation. *Brit. Med. J.* 1938; 2:875–883.

17. Hoch PH. Discussion of D. E. Cameron, "A Theory of Diagnosis," in *Current Problems in Psychiatric Diagnosis*, ed. Hoch PH, Zubin J. New York, Grune & Stratton; 1953. 46–50.

18. Partridge M. Some reflections on the nature of affective disorders arising from the results of prefrontal leucotomy. *J. Ment. Sci.* 1949; 95:795–825.

19. Gillespie RD. Clinical differentiation of types of depression. *Guy Hosp. Rep.* 1929; 79:306–344.

20. Candolle AP. de *Essai sur les propriétés medicales des plantes, comparées avec leurs formes extérieures et leur classification naturelle.* Paris, Crochard; 1816.

21. Kraepelin E. "Manic-Depressive Insanity and Paranoia," in *Textbook of Psychiatry*, trans. Barclay RM. Edinburgh, Livingstone; 1913.

22. Heron MJ. A note on the concept endogenous-exogenous. *Brit. J. Med. Psychol.* 1965; 38:241.

23. Klein DF, Wender PH. *Understanding Depression.* New York, Oxford; 1993.

24. Crichton-Miller H. Discussion of the diagnosis and treatment of the milder forms of the manic-depressive psychosis. *Proc. Roy. Soc. Med.* 1930; 23:883–886.

25. Boyle H. Discussion on the diagnosis and treatment of the milder forms of the manic-depressive psychosis. *Proc. Roy. Soc. Med.* 1930; 23:890–892.

26. Buzzard EF. Discussion of the diagnosis and treatment of the milder forms of the manic-depressive psychosis. *Proc. Roy. Soc. Med.* 1930; 23:881–883.

27. Kiloh LG, Garside RF. The independence of neurotic depression and endogenous depression. *Brit. J. Psychiat.* 1963; 109:451–463.

28. Carney MWP, Roth M, Garside RF. The diagnosis of depressive syndromes and the prediction of E.C.T. response. *Brit. J. Psychiat.* 1965; 3:659–674.

29. Hamilton M, White J. Clinical syndromes in depressive states. *J. Ment. Sci.* 1959; 105:485–498.

30. Hamilton M. A rating scale for depression. *J. Neurol. Neurosurg. Psychiat.* 1960a; 23:56–61.

31. Rose JT. Reactive and endogenous depressions—responses to E.C.T. *Brit. J. Psychiat.* 1963; 109:213–217.

32. Shagass C, Jones AL. A neurophysiological test for psychiatric diagnosis: results in 750 patients. *Amer. J. Psychiat.* 1958; 114:1002–1009.

33. Ackner B, Pampiglione G. An evaluation of the sedation threshold test. *J. Psychosom. Res.* 1959; 3:271–281.

34. Roberts JM. Prognostic factors in the electro-shock treatment of depressive states; II. The application of specific tests. *J. Ment. Sci.* 1959; 105:703–713.

35. Shagass C, Schwartz M. Cortical excitability in psychiatric disorder—preliminary results. *Third World Congr. of Psychiatry Proc.* 1961; 1:441–446.

36. Sloane RB, Lewis DJ, Slater P. Diagnostic value of blood pressure responses in psychiatric patients. *Arch. Neurol. Psychiat.* 1957; 77:540–542.

37. Rees L. "Constitutional Factors and Abnormal Behavior," in *Handbook of Abnormal Psychology*, ed. Eysenck HJ. New York, Basic Books; 1960.

38. Kennedy F, Wiesel B. The clinical nature of "manic-depressive equivalents" and their treatment. *Trans. Amer. Neurol. Ass.* 1946; 71:96–101.

39. Kral VA. Masked depression in middle-aged men. *Canad. Med. Ass. J.* 1958; 79:1–5.

40. Denison R, Yaskin JC. Medical and surgical masquerades of the depressed state. *Penn. Med. J.* 1944; 47:703–707.

41. Lewis A. Melancholia: a clinical survey of depressive states. *J. Ment. Sci.* 1934; 80:277–378.

42. Castelnuovo-Tedesco P. *Depressions in Patients with Physical Disease.* Cranbury, NJ: Wallace Laboratories; 1961.

43. Simonson M. Phenothiazine depressive reaction. *J. Neuropsychiat.* 1964; 5:259–265.

44. Ayd FJ Jr. Drug-induced depression—fact or fallacy. *New York J. Med.* 1958; 58:354–356.

45. Schwab JJ, Clemmons RS, Bialow B, Duggan V, Davis B. A study of the somatic symptomatology of depression in medical inpatients. *Psychosomatics* 1965; 6:273–277.

46. Yaskin JC. Nervous symptoms as earliest manifestations of carcinoma of the pancreas. *J. Amer. Med. Ass.* 1931; 96:1664–1668.

47. Yaskin JC, Weisenberg TH, Pleasants H. Neuropsychiatric counterfeits of organic visceral disease. *J. Amer. Med. Ass.* 1931; 97:1751–1756.

48. Dovenmuehle RH, Verwoerdt A. Physical illness and depressive symptomatology. I. Incidence of depressive symptoms in hospitalized cardiac patients. *J. Amer. Geriat. Soc.* 1962; 10:932–947.

49. Michael RP, Gibbons JL. "Interrelationships Between the Endocrine System and Neuropsychiatry," *International Review of Neurobiology*, ed. Pfeifer C, Smythies J. New York: Academic Press; 1963.

Chapter 5. Psychotic Versus Nonpsychotic Depression

1. Hoch PH. Discussion of D. E. Cameron, "A Theory of Diagnosis," in *Current Problems in Psychiatric Diagnosis*, ed. Hoch PH, Zubin J. New York: Grune & Stratton 1953; 46–50.

2. Kraepelin, E. "Manic-Depressive Insanity and Paranoia," in *Textbook of Psychiatry*, trans. Barclay RM. Edinburgh: Livingstone; 1913.

3. Paskind, HA. Manic-depressive psychosis in private practice: length of attack and length of interval. *Arch. Neurol. Psychiat.* 1930b; 23:789–794.

4. American Psychiatric Association. *Diagnostic and Statistical Manual of Mental Disorders (DSM-IV)* (4th ed., textual revisions). Washington, DC, APA; 2000.

5. Kiloh LG, Garside RF. The independence of neurotic depression and endogenous depression. *Brit. J. Psychiat.* 1963; 109:451–463.

6. Carney MWP, Roth M, Garside RF. The diagnosis of depressive syndromes and the prediction of E.C.T. response. *Brit. J. Psychiat.* 1965; 3:659–674.

7. Sandifer MG Jr, Wilson IC, Green L. The two-type thesis of depressive disorders. *Amer. J. Psychiat.* 1966; 123:93–97.

8. Schwab JJ, Bialow M, Holzer C. A comparison of two rating scales for depression. *J. Clin. Psychol.* 1967; 23:94–96.

9. American Psychiatric Association. *Diagnostic and Statistical Manual: Mental Disorders*. Washington, DC, APA; 1952.

10. Ascher E. A criticism of the concept of neurotic depression. *Amer. J. Psychiat.* 1952; 108:901–908.

11. Ward CH, Beck AT, Mendelson M, Mock JE, Erbaugh JK. The psychiatric nomenclature: reasons for diagnostic disagreement. *Arch. Gen. Psychiat. (Chicago)* 1962; 7:198–205.

12. Mapother E. Discussion on manic-depressive psychosis. *Brit. Med. J.* 1926; 2:872–876.

13. Lewis A. Melancholia: a clinical survey of depressive states. *J. Ment. Sci.* 1934; 80:277–378.

14. Cassidy WL, Flanagan NB, Spellman M. Clinical observations in manic-depressive disease: a quantitative study of 100 manic-depressive patients and 50 medically sick controls. *J. Amer. Med. Ass.* 1957; 164:1535–1546.

15. Campbell JD. *Manic-Depressive Disease*. Philadelphia: Lippincott; 1953.

16. Kraines SH. *Mental Depressions and Their Treatment*. New York: Macmillan; 1957.

17. Robins E, Gassner S, Kayes J, Wilkinson RH, Murphy EG. The communication of suicidal intent: a study of 134 consecutive cases of successful (completed) suicide. *Amer. J. Psychiat.* 1959; 115:724–733.

18. Winokur G, Pitts, FN. Affective disorder. IV. A family history study of prevalances, sex differences, and possible genetic factors. *J. Psychiat. Res.* 1965; 3:113–123.

19. Bleuler, E. *Textbook of Psychiatry*, trans. Brill AA. New York, Macmillan; 1924.

20. Wexberg E. Zur Klinik und Pathogenese der leichten Depressionzustände. *Z. Neurol. Psychiat.* 1928; 112:549–574.

21. Paskind HA. Brief attacks of manic-depression. *Arch. Neurol. Psychiat.* 1929; 22:123–134.

22. Harrowes W McC. The depressive reaction types. *J. Ment. Sci.* 1933; 79:235–246.

23. Cheney CO. *Outlines for Psychiatric Examinations*. Albany: New York State Dept. of Mental Hygiene; 1934.

24. Beck AT, Valin S. Psychotic depressive reactions in soldiers who accidentally killed their buddies. *Amer. J. Psychiat.* 1953; 110:347–353.

25. Foulds GA. Psychotic depression and age. *J. Ment. Sci.* 1960; 106:1394.

Chapter 6. Bipolar Disorders

1. Kraepelin E. "Manic-Depressive Insanity and Paranoia," in *Textbook of Psychiatry*, trans. Barclay, R. M. Edinburgh, Livingstone; 1913.

2. Meyer A. "The Problems of Mental Reaction Types" (1908), in *The Collected Papers of Adolf Meyer*. Baltimore, Johns Hopkins Univ. Press 1951; 2:591–603.

3. American Psychiatric Association. *Diagnostic and Statistical Manual: Mental Disorders*. Washington, DC, APA; 1952.

4. Zilboorg G. "Manic-Depressive Psychoses," in *Psychoanalysis Today: Its Scope and Function*, ed. Lorand S. New York: Covici, Friede; 1933. 229–245.

5. Loftus TA. *Meaning and Methods of Diagnosis in Clinical Psychiatry*. Philadelphia: Lea & Febiger; 1960.

6. American Psychiatric Association. *Diagnostic and Statistical Manual of Mental Disorders (DSM-IV)* (4th ed., textual revisions). Washington, DC, APA; 2000

7. Angst J. The course of affective disorders. *Psychopathol.* 1986; 19:47–52.

8. Sharma V, Khan M, Smith A. A closer look at treatment resistant depression: is it due to a bipolar diathesis? *J. Aff. Disord.* 2005; 84:251–257.

9. Johnson GF. Lithium in depression: a review of the antidepressant and prophylactic effects of lithium. *Austral. New Zeal. J. Psychiatry* 1987; 21:356–365.

10. Hantouche EG, Akiskal HS. Bipolar II vs. unipolar depression: psychopathologic differentiation by dimensional measures. *J. Aff. Disord.* 2005;84:127-132.

11. Serretti A, Olgiati P. Profiles of "manic" symptoms in bipolar I, bipolar II and major depressive disorders. *J. Aff. Disord.* 2005; 84:159–166.

12. Akiskal HS, Benazzi F. Atypical depression: a variant of bipolar II or a bridge between unipolar and bipolar II? *J. Aff. Disord.* 2005; 84:209–217.

13. Cameron N. The place of mania among the depressions from a biological standpoint. *J. Psych.* 1942; 14:181–195.

14. Rennie T. Prognosis in manic-depressive psychoses. *Amer. J. Psychiat.* 1942; 98:801–814.

15. Clayton PJ, Pitts FN, Winokur G. Affective disorder IV. Mania. *Compr. Psychiat.* 1965; 6:313.

16. Richter PR. *Biological Clocks in Medicine and Psychiatry*. Springfield, IL: Thomas; 1965.

17. Bunney WE, Hartmann EL. A study of a patient with 48-hour manic-depressive cycles: I. An analysis of behavioral factors. *Arch. Gen. Psychiat. (Chicago)* 1965; 12:611.

18. Titley WB. Prepsychotic personality of patients with involutional melancholia. *Arch. Neurol. Psychiat* 1936; 36:19–33.

19. Kohn M, Clausen J. Social isolation and schizophrenia. *Amer. Sociol. Rev.* 1955; 20:265–273.

20. Leahy RL. Decision-making and mania. *J. Cog. Psychother.* 1999; 13:83–105.

21. Newman CF, Leahy RL, Beck AT, Reilly-Harrington NA, Gyulai L. *Bipolar Disorder: A Cognitive Approach*. Washington, DC, APA; 2001.

22. Johnson SL, Sandrow D, Meyer B, Winters R, Miller I, Solomon D, Keitner G.

Increases in manic symptoms after life events involving goal attainment. *J. Abnorm. Psych.* 2000; 109:721–727.

Chapter 7. Involutional Depression

1. American Psychiatric Association. *Diagnostic and Statistical Manual of Mental Disorders (DSM-IV)* (4th ed., textual revisions). Washington, DC, APA; 2000.
2. Kraepelin E. "Manic-Depressive Insanity and Paranoia," in *Textbook of Psychiatry*, trans. Barclay RM. Edinburgh, Livingston; 1913.
3. Thalbitzer S. *Acta Psychiat. Scand. Suppl.* 1905. Cited in Lundquist G, Prognosis and course in manic-depressive psychoses. *Acta Psychiat. Neurol. Suppl.* 1945; 35:8.
4. Dreyfus, G. The prognosis of involution melancholia. *Arch. Neurol. Psychiat.* 1907; 7:1–37. Quoted in Hoch A, MacCurdy JT, The prognosis of involution melancholia. *Arch. Neurol. Psychiat.* 1922; 7.
5. Kirby GH. *Arch. Neurol. Psychiat.* 1908; 36:19–33. Quoted in Titley WB, Prepsychotic personality of patients with involutional melancholia. *Arch. Neurol. Psychiat.* 1936; 36:19–33.
6. Hoch A, MacCurdy JT. The prognosis of involution melancholia. *Arch. Neurol. Psychiat.* 1922; 7:1.
7. Cheney CO. *Outlines for Psychiatric Examinations.* Albany: New York State Dept. of Mental Hygiene; 1934.
8. Henderson D, Gillespie RD. *Textbook of Psychiatry* (9th ed.). London: Oxford Univ. Press; 1963.
9. Stengel E. Classification of mental disorders. *Bull. WHO.* 1959; 21:601–663.
10. Palmer HD, Hastings DW, Sherman SH. Therapy in involutional melancholia. *Amer. J. Psychiat.* 1941; 97:1086–1111.
11. Ripley HS, Shorr E, Papanicolaou GN. The effect of treatment of depression in the menopause with estrogenic hormone. *Amer. J. Psychiat.* 1940; 96:905–914.
12. Henderson D, Gillespie RD. *Textbook of Psychiatry* (9th ed.). London: Oxford Univ. Press; 1963.
13. Matthews KA, Wing RR, Kuller LH, Meilhan EN, Kelsey SF, Costello EJ, Caggiula AW. Influence of natural menopause on psychological characteristics and symptoms of middle-aged healthy women. *J. Consult. Clin. Psych.* 1990; 58:345–351.
14. Cameron N. "The Functional Psychoses," in *Personality and the Behavior Disorders*, ed. Hunt J McV. New York, Ronald Press; 1944, 861–921.
15. Sawyer JE III. Personal communication; 2005.
16. State of New York Department of Mental Hygiene; 1960.
17. Berger H. Ueber periodische schwankungen in der schnelligkeit der aufeinandfolge willkürlicher bewegungen. *Z. Psychol. Physiol. Sinnesorg* 1908; 1:321–331.
18. Driess H. Über der gestaltung und unterteilung in der involution auftretenden depressionen. *Z. Psych. Hyg.* 1942; 14:65–77.
19. Malamud W, Sands SL, Malamud I. The involutional psychoses: a socio-psychiatric study. *Psychosom. Med.* 1941; 3:410–426.
20. Cassidy WL, Flanagan NB, Spellman M. Clinical observations in manic-depressive disease: a quantitative study of 100 manic-depressive patients and 50 medically sick controls. *J. Amer. Med. Ass.* 1957; 164:1535–1546.
21. Hopkinson G. A genetic study of affective illness in patients over 50. *Brit. J. Psychiat.* 1964; 110:244–254.
22. Titley WB. Prepsychotic personality of patients with involutional melancholia. *Arch. Neurol. Psychiat.* 1936; 36:19–33.

23. Palmer HD, Sherman SH. The involutional melancholia process. *Arch. Neurol. Psychiat.* 1938; 40:762–788.

24. Beck AT. *Depression: Causes and Treatment.* Philadelphia, Univ. Pennsylvania Press; 1967.

25. Newmann JP. Aging and depression. *Psych. Aging* 1989; 4:150–165.

Chapter 8. Schizoaffective Disorder

1. American Psychiatric Association. *Diagnostic and Statistical Manual: Mental Disorders.* Washington, DC, APA; 1952.

2. Clark JA, Mallet BA. Follow-up study of schizophrenia and depression in young adults. *Brit. J. Psychiat.* 1963; 109:491–499.

3. Lewis NDC, Piotrowski ZS. "Clinical Diagnosis of Manic-Depressive Psychosis," in *Depression*, ed. Hoch PH, Zubin J. New York: Grune & Stratton; 1954:25–38.

4. Kirby GH. The catatonic syndrome and its relation to manic-depressive insanity. *J. Nerv. Ment. Dis.* 1913; 40:691–704.

5. Hoch A. *Benign Stupors: A Study of a New Manic-Depressive Reaction Type.* New York, Macmillan; 1921.

6. Kasanin JS. The acute schizoaffective psychoses. *Amer. J. Psychiat.* 1933; 13:97–126.

7. Vaillant GE. An historical review of the remitting schizophrenias. *J. Nerv. Ment. Dis.* 1964a; 138:48–56.

8. Hoch PH, Rachlin HL. An evaluation of manic-depressive psychosis in the light of follow-up studies. *Amer. J. Psychiat.* 1941; 97:831–843.

9. Rachlin HL. A followup study of Hoch's benign stupor cases. *Amer. J. Psychiat.* 1935; 92:531.

10. Rachlin HL. A statistical study of benign stupor in five New York state hospitals. *Psychiat. Quart.* 1937; 11:436–444.

11. Cheney CO. *Outlines for Psychiatric Examinations.* Albany, New York State Dept. of Mental Hygiene; 1934.

12. Vaillant GE. Natural history of remitting schizophrenias. *Amer. J. Psychiat.* 1963a; 120:367–375.

13. Lewis NDC, Hubbard LD. The mechanisms and prognostic aspects of the manic-depressive schizophrenic combinations. *Res. Pub. Ass. Res. Nerv. Ment. Dis.* 1931; 11:539–608.

14. American Psychiatric Association. *Diagnostic and Statistical Manual of Mental Disorders (DSM-IV)* (4th ed., textual revisions). Washington, DC, APA; 2000.

15. Henderson D, Gillespie RD. *Textbook of Psychiatry* (9th ed.) London, Oxford Univ. Press; 1963.

16. Hunt RR, Appel KE. Prognosis in psychoses lying midway between schizophrenic and manic-depressive psychoses. *Amer. J. Psychiat.* 1936; 93:313–339.

17. Zubin J, Sutton S, Salzinger K, Salzinger S, Burdock E, Peretz D. "A biometric Approach to Prognosis in Schizophrenia," in *Comparative Epidemiology of the Mental Disorders*, ed. Hoch PH, Zubin J. New York, Grune & Stratton 1961; 143–203.

18. Albee G. The prognostic importance of delusions in schizophrenia. *J. Abnorm. Soc. Psychol.* 1951; 46:208–212.

19. Vaillant GE. Manic-depressive heredity and remission in schizophrenia. *Brit. J. Psychiat.* 1963b; 109:746–749.

20. Albee GW. Patterns of aggression in psychopathology. *J. Consult. Psychol.* 1950; 14:465–468.

21. Feldman D, Pascal GR, Swenson CH. Direction of aggression as a prognostic variable in mental illness. *J. Consult. Psychol.* 1954; 18:167.

22. Phillips L, Ziegler E. Role orientation, the action-thought dimension, and outcome in psychiatric disorder. *J. Abnorm. Soc. Psychol.* 1964; 68:381–389.

23. Vaillant GE. Prospective prediction of schizophrenic remission. *Arch. Gen. Psychiat. (Chicago).* 1964b; 11:509–518.

24. Williams PV, McGlashan TH. Schizoaffective psychosis, I: comparative long-term outcome. *Arch. Gen. Psychiat.* 1987; 44, 130-137.

25. Evans JD, Heaton RK, Paulsen JS, McAdams LA, Heaton SC, Jeste DV. Schizoaffective disorder: a form of schizophrenia or affective disorder? *J. Clin. Psychiat.* 1999; 60:874–882.

26. Kendler KS, McGuire M, Gruenberg AM, Walsh D. Examining the validity of DSM-III-R schizoaffective disorder and its putative subtypes in the Roscommon family study. *Amer. J. Psychiat.* 1995; 152:755–764.

27. Maj M, Starace F, Pirozzi R. Family study of DSM-III-R schizoaffective disorder, depressive type, compared with schizophrenia and psychotic and nonpsychotic major depression. *Amer. J. Psychiat.* 1991; 148:612–616.

28. Taylor MA. Are schizophrenia and affective disorder related? a selective literature review. *Amer. J. Psychiat.*1992; 149:22–32.

29. Bertelsen A, Gottesman II. Schizoaffective psychoses: genetical clues to classification. *Amer. J. Med. Gen.* 1995; 60:7–11.

Chapter 9. Biological Studies of Depression

1. Wong M, Licinio J. Research and treatment approaches to depression. *Nature Rev. Neurosci.* 2001; 2:343–351.

2. Beck AT. *Depression: Causes and Treatment.* Philadelphia: Univ. Pennsylvania Press; 1967.

3. Thase ME, Howland RH. "Biological Processes in Depression: An Updated Review and Integration," in *Handbook of Depression* (2nd ed.), ed. Beckham EE, Leber WR. New York: Guilford; 1995. 213–279.

4. Dubovsky SL, Buzan R. "Mood Disorders," in *Textbook of Psychiatry*, ed. Hales RE, Yudofsky SC, Talbott JA. Washington, DC, American Psychiatric Press; 1999. 479–565.

5. Kretschmer E. *Physique and Character*, trans. Sprout WJH. New York, Harcourt; 1925.

6. Rees L. "Constitutional Factors and Abnormal Behavior," in *Handbook of Abnormal Psychology*, ed. Eysenck HJ. New York, Basic Books; 1960.

7. Clegg JL. The association of physique and mental condition. *J. Ment. Sci.* 1935; 81:297–316.

8. Burchard EML. Physique and psychosis: an analysis of the postulated relationship between bodily constitution and mental disease syndrome. *Compr. Psychol. Monogr.* 1936; 13:1.

9. Wittman P, Sheldon W, Katz CJ. A study of the relationship between constitutional variations and fundamental psychotic behavior reactions. *J. Nerv. Ment. Dis.* 1948; 108:470–476.

10. Anastasi A, Foley JP. *Differential Psychology: Individual and Group Differences in Behavior.* New York, Macmillan; 1949.

11. Farber ML. Critique and investigation of Kretschmer's theory. *J. Abnorm. Soc. Psychol.* 1938; 33:398.

12. Rees L. Physical constitution, neurosis, and psychosis. *Proc. Roy. Soc. Med.* 1944; 37:635–638.

13. Bellak, L. *Manic-Depressive Psychosis and Allied Conditions.* New York, Grune & Stratton; 1952.

14. Fagiolini A, Kupfer DJ, Rucci P, Scott JA, Novick DM, Frank E. Suicide attempts and ideation in patients with bipolar I disorder. *J. Clin. Psychiat.* 2004; 65, 509–514.

15. Kallmann F. "Genetic Aspects of Psychoses," in Milbank Memorial Fund, *Biology of Mental Health and Disease.* New York, Hoeber; 1952:283–302.

16. Tienari P. Psychiatric illness in identical twins. *Acta Psychiat. Scand. Suppl.* 1963; 171.

17. Gregory IW. *Psychiatry: Biological and Social.* Philadelphia, Saunders; 1961.

18. Slater E. Psychiatric and neurotic illnesses in twins. Medical Research Council Special Report Series 278. London, HMSO; 1953.

19. Shields J. *Monozygotic Twins Brought Up Apart and Brought Up Together.* London, Oxford Univ. Press; 1962.

20. Stenstedt A. A study in manic-depressive psychosis: clinical, social, and genetic investigations. *Acta Psychiat. Scand. Suppl.* 1952; 79.

21. Winokur G, Pitts FN. Affective disorder. IV. A family history study of prevalances, sex differences, and possible genetic factors. *J. Psychiat. Res.* 1965; 3:113–123.

22. Fremming K. *The Expectation of Mental Infirmity in a Sample of the Danish Population.* London: Cassell; 1951.

23. Taylor L, Faraone SV, Tsuang MT. Family, twin, and adoption studies of bipolar disease. *Curr. Psychiat. Rep.* 2002; 4:130–133.

24. McGuffin P, Rijsdijk F, Andrew M, Sham P, Katz R, Cardno A. The heritability of bipolar affective disorder and the genetic relationship to unipolar depression. *Arch. Gen. Psychiat.* 2003; 60:497–502.

25. Sevy S, Mendlewicz J, Mendelbaum K. "Genetic Research in Bipolar Illness," in *Handbook of Depression* (2nd ed.), ed. Beckham EE, Leber WR. New York, Guilford; 1995. 203-212.

26. Wallace J, Schneider T, McGuffin P. "Genetics of Depression," in *Handbook of Depression*, ed. Gotlib IH, Hammen CL. New York, Guilford; 2002.

27. Cleghorn RA, Curtis GC. Psychosomatic accompaniments of latent and manifest depressive affects. *Canad. Psychiat. Ass. J. Suppl.* 1959; 4:S13–S23.

28. McFarland RA, Goldstein H. The biochemistry of manic-depressive psychosis. *Amer. J. Psychiat.* 1939; 92:21–58.

29. Gildea EF, McLean,VL, Man EB. Oral and intravenous dextrose tolerance curves of patients with manic-depressive psychosis. *Arch. Neurol. Psychiat.* 1943; 49:852–859.

30. Pryce IG. Melancholia, glucose tolerance, and body weight. *J. Ment. Sci.* 1958; 104:421–427.

31. Whittier JR, Korenzi C, Goldschmidt L, Haydu G. The serum cholesteral "sign" test in depression. *Psychosomatics* 1964; 5:27–33.

32. Cameron N. The place of mania among the depressions from a biological standpoint. *J. Psychol.* 1942; 14:181–195.

33. Birmaher B, Heydl P. Biological studies in depressed children and adolescents. *Internat. J. Neuropsychopharmacol.* 2001; 4:149–157.

34. Gjessing R. Disturbances of somatic functions in catatonia with a periodic course, and their compensation. *J. Ment. Sci.* 1938; 84:608–621.

35. Klein R, Nunn RF. Clinical and biochemical analysis of a case of manic-depressive psychosis showing regular weekly cycles. *J. Ment. Sci.* 1945; 91:79–88.

36. Crammer JL. Water and sodium in two psychotics. *Lancet.* 1959; 1:1122–1126.

37. Gibbons JL. Total body sodium and potassium in depressive illness. *Clin. Sci.* 1960; 19:133–138.

38. Russell GFM. Body weight and balance of water, sodium, and potassium in depressed patients given electroconvulsive therapy. *Clin. Sci.* 1960; 19:327–336.

39. Coppen AJ, Shaw DM. Mineral metabolism in melancholia. *Brit. Med. J.* 1963; 2:1439–1444.

40. Lobban M, Tredre B, Elithorn A, Bridges P. Diurnal rhythm of electrolyte excretion in depressive illness. *Nature (London).* 1963; 199:667–669.

41. Anderson W McC, Dawson J. The clinical manifestations of depressive illness with abnormal acetyl methyl carbinol metabolism. *J. Ment. Sci.* 1962; 108:80–87.

42. Assael M, Thein M. Blood acetaldehyde levels in affective disorders. *Israel Ann. Psychiat.* 1964; 2:228–234.

43. Flach F. Calcium metabolism in states of depression. *Brit. J. Psychiat.* 1964; 110:588.

44. Cade J. FJ. A significant elevation of plasma magnesium levels in schizophrenia and depressive states. *Med. J. Aust.* 1964; 1:195–196.

45. Gershon S, Yuweiler A. Lithium ion: a specific psychopharmacological approach to the treatment of mania. *J. Neuropsychiat.* 1960; 1:229–241.

46. Gibbons JL. Electrolytes and depressive illness. *Postgrad. Med. J.* 1963; 39:19–25.

47. Mullen PE, Linsell CR, Parker D. Influence of sleep disruption and calorie restriction on biological markers of depression. *Lancet* 1986; 328(8515):1051–1055.

48. Schottstaedt WW, Grace WJ, Wolff HG. Life situations, behaviour, attitudes, emotions, and renal excretions of fluid and electrolytes. IV. Situations associated with retention of water, sodium, and potassium. *J. Psychosom. Res.* 1956; 1:287–291.

49. Michael RP, Gibbons JL. "Interrelationships Between the Endocrine System and Neuropsychiatry," in *International Review of Neurobiology*, ed. Pfeifer C, Smythies J. New York: Academic Press; 1963.

50. Board F, Wadeson R, Persky H. Depressive affect and endocrine function. *Arch. Neurol. Psychiat.* 1957; 78:612–620.

51. Curtis GC, Cleghorn RA, Sourkes TL. The relationship between affect and the excretion of adrenaline, noradrenaline, and 17-hydroxycorticosteroids. *J. Psychosom. Res.* 1960; 4:176.

52. Gibbons JL, McHugh PR. Plasma cortisol in depressive illness. *J. Psychiat. Res.* 1962; 1:162–171.

53. Kurland HD. Steroid excretion in depressive disorders. *Arch. Gen. Psychiat. (Chicago)* 1964; 10:554–560.

54. Gibbons JL. Cortisol secretion rate in depressive illness. *Arch. Gen. Psychiat. (Chicago)* 1964; 10:572–575.

55. Bunney WE, Mason JD, Roatch JF, Hamburg DA. A psycho endocrine study of severe psychotic depressive cases. *Amer. J. Psychiat.* 1965; 122:72.

56. Bunney WE, Hartmann EL, Mason JW. Study of a patient with 48-hour manic-depressive cycles. II. Strong positive correlation between endocrine factors and manic-depressive patterns. *Arch. Gen. Psychiat. (Chicago).* 1965; 12:619.

57. Bunney WE, Fawcett JA. Possibility of a biochemical test for suicidal potential: an analysis of endocrine findings prior to three suicides. *Arch. Gen. Psychiat. (Chicago).* 1965; 13:232–239.

58. Tiemeier H. Review: Biological risk factors for late life depression. *European J. Epidemiol.* 2003; 18:745.

59. Parker KJ, Schatzberg AF, Lyons DM. Neuroendocrine aspects of hypercortisolism in major depression. *Hormones Behav.* 2003; 43:60–66.

60. Brody EB, Man EB. Thyroid function measured by serum precipitable iodine determinations in schizophrenic patients. *Amer. J. Psychiat.* 1950; 107:357–359.

61. Gibbons JL, Gibson JG, Maxwell AE, Willcox DRC. An endocrine study of depressive illness. *J. Psychosom. Res.* 1960; 5:32–41.

62. Joffe R, Segal Z, Singer W. Change in thyroid hormone levels following response to cognitive therapy for major depression. *Amer. J. Psychiat.* 1996; 153:411–413.

63. Funkenstein DH. "Discussion of Chapters 10–11: Psychophysiologic Studies of Depression: Some Experimental Work," in *Depression*, ed. Hoch PH, Zubin J. New York, Grune & Stratton; 1954.

64. Feinberg I. Current status of the Funkenstein Test. *Arch. Neurol. Psychiat.* 1958; 80:488.

65. Hamilton M. Quantitative assessment of the Mecholyl (Funkenstein) test. *Acta Neurol. Scand.* 1960b; 35:156–162.

66. Rose JT. Autonomic function in derpression: a modified metacholine test. *J. Ment. Sci.* 1962; 108:624–641.

67. Strongin EI, Hinsie LE. Parotid gland secretions in manic-depressive patients. *Amer. J. Psychiat.* 1938; 94:1459.

68. Peck RE. The SHP Test: an aid in the detection and measurement of depress. *Arch. Gen. Psychiat.* (*Chicago*). 1959; 1:35–40.

69. Gottlieb G, Paulson G. Salivation in depressed patients. *Arch. Gen. Psychiat.* (*Chicago*) 1961; 5:468–471.

70. Busfield BL, Wechsler H. Studies of salivation in depression: a comparison of salivation rates in depressed, schizoaffective depressed, nondepressed hospitalized patients, and in normal controls. *Arch. Gen. Psychiat.* (*Chicago*). 1961; 4:10.

71. Busfield BL, Wechsler H, Barnum WJ. Studies of salivation in depression II. Physiological differentiation of reactive and endogenous depression. *Arch. Gen. Psychiat.* (*Chicago*). 1961; 5:472–477.

72. Davies BM, Gurland JB. Salivary secretion in depressive illness. *J. Psychosom. Res.* 1961; 5:269–271.

73. Palmai G, Blackwell B. The diurnal pattern of salivary flow in normal and depressed patients. *Brit. J. Psychiat.* 1965; 111:334–338.

74. Ship II, Burket LW. "Oral and Dental Problems," in *Clinical Features of the Older Patient*, ed. Freeman JT. Springfield, Ill., Thomas; 1965.

75. Shagass C, Naiman J, Mihalik J. An objective test which differentiates between neurotic and psychotic depression. *Arch. Neurol. Psychiat.* 1956; 75:461–471.

76. Ackner B, Pampiglione G. An evaluation of the sedation threshold test. *J. Psychosom. Res.* 1959; 3:271–281.

77. Nymgaard K. Studies on the sedation threshold: A. Reproducibility and effect of drugs. B. Sedation threshold in neurotic and psychotic depression. *Arch. Gen. Psychiat.* (*Chicago*) 1959; 1:530–536.

78. Martin I, Davies BM. Sleep thresholds in depression. *J. Ment. Sci.* 1962; 108:466–473.

79. Friedman AS, Granick S, Freeman L, Stewart M. Cross-validation of the low (EEG) sedation threshold of psychotic depressives. Paper presented at Annual Meeting of American Psychological Association. Chicago, September 1965.

80. Friedman AS. Personal communication; 1966.

81. Farley P. The anatomy of despair. *New Scientist* 2004; 182:42.

82. Sheline YI, Sanghavi M, Mintun MA, Gado M. Depression duration but not age predicts hippocampal volume loss in women with recurrent major depression. *J. Neurosci.* 1999; 19:5034–5043.

83. McEwen BS, Sapolsky RM. Stress and cognitive function. *Curr. Opin. Neurobiol.* 1995; 5(2):205–216.

84. Frodl T, Meisenzahl EM, Zetzsche T, Höhne T, Banac S, Schorr C, et al. Hippocampal and amygdala changes in patients with major depressive disorder and healthy controls during a 1-year follow-up. *J. Clin. Psychiat.* 2004; 65:492–499.

85. Duman RS, Heninger GR, Nestler EJ. A molecular and cellular theory of depression. *Arch. Gen. Psychiat.* 1997; 54:597–606.

86. Santarelli L, Saxe M, Gross C, Surget A, Battaglia F, Dulawa S, et al. Requirement of hippocampal neurogenesis for the behavioral effects of antidepressants. *Science* 2003; 301:805–809.

87. Sheline YI, Gado MH, Kraemer HC. Untreated depression and hippocampal loss. *Amer. J. Psychiat.* 2003; 160:1516-1518.

88. Holden C. Future brightening for depression treatments. *Science* 2003; 302:810–813.

89. Vaidya VA, Duman RS. Depression-emerging insights from neurobiology. *Brit. Med. Bull.* 2001; 57:61–79.

90. Duman RS. Genetics of childhood disorders: XXXIX. Stem cell research, part 3: Regulation of neurogenesis by stress and antidepressant treatment. *J. Acad. Child Adolesc. Psychiat.* 2002; 41:745-748.

91. Jacobs BL. Depression: the brain finally gets into the act. *Curr. Dir. Psychol. Sci.* 2004; 13:103–106.

92. Whatmore GB, Ellis RM Jr. Some neurophysiologic aspects of depressed states: an electromyographic study. *Arch. Gen. Psychiat. (Chicago).* 1959; 1:70–80.

93. Whatmore G, Ellis RM. Further neurophysiologic aspects of depressed states: an electromyographic study. *Arch. Gen. Psychiat. (Chicago).* 1962; 6:243–253.

94. Goldstein IG. The relationship of muscle tension and autonomic activity to psychiatric disorders. *Psychosom. Med.* 1965; 27:39–52.

95. Diaz-Guerrero R, Gottlieb JS, Knott JR. The sleep of patients with manic-depressive psychosis, depressive type: an electroencephalographic study. *Psychosom. Med.* 1946; 8:399–404.

96. Oswald I, Berger RJ, Jaramillo RA, Keddie KMG, Olley PC, Plunkett GB. Melancholia and barbiturates: a controlled EEG, body and eye movement study of sleep. *Brit. J. Psychiat.* 1963; 109:66–78.

97. Zung WWK, Wilson WP, Dodson WE. Effect of depressive disorders on sleep EEG responses. *Arch. Gen. Psychiat. (Chicago).* 1964; 10:439–445.

98. Gresham SC, Agnew HW, Williams RL. The sleep of depressed patients: an EEG and eye movement study. *Arch. Gen. Psychiat. (Chicago).* 1965; 13:503–507.

99. Mendels J, Hawkins DR, Scott J. The psychophysiology of sleep in depression. Paper presented at Annual Meeting of the Association of the Psychophysiological Study of Sleep. Gainesville, FL, March 1966.

100. Simons AD, Gordon JS, Monroe SM, Thase ME. Toward an integration of psychologic, social, and biologic factors in depression: effects on outcome and course of cognitive therapy. *J. Consult. Clin. Psych.* 1995; 63:369–377.

101. Thase ME, Fasiczka AL, Berman SR, Simons AD, Reynolds CF. Electroencephalographic sleep profiles before and after cognitive behavior therapy of depression. *Arch. Gen. Psychiat.* 1998; 55:138–144.

102. Paulson GW, Gottlieb G. A longitudinal study of the electroencephalographic arousal response in depressed patients. *J. Nerv. Ment. Dis.* 1961; 133:524–528.

103. Shagass C, Schwartz M. Cerebral cortical reactivity in psychotic depressions. *Arch. Gen. Psychiat. (Chicago).* 1962; 6:235–242.

104. Wilson WP, Wilson NJ. Observations on the duration of photically elicited arousal responses in depressive illness. *J. Nerv. Ment. Dis.* 1961; 133:438–440.

105. Driver MV, Eilenberg MD. Photoconvulsive threshold in depressive illness and the effect of E.C.T. *J. Ment. Sci.* 1960; 106:611–617.

106. Quraishi S, Frangou S. Neuropsychology of bipolar disorder: a review. *J. Aff. Disord.*2002; 72:209–226.

107. Shenal BV, Harrison DW, Demaree HA. The neuropsychology of depression: a literature review and preliminary model. *Neuropsych. Rev.* 2003; 13:33–42.

108. American Psychiatric Association. *Diagnostic and Statistical Manual of Mental Disorders (DSM-IV)* (4th ed., textual revisions). Washington, DC, APA; 2000.

109. Mann JJ. Neurobiology of suicidal behaviour. *Nature Reviews Neuroscience* 2003; 4:819–828.

110. Goldapple K, Segal Z, Garson C, Lau M, Bieling P, Kennedy S, Mayberg H. Modulation of cortical-limbic pathways in major depression: treatment-specific effects of cognitive behavior therapy. *Arch. Gen. Psychiat.* 2004; 61:34–41.

Chapter 10. Psychological Studies

1. Beck AT. A systematic investigation of depression. *Compr. Psychiat.* 1961; 2:162–170.

2. Beck AT. Thinking and depression: 1. Idiosyncractic content and cognitive distortions. *Arch. Gen. Psychiat.* 1963; 9:324–333.

3. Beck AT. Thinking and depression: 2. Theory and therapy. *Arch. Gen. Psychiat.* 1964; 10:561–571.

4. Beck AT. *Depression: Causes and Treatment*. Philadelphia: Univ. Pennsylvania Press; 1967.

5. Beckham EE, Leber WR (Eds.) *Handbook* of Depression: Treatment, Assessment, and Research. Homewood, IL: Dorsey Press;1985.

6. Dubovsky SL, Buzan R. "Mood Disorders." In *Textbook of Psychiatry*, ed. Hales RE, Yudofsky SC, Talbott JA. Washington, DC;American Psychiatric Press; 1999. 479–565.

7. Paykel ES. "Treatment of Depression in the United Kingdom," in *Treatment of Depression: Bridging the 21st Century*, ed. Weissman MM. Washington, D.C.: American Psychiatric Press; 2001. 135-149.

8. Rapaport D. (1945): *Diagnostic Psychological Testing: The Theory, Statistical Evaluation, and Diagnostic Application of a Battery of Tests*, vol. 1. Chicago: Yearbook; 1945.

9. Beck, A. T., Feshbach, S., and Legg, D. (1962): The clinical utility of the digit symbol test. *J. Consult. Psychol.* 26:263–268.

10. Granick, S. (1963): Comparative analysis of psychotic depressives with matched normals on some untimed verbal intelligence tests. *J. Consult. Psychol.* 27:439–443.

11. Friedman, A. S. (1964): Minimal effects of severe depression on cognitive functioning. *J. Abnorm. Soc. Psychol.* 1964; 69:237–243.

12. Loeb A, Beck AT, Diggory JC, Tuthill R. The effects of success and failure on mood, motivation, and performance as a function of predetermined level of depression. Unpublished study; 1966.

13. Shapiro MB, Campbell D, Harris, Dewsberry JP. Effects of E.C.T. upon psychomotor speed and the "distraction effect" in depressed psychiatric patients. *J. Ment. Sci.* 1958; 104:681–695.

14. Tucker JE, Spielberg MJ. Bender-Gestalt Test correlates of emotional depression. *J. Consult. Psychol.* 1958; 22:56.

15. Payne RW, Hirst HL. Overinclusive thinking in a depressive and a control group. *J. Consult. Psychol.* 1957; 21:186–188.

16. Hemphill RE, Hall KRL, Crookes TG. A preliminary report on fatigue and pain tolerance in depressive and psychoneurotic patients. *J. Ment. Sci.* 1952; 98:433–440.

17. Wadsworth WV, Wells BWP, Scott RF. A comparative study of the fatigability of a group of chronic schizophrenics and a group of hospitalized non-psychotic depressives. *J. Ment. Sci.* 1962; 108:304–308.

18. Dixon NF, Lear TE. Perceptual regulation and mental disorder. *J. Ment. Sci.* 1962; 108:356–361.

19. Mezey AG, Cohen SI. The effect of depressive illness on time judgment and time experience. *J. Neurol. Neurosurg. Psychiat.* 1961; 24:269–270.

20. Fisher S. Depressive affect and perception of up-down. *J. Psychiat. Res.* 1964; 2:25.

21. Rosenblatt BP. The influence of affective states upon body image and upon the perceptual organization of space. Ph.D. Dissertation, Clark University, Worcester, MA; 1956.

22. Wapner S, Werner H, Krus DM. The effect of success and failure on space localization. *J. Personality* 1957; 25:752–756.

23. Polyakova M. The effect of blood from manic-depressive psychotics on the higher nervous activity (behavior) of animals. *Zh. Nevropat. I Psikhiat.* 1961; 61:104–108.

24. Loeb A, Feshbach S, Beck AT, Wolf A. Some effects of reward upon the social perception and motivation of psychiatric patients varying in depression. *J. Abnorm. Soc. Psychol.* 1964; 68:609–616.

25. Harsch OH, Zimmer H. An experimental approximation of thought reform. *J. Consult. Psychology* 1965; 29:475–479.

26. Wilson DC. Families of manic-depressives. *Dis. Nerv. Syst.* 1951; 12:362–369.

27. Cohen MB, Baker G, Cohen RA, Fromm-Reichmann F, Weigert EV. An intensive study of twelve cases of manic-depressive psychosis. *Psychiat.* 1954; 17:103–157.

28. Gibson RW. *Comparison of the Family Background and Early Life Experience of the Manic-Depressive and Schizophrenic Patient.* Final Report on Office of Naval Research Contract (Nonr-751(00)). Washington, DC, Washington School of Psychiatry; 1957.

29. Becker J. Achievement-related characteristics of manic-depressives. *J. Abnorm. Soc. Psychol.* 1960; 60:334–339.

30. Spielberger CD, Parker JB, Becker J. Conformity and achievement in remitted manic-depressive patients. *J. Nerv. Ment. Dis.* 1963; 137:162–172.

31. Becker J, Spielberger CD, Parker JB. Value achievement and authoritarian attitudes in psychiatric patients. *J. Clin. Psychol.* 1963; 19:57–61.

32. Beck AT, Stein D. The self concept in depression. Unpublished study; 1960.

33. Beck AT, Steer RA, Epstein N, Brown G. Beck Self-Concept Test. *Psych. Assess.* 1990; 2:191–197.

34. Laxer RM. Self-concept changes of depressive patients in general hospital treatment. *J. Consult. Psychol.* 1964; 28:214–219.

35. Abraham K. "Notes on the Psychoanalytic Investigation and Treatment of Manic-Depressive Insanity and Allied Conditions" (1911), in *Selected Papers on Psychoanalysis*. New York: Basic Books; 1960:137–156.

36. Freud S. "Mourning and Melancholia" (1917), in *Collected Papers*, vol. 4. London: Hogarth Press and Institute of Psychoanalysis; 1950: 152–172.

37. Rado S. The problem of melancholia. *Int. J. Psychoanal.* 1928; 9:420–438.

38. Mendelson, M. *Psychoanalytic Concepts of Depression.* Springfield, IL, Thomas; 1960.

39. Beck AT, Valin S. Psychotic depressive reactions in soldiers who accidentally killed their buddies. *Amer. J. Psychiat.* 1953; 110:347–353.

40. Saul LJ, Sheppard E. An attempt to quantify emotional forces using manifest dreams: a preliminary study. *J. Amer. Psychiat. Ass.* 1956; 4:486–502.

41. Beck AT, Ward CH, Mendelson M, Mock J, Erbaugh J. An inventory for measuring depression. *Arch. Gen. Psychiat. (Chicago).* 1961; 4:561–571.

42. Beck AT, Hurvich MS. Psychological correlates of depression. 1. Frequency of "masochistic" dream content in a private practice sample. *Psychosom. Med.* 1959; 21:50–55.

43. Goldhirsh MI. Manifest content of dreams of convicted sex offenders. *J. Abnorm. Soc. Psychol.* 1961; 63:643–645.

44. Alexander F, Wilson GW. Quantitative dream studies: a methodological attempt at a quantitative evaluation ofpsychoanalytic material. *Psychoanal. Quart.* 1935; 4:371–407.

45. Sheppard E, Saul LJ. An approach to a systematic study of ego function. *Psychoanal. Quart.* 1958; 27:237–245.

46. Hollingshead AB. *Two Factor Index of Social Position* (Mimeographed paper). New Haven, CT, AB Hollingshead; 1957.

47. Gregory IW. *Psychiatry: Biological and Social.* Philadelphia, Saunders; 1961.

48. Brown F. Depression and childhood bereavement. *J. Ment. Sci.* 1961; 107:754–777.

49. Lorr M. Classification of the behavior disorders. *Ann. Rev. Psychol.* 1961; 12:195–216.

50. Pitts FN Jr, Meyer J, Brooks M, Winokur G. Adult psychiatric illness assessed for childhood parental loss, and psychiatric illness in family members—a study of 748 patients and 250 controls. *Amer. J. Psychiat. Suppl.* 1965; 121:i–x.

51. Schwab JJ, Clemmons RS, Bialow B, Duggan V, Davis B. A study of the somatic symptomatology of depression in medical inpatients. *Psychosomat.* 1965; 6:273–277.

52. Schwab JJ, Bialow M, Martin PC, Clemmons R The use of the Beck Depression Inventory with medical inpatients. *Acta Psychiat. Scand.* 1967; 43:255–266.

53. Gregory IW. Retrospective data concerning childhood loss of a parent: II. Category of parental loss by decade of birth, diagnosis and MMPI. *Arch. Gen. Psychiat. (Chicago)* 1966; 15:362–367.

54. American Psychiatric Association *Diagnostic and Statistical Manual: Mental Disorders.* Washington, DC, APA; 1952.

55. Schafer R. *The Clinical Application of Psychological Tests.* New York: Internat. Univ. Press; 1948.

56. Payne RW, Hewlett JH. "Thought Disorder in Psychotic Patients," in *Experiments in Personality,* ed. Eysenck HH. London: Routledge; 1961. 3–104.

57. Cohen B, Senf R, Huston P. Perceptual accuracy in schizophrenia, depression, and neurosis, and affects of amytal. *J. Abnorm. Soc. Psychol.* 1956; 52:363–367.

58. Kraines SH. *Mental Depressions and Their Treatment.* New York, Macmillan; 1957.

59. Kasanin JS. *Language and Thought in Schizophrenia.* Berkeley, Univ. Calif. Press; 1944.

60. Gottschalk L, Gleser G, Springer K. Three hostility scales applicable to verbal samples. *Arch. Gen. Psychiat. (Chicago).* 1963; 9:254–279.

61. Beck AT. Cognitive models of depression. *J. Cog. Psych* 1987; 1:5-37.

62. Clark DA, Beck AT, with Alford BA. *Scientific Foundations of Cognitive Theory and Therapy of Depression.* New York: Wiley; 1999.

63. Haaga DAF, Dyck MJ, Ernst D. Empirical status of cognitive theory of depression. *Psych. Bul.* 1991; 110:215–236.

64. Scher C, Ingram R, Segal Z. Cogntive reactivity and vulnerability: Empirical evaluation of construct activation and cognitive diatheses in unipolar depression. *Clin. Psych. Rev.* 2005; 25:487–510.

Chapter 11. Theories of Depression

1. Alford BA, Beck AT. "Psychotherapeutic Treatment of Depression and Bipolar Disorder," In *The Physician's Guide to Depression and Bipolar Disorder* , ed. Evans DL, Charney DS. New York, McGraw-Hill; 2006. 63–93.

2. Ferster CB. "Behavioral Approaches to Depression," in *The Pychology of Depression: Contemporary Theory and Research*, ed. Friedman RJ, Katz MM. Washington, DC, Hemisphere; 1974.

3. Seligman MEP, Groves D. Non-transient learned helplessness. *Psychonom. Sci.* 1970; 19:191–192.

4. Seligman MEP. "Depression and Learned Helplessness," in *The Psychology of Depression: Contemporary Theory and Research*, ed. Friedman RJ, Katz MM. Washington, DC, Hemisphere; 1974.

5. Lewinsohn PM. "A Behavioral Approach to Depression," in *The Psychology of Depression: Contemporary Theory and Research*, ed. Friedman RJ, Katz MM. Washington, DC, Hemisphere; 1974.

6. Dubovsky SL, Buzan R. "Mood Disorders," in *Textbook of Psychiatry*, ed. Hales RE, Yudofsky SC, Talbott JA Washington, DC, American Psychiatric Press; 1999. 479–565.

7. Gotlib IH, Hammen CL. (Eds.). *Handbook of Depression*. New York, Guilford; 2002.

8. Hollon SD, Haman KL, Brown LL. "Cognitive Behavioral Treatment of depression," in *Handbook of Depression*, ed. Gotlib IH, Hammen CL. New York, Guilford; 2002. 383–403.

9. Beck AT. Cognitive models of depression. *J. Cog. Psychother.* 1987; 1:5–37.

10. Gilbert P. *Human Nature and Suffering*. Hillsdale, NJ, Erlbaum; 1989.

11. Nesse RM. Is depression an adaptation? *Arch. Gen. Psychiat.* 2000; 57:14–20.

12. Skinner BF. Behaviorism at fifty. *Science* 1963; 140:951–958.

13. Skinner BF. Selection by consequences. *Science* 1981; 213:501–504.

14. Alford BA, Beck AT. *The Integrative Power of Cognitive Therapy*. New York, Guilford Press; 1997.

15. Rado S. The problem of melancholia. *Int. J. Psychoanal.* 1928; 9:420–438.

16. Gero G. The construction of depression. *Int. J. Psychoanal.* 1936; 17:423–461.

17. Klein M. "A Contribution to the Psychogenesis of Manic-Depressive States" (1934), in *Contributions to Psycho-Analysis 1921–1945*. London, Hogarth Press and Institute of Psychoanalysis; 1948,. 282–310.

18. Bibring E. "The Mechanism of Depression," in *Affective Disorders*, ed. Greenacre P. New York: Internat. Univ. Press; 1953, 13–48.

19. Jacobson E. Transference problems in the psychoanalytic treatment of severely depressive patients. *J. Amer. Psychoanal. Ass.* 1954; 2:595–606.

20. Hammerman S. Ego defect and depression. Paper presented at Philadelphia Psychoanalytic Society. Philadelphia, November 7, 1962.

21. Zetzel, E. R. The predisposition to depression. *Canad. Psychiat. Ass. J. Suppl.* 1966; 11:236–249.

22. Abraham K. "Notes on the Psychoanalytic Investigation and Treatment of

Manic-Depressive Insanity and Allied Conditions" (1911), in *Selected Papers on Psychoanalysis*. New York, Basic Books; 1960, 137–156.

23. Balint M. New beginning and the paranoid and the depressive syndromes. *Int. J. Psychoanal.* 1952; 33:214–224.

24. Cohen MB, Baker G, Cohen RA, Fromm-Reichmann F, Weigert EV. An intensive study of twelve cases of manic-depressive psychosis. *Psychiatry* 1954; 17:130–137.

25. Abraham K. "The First Pregenital Stage of the Libido" (1916), in *Selected Papers on Psychoanalysis*. New York, Basic Books; 1960, 248–279.

26. Jacobson E. "Contribution to the Metapsychology of Cyclothymic Depression," in *Affective Disorders*, ed. Greenacre P. New York: Internat. Univer. Press; 1953, pp. 49–83.

27. Lichtenberg P. A definition and analysis of depression. *Arch. Neurol. Psychiat.* 1957; 77:516–527.

28. Schwartz DA. Some suggestions for a unitary formulation of the manic-depressive reactions. *Psychiatry* 1961; 24:238–45.

29. Arieti S. (1959): "Manic-Depressive Psychosis," in *American Handbook of Psychiatry*, ed. Arieti S, vol. 1. New York, Basic Books; 1959. 419–454.

30. Tellenbach H. *Melancholie*. West Berlin, Springer; 1961.

31. Schulte W. Nichttraurigseinkönnen im Kern melancholischen Erlebens. *Nervenartz* 1961; 32:314–320.

32. Kraines SH. Manic-depressive syndrome: a diencephalic disease. Paper presented at Annual Meeting of the American Psychiatric Association, New York, May 6, 1965.

33. Shenal BV, Harrison DW, Demaree HA. The neuropsychology of depression: a literature review and preliminary model. *Neuropsych. Rev.* 2003; 13:33–42.

34. Schildkraut J. The catecholamine hypothesis of affective disorders: a review of support evidence. *Amer. J. Psychiat.* 1965; 122:509–522.

35. Willner P. "Animal models of Depression," in *Handbook of Depression and Anxiety: A Biological Approach*, ed. den Boer JS, Sitsen JM. New York: Dekker; 1994. 291–316.

36. Hayhurst H, Cooper Z, Paykel ES, Vernals S, Ramana R. Expressed emotion and depression: a longitudinal study. *Brit. J. Psychiat.* 1997; 171:439–443.

37. Beck AT. *Depression: Causes and Treatment*. Philadelphia: Univ. Pennsylvania Press; 1967.

Chapter 12. Cognition and Psychopathology

1. Abraham K. "The First Pregenital Stage of the Libido" (1916), in *Selected Papers on Psychoanalysis*. New York: Basic Books, 1960, 248–279.

2. Rado S. The problem of melancholia. *Int. J. Psychoanal.* 1928; 9:420–438.

3. Freud S. (1917): "Mourning and Melancholia" (1950), in *Collected Papers*, vol. 4. London, Hogarth Press and Institute of Psychoanalysis. 152–172.

4. Adler KA. Depression in the light of individual psychology. *J. Indiv. Psych.* 1961; 17:56–67.

5. Klein M. "A Contribution to the Psychogenesis of Manic-Depressive States" (1934), in *Contributions to Psycho-Analysis 1921–1945*. London: Hogarth Press and Institute of Psychoanalysis; 1948.

6. Grinker R, Miller J, Sabshin M, Nunn R, Nunnally J. *The Phenomena of Depressions*. New York: Hoeber; 1961.

7. Campbell JD. *Manic-Depressive Disease*. Philadelphia: Lippincott; 1953.

8. Kraines SH. Manic-depressive syndrome: a diencephalic disease. Paper presented at Annual Meeting of the American Psychiatric Association. New York, May 6, 1965.

9. Diethelm O, Hefferman T. Felix Platter and psychiatry. *J. Hist. Behav. Sci.* 1965; 1:10–23.

10. Jelliffe SE . Some historical phases of the manic-depressive synthesis. *Ass. Res. Nerv. Ment. Proc.* 1931; 11:3–47.

11. Kelly GA. *The Psychology of Personal Constructs.* New York: Norton; 1955, vol. 1.

12. Harvey OJ, Hunt DE, Schroeder HM. *Conceptual Systems and Personality Organization.* New York: Wiley; 1961.

13. Ellis A. *Reason and Emotion in Psychotherapy.* New York: Lyle Stuart; 1962.

14. Arieti S. Studies of thought processes in contemporary psychiatry. *Amer. J. Psychiat.* 1963; 120:58–64.

15. Ellis A. Reflections on rational-emotive therapy. *J. Consult. Clin. Psych.* 1993; 61:199–201.

16. Rholes WS, Riskind JH, Neville B. The relationship of cognitions and hopelessness to depression and anxiety. *Soc. Cog.* 1985; 54:36–50.

17. Alford BA, Lester JM, Patel RJ, Buchanan JP, Giunta LC. Hopelessness predicts future depressive symptoms: a prospective analysis of cognitive vulnerability and cognitive content specificity. *J. Clin. Psych.* 1995; 51:331–339.

18. Kendall PC, Hollon SD, Beck AT, Hammen CL, Ingram RE. Issues and recommendations regarding use of the Beck Depression Inventory. *Cog. Ther. Res.* 1987; 11:289–299.

19. Beck AT. Cognitive therapy: a 30-year retrospective. *Amer. Psychologist* 1991; 46:368–375.

20. Rush AJ, Weissenburger J, Eaves G. Do thinking patterns predict depressive symptoms? *Cog. Ther. Res.* 1986; 10:225–236.

21. Teasdale JD, Fennell MJV. Immediate effects on depression of cognitive therapy interventions. *Cog. Ther. Res.* 1982; 6:343–352.

22. Beck AT, Kovacs M, Weissman A. Hopelessness and suicidal behavior: an overview. *J. Amer. Med. Assoc.* 1975; 234:1146–1149.

23. Beck AT, Brown G, Berchick RJ, Stewart BL, Steer RA. Relationship between hopelessness and ultimate suicide: a replication with psychiatric outpatients. *Amer. J. Psychiat.* 1990; 147:190–195.

24. Beck AT, Steer RA, Kovacs M, Garrison B. Hopelessness and eventual suicide: a 10-year prospective study of patients hospitalized with suicidal ideation. *Ame. J. Psychiat.* 1985; 142:559–563.

25. Rush AJ, Kovacs M, Beck AT, Weissenburger J, Hollon SD. Differential effects of cognitive therapy and pharmacotherapy on depressive symptoms. *J. Aff. Disord* 1981; 3:221–229.

26. Rush AJ, Beck AT, Kovacs M, Hollon SD. (1977). Comparative efficacy of cognitive therapy and pharmacotherapy in the treatment of depressed outpatients. *Cog. Ther. Res.* 1977; 1:17–37.

27. Roseman IJ, Evdokas A. (2004). Appraisals cause experienced emotions: experimental evidence. *Cog. Emot.* 2004; 18:1–28.

28. Loeb A, Feshbach S, Beck AT, Wolf A. Some effects of reward upon the social perception and motivation of psychiatric patients varying in depression. *J. Abnorm. Soc. Psychol.* 1964; 68:609–616.

29. Friedman AS. Minimal effects of severe depression on cognitive functioning. *J. Abnorm. Soc. Psychol.* 1964; 69:237–243.

30. Editorial (1963): Thinking disorder in neurosis. *J. Amer. Med. Assoc.* 1963; 186:946.

31. Overall J, Gorham D. Basic dimensions of change in the symptomatology of chronic schizophrenics. *J. Abnorm. Soc. Psychol.* 1961; 63:597–602.

32. Charcot JM. (1890). Cited by White RW in *The Abnormal Personality*. New York: Ronald Press, 1956. 25.

33. Salkovskis PM, Wroe AL, Gledhill A, Morrison N, Forrester E, Richards C et al. Responsibility attitudes and interpretations are characteristic of obsessive compulsive disorder. *Behaviour Research and Therapy* 2000; 38:347–372.

Chapter 13. Development of Depression

1. Jacobson E. "Contribution to the Metapsychology of Cyclothymic Depression," in *Affective Disorders*, ed. Greenacre, P. New York, Internat. Univer. Press; 1953:49–83.

2. Bibring E. "The Mechanism of Depression," in *Affective Disorders*, ed. Greenacre P. New York, Internat. Univ. Press; 1953:13–48.

3. Kelly GA. *The Psychology of Personal Constructs*. New York, Norton; 1955 vol. 1.

4. Cassidy WL, Flanagan NB, Spellman M. Clinical observations in manic-depressive disease: a quantitative study of 100 manic-depressive patients and 50 medically sick controls. *J. Amer. Med. Ass.* 1957; 164:1535–1546.

5. Beck AT. *Depression: Causes and Treatment*. Philadelphia: Univ. Pennsylvania Press; 1967.

6. Scher C, Ingram R, Segal Z. Cognitive reactivity and vulnerability: empirical evaluation of construct activation and cognitive diatheses in unipolar depression. *Clin. Psych. Rev.* 2005; 25:487–510.

7. Teasdale JD, Dent J. Cognitive vulnerability to depression: an investigation of two hypotheses. *Brit. J. Clin. Psych.* 1987; 26:113–126.

8. Miranda J, Persons JB. Dysfunctional attitudes are mood-state dependent. *J. Abnorm. Psych.* 1988; 97:76–79.

9. Miranda J, Persons JB, Byers CN. Endorsement of dysfunctional beliefs depends on current mood state. *J. Abnorm. Psych.*1990; 99:237–241.

10. Ingram RE, Bernet CZ, McLaughlin SC. Attentional allocation processes in individuals at risk for depression. *Cog. Ther. Res.* 1994; 18:317–332.

11. Hedlund S, Rude SS. Evidence of latent depressive schemas in formally depressed individuals. *J. Abnorm. Psych.* 1995; 104:517–525.

12. Roberts JE, Kassel JD. Mood state dependence in cognitive vulnerability to depression: the roles of positive and negative affect. *Cognitive Therapy and Research* 1996; 20:1–12.

13. Dykman BM. A test of whether negative emotional priming facilitates access to latent dysfunctional attitudes. *Cognit. Emot.* 1997; 11:197–222.

14. Gilboa E, Gotlib IH. Cognitive biases and affect persistence in previously dysphoric and never-dysphoric individuals. *Cognit. Emot.* 1997; 11:517–538.

15. Miranda J, Gross JJ, Persons JB, Hahn J. Mood matters: Negative mood induction activates dysfunctional attitudes in women vulnerable to depression. *Cognitive Therapy and Research* 1998; 22:363–376.

16. Solomon A, Haaga DAF, Brody C, Kirk L, Friedman, DG. Priming irrational beliefs in recovered-depressed people. *J. Abnorm. Psych.* 1998; 107:440–449.

17. Brosse AL, Craighead LW, Craighead WE. Testing the mood-state hypothesis

among previously depressed and never-depressed individuals. *Behav. Ther.* 1999; 30:97–115.

18. Segal ZV, Gemar MC, Williams S. Differential cognitive response to a mood challenge following successful cognitive therapy or pharmacotherapy for unipolar depression. *J. Abnorm. Psych.* 1999; 108:3–10.

19. Taylor L, Ingram RE. Cognitive reactivity and depressotypic Information processing in children of depressed mothers. *J. Abnorm. Psych.* 1999; 108:202–210.

20. Ingram RE, Ritter J. Vulnerability to depression: Cognitive reactivity and parental bonding in high-risk individuals. *J. Abnorm. Psych.* 2000; 109:588–596.

21. McCabe SB, Gotlib IH, Martin RA. Cognitive vulnerability for depression: Deployment of attention as a function of history of depression and current mood state. *Cog. Ther. Res.* 2000; 24:427–444.

22. Gemar MC, Segal ZV, Sagrati S, Kennedy SJ. Mood-induced changes on the implicit association test in recovered depressed patients. *J. Abnorm. Psych.* 2001; 110:282–289.

23. Murray L, Woolgar M, Cooper P, Hipwell A. Cognitive vulnerability to depression in 5-year-old children of depressed mothers. *J. Child Psych. Psychiat. Al. Disc.* 2001; 42:891–899.

24. Timbremont B, Braet C. Cognitive vulnerability in remitted depressed children and adolescents. *Behav. Res. Ther.* 2004; 42:423–437.

25. Barnett PA, Gotlib IH. Dysfunctional attitudes and psychosocial stress: the differential prediction of future psychological symptomatology. *Motiv. Emot.* 1988; 12:251–270.

26. Barnett PA, Gotlib IH. Cognitive vulnerability to depressive symptoms among men and women. *Cog. Ther. Res.* 1990; 14:47–61.

27. Kwon S, Oei TPS. Differential casual roles of dysfunctional attitudes and automatic thoughts in depression. *Cog. Ther. Res.* 1992; 16:309–328.

28. Brown GP, Hammen CL, Craske MG, Wickens TD. Dimensions of dysfunctional attitudes as vulnerabilities to depressive symptoms. *J. Abnorm. Psych.* 1995; 104:431–435.

29. Dykman BM, Johll M. Dysfunctional attitudes and vulnerability to depressive symptoms: a 14-week longitudinal study. *Cog. Ther. Res.* 1998; 22:337–352.

30. Shirk SR, Boergers J, Eason A, Van Horn M. Dysphoric interpersonal schemata and preadolescents' sensitization to negative events. *J. Clin. Child Psych.* 1998; 2:54–68.

31. Joiner TE, Metalsky GI, Lew A, Klocek J. Testing the causal mediation component of Beck's theory of depression: evidence for specific mediation. *Cog. Ther. Res.* 1999; 23:404–412.

32. Lewinsohn PM, Joiner TE Jr, Rohde P. Evaluation of cognitive diathesis-stress models in predicting major depressive disorder in adolescents. *J. Abnorm. Psych.* 2001; 110:203–215.

33. Abela JR, D'Alessandro DU. Beck's cognitive theory of depression: a test of the diathesis-stress and causal mediation components. *Brit. J. Clin. Psych.* 2002; 41:111–128.

34. Beevers CG, Carver CS. Attentional bias and mood persistence as prospective predictors of dysphoria. *Cog. Ther. Res.* 2003; 27:619–637.

35. Hankin BL, Abramson LY, Miller N, Haeffel GJ. Cognitive vulnerability-stress theories of depression: examining affective specificity in the prediction of depression versus anxiety in three prospective studies. *Cog. Ther. Res.* 2004; 28:309–345.

36. Heim C, Meinlschmidt G, Nemeroff CB. Neurobiology of Early-Life Stress. *Psychiat. Ann.* 2003; 33:18–26.

37. Nemeroff CB, Vale WW. The Neurobiology of depression: inroads to treatment and new drug discovery. *J. Clin. Psychiat.* 2005; 66:5–13.

38. Penza KM, Heim C, Nemeroff CB. Neurobiological effects of childhood abuse: implications for the pathophysiology of depression and anxiety. *Arch. Women's Mental Health* 2003; 6:15–22.

39. Caspi A, Sugden K, Moffitt TE, Taylor A, Craig IW, Harrington HL, et al. Influence of life stress on depression: moderation by a polymorphism in the 5-HTT gene. *Science* 2003; 301:386–389.

40. Hayden EP, Klein DN. Outcome of dysthymic disorder at 5-year follow-up: the effect of familial psychopathology, early adversity, personality, comorbidity, and chronic stress. *Amer. J. Psychiat.* 2001; 158:1864–1870.

41. Dougherty LR, Klein DN, Davila J. A growth curve analysis of the course of dysthymic disorder: the effects of chronic stress and moderation by adverse parent-child relationships and family history. *J. consult. Clin. Psych.* 2004; 72(6):1012–1021.

42. Kendler KS, Thornton LM, Gardner CO. Genetic risk, number of previous depressive episodes, and stressful life events in predicting onset of major depression. *Amer. J. Psychiat.* 2001; 158:582–586.

43. Rapaport D. *Organization and Pathology of Thought.* New York, Columbia Univ. Press; 1951.

44. Allport FH. *Theories of Perception and the Concept of Structure.* New York, Wiley; 1955.

45. Bruner JS, Goodnow JJ, Austin GA. *A Study of Thinking.* New York, Wiley; 1956.

46. Festinger L. *A Theory of Cognitive Dissonance.* Evanston, IL, Harper & Row; 1957.

47. Osgood CE. "A Behavioristic Analysis of Perception and Language as Cognitive Phenomena," in *Contemporary Approaches to Cognition,* ed. Bruner s et al. Cambridge, MA, Harvard Univ. Press; 1957:75–119.

48. Sarbin TR, Taft R, Bailey DE. *Clinical Inference and Cognitive Theory.* New York, Holt; 1960.

49. Harvey OJ, Hunt DE, Schroeder HM. *Conceptual Systems and Personality Organization.* New York, Wiley; 1961.

50. Ellis A. *Reason and Emotion in Psychotherapy.* New York, Lyle Stuart; 1962.

51. Freud S. *Basic Writings,* trans. Brill AA. New York, Modern Library; 1938.

52. Horney K. *Our Inner Conflicts.* New York, Norton; 1945.

53. Rogers CR. *Client-Centered Therapy.* Boston, Houghton-Mifflin; 1951.

54. Piaget J. *The Moral Judgment of the Child,* trans. Gabain M. Glencoe, IL, Free Press; 1948.

55. Postman L. "Toward a General Theory of Cognition," in *Social Psychology at the Crossroads,* ed. Rohrer JH, Sherif M. New York, Harper; 1951.

56. English HB, English AC. *A Comprehensive Dictionary of Psychological and Psychoanalytical Terms.* New York, Longmans; 1958.

57. Alford BA, Beck AT. *The Integrative Power of Cognitive Therapy.* New York, Guilford Press; 1998.

58. Beck AT. "Beyond Belief: A Theory of Modes, Personality, and Psychopathology," in *Frontiers of Cognitive Therapy,* ed. Salkovsikis PM. New York, Guilford; 1996. 1–25.

59. Clark DA, Beck AT, with Alford BA. *Scientific Foundations of Cognitive Theory and Therapy of Depression.* New York, Wiley; 1999.

60. Epstein S. Integration of the cognitive and the psychodynamic unconscious. *Amer. Psych.* 1994; 49:709–724.

61. Mandler G. *Mind and Emotion*. Malabar, FL: Krieger; 1982.

62. Mischel W, Shoda Y. A cognitive-affective system theory of personality: reconceptualizing situations, dispositions, dynamics, and invariance in personality structure. *Psych. Rev.* 1995; 102:246–268.

63. Oatley K, Johnson-Laird PN. Towards a cognitive theory of emotion. *Cognit. Emotion* 1987; 1:29–50.

64. Teasdale JD, Barnard PJ. *Affect, Cognition and Change: Remodelling Depressive Thought*. Hove, UK, Lawrence Erlbaum; 1993.

65. Nolen-Hoeksema S. "Gender Differences in Depression," in *Handbook of Depression*, ed. Gotlib IH, Hammen, CL. New York, Guilford; 2002. 492–509.

66. Papageorgiou C, Wells A. (Eds.) *Depressive Rumination: Nature, Theory, and Treatment*. Chichester, Endland; 2004.

67. Nolen-Hoeksema S, Larson J, Grayson C. Explaining the gender difference in depressive symptoms. *J. Personal. Soc. Psych.* 1999; 77:1061–1072.

68. Nolen-Hoeksema S. The role of rumination in depressive disorders and mixed anxiety/depressive symptoms. *J. Abnorm. Psych.* 2000; 109:504–511.

69. Roseman IJ, Evdokas A. Appraisals cause experienced emotions: experimental evidence. *Cognition and Emotion* 2004; 18:1–28.

70. Feshbach S. Personal communication; 1965.

Chapter 14. Somatic Therapies

1. Marangell LB, Yudofsky SC, Silver JM. "Psychopharmacology and Electroconvulsive Therapy," in *Textbook of Psychiatry*, ed. Hales RE, Yudofsky SC, Talbott JA. Washington, DC, American Psychiatric Press; 1999. 1025–1132.

2. American Psychiatric Association. *Practice Guidelines for the Treatment of Psychiatric Disorders: Compendium 2000*. Washington DC, APA; 2000.

3. Dubovsky SL, Buzan R. "Mood Disorders," in *Textbook of Psychiatry*, ed. Hales RE, Yudofsky SC, Talbott JA. Washington, DC, American Psychiatric Press; 1999. 479–565.

4. Kline N. Practical management of depression. *J. Amer. Med. Ass.* 1964; 190:732–740.

5. Hordern A. The antidepressant drugs. *New Eng. J. Med.* 1965; 272:1159–1169.

6. Brady JP. Review of controlled studies of imipramine. Unpublished study. 1963.

7. Cole JO. Therapeutic efficacy of antidepressant drugs. *J. Amer. Med. Ass.* 1964; 190:448–455.

8. Klerman GL, Cole JO. Clinical pharmacology of imipramine and related antidepressant compounds. *Pharmacol. Rev.* 1965; 17:101–141.

9. Friedman AS, Granick S, Cohen HW, Cowitz B. Imipramine (Tofranil) vs. placebo in hospitalized psychotic depressives. *J. Psychiat. Res.* 1966; 4:13–36.

10. Quitkin FM, Rabkin JG, Gerald J, Davis JM, Klein DF. Validity of clinical trials of antidepressants. *Am J Psychiatry* 2000; 157:327–337.

11. Wechsler H, Grosser G, Greenblatt M. Research evaluating antidepressant medications on hospitalized mental patients: a survey of published reports during a five year period. *J. Nerv. Ment. Dis.* 1965; 141:231–239.

12. Davis J. Efficacy of tranquilizing and antidepressant drugs. *Arch. Gen. Psychiat.* 1965; 13:552–572.

13. Fiedorowicz JG, Swartz KL. The role of monoamine oxidase inhibitors in current psychiatric practice. *J Psychiatr Pract* 2004; 10:239–248.

14. Potter WZ, Rudorfer MV, Manji H. The pharmacologic treatment of depression. *New England J. Med.* 1991; 325:633–642.

15. Paykel ES. "Treatment of Depression in the United Kingdom," in *Treatment of Depression: Bridging the 21st Century*, ed. Waissman MM. Washington, DC, American Psychiatric Press; 2001. 135–149.

16. Stafford RS, MacDonald EA, Finkelstein SN. National patterns of medication treatment for depression, 1987 to 2001. *Prim. Car. Companion. J Clin. Psychiat.* 2001; 3:232–235.

17. Masand PS, Gupta S. Selective serotonin-reuptake inhibitors: an update. *Harv. Rev. Psychiat.* 1999; 7:69–84.

18. Pirraglia PA, Stafford RS, Singer DE. Trends in prescribing of selective serotonin reuptake inhibitors and other newer antidepressant agents in adult primary care. *Prim. Care Companio. J Clin. Psychiat.* 2003; 5:153–157.

19. Ma J, Lee KV, Stafford RS. Depression treatment during outpatient visits by U.S. children and adolescents. *J. Adolesc. Health.* 2005; 37:434–42.

20. Satel SL, Nelson JC. Stimulants in the treatment of depression: a critical overview. *J. Clin. Psych.* 1989; 50:241–249.

21. Johnson GF. Lithium in depression: a review of the antidepressant and prophylactic effects of lithium. *Austral. New Zeal. J. Psychiat.* 1987; 21:356–365.

22. Sharma V, Khan M, Smith A. A closer look at treatment resistant depression: is it due to a bipolar diathesis? *J. Aff. Disord.* 2005; 84:251–257.

23. Kessing LV, Sondergard L, Kvist K, Andersen PK. Suicide risk in patients treated with lithium. *Arch. Gen Psychiat.* 2005; 62:860–866.

24. Baldessarini RJ, Tonodo L, Hennen J, Viguera AC. Is lithium still worth using? an update of selected recent research. *Harv. Rev. Psychiat.* 2002; 10:59–75.

25. Parker G. "New" and "old" antidepressants: all equal in the eyes of the lore? *Brit. J. Psychiat.* 2001; 179:95–96.

26. Fava M. Management of nonresponse and intolerance: switching strategies. *J. Clin Psychiat.* 2000; 61 (Suppl 2):10–12.

27. Rush AJ, Trivedi HM, Wisniewski SR, Stewart JW, Nierenberg AA, Thase ME, et al. Bupropion-sr, sertraline, or vernlafaxine-xr after failure of SSRIs for depression. *New England J. Med.* 2006; 354:1231–1242.

28. Marangell LB. Switching antidepressants for treatment-resistant major depression. *J. Clin. Psychiat.* 2001; 62:12–17.

29. Thase ME, Rush AJ, Howland RH, Kornstein SG, Kocsis JH, Gelenberg AJ, et al. Double-blind switch study of imipramine or sertraline treatment of antidepressant-resistant chronic depression. *Arch. Gen. Psychiat.* 2002; 59:233–239.

30. Lam RW, Dante DC, Cohen NL, Kennedy SH. Combining antidepressants for treatment-resistant depression: a review. *J. Clin. Psychiat.* 2002; 63:685–693.

31. Coryell W. Augmentation strategies for inadequate antidepressant response: A review of placebo-controlled studies. *Ann. Clin. Psychiat.* 2000; 12:141–146.

32. Hollon SD, Jarrett RB, Nierenberg AA, Thase ME, Trivedi MD, Rush AJ. Psychotherapy and medication in the treatment of adult and geriatric depression: which monotherapy or combined treatment? *J. Clin. Psychiat.* 2005; 66:455–468.

33. Mendlewicz, J. Optimising antidepressant use in clinical practice: towards criteria for antidepressant selection. *Brit. J. Psychiat.* 2001: 179 (Suppl. 42), s1-s3.

34. Freudenstein U, Jagger C, Arthur A, Donner-Banzhoff N. Treatments for late life depression in primary care: a systematic review. *Family Practice* 2001; 18:321–327.

35. Baldwin RC. Refractory depression in late life: a review of treatment options. *Rev. Clin. Geront.* 1996; 6:343–348.

36. Satel SL, Nelson JC. Stimulants in the treatment of depression: A critical overview. *J. Clin. Psychiat.* 1989; 50, 241–249.

37. Snow LH, Rickels K. The controlled evaluation of imipramine and amitriptyline in hospitalized depressed psychiatric patients. *Psychopharmacol.*1964; 5:409–416.

38. Rickels K. Psychopharmacological agents: a clinical psychiatrist's individualistic point of view: patient and doctor variables. *J. Nerv. Ment. Dis.* 1963; *136*:540–549.

39. Rickels K, Ward CH, Schut L. Different populations, different drug responses: comparative study of two anti-depressants, each used in two different patient groups. *Amer. J. Med. Sci.* 1964; 247:328–335.

40. Grosser GH, Freeman H. "Differential Recovery Patterns in the Treatment of Acute Depression," in *Proceedings of the Third World Congress of Psychiatry*. University of Toronto Press and Montreal, McGill Univ. Press 1961; 2:1396–1402.

41. DiMasico A, Klerman GL. "Experimental Human Psychopharmacology: The Role of Non-Drug Factors," in *The Dynamics of Psychiatric Drug Therapy*, ed. Sarwer-Fober GJ. Springfield, IL, Thomas, 1960:56–97.

42. Bolwig TG. Commentary: Recent developments and controversies in depression. *The Lancet*. 2006; 367:1235–1237.

43. Summerfield D. Commentary: Recent developments and controversies in depression. *The Lancet*. 2006; 367:1235–1237.

44. Greenberg RP, Bornstein RF, Greenberg MD, Fisher S. A meta-analysis of antidepressant outcome under "blinder" conditions. *J. Consult. Clin. Psychol.* 1992; 60:664–669.

45. Moncrieff J, Wessely S, Hardy R. Meta-analysis of trials comparing antidepressants with active placebos. *Brit. J. Psychiat.* 1998; 172:227–231.

46. Moncrief J. The anit-depressant debate. *Brit. Psychiat.* 2002; 180:193–194.

47. Ayd FJ. Chemical remedies for depression. *Med. Sci.* 1964; 15:37–44.

48. Hu XH, Bull SA, Hunkeler EM, Ming E, Lee JY, Fireman B, Markson LE. Incidence and duration of side effects and those rated as bothersome with selective serotonin reuptake inhibitor treatment for depression: patient report versus physician estimate. *J. Clin. Psychiat.* 2004; 65:959–965.

49. Culpepper L., Davidson JRT, Dietrich AJ, Goodman WK, Kroenke K, Schwenk TL. Suicidiality as a possible side effect of antidepressant treatment. *J. Clin. Psychiat* .2004; 65:742–749.

50. Holmberg G. Biological aspects of electro-convulsive therapy." *Internat. Rev. Neurobiol.* (ed. Preiffer C, Smythies J.). 1963; 5:389–406.

51. Cronholm B, Molander L. Memory disturbances after electroconvulsive therapy: 5. Conditions one month after a series of treatments. *Acta Psychiat. Scand.* 1964; 40:212.

52. Kalinowsky LB, Hoch PH. *Somatic Treatments in Psychiatry*. New York: Grune & Stratton; 1961.

53. Holden C. Future brightening for depression treatments. *Science* 2003; 302:810–813.

54. Sterling P. ECT damage is easy to find if you look for it. *Nature* 2000; 403:242.

55. Fink M. ECT has proved effective in treating depression. *Nature* 2000; 403:826.

56. Carney S, Cowen P, Geddes J, Goodwin G, et al. Efficacy and safety of electroconvulsive therapy in depressive disorders: A systematic review and meta-analysis. *The Lancet*. 2003; 361:799–808.

57. Kho KH, van Vreeswijk F, Simpson S, Zwinderman AH. A meta-analysis of electroconvulsive therapy efficacy in depression. *J. ECT.* 2005; 19:139–147.

58. Pridmore S. Substitution of rapid transcranial magnetic stimulation treatments for electroconvulsive therapy treatments in a course of electroconvulsive therapy. *Depress. Anx.* 2000; 12:118–123

59. Pridmore S, Bruno R, Turnier-Shea Y, Reid P, Rybak M. Comparison of unlim-

ited numbers of rapid transcranial magnetic stimulation (rTMS) and ECT treatment sessions in major depressive episode.*Internat. J. Neuropsychopharm.* 2000; 3:129–134.

60. Grunhaus L, Dannon PN, Schreiber S, Dolberg OH, Amiaz R, Ziv R, Lefkifker E. Repetitive transcranial magnetic stimulation is as effective as electroconvulsive therapy in the treatment of nondelusional major depressive disorder: an open study. *Biol. Psychiat.* 2000; 47:314–324.

61. Grunhaus L, Schreiber S, Dolberg OT, Polak D, Dannon PN. A randomized controlled comparison of electroconvulsive therapy and repetitive transcranial magnetic stimulation in severe and resistant nonpsychotic major depression. *Biol. Psychiat.* 2003; 53:324–331.

62. Smeraldi E, Zanardi R, Benedetti F, Di Bella D, Perez J, Catalano M. Polymorphism within the promoter of the serotonin transporter gene and antidepressant efficacy of fluvoxamine. *Mol. Psychiatry* 1998; 3:508–11.

63. Pollock BG, Ferrell RE, Mulsant BH, Mazumdar S, Miller M, Sweet RA, et al. Allelic variation in the serotonin transporter promoter affects onset of paroxetine treatment response in late-life depression. *Neuropsychopharmacol.* 2000; 23:587–590.

64. Rausch JL, Johnson ME, Fei YJ, Li JQ, Shendarkar N, Hobby HM, et al. Initial conditions of serotonin transporter kinetics and genotype: influence on SSRI treatment trial outcome. *Biol. Psychiat.* 2002; 51:723–32.

Chapter 15. Psychotherapy

1. Butler AC, Chapman JE, Forman EM, Beck AT. The empirical status of cognitive-behavioral therapy: a review of meta-analyses. *Clin. Psych. Rev.* 2006; 26,17–31.

2. Chambless DL, Ollendick TH. Empirically supported psychological interventions: controversies and evidence. *Ann. Rev. Psych.* 2001; 52:685–716.

3. Beck AT, Rush AJ, Shaw BF, Emery G. *Cognitive Therapy of Depression.* New York, Guilford; 1979.

4. Campbell JD. *Manic-Depressive Disease.* Philadelphia, Lippincott; 1953.

5. Wilson DC. Dynamics and psychotherapy of depression. *J. Amer. Med. Ass.* 1955; 158:151–153.

6. Kraines SH. *Mental Depressions and Their Treatment.* New York, Macmillan; 1957.

7. Ayd FJ Jr. *Recognizing the Depressed Patient.* New York, Grune & Stratton; 1961.

8. Arieti S. The psychotherapeutic approach to depression. *Amer. J. Psychother.* 1962; 16:397–406.

9. Gibson RW. Psychotherapy of manic-depressive states. *Psychiat. Res. Rep. Amer. Psychiat. Ass.* 1963; 17:91–102.

10. Regan PF. Brief psychotherapy of depression. *Amer. J. Psychiat.* 1965; 122:28–32.

11. Bonime W. A psychotherapeutic approach to depression. *Contemporary Psychoanalysis* 1965; 2:48–53.

12. Loeb A, Beck AT, Diggory JC, Tuthill R. The effects of success and failure on mood, motivation, and performance as a function of predetermined level of depression. Unpublished study. 1966.

13. Ursano RJ, Silberman EK. "Psychoanalysis, Psychoanalytic Psychotherapy, and Supportive Psychotherapy." In *Textbook of Psychiatry*, ed. Hales RE, Yudofsky SC, Talbott JA. Washington, DC, American Psychiatric Press; 1999. 479–565.

14. American Psychiatric Association. D *Diagnostic and Statistical Manual of Mental Disorders* (*DSM-IV*) (4th ed., textual revisions). Washington, DC, APA; 2000.

15. Dewald PA. The process of change in psychoanalytic psychotherapy. *Arch. Gen. Psychiat.* 1978; 35:535–542.

16. Freud S. *Analysis Terminable and Interminable* (Standard Edition, Vol. 23.); 1937.

17. Corsini RJ, Wedding D. (Eds.). *Current Psychotherapies.* Itasca, IL, Peacock; 2000.

18. Arlow JA. "Psychoanalysis," in *Current Psychotherapies*, ed. Corsini RJ, Wedding D. Itasca,IL, Peacock Publishers; 2000. 16–53.

19. Thase ME, Friedman ES, Howland RH. Management of treatment-resistant depression: psychotherapeutic perspectives. *J. Clin. Psychiat.* 2001; 62(suppl 18):18–24.

20. Lam DH, Watkins ER, Hayward P, Bright J, Wright K, Kerr N, et al. A randomized controlled study of cognitive therapy for relapse prevention for bipolar affective disorder. *Arch. Gen. Psychiat.* 2003; 60:145–152.

21. Beck AT. *Depression: Causes and Treatment.* Philadelphia: Univ. Pennsylvania Press; 1967.

22. Markowitz JC. Learning the new psychotherapies. In *Treatment of Depression: Bridging the 21st Century*, ed. Weissman MM. Washington, DC, American Psychiatric Press; 2001. 135–149.

23. Markowitz JC. Interpersonal psychotherapy for chronic depression. *J. Clin. Psych.* 2003; 59(8):847–858.

24. Weissman MM, Markowitz JC, Klerman GL. *Comprehensive Guide to Interpersonal Psychotherapy.* New York, Basic; 2000.

25. Paykel ES. Treatment of depression in the United Kingdom. In *Treatment of Depression: Bridging the 21st Century*, ed. Weissman MM. Washington, DC: American Psychiatric Press; 2001. 135–149.

26. Frank E, Kupfer DJ, Perel JM, Cornes C, Jarrett DB, Mallinger AG, et al. Three-year outcomes for maintenance therapies in recurrent depression. *Arch. Gen. Psychiat.* 1990; 47:1093–1099.

27. Hinrichsen GA. Interpersonal psychotherapy for depressed older adults. *J. Geriat. Psychiat.* 1997; 30:239–257.

28. Freud S. "Mourning and Melancholia" (1917), in *Collected Papers*, vol. 4. London, Hogarth Press and Institute of Psychoanalysis; 1950:152–172.

29. Beck AT. How an anomalous finding led to a new system of psychotherapy. *Nature Med.* 2006; 12(10):xiii–xv.

30. Beck AT. Cognitive therapy: nature and relation to behavior therapy. *Behav. Ther.* 1970; 1:184–200.

31. Alford BA, Beck AT. Therapeutic interpersonal support in cognitive therapy. *J. Psychother. Integ.* 1997; 7:275–289.

32. Safran JD, Segal ZV. *Interpersonal Process in Cognitive Therapy.* New York, Basic Books; 1990.

33. Alford BA, Beck AT. "Psychotherapeutic Treatment of Depression and Bipolar Disorder," in *Physician's Guide to Depression and Bipolar Disorder*, ed. Evans DL, Charney DS. New York, McGraw-Hill; 2006. 63–93

34. Beck AT. "Cognitive Therapy of Depression: New Perspectives," in *Treatment of Depression: Old Controversies and New Approaches*, ed. Clayton PJ, Barrett JE. New York, Raven Press; 1982:265–290.

35. Jacobson, Dobson, Truax, Addis, Koerner, Gollan, Gortner, Prince. A component analysis of cognitive-behavioral treatment for depression. *J. Consult. Clin. Psych.* 1996; 64(2):295–304.

36. Dimidjian S, Hollon SD, Dobson KS, Schmaling KB, Kohlenberg RJ, Addis ME, et al. Randomized trial of behavioral activation, cognitive therapy, and antidepressant medication in the acute treatment of adults with major depression. *J. Consult. Clin. Psych.* 2006; 74:658–670.

37. Ellis A. *Reason and Emotion in Psychotherapy*. New York, Lyle Stuart; 1962.

38. Newman CF, Leahy RL, Beck AT, Reilly-Harrington NA, Gyulai L. *Bipolar Disorder: A Cognitive Approach*. Washington, DC, APA; 2001.

39. Baldessarini RJ, Tonodo L, Hennen J, Viguera AC. Is lithium still worth using? an update of selected recent research. *Harv. Rev. Psychiat.* 2002; 10:59–75.

40. Colom F, Vieta E, Martinez-Aran A, Reinares M, Goikolea JM, Benabarre A, et al. A randomized trial on the efficacy of group psychoeducation in the prophylaxis of recurrences in bipolar patients whose disease is in remission. *Arch. Gen. Psychiat.* 2003; 60:402–407.

41. Brown GK, Have TT, Henriques GR, Xie SX, Hollander JE, Beck AT. Cognitive therapy for the prevention of suicide attempts: a randomized controlled trial. *J. Amer. Med. Assoc.* 2005; 294:563–570.

42. Klein DN, Santiago NJ, Vivian D, Arnow BA, Blalock JA, Dunner DL, et al. Cognitive-behavioral analysis system of psychotherapy as a maintenance treatment for chronic depression. *J. Consult. Clin. Psych.* 2004; 72(4):681–688.

43. Bockting CLH, Schene AH, Spinhoven P, Koeter MWJ, Wouters LF, Huyser J, Kamphuis JH, DELTA Study Group. Preventing relapse/recurrence in recurrent depression with cognitive therapy: a randomized controlled trial. *J. Consult. Clin. Psych.* 2005; 73:647–657.

44. Beck AT. *Cognitive Therapy and the Emotional Disorders*. New York: International Univ. Press; 1976.

45. Moore RG. It's the thought that counts: the role of intentions and meta-awareness in cognitive therapy. *J. Cog. Psychother.* 1996; 10:255–269.

46. Reisberg D. *Cognition: Exploring the Science of Mind*. New York, Norton; 1997.

47. Simons AD, Murphy GE, Levine JL, Wetzel RD. Cognitive therapy and pharmacotherapy for depression: sustained improvement over one year. *Arch. Gen. Psych.* 1986; 43:43–48.

48. Robins CJ, Hayes AM. An appraisal of cognitive therapy. *J. Consult. Clin. Psych.* 1993; 61:205–214.

49. Rush AJ, Kovacs M, Beck AT, Weissenburger J, Hollon SD. Differential effects of cognitive therapy and pharmacotherapy on depressive symptoms. *J. Affect. Disord.* 1981; 3:221–229.

50. Rush AJ, Beck AT, Kovacs M, Hollon SD. Comparative efficacy of cognitive therapy and pharmacotherapy in the treatment of depressed outpatients. *Cog. Ther. Res.* 1994; 1:17–37.

51. Segal ZV, Ingram RE. Mood priming and construct activation in tests of cognitive vulnerability to unipolar depression. *Clin. Psych. Rev.* 1994; 14(7):663–695.

52. Alloy LB, Abramson LY, Neeren AM, Walshaw PD, Urosevic S, Nusslock R. "Psychosocial Risk factors for Bipolar disorder: current and early environment and cognitive styles," in *The Psychology of Bipolar Disorder: New Developments and Research Strategies*, ed. Jones S, Bentall R. Oxford, Oxford. Univ. Press; 2006.

53. Alloy LB, Abramson LY, Walshaw PD, Neeren AM. Cognitive vulnerability to unipolar and bipolar mood disorders. *J. Soc. Clin. Psych.* 2006; 25(7):726–754.

54. Oei TPS, Free ML. Do cognitive behaviour therapies validate cognitive models of mood disorders? a review of the empirical evidence. *Int. J. Psych.* 1995; 30:145–179.

Chapter 16. Evaluating Depression Treatments

1. Klein DF. *Understanding Depression: A Complete Guide to Its Diagnosis and Treatment.* New York, Oxford Univ. Press; 1993.

2. Butler AC, Chapman JE, Forman EM, Beck AT. The empirical status of cognitive-behavioral therapy: a review of meta-analyses. *Clin. Psych. Rev.* 2006; 26:17–31.

3. Dobson KS. A meta-analysis of the efficacy of cognitive therapy for depression. *J. Consult. Clin. Psych.* 1989; 57,3:414–419.

4. Hollon SD, DeRubeis RJ, Evans MD. "Cognitive Therapy in the Treatment and Prevention of Depression," in *Frontiers of Cognitive Therapy*, ed. Salkovskis PN. New York, Guilford; 1996, 293–317.

5. Robins CJ, Hayes AM. An appraisal of cognitive therapy. *J. Consult. Clin. Psych.* 1993; 61:205–214.

6. Bailar JC. The promise and problems of meta-analysis. *New England J. Med.* 1997; 337:559.

7. DeRubeis RJ, Hollon SD, Amsterdam JD, Shelton RC, Young PR, Salomon RM, et al. Cognitive therapy vs. medications in the treatment of moderate to severe depression. *Arch. Gen. Psychiat.* 2005; 62:409–436.

8. Hollon SD, DeRubeis RJ, Evans MD, Weimer MJ, Garvey MJ, Grove WM, Tuason VB. Cognitive therapy and pharmacotherapy for depression: singly and in combination. *Arch. Gen. Psychiat.* 1992; 49:774–781.

9. Elkin I, Shea MT, Watkins JT, Imber SD, Sotsky SM, Collins JF, et al. National Institute of Mental Health Treatment of Depression Collaborative Research Program: general effectiveness of treatments. *Arch. Gen. Psychiat.* 1989; 46:971–982.

10. Bowers WA. Treatment of depressed in-patients: cognitive therapy plus medication, relaxation plus medication, and medication alone. *Brit. J. Psychiat.* 1990; 156:73–78.

11. Jacobson N.S, Hollon SD. Prospects for future comparisons between drugs and psychotherapy: lessons from the CBT-versus-pharmacotherapy exchange. *J. Consult. Clin. Psych.* 1996; 64:104–108.

12. Miller IW, Norman WH, Keitner GI, Bishop SB, Dow MG. Cognitive-behavioral treatment of depressed inpatients. *Behav. Ther.* 1989; 20:25–47.

13. Covi L, Lipman RS. Cognitive behavioral group psychotherapy combined with imipramine in major depression. *Psychopharm. Bull.* 1987; 23:173–176.

14. Beck AT, Hollon SD, Young JE, Bedrosian RC, Budenz D. Treatment of depression with cognitive therapy and amitriptyline. *Arch. Gen. Psychiat.* 1985; 42:142–148.

15. Murphy GE, Simons AD, Wetzel RD, Lustman PJ. Cognitive therapy and pharmacotherapy: singly and together in the treatment of depression. *Arch. Gen. Psychiat.* 1984; 41:33–41.

16. Blackburn IM, Bishop S, Glen AIM, Whalley LJ, Christie JE. The efficacy of cognitive therapy in depression: A treatment trial using cognitive therapy and pharmacotherapy, each alone and in combination. *Brit. J. Psychiat.* 1981; 139:181–189.

17. Rush AJ, Beck AT, Kovacs M, Hollon SD. Comparative efficacy of cognitive therapy and pharmacotherapy in the treatment of depressed outpatients. *Cog. Ther. Res.* 1977; 1:17–37.

18. Kendall PC. Empirically supported psychological therapies. *J. Consult. Clin. Psych.* 1998; 26:27–38.

19. Chambless DL, Hollon SD. Defining empirically supported therapies. *J. Consult. Clin. Psych.* 1998; 66:7–18.

20. Goldfried MR, Wolfe BE. Psychotherapy practice and research: repairing a strained alliance. *Amer. Psych.* 1996; 51:1007–1016.

21. Jonas WB. Clinical trials for chronic disease: Randomized, controlled clinical trials are essential. *J. NIH Res.* 1997; 9:33–39.

22. Persons JB, Bostrom A, Bertagnolli A. Results of randomized controlled trials of cognitive therapy for depression generalize to private practice. Paper presented at 30th Annual Convention of the Association for the Advancement of Behavior Therapy, New York; 1996.

23. Task Force on Promotion and Dissemination of Psychological Procedures, Division of Clinical Psychology. Training in and dissemination of empirically validated psychological treatments: report and recommendations, *Clin. Psych.* 1995; 48:3–23.

24. Thase ME, Greenhouse JB, Frank E, Reynolds CF, Pilkonis PA, Hurley K, et al. Treatment of major depression with psychotherapy or psychotherapy-pharmacotherapy combinations. *Arch. Gen. Psychiat.*1997; 54:1009–1015.

25. Hollon SD, Shelton RC, Davis DD. Cognitive therapy for depression: Conceptual issues and clinical efficacy. *J. Consult. Clin. Psych.* 1993; 61:2,270–275.

26. Dobson KS, Pusch D, Jackman-Cram S. Further evidence for the efficacy of cognitive therapy for depression: multiple outcome measures and long-term effects. Paper presented at the 25th Annual Convention of the Association for the Advancement of Behavior Therapy, New York, New York; 1991.

27. Williams JMG. "Depression," in *Science and Practice of Cognitive Behaviour Therapy*, ed. Clark DM, Fairburn CA. Oxford: Oxford Univ. Press; 1997, 259–283.

28. McLean P, Taylor S. Severity of unipolar depression and choice of treatment. *Behav. Res. Ther.* 1992; 30:5, 443–451.C

29. Ahmed I, Soares KVS, Seifas R, Adams CE. Randomized controlled trials in Archives of General Psychiatry (1959–1995): a prevalence study. *Arch. Gen. Psychiat.* 1998; 55:754–755.

30. Jarrett RB, Schaffer M, McIntire D, Witt-Browder A, Kraft D, Risser RC. Treatment of atypical depression with cognitive therapy or phenelzine: a double-blind, placebo-controlled trial. *Arch. Gen. Psychiat.* 1999; 56:431–437.

31. Judd LL. The clinical course of unipolar major depressive disorders. *Arch. Gen. Psychiat.*1997; 54:989–991.

32. Hollon SD, DeRubeis RJ, Seligman MEP. Cognitive therapy and the prevention of depression. *Appl. Prev. Psych.y* 1992; 1:89–95.

33. Hollon SD, DeRubeis RJ, Shelton RC, Amsterdam JD, Salomon RM, O'Reardon JP, et al. Prevention of relapse following cognitive therapy vs medications in moderate to severe depression. *Arch. Gen. Psychiat.* 2005; 62:417–422.

34. Jarrett RB, Basco MR, Risser R, Ramanan J, Marwill M, Kraft D, Rush AJ. Is there a role for continuation phase cognitive therapy for depressed outpatients? *J. Consult. Clin. Psych.* 1998; 66:1036–1040.

35. Evans MD, Hollon SD, DeRubeis RJ, Grove WM, Garvey MJ, Tuason VB. Differential relapse following cognitive therapy and pharmacotherapy for depression. *Arch. Gen. Psychiat.* 1992; 49:802–808.

36. Shea MT, Elkin I, Imber SD, Sotsky SM, Watkins JT, Collins JF, et al. Course of depressive symptoms over follow-up: findings from the National Institute of Mental Health Treatment of Depression Collaborative Research Program. *Arch. Gen. Psychiat.* 1992; 49:782–787.

37. Blackburn IM, Eunson KM, Bishop S. A two-year naturalistic follow-up of depressed patients treated with cognitive therapy, pharmacotherapy and a combination of both. *J. Affect. Disord.* 1986; 10:67–75.

38. Simons AD, Murphy GE, Levine JL, Wetzel RD. Cognitive therapy and pharmacotherapy for depression: sustained improvement over one year. *Arch. Gen. Psychiat.* 1986; 43:43–48.

39. Kovacs M, Rush AJ, Beck AT, Hollon SD. Depressed outpatients treated with cognitive therapy or pharmacotherapy: A one-year follow-up. *Arch. Gen. Psychiat.* 1981; 38:33–39.

40. Rush A., Kovacs M, Beck AT, Weissenburger J, Hollon S. D. Differential effects of cognitive therapy and pharmacotherapy on depressive symptoms. *J. Affect. Disord.* 1981; 3:221–229.

41. Vos T, Haby MM, Barendregt JJ, Kruijshaar M, Corry J, Andrews G. The burden of major depression avoidable by longer-term treatment strategies. *Arch. Gen. Psychiat.* 2004; 61:1097–1103.

42. Segal ZV, Gemar MC, Williams S. (1999). Differential cognitive response to a mood challenge following successful cognitive therapy or pharmacotherapy for unipolar depression. *J. Abnorm. Psych.* 1999; 108:3–10.

43. Hollon SD, Jarrett RB, Nierenberg AA, Thase ME, Trivedi MD, Rush AJ. Psychotherapy and medication in the treatment of adult and geriatric depression: which monotherapy or combined treatment? *J. Clin. Psychiat.* 2005; 66:455–468.

44. DeRubeis RJ, Gelfand LA, Tang TZ, Simons AD. Medications versus cognitive behavior therapy for severely depressed outpatients: mega-analysis of four randomized comparisons. *Amer. J. Psychiat.* 1999; 156:1007–1013.

45. Rush, AJ. STAR*D: What have we learned? *Amer. J. Psychiat.* 2007; 164:201–204.

Afterword

1. Siegle GJ, Carter CS, Thase ME. Use of fMRI to predict recovery from unipolar depression with Cognitive Behavior Therapy. *Amer. J. Psychiat.* 2006; 163:735–738.

2. Mayberg HS. Defining neurocircuits in depression: insights from functional neuroimaging studies of diverse treatments. *Psych. Ann.* 2006; 36:258–267.

3. Ressler KJ, Mayberg HS. Targeting abnormal neural circuits in mood and anxiety disorders: from the laboratory to the clinic. *Nat. Neurosci.* 2007; 10(9):1116–1124.

4. Clark DA, Beck AT, Alford BA. *Scientific Foundations of Cognitive Theory and Therapy of Depression.* New York, Wiley; 1999.

5. Scher C, Ingram R, Segal Z. Cognitive reactivity and vulnerability: empirical evaluation of construct activation and cognitive diatheses in unipolar depression. *Clin. Psych. Rev.* 2005; 25:487–510.

6. Dozois DJA, Beck AT. Cognitive schemas, beliefs and assumptions, in *Risk Factors for Depression*, ed. Dobson KS, Dozois DJA. Oxford, Elsevier in press.

7. Garratt G, Ingram RE, Rand KL, Sawalani G. Cognitive processes in cognitive therapy: evaluation of the mechanisms of change in the treatment of depression. *Clin. Psych. Rev*, in press.

8. Caspi A, Sugden K, Moffitt TE, Taylor A, Craig IW, Harrington HL, et al. Influence of life stress on depression: moderation by a polymorphism in the 5-HTT gene. *Science* 2003; 301:386–389.

9. Canli T, Lesch K. Long story short: the serotonin transporter in emotion regulation and social cognition. *Nature Neurosci.* 2007; 10:1103–1109.

10. Beevers CG, Gibb BE, McGeary JE, Miller IW. Serotonin transporter genetic variation and biased attention for emotional word stimuli among psychiatric inpatients. *J Abnorm. Psych.* 2007; 116:208–212.

11. Gibb BE, Uhrlass DJ, Grassia M. Hopelessness theory of depression in children: concurrent and predictive validity of the causes, consequences, and self-characteristics dimensions. Paper presented at the annual meeting of the Association for Behavioral and Cognitive Therapies, Philadelphia, 2007.

12. Munafò MR, Brown SM, Hariri AR. Serotonin transporter (5-HTTLPR) genotype and amygdala activation: a meta-analysis. *Biol Psychiat.* 2008; 63:852–857.

13. Hariri AR, Mattay VS, Tessitore A, Kolachana B, Fera F, Goldman D, et al. Serotonin transporter genetic variation and the response of the human amygdala. *Science* 2002; 297:400–403.

14. Hariri AR, Drabant EM, Munoz KE, Kolachana BS, Mattay VS, Egan MF, Weinberger DR. A susceptibility gene for affective disorders and the response of the human amygdala. *Arch. Gen. Psychiat.* 2005; 62:146–152.

15. Heinz A, Braus DF, Smolka MN, Wrase J, Puls I, Hermann D, et al. Amygdala-prefrontal coupling depends on a genetic variation of the serotonin transporter. *Nat. Neurosci.* 2005; 8:20–21.

16. Canli T, Omura K, Haas BW, Fallgatter A, Constable RT, Lesch KP. Beyond affect: A role for genetic variation of the serotonin transporter in neural activation during a cognitive attention task. *Proc. Natl. Acad. Sci. USA.* 2005; 102:12224–12229.

17. Pezawas L, Meyer-Lindenberg A, Drabant EM, Verchinski BA, Munozm KE Kolachana BS, Egan MF, Mattay VS, Hariri AR, Weinberger DR. 5-HTTLPR polymorphism impacts human cingulate-amygdala interactions: A genetic susceptibility mechanism for depression. *Nat. Neurosci.* 2005; 8:828–834.

18. Bertolino A, Arciero G, Rubino V, Latorre V, De Candia M, Mazzola V, et al. Variation of human amygdala response during threatening stimuli as a function of 5-HTTLPR genotype and personality style. *Biol. Psychia.* 2005; 57:1517–1525.

19. Furmark T, Tillfors M, Garpenstrand H, Marteinsdottir I, Langstrom B, Oreland L, Fredrikson M. Serotonin transporter polymorphism related to amygdala excitability and symptom severity in patients with social phobia. *Neurosci. Lett.* 2004; 362:189–192.

20. Dannlowski U, Ohrmann P, Bauer J, Kugel H, Arolt V, Heindel W, Kersting A, Baune BT. Suslow T. Amygdala reactivity to masked negative faces is associated with automatic judgmental bias in major depression: a 3 T fMRI study. *J. Psychiat. Neurosci.* 2007; 32:423–429.

21. Gotlib IH, Joormann J, Minor KL, Hallmayer J. HPA axis reactivity: a mechanism underlying the associations among 5-HTTLPR, stress, and depression. *Biol. Psychiat.* in press.

22. Manji HK, Drevets WC, Charney DS. The cellular neurobiology of depression. *Nat. Med.* 2001; 7:541–547.

23. Akil H. Stressed and depressed. *Na. Med.* 2005; 11:116–118.

24. Heim C, Meinlschmidt G, Nemeroff CB. Neurobiology of early-life stress. *Psychiat. Ann.* 2003; 33:18–26.

25. Beck AT, Rush AJ, Shaw BF, Emery G. *Cognitive Therapy of Depression.* New York, Guilford Press; 1979.

26. Beck AT. How an anomalous finding led to a new system of psychotherapy. *Nat. Med.* 2006; 12(10):xiii–xv.

27. Goel V, Dolan RJ. Explaining modulation of reasoning by belief. *Cognition* 2003; 87:B11–22.

28. Beck AT. The evolution of the cognitive model of depression and its neurobiological correlates. *Am. J. Psychiat.* 2008; 165(8):969–77.

Name Index

Subject Index